SINGING THE ETHOS OF GOD

D0886113

SINGING THE ETHOS OF GOD

On the Place of Christian Ethics in Scripture

BRIAN BROCK

WILLIAM B. EERDMANS PUBLISHING COMPANY
GRAND RAPIDS, MICHIGAN / CAMBRIDGE, U.K.

© 2007 Brian Brock
All rights reserved

Published 2007 by
Wm. B. Eerdmans Publishing Co.
2140 Oak Industrial Drive N.E., Grand Rapids, Michigan 49505 /
P.O. Box 163, Cambridge CB3 9PU U.K.
www.eerdmans.com

Printed in the United States of America

12 11 10 09 08 07   7 6 5 4 3 2 1

Library of Congress Cataloging-in-Publication Data

Brock, Brian.
Singing the ethos of God: on the place of christian ethics in scripture/
Brian Brock.
p.   cm.
Includes bibliographical references.
ISBN 978-0-8028-0379-5 (pbk.: alk. paper)
1. Ethics in the Bible.   2. Christian ethics — Biblical teaching.
3. Christian ethics.   I. Title.

BS680.E84B74   2007
241.5 — dc22

2006036404

An earlier version of chapter 5 was published as "Bonhoeffer and the Bible in Christian Ethics: Psalm 119, the Mandates, and Ethics as a 'Way,'" in *Studies in Christian Ethics* 18, no. 3 (December 2005).

Der wäre ein Narr, der beim Ergreifen seiner Gelegenheit nicht nach Vorbildern und Meistern, nach Kameraden und Brüdern fragen wollte. Wer eine Gelegenheit wirklich mit mehr oder weniger Genauigkeit entdeckt und mit mehr oder weniger Festigkeit ergreift, der hat das außer Gott bestimmt auch immer irgendwelchen anderen Menschen zu verdanken, die ihn aus der Nähe oder aus der Ferne so oder anders dazu anzuregen, zu ermuntern und auszurüsten wußten.

Kirchliche Dogmatik, III.4, 672

In gratitude to my teachers, for bequeathing their loves.
  Michael Banner, of Augustine,
  Bernd Wannenwetsch, of Luther, and
  Hans Ulrich, of the Psalms.

זְמִרוֹת הָיוּ־לִי חֻקֶּיךָ בְּבֵית מְגוּרָי

PSALM 119:54

Contents

CONTENTS

viii

The Problem of Estrangement from Scripture in Christian Ethics

For some time now, many Christians have had a niggling worry that the Bible is a document from another time and place and that its moral certainties could never be their own. Over the decades, this uncertainty has percolated into the contemporary mind, which now commonly holds that the Bible provides only useless or positively misleading bearings in a modern moral landscape.

We are all strangers to the moral world of Scripture, but not all of us remain strangers. In his *Confessions,* Augustine provides us with one account of how we might overcome this estrangement. When he was a bright young rhetor, he says, Scripture was irrelevant to the hedonistic and irresponsible "liberty of the runaway."[1] When he tired of that life over time, he discovered in the Manichean sect a bracing moral seriousness, a Christ exalted in suitably eloquent language, and a luminous praise of creation. His respect for the Manichean saints brought a familiarity with the Bible, but along with it came a disdain for its rhetorical simplicity and its stories of the ridiculously mundane sainthood of God's servants and prophets (III.v; VI.x). Yet Augustine harbored a slight worry that the Manicheans, with their saintly lives and impressive metaphysics and hermeneutics, faltered when trying to interpret some passages of Scripture (III.xi).

The warm personality and rhetorical sophistication of Ambrose, the bishop of Milan, brought Augustine face to face for the first time with an orthodox Christianity worth listening to. Surprisingly, Ambrose took the Old Testament seriously — even as life-giving (V.xiii-xiv). Week after week, Au-

---

1. St. Augustine, *Confessions,* trans. and intro. Henry Chadwick (Oxford: Oxford University Press, 1991), III.iii (references to the *Confessions* hereafter cited parenthetically within the text).

gustine returned to hear Ambrose preach, and, in his respect for this one Catholic saint, he discovered that his objections to the church and his ridicule of the biblical saints had been exposed as straw men (VI.iii,iv). Faced with these realizations and the undeniable power of Ambrose's life and biblical interpretation, Augustine embraced Christianity and, with it, its Scripture.

This conversion, he soon discovered, was not a onetime event, but an ongoing renewal of his understanding of moral wholeness. It was a transformation taking the form of a journey into Scripture. As part of this journey, he retrospectively came to understand that his earlier estrangement from Scripture was primarily a moral estrangement. The roots of this alienation were partially innate and partially learned in the various social circles in which he had moved. Each person he knew, in his or her own way, had facilitated his rationalizing away any moral challenge from Scripture (VI.v). Beginning with the belief that Scripture was morally irrelevant, and later laughable on the basis of *its* moral vision, he eventually realized that his estrangement from Scripture lay within *him* and his refusal to allow it to question him.

This was a discovery with two faces. On one hand, he now saw how communities can blind us to Scripture, making it inaccessible; on the other, it was a lesson in the indispensability of God's own speaking as God broke through this trained deafness and moral debilitation. God alone could make Scripture sweet, displacing his bitter distaste for it. He could not follow his own *eros* to find God, nor could even Ambrose's teaching and moral example prove the truth of Catholic Christianity (VI.v). It was God's own voice, Augustine said, that "called and cried out loud and shattered my deafness. You were radiant and resplendent, you put to flight my blindness. You were fragrant, and I drew in my breath and now pant after you. I tasted you and I feel but hunger and thirst for you. You touched me and I am set on fire to attain the peace which is yours" (X.xxvii).

This God-given delight in God led him with ever-increased joy to Scripture, especially the Psalms, and his praying of the Psalms kindled a genuine love for God that put to flight his untruth, deceit, and vanity (VII.xi). The moral confusion that had estranged him from Scripture had made him a blind and bitter critic, "barking at the scriptures which drip the honey of heaven and blaze with your light" (IX.iv). He had come full circle: from ignorance, through hostility, to a love of Scripture and an awe of its moral power. He ends his account of this transformation with a prayer for delight in Scripture, for nourishment from it, and to be brought into all perfection through ever-deepening insights into its meaning (XI.ii). Not only does he seek his own perfection (moral and otherwise) in searching Scripture, but he is taught by Scripture to love all those who are enemies of it, as he once was, that they might die to themselves and live in God. This is not built on a claim to have completely understood himself, God, or Scripture: he confesses that God must judge the accuracy of all such interpretations. Augustine can affirm only that God knows who he is, and that he must cling to God to discover himself in enjoying God's beauty and in learning the path of righteousness from Scripture (XII.xiv).

We need not take Augustine's example as normative to see that the range of considerations drawn into his autobiographical account is richer than most contemporary treatments of the role of the Bible in Christian ethics. He is aware that one must be morally transformed to read Scripture, and that we learn to read the Bible in communities of tradition. He also assumes that the way that the Bible shapes Christian action is not adequately described by cataloging the moral teachings of Scripture; but he demands an account of all reality that is drawn from the whole Bible, including its "non-moral" teachings. These are familiar points in the contemporary discussion, but Augustine also adds unfamiliar elements, such as his emphasis on the role played by affections and senses in directing our moral lives, and the way Scripture shapes them. Most strikingly, in reflecting on his own experience, Augustine discovered what historical criticism has recently retaught the modern church: that the Bible is morally a stranger thing than we have yet grasped.

Contemporary scholarship has most often come to this conclusion by noting that academic biblical scholars and Christian ethicists have been methodologically estranged for some decades. This book will trace a range of contemporary attempts to go through or around the presuppositions that keep us, interminably, at arm's length from the Bible. It will suggest that the time has come to move beyond the initial question behind that discussion, "How do we bridge the varying degrees of estrangement between biblical studies and Christian ethics?"[2] However, my aim here is not to render the Bible more familiar. It is as strange and eternally different from our common sense as is Christ himself. But I do hope to discover some roads into this

2. The 1976 edition of *Bible and Ethics in the Christian Life* by Bruce Birch and Larry Rasmussen was one of the earliest attempts in Christian ethics to reintroduce the question into scholarly discussion in this form. This book was not widely known, but it framed Thomas Ogletree's much more influential work, *The Use of the Bible in Christian Ethics* (Philadelphia: Fortress Press, 1983). Ogletree's aim was to give students of Christian ethics access to the results of biblical studies for contemporary moral deliberation. Though Ogletree's approach took its cues from the formulation of the question by Birch and Rasmussen ("I see my own work as a continuation of their important contribution" [p. 14, n. 15]), and brought it to a wider audience, it is the second edition of Birch and Rasmussen that has proved to have the more enduring influence (cf. ch. 2).

strange world while resisting the kind of theologizing that avoids vulnerability in the quest to mechanically ensure that one remains on the right side of God and humans (Job 12:4). The analytical task is properly to understand the *way* we are foreigners in the Bible's world, to thematize its foreignness in a theologically illuminating fashion, and to do so as an exploration of the idea that Christian thinking and action are first and properly understood as aspects of a conversation with God.

Throughout most of the Christian exegetical tradition, the Bible has been read as a document reiterating the morally stupendous claim that all reality is created and remade by God's overflowing goodness. To take this claim seriously is to give up the attempt to fit the Bible into a preconceived moral universe and to begin, instead, to wrestle with the methodological questions raised by the moral strangeness of this basic claim. It is an unfamiliar starting point, and it will yield unfamiliar methodological presuppositions. But if those who take the Bible's moral strangeness seriously look quixotic from the vantage point of modern readers, they in turn see modern readers as self-insulated travelers who, despite being physically present in foreign lands, are impoverished by reading everything through the categories and perceptions of their home culture.

To ease us into the exegetical tradition, I have chosen to begin in the broad heartland of Christian exegesis of the Psalms. That book is arguably the most important and familiar of all biblical books to Christians throughout history, and thus it is an obvious place to meet past readers of Scripture.[3] The Psalms were especially prominent in the first few centuries of the Christian era, generating far more commentaries than any other biblical book. More importantly, by at least the fourth century, the book of Psalms was being used as a *Psalter*,[4] a songbook that was in constant — often daily — liturgical and private use. The influence of the Psalter on Western theology was assured when the performance of the Psalms was made the central activity of Western monastic life; at the same time, though, the Psalms remained the property of laypeople as no other book.[5] We must ask about the theological significance

3. See William Holladay, *The Psalms through Three Thousand Years: Prayerbook of a Cloud of Witnesses* (Minneapolis: Fortress Press, 1996), Part 2: "The Psalter through History," pp. 95-286.

4. Günter Bader, *Psalterium affectum palestra: Prolegomena zu einer Theologie des Psalters* (Tübingen: J. C. B. Mohr [Paul Siebeck], 1996), pp. 5-15.

5. Brian Daley, "Is Patristic Exegesis Still Usable? Some Reflections on Early Christian Interpretation of the Psalms," in Ellen Davis and Richard Hays, eds., *The Art of Reading Scripture* (Grand Rapids: Eerdmans, 2003), pp. 80-81; Holladay, *The Psalms through Three Thousand Years*, p. 178.

of *singing* this book, and why the early church found the performance of the Psalter so important. My choice to look in some depth at the exegesis of Augustine and Luther, both of whom loved the Psalter above all other biblical books, is intended to push us out into this central stream of historical Christian exegetical practice.

To combat the modern obsession with method, I approach this exegetical tradition as an ineradicably social "acoustic space," within which one learns practical skills of handling and appropriating Scripture. It is a conversation we cannot summarize or mine for methodological insights, but to which we must become attuned, thus opening our questions themselves to subtle and unexpected reformulations. This is, of course, a theologically grounded interpretation of the Christian tradition, but one that I hope to show finds its footing in Scripture. We can make the point by simply saying that a good book is always better than its summary, and, as such, Scripture cannot be summarized. Nor can the exegetical tradition through which we approach it. The heart and soul of theology is its immersion in the exegetical tradition of the Christian faith, an insight I have tried simultaneously to display and defend. The real methodological lessons of this book can be learned in its second part, where, rather than summarizing the hermeneutics of Augustine and Luther, I show them — and listen to them — at work interpreting Scripture.

Watching the saints interpret Scripture allows us to discover that the concerns of contemporary exegetes are not as foreign to the precritical tradition as was once supposed, especially regarding the interpretation of the Psalms.[6] After a comprehensive survey of the various hermeneutical strategies displayed in the two thousand years of Christian Psalms exegesis, redaction critic David Mitchell concludes: "A historical perspective at the end of the twentieth century seems to suggest that western scholarship from about 1820 to 1970 is, in some respects, a hiatus in Psalms interpretation, during which scholarly opinion diverged sharply from what must be considered, historically speaking, the dominant views. These traditional interpretational norms deserve reconsideration."[7] Taking up this gauntlet demands much crossing of modern disciplinary boundaries, a daunting task guaranteed to produce scholarly angst. To avoid confusing readers (and librarians), let me be clear: this is not a book of church history, biblical studies, or philosophical

6. For a review of contemporary methodological developments in biblical criticism of the Psalms down to the 1980s, see Patrick D. Miller, *Interpreting the Psalms* (Philadelphia: Fortress Press, 1986), ch. 1.

7. David C. Mitchell, *The Message of the Psalter: An Eschatological Programme in the Book of Psalms* (Sheffield, UK: Sheffield Academic Press, 1997), p. 65.

ethics. It is a study in Christian moral theology that I have undertaken by way of an analysis of the practices of the Christian exegetical tradition. I hope that the methodological antecedents for such an approach will become clear in the course of recovering some forgotten strands of the Christian exegetical tradition.

The *Leitmotiv* of foreignness also provides an explanation of a practical feature of the book's last two parts: the citation of verses under discussion in several languages. The printing of the Hebrew text of the Psalms reminds us that we should not expect the conceptual distinctions they set up to cohere with our own. The foreignness of this alphabet and grammar suggests the magnitude of the transformation that reading Scripture demands of us. This textual and conceptual foreignness is exponentially increased when we engage with the two thousand years of the Christian exegetical tradition.

Augustine was the last ancient, Luther the last medieval. This is a statement about the forms of their thinking, the ages it came so deeply to shape, and the Bibles they used. Their writings provide access to social worlds and Bibles that are no longer immediately present. There have been at least three great Bibles in Western Christianity: the Greek Septuagint, the Hebrew Old Testament on which it rested, and the Latin Vulgate. The Greek is properly listed first because it was the Scripture of the writers of the New Testament.[8] Augustine lived during the Western church's transition from the primacy of the Greek Septuagint to Jerome's Latin Vulgate,[9] which was ascendant until Luther's inauguration of the age of vernacular translations.

Augustine's exegesis is of a Latin translation of the Greek Bible, as a thinker trained in ancient rhetoric and philosophy and deeply engaged with the political questions of a dying Roman Empire. His was a sweeping theology that was largely responsible for the establishment of Jerome's Vulgate in the church that followed him. Thus, just as the Hebrew text opens the biblical Israel's world of thought and social practice, so do Greek and Latin translations contain their own thought worlds, marked in chapter 6 of this book by the inclusion of the Vulgate translation.[10] Luther contended that the Vulgate and the theology that accrued to it came, in time, to eclipse critical Hebrew

8. The hermeneutical and theological issues raised by the church's holding multiple authoritative translations are ones that have not been sufficiently explored. For the importance of this exploration, see Francis Watson, "Mistranslation and the Death of Christ: Isaiah 53 LXX and its Pauline Reception" (forthcoming).

9. We might note here that Jerome's Vulgate never became the church's liturgical text, and his Psalter was never a standard sung version.

10. Augustine did not always work from the Vulgate, but I have included the Vulgate to represent the several Latin translations he did use; see discussion in ch. 6, p. 115 n. 26.

thought structures, which inspired his own translation efforts. These observations clarify why the Bible *should* feel strange to us, sensitizing us to the interrelationships of translations and theology. Luther's translation of the Hebrew into German, in which he was engaging in polemical battles against contemporary interpretations of the Vulgate, is marked in chapter 7 by the bridging of Hebrew and English with his German translations.

Being able to discuss the theological implications of this layering of language is a gift of the humanist Renaissance. That Luther was well aware and appreciative of the new textual tools it offered suggests that the supposed antagonism between theology and "secular" biblical criticism may rest on an illusory distinction. By placing the different ages of the Hebrew Psalms — Augustine's late-antiquity Latin, Luther's high-medieval German, and our own English translations — in close proximity, we can pose a running challenge to a contemporary intellectual context focused on hermeneutical method. For millennia, Israel and the church have not gathered around methodological agreement, or even a definitive translation or canon. They have translated, read, argued, and gathered for worship around a group of texts they called Scripture, which functioned to orient their praise of God and God's works.

The contemporary academic Bible-and-ethics discussion remains largely determined by the question of *how* Scripture might be understood as a moral guide, preparing for exegesis rather than engaging in it. In so doing, such treatments rarely glimpse the possibility that exegesis might be a form of praise. My suggestion, learned from Augustine and Luther, is that exegesis should find its proper form only as praise of a God who is present with creatures. This raises a set of deep methodological challenges in an age founded on the claim that it is methodological detachment rather than praise that guarantees intellectual clarity and fecundity. Postcritical biblical exegesis seeks to marry these divergent impulses of modern critical approaches, but within an appreciation of the assurance and richness of the exegetical tradition. Augustine and Luther may or may not be useful in providing exegetical tools, but they undoubtedly reintroduce modern Christians to the joy and profundity of biblical interpretation without embarrassment.

Such a beginning expresses the theological presupposition that no exegetical or devotional method can overcome God's proper otherness. In the final analysis, it is not our historical or moral distance from the Bible that renders it foreign to us, nor the gap between time and eternity, but the gap between the ways of God and those of humanity. God is not foreign to us on some general criterion, but as another person: it is precisely in God's incarnation that God's difference from us becomes visible (John 1:14). The Psalms are foreign because they open into the manifold life of the trinitarian God; and this conclusion allows us theologically to clarify how they are foreign. The foreignness proper to faith is an eschatological foreignness. Christ is the chorus of a new song that, in its announcement of good news to the world, unleashes a critical impulse within history. Singers are made "strangers and aliens" in a rebellious world by having their eyes opened to the profundity of the Godhead and the perfection of God's works.

Because it is in becoming one of us that God's foreignness becomes visible, we learn that the Bible is both other and external—and yet approachable. This allows God's working to assume a substantive role in our hermeneutical theory, contrasting with philosophical hermeneutics discourses in which the divine self-impartation plays no role. In being part of God's path to us, Scripture is foreign with Christ's foreignness, but not a stranger that we cannot come to know, nor an otherworldly alien. Nor is its foreignness that of modern liberalism, within which otherness becomes an end in itself. Its foreignness finds its origin in God's inexhaustible holiness rather than Scripture's effectiveness as a moral source or guide. Because it is outside us, the *verbum externum*, it can, as gospel, console and teach us.

The verb of this book's title, "singing," emphasizes that this is not a book about reading or moral transformation taken on its own. The metaphor of singing (more than that of reading or thinking) draws attention to the way an external word can claim human action and affections and thus be internalized as a way of life. The metaphor is developed via a more technical claim that language worlds, if we enter them, can orient and shape our lives. This claim is not based on general observations about the functioning of all languages; rather, it is a description of what happens when we are immersed in Scripture. The main job of Christian ethics is not formal but material: it must facilitate our coming into contact with its proper source, and only secondarily do we learn to describe and clarify what we experience there. What this study discovers in the church's singing of the Psalter is that through each psalm we enter the world of praise in which all human life is comprehended within God's work—and is thus renewed.

Praising God transforms the many rationalities and languages of this world. Praise leads Christians out of conformity to this world by transforming perception and knowledge so that we may discern what God intends for us, the good and acceptable and perfect (Rom. 12:2). In praise the world's true unity becomes visible to us, as our prior categories for perceiving diversity are radically reconfigured. It is the task of this book to show how the unity that praise creates lies not in the first place in hermeneutical acuity but in God's inexhaustibility in renewing language, human life, and all creation. Within the working of God in human history, Scripture is a unique invitation to praise, channeling the Spirit-given desire to "sing to Yahweh all my life, and celebrate my God with music as long as I live" (Ps. 104:33).[11] Singing, as Luther puts it, includes "not only making melody or shouting but also every sermon or public confession by which God's work, counsel, grace, help, comfort, victory, and salvation are glorified before the world."[12]

This praise has a critical function in revealing how this song of superabundance really does differ from other songs and languages, and so from other ways of life. The Psalms overturn the claim that our lives are what we make them by teaching us that the activities of life are meant for returning to God as praise. It is the Psalms' own rhythms and grammar of praise that supply the church with the resources necessary to make it aware of its captivity. As it says in the Jewish midrash on Psalm 137:1, if the faithful had once repented and taken these songs on their lips, they would not now find themselves in captivity.[13] The loss of the desire and ability to sing *is* the captivity of the community of faith, a captivity of thought to ideology, of action to futile pursuits.

Thus is reading as praise more critical than critical theory. Critical theory can only problematize, erase, and close down false readings by questioning them. This may enrich the church's exegesis by exposing cases where the Bible is being read in a self-serving or self-referential way. But it is the positive nature of praise that concerns us here. If our quest is to understand how God enters our world, we must not only criticize false readings, but must do so by way of positive displacement. Because its tools work by negation, criticism ends in a question about the way forward: the gospel presents a way forward and thus exposes the deadness of worldly life. No amount of criticism is capable of forcing God to make an appearance; therefore, Christian hermeneutics and ethics are only Christian insofar as they are an expression of the good news.

This allows us to reframe the whole Bible-and-ethics discussion in terms of this question: What role does the Bible play in God's generation of a holy people? More importantly, how do we participate in this regeneration? The bulk of the analysis of Part III is concerned with articulating the logic and processes of this renewal rather than attempting to develop yet another hermeneutical method. The Psalter is remarkably unified as a reflection on the path from lostness into God's story, incorporating us into God's not-yet-

---

11. All biblical quotations are from the New Revised Standard Version, unless otherwise specified.

12. Martin Luther, "Psalm 118," *Luther's Works: Vol. 14, Selected Psalms III*, ed. Jaroslav Pelikan (St. Louis: Concordia Publishing House, 1958), p. 81.

13. William Braude, trans., *The Midrash on the Psalms*, vol. 2 (New Haven: Yale University Press, 1959), p. 331.

completed journey.[14] I will argue that such an understanding of the Psalms both properly situates the foreignness of the Bible as the foreignness of life with God and indicates the proper response of faith. The soteriological moment becomes the launching pad for an investigation of widespread contemporary confusion about the Bible's proper methodological role in Christian ethics. This focus is suggested by the psalmists' refusal to ground their hope in conceptual certainties and their assurance that the false certainties of misdirected faith and life are inherently unstable. In doing so, they train the faithful in the practices of collaborating with their own transformation.

Though I begin from the Psalms, an investigation such as this might begin elsewhere in the biblical canon. But if it is true, as has often been suggested, that the Psalter is a "little Bible," there will be good reasons for repeating the study beginning elsewhere in the canon. The essential point is that the problem of theological reading is not finding a single key to Scripture but a place to begin to read. This book does not intend to be a watertight establishing of a particular approach to Scripture, but it aims to indicate the richness of one proposal. I am painfully aware that, however careful I am in presenting my case, it will be easy to be critical of this book, should that be the reader's intention. However, I hope that the general direction of the inquiry will become clear, and therefore illuminating. Even if my attempt is judged unsuccessful, I hope that it will encourage other and better attempts to work out the basic theological insights.

The foregoing suggests a three-part construction, and the titles of the three parts indicate their methodological orientation: Part I "learns" to "read" the Bible, gleaning insights into methodological options from the contemporary discussion. Part II "listens" to the "saints," seeking to immerse us in the exegetical practice of two of the church's great biblical interpreters. Its aim is to widen the focus of inquiry beyond methodological questions by letting us get a feel for the many unfamiliar ways their thought moves as they exposit Scripture. Part III follows this progression to its logical conclusion by taking up a first-person relationship with Scripture—thus "singing" the "ethos of God." It attempts exegesis in dialogue with saints past and present, having learned from them that biblical interpretation in Christian ethics is in the service of God's praise, to which it calls the world.

14. "It is really surprising to see how homogeneous the picture of the divine is in the psalms. The inner tension of the historical 'development' in Israel's religion and its conception of God is little felt in the book of Psalms." Sigmund Mowinckel, *The Psalms in Israel's Worship*, vol. 1 (Oxford: Oxford University Press, 1962), p. 97.

These sections unfold as follows. Part I surveys contemporary accounts of the role of the Bible in Christian ethics. Leaving aside treatments that aspire to no more than a *description* of the ethical teaching of parts or the whole of Scripture, it focuses on accounts that suggest that the Bible is morally *normative* for the contemporary church. Within this limit, I have tried to refer to all significant treatments of the last decades, making this part suitable as an introduction to the field. My aim, however, is not only to describe how theologians use Scripture to generate moral claims, but to draw out the most important insights of each strand to advance the thesis of the book.[15] Each chapter treats proposals that are important, provide constructive insights, and display the many points of methodological debate within the discussion. To clarify the nuances of this dialogue, I have often placed methodologically "pure" types next to examples of attempts to try to blend different approaches. I hope that such a treatment allows a sort of map of the nodes of methodological clarity or consensus to emerge, and thus a sense of the perceptions shaping contemporary work to link these nodes. In focusing solely on the recent discussion, Part I also has a wider aim: to whet the reader's appetite to encounter the tradition afresh. The survey of the contemporary discussion reveals it to be quite often shaped by the typically modern emphasis on hermeneutical method and a concomitant distance from detailed engagement with biblical content.

In Part II we move into an entirely different atmosphere, immersing ourselves in the exegetical moral theologies of Augustine (ch. 6) and Luther (ch. 7). From their Psalms exegesis we learn that the foreignness of the Bible, properly understood, is the foreignness of life in the Spirit within which faith awakens to discover itself. In this sense, the disciples have no advantage: we are all contemporaries with Christ.[16] Part II thus makes a transition into the constructive work of Part III by conceiving the reading of Scripture not in terms of hermeneutical method but as part of entering God's story. This

15. A brief survey is offered in J. Ian McDonald, *The Crucible of Christian Morality* (London: Routledge, 1998), pp. 1-6. Jeffrey Siker provides a book-length account in *Scripture and Ethics: Twentieth Century Portraits* (Oxford: Oxford University Press, 1997). Like Siker, I describe contemporary methodological approaches to the question, but unlike him, I compare modern approaches *as a group* within the wider Christian exegetical tradition. He surveys modern writers as part of the modern quest to increase the methodological reflexivity of Christian moral argumentation from Scripture (a central theme here of ch. 1); I raise questions about this trajectory in order to emphasize the methodological importance of engaging with the content of Scripture.

16. Soren Kierkegaard (Johannes Climacus), *Philosophical Fragments: Kierkegaard's Writings, VII,* ed. and trans. Howard Hong and Edna Hong (Princeton, NJ: Princeton University Press, 1985), ch. IV: "The Situation of the Contemporary Follower."

yields a further suggestion that the Bible is a divine gift that leads us deeper into the awareness that the foreignness of life in the Spirit is humanity's proper home. The permanent provisionality of such a home may nevertheless become richly inhabitable in a way that a raw and bewildered estrangement from Scripture can never be. Such an understanding of exegesis exposes the way that the unity of the Christian tradition, the rule of faith, and the community's struggle to understand Scripture are in God's working alone. My working hypothesis is that, insofar as there are legitimate concerns expressed in the different strands of the contemporary Bible-and-ethics discussion, these can only become visible in their interrelationship and unity within an account of how God uses Scripture to claim humanity.

This hypothesis leads to the exploration of Part III, in which I suggest how this close attention to the Christian tradition recasts our understanding of the role of the Bible in Christian ethics. Its discovery is that contemporary methodologies have inverted the theologically proper question about the role of Scripture in Christian ethics, which is: What is the place of Christian ethics within Scripture? The heart of Part III is chapter 9's exemplary and provisional answer to this question. Here I read Psalms 130 and 104 to examine how they conceive of — and thus situate — Christian ethics within the world of God's work and Scripture. Chapter 8 undertakes to describe as many of the exegetical presuppositions of the final chapter as possible, and elucidates why hermeneutics must be understood as the clarification of the ongoing processes of exegesis, and not its source.

This book's emphasis on theology done in the flow of life prompts the biographical admission that this book was conceived and written during a decade in which I, joined in time by my longsuffering wife, Stephanie, and later our son Adam, moved house at least ten times, five of them internationally. Clearly, the hermeneutical perplexities that shape the book were easily conceivable within the many experiences of foreignness that such a life affords, with all of its disorientation and insecurity, and the necessity for hope.

The breadth of material demanded by the theme of this book presented a source of academic anxiety in its own right. For this the living community of saints is God's greatest help and comfort. I have often had recourse to friends from whom I have received indispensable help. Chief Rabbi Jonathan Sacks, Reinhard Hütter, and David Williams provided stimulation and feedback in the earliest stages of formulating my thoughts. Walter Moberly, Jamie Grant, Francis Watson, John Webster, Jan Fokkelman, Douglas Knight, and Ovidiu Creanga each provided invaluable critical, conceptual, and personal support. I am especially grateful to those who made the sacrifice of reviewing the whole manuscript: Hans Ulrich, Bernd Wannenwetsch, Stefan Heuser, Francesca Murphy, Stephanie Brock, Martin Wendte, Andy Draycott, Simon Perry and Rob Price, and to those who helped with proofreading the "foreign" languages, Peter Williams and Scot Becker. Special thanks to Stephanie Brock, Andy Draycott, Andy Odle, Scott Prather, and Annie Vaughan for their help with proofreading and indexing.

Indeed, the project has been collaborative from the roots up, growing from the study group "The Psalms as a Discursive Forum for Ethics," which was conceived and led by Professor Hans Ulrich at Friedrich Alexander Universität, Erlangen-Nürnberg since 2000. In so many ways, the uniqueness of this book is due to Professor Ulrich's theological insights. Group members Stefan Heuser and Picu Ocoleanu were continual conversation partners throughout the book's genesis. That the book grew from conversations is not merely incidental but integrally related to the ecclesial way of life it defends. Through such collaboration we learn how different cultures and languages are drawn together in praise. The book is written in English, despite my being the only native English speaker of my dialogue partners, yet easily could have sprung from that research community in a different language. The importance of this claim will become clear as later chapters indicate how reading the Bible at specific, embodied places, which demands the continual crossing of all kinds of borderlines, is possible only as an artifact of God's peace. Finally, I owe a debt of gratitude to the faculty of the Department of Divinity at the University of Aberdeen, whose unstinting academic, financial, and logistical support enriched the content and enabled the speedy completion of this work.

PART I

Learning about Reading the Bible for Ethics

CHAPTER 1

Reading Self-Consciously:
The Hermeneutical Solution

The chapters of Part I offer a brief survey of contemporary discussions of the role of the Bible in Christian ethics, grouping proposals that share ways of framing problems and solutions. The authors surveyed in this chapter, for instance, agree that the problem to be overcome is the use of the Bible to generate ethical claims by which others are oppressed. They propose solutions in which methodological self-awareness plays the leading role. Reading that more self-consciously considers its effects on a wider range of people by being more aware of its social and political context is less likely to be oppressive and therefore more just. Elisabeth Schüssler Fiorenza, Daniel Patte, and Charles Cosgrove agree that the key to a more just and ethical reading of the Bible is to encourage those who interpret the Bible to become more self-aware of the impact of their biblical exegesis on the lives of others.

We begin with this set of authors because they raise an important question for the study of the Bible in Christian ethics: What is ethical *interpretation?* This question stands one step behind the familiar question about how to grasp what the Bible might say about how we should act. The authors in this chapter remind us that interpretation is already an action, and thus the way we *read,* that is, our hermeneutics, is susceptible to moral analysis. Ethical questions, it turns out, arise not only from the moral claims made in the Bible but in the very processes of our making moral arguments from it at all. In asking about ethical interpretation, we enter an important examination of how our hermeneutical presuppositions may in themselves be unethical. The authors represented in this chapter remind us that we may have already become demagogues if our hermeneutics of the Bible has oppressive assumptions built into its structure.

Elisabeth Schüssler Fiorenza:
Confronting Oppression in Biblical Studies

Rhetoric and Ethic: The Politics of Biblical Studies is Elisabeth Schüssler Fiorenza's most explicit foray into the question of the Bible's place in morality. Its first chapter is interesting because it is not a theoretical treatise but the text of a performance of her ethical theory, "a rhetorical-historical event rather than just a theoretical exploration,"[1] which she delivered as the presidential address to the 1988 Annual Meeting of the Society of Biblical Literature. As the first female president of the SBL, Schüssler Fiorenza used that address to enact what she would call the prototypical ethical act: goading the society to be more politically aware and, more importantly, acknowledging that their interpretative practices had been using their "scientific expertise" to systematically silence many readers of the Bible. Despite being shrugged off by many (*Rhetoric and Ethic*, pp. 33-34), the address seems to have had some success as a "rhetorical-historical event." Several scholars, among them Patte and Cosgrove, took up the program for ethical biblical interpretation that Schüssler Fiorenza proposed in the address and elaborated in *Rhetoric and Ethic*.

Schüssler Fiorenza's starting point is to admit her feminist presuppositions and challenge the members of the society also to throw aside their mantle of modern scientific objectivity.[2] For her, feminism is the struggle to have women recognized as full agents in the public, democratic sphere of human relations, a struggle carried out through public speech. As a participant in this struggle, she had come to find that "scientific objectivity" was a club wielded by many in the society to silence her and other minority voices. On her own terms, what to say in her SBL presidential address represented a deci-

---

1. Elisabeth Schüssler Fiorenza, *Rhetoric and Ethic: The Politics of Biblical Studies* (Minneapolis: Fortress Press, 1999), p. 13 (page references to this book hereafter cited parenthetically in text).

2. A note on my usage of the term "modernity." In the English-speaking world, much of the scholarly discussion in moral philosophy (influenced as it is by thinkers such as Adam Smith and John Rawls), as well as most popular thought, rests on a thorough appropriation of the early Enlightenment (Descartes to Kant). German thought is much more explicitly aware of the later Enlightenment (referred to as *Moderne,* including Fichte, Schelling, Schleiermacher, and Hegel) and has been marked by an awareness of the shortcomings of the early Enlightenment (referred to as *Neuzeit*). By noting this differentiation, we are able to more closely discriminate between the positive and destructive aspects of the post-Enlightenment age. This frees Anglo-American theology to move beyond the blanket antimodern polemics that have often — effectively and properly — reopened closed debates to begin to appreciate the aspects of wisdom of the modern world, of which it is a beneficiary and participant.

4

sion between validating the society's practices by following precedent and summarizing the state of the discipline, suggesting future directions, and so forth, or speaking out in order to challenge the society to be a more ethical community (p. 4). In choosing the latter, she was true to the deeply ethical cast of her own research program, in which feminism is conceived as "a theory and practice of justice that seeks not just to understand but to change relations of marginalization and domination" (p. 7).

Her speech began by drawing on the hermeneutical turn of Western philosophy that is most clearly seen in the works of Derrida, Rorty, Gadamer, and Ricoeur (pp. 58-61) to point out that "[b]iblical interpretation, like all scholarly inquiry, is a communicative practice that involves interests, values, and visions" (p. 18). There is no such thing as the "value-free" interpretation of Scripture that the society had long been claiming to discover through its positivist and supposedly politically and religiously detached approach to scholarship. Scholarly communities are also communities that claim authority and wield it to "ostracize or embrace, to foster or restrict membership, to recognize and define what 'true scholarship' entails" (p. 22). By rehearsing in detail the society's demographic history, Schüssler Fiorenza illustrated the way the SBL had used its authority to canonize texts and approaches, name its heroes (saints) and heretics, and, in so doing, systematically exclude female interpreters and interpretations of the Bible.

While rejecting many readings of the Bible as "unscientific," the guild had colonized the space marked out by the biblical canon in which many other communities have an interest, using the mantle of "science" to establish a "true" meaning that would negate all other meanings. Their ethical credo had been that "the biblical critic needs to stand outside the common circumstances of collective life and [it] stresses the alien character of biblical materials. What makes biblical interpretation possible is radical detachment and emotional, intellectual, and political distancing" (p. 24). The sad result, she said, was generations of academics and students who had been taught to abstract their readings (and ultimately themselves) from the historical location of reading, systematically blinding themselves to the injustices such practices inflicted on those around them.

Schüssler Fiorenza's solution is to begin by asking simply that biblical scholars admit that they have an investment in certain causes, that they have hopes for their research to come out one way rather than another, and that this personal stake is not incidental to their research. She insists that biblical interpretation will always be a rhetorical act that shapes and changes power relationships, and that any improvement in the situation will depend on biblical scholars no longer aspiring to be "professionalized intellectuals," but rather becoming more self-conscious about the effects of their interpretations on sociopolitical dynamics. In *Rhetoric and Ethic,* Schüssler Fiorenza elaborates her vision of "a theoretical and institutional change that would foster a biblical rhetoric and ethics of justice and well-being. Biblical scholars are called to contribute as critical transformative intellectuals to a radical democratic biblical vision for the overcoming of domination in the global *cosmopolis* that is our spiritual home" (p. 14).

The backbone of this new discipline is rhetorical criticism: "The reconceptualization of biblical studies in rhetorical rather than scientistic terms would provide a research framework not only for integrating historical archaeological, sociological, literary and theological approaches as perspectival readings of texts, but also for raising ethical-political and religious-theological questions as constitutive of the interpretative process" (p. 26). Understanding biblical studies in this way suggests a bi-directional understanding of the responsibility of the exegete. One direction is toward the text, yielding an "ethics of critical reading." This ethics stays true to the text by its awareness of the plurality of interpretations, yet insists that all interpretations allow themselves to be limited by the text. In so doing, Schüssler Fiorenza says, it keeps the text alive as a "foreign" entity by showing how it constantly differs from and thus challenges our experiences and interests (p. 27).

A second responsibility is toward others. An "ethics of responsibility" makes it incumbent on interpreters to take responsibility for the theoretical and interpretative models they have chosen, as well as the ethical consequences of their use of those models. Here Schüssler Fiorenza is heavily influenced by the responsibility ethic of Jürgen Habermas (p. 64, n. 29). Such an ethic takes responsibility for the ethical impact that the Bible and its subsequent interpretations have had in the past, and it seeks actively to combat these through more just rereadings of the text (p. 28). It promotes and nurtures a sphere of "radical democratic equality" where all voices are heard, thus destabilizing the concepts and communities that have used the Bible to maintain oppressive patriarchal, racist, and colonial structures. Biblical studies can only speak to church, synagogue, mosque, and civil society as they serve the breaking down of this oppressive "scientistic hegemonic ethos of the center" to build up the region of equality she calls the *ekklesia.* "Since *ekklesia* is not primarily a religious but a political term, such a change would position biblical scholarship in the public sphere of the polis and transform it into a critical discourse that seeks to further the well-being of all the inhabitants of the *cosmo-polis* today" (p. 11).

This critical rhetorical analysis reformulates the concept of research in biblical studies:

Biblical studies must engage in critical readings and evaluations of biblical discourses in terms of a public, radical democratic ethos. It must ask: How has this text been used and how is it used today to defy or corroborate hegemonic political systems, laws, science, medicine, or public policy? How has biblical interpretation been used and how is the Bible still used either to challenge or to protect powerful interests and to engender sociocultural, political, and religious change? How is the Bible used to define public discourse and groups of people? What is the vision of society that is articulated in and through biblical texts? Is, and how is, Scripture used to marginalize certain people, to legitimate racism and other languages of hate, or is it used to intervene in discourses of justice? Such questions must become as central as exegetical-historical and literary-anthropological questions still are and have been. (p. 33)

Schüssler Fiorenza's aim in this work is not systematically to integrate the practical outworking of "critical reading" and "ethical responsibility," but to show how they yield a new and more just set of questions not previously allowed to be on the agenda of biblical scholars.

Thus the book's second part, in which Schüssler Fiorenza turns to Paul's writings, provides only a sketch of how she believes such a hermeneutics might be played out. She uses a process of exegetical excavation to recover egalitarian positions she believes to have been suppressed by Paul's rhetoric. The early Christianity that Paul is attacking she understands to be radically egalitarian, as stated in Galatians 3:28, which she takes as a classic statement of her own ethical egalitarianism.[3] Having thus shown her understanding of radical egalitarianism to be coherent with Paul, she does not claim that it is based on or derived from his writings. Paul's writings are key for Schüssler Fiorenza because they are taken seriously by many and thus can serve to expose the strategies of the unjust, who use them to try to suppress the truth. Yet because they do not fully suppress what is just, studying biblical suppression strategies sensitizes us to the ways that unjust and dominating attitudes can be couched in religious language to suppress others' voices (most notably those of women). Paul's oppressive rhetorical practices teach contemporary biblical scholars how to recognize a bigoted hermeneutic when they see one. Yet these repressive writings retain shadows and memories of a nonrepressive Jesus movement viable today.

It would be worth the effort but beyond the scope of this book to analyze the ethics of Schüssler Fiorenza's *In Memory of Her*. She does not directly

---

3. "There is no longer Jew or Greek, there is no longer slave or free, there is no longer male and female; for all of you are one in Christ Jesus."

7

address the role of Scripture in ethics in that book; but a close study would be interesting because it is a genealogy with obvious ethical implications that relies on Scripture, not directly but indirectly, for its counter-history of faith.[4] Her counter-history does not establish or assume Scripture as morally normative in any straightforward way. At best the text points to, but cannot criticize, the normative experience of the community. For Schüssler Fiorenza, the living community of women is itself its own Scripture,[5] a claim that refers to the image of God's *basileia* ("kingdom") or "God's people" taken from Scripture but not defined in its content by reference to Scripture.[6]

The remainder of Part I will continue to follow how various writers understand the Bible to inform normative views of the male-female relationship. Schüssler Fiorenza has made this question central to her ethical program, and cast it in terms of sexual equality. The aim in doing so is not to develop a theology of sexuality. Because the Bible so often appears to support "old-fashioned" patriarchalism on that question, tracing the various ways writers in later chapters deal with this feature of Scripture will serve an analytical role. I need only note at this point that if Schüssler Fiorenza rejects almost all of the Bible's references to the male-female relationship as legitimating oppression, and does so on the basis of one passage that she holds as genuine on historical and ethical grounds, we are justified in concluding that she has little interest in grounding her main moral axiom on the moral claim of Scripture.

Schüssler Fiorenza's ethos of critical responsibility is a blueprint rather than a finished project. Its focus on a critical relationship to the text and ethical responsibility to others seems to give little attention to communities that view the Bible as morally authoritative. It is at this point that Daniel Patte begins to develop Schüssler Fiorenza's program of ethical interpretation.

---

4. I refer to the ethical approach popularized in modernity by Friedrich Nietzsche's *On the Genealogy of Morality*, which can be read as an inversion of Augustine's Christian renarration of pagan virtue in *The City of God*.

5. "The focal point of early Christian self-understanding was not a holy book or cultic rite, not mystic experience and magic invocation, but a set of relationships: the experience of God's presence among one another and through one another. . . . *Christian* spirituality means eating together, sharing together, drinking together, talking with each other, receiving each other, experiencing God's presence through each other, and, in doing so, proclaiming the gospel as God's alternative vision for everyone, especially for those who are poor, outcast, and battered." Schüssler Fiorenza, *In Memory of Her: A Feminist Theological Reconstruction of Christian Origins*, 2nd ed. (London: SCM Press, 1995), p. 345; cf. p. 349.

6. *In Memory of Her*, pp. 111, 349.

Daniel Patte:
Biblical Studies as Servant and Critic of Faith Communities

Schüssler Fiorenza's call found an immediate hearer in Daniel Patte, whose *Ethics of Biblical Interpretation: A Reevaluation* made its way into print even before Schüssler Fiorenza's revised lecture was published. Explicitly locating his project within the definitions of ethics and biblical studies set out by Schüssler Fiorenza, Patte encounters two problems. The first is a worry that her focus on rhetoric undercuts the method of the "critical reading" that grounds biblical studies. He proposes a sequential model that restores the balance disrupted by setting critical reading *within* rhetorical criticism. "Once the characteristics of 'the biblical text and its meanings' have been satisfactorily established, the issue of ethical accountability can be raised about the results of this academic endeavour."[7] Biblical criticism must be allowed to function without its method being shaped by rhetorical considerations.

The second problem Patte identifies is that he does not speak as someone marginalized by the guild but as a "European American critical exegete." Therefore, rather than being able to champion the outsider as an outsider, he has the task of becoming more self-conscious about his own reading more accountable, and thus more just. Unlike Schüssler Fiorenza, who at least suggests she has the ability to interpret in an egalitarian way, Patte admits he must still learn to do it while staying true to his "critical vocation." His vocation, he says, is to use the tools of biblical criticism to halt the destructive effects of biblical fundamentalism, in his words, to free people from evangelical fundamentalist obscurantism and its alienating, dehumanizing, and sect-multiplying effects (p. 79). The opposite of this fundamentalism he understands to be hermeneutical accountability and transparency (p. 2). The methodological problem for Patte is how to play this policing role without encouraging the very forms of repressive biblical criticism that Schüssler Fiorenza has so sharply attacked.

Patte settles on a form of biographical self-analysis that he hopes will facilitate the paradigm shift in biblical studies he sees as already under way. Patte speaks in the first person throughout his book, and he gives the details of his search to leave aside a self-identity as a "professionalized exegete" to become a "critical transformative intellectual." His basic conviction is that, to be just, we must constantly admit our biases and review the strategies of interpretation we use. Just interpreters know that there are no final moral answers,

---

7. Daniel Patte, *Ethics of Biblical Interpretation: A Reevaluation* (Louisville: Westminster John Knox Press, 1995), p. 7 (page references to this book hereafter cited parenthetically in text).

only a continual process of bringing one's pre-understandings and their ethical impact to light (pp. 5, 12, 102).

Having admitted that he is part of the "oppressive scientist hegemonic ethos of the centre," Patte movingly describes his struggles to become a more just reader. The first step in this process for him was realizing and admitting, after a long and painful struggle, that a close friend was quite right to accuse his studies of Paul and Matthew of conveying at least latent anti-Semitic sentiments. At the same time, he found himself confronted by his African-American students at Vanderbilt and had to admit their charge that he was asking them to deny their whole culture with his exegetical practices. Not only was his "science" not neutral, it was fundamentally anti-Semitic and racist. He realized that his methods had to be faulty if they demanded that "Christian feminists, African-Americans, third world churches, Jews and many other groups, (potentially anyone who is not a European-American male) renounce their own experiences and their own cultures, forsake their own identities, and deny the validity of their own concerns and interests" (pp. 20-21).

His solution to this predicament is to validate all "interested" readings, which he calls "ordinary" readings. It will be important for the reader to keep in mind, throughout the remainder of this book, the distinction Patte is working with here. Modern biblical criticism was founded on the commitment to treat the Bible as a *text,* susceptible to interpretation by scholarly tools of inquiry as is any other book. On this model, scholarly rigor is only possible by keeping faith claims out of biblical interpretation. Those who read the Bible from within the whole complex of doctrines, tradition, and communal practice; take it to be morally authoritative; and are personally invested in their interpretations are thus defined as those who take the Bible to be *Scripture.* In the terms of modern biblical scholarship, those who take the Bible as Scripture tend to the irrationality of reading much more into the text than it warrants, or conversely, of overlooking what it actually says. This formulation of the discipline has been a powerful one in the rise of biblical studies as a discipline, but it is a consensus that is breaking down (and is questioned in various ways by the exegetes represented in chapters 2–5 of this volume).

Patte wishes to remain part of the modern tradition of biblical criticism, that is, to treat the Bible as a text. Rather than unjustly suppressing the readings of those who take the Bible to be Scripture, as the critical method does, he offers his services as a critic to clarify and sharpen these ordinary readings. His offer is to bring objective analysis to the table in order to make ordinary faith communities accountable to themselves. He allows each ordinary reading community to develop its own biblical topography, picking up features that it considers important and explaining how they fit together. The critical exegete's task is essentially one of clarifying this biblical topography. Criticism cannot generate readings, but it can map those of ordinary communities, making them more transparent by elucidating the level of order on which a given reading draws. Thus can the critical exegete affirm that the Bible, when taken as Scripture, can liberate and change people, while offering to help those so liberated to pay closer attention to the features of the text. This sets up a barrier (the text) against those who promote injustice by illegitimately (noncritically) co-opting the text as warrant for making moral claims by which they can condemn others (pp. 27-30).

Ethics, for Patte as for Schüssler Fiorenza, is the attempt to establish interpretative frameworks that allow all fully to participate in political life. It is a "methodological quest" (p. 9) in that it systematically refuses the validity of any statements about the content of the moral life, specifying only the procedures that should lead to each community's attaining its own vision of truth. Patte's "conception of ethics (of biblical interpretation) is primarily based upon the view that the ethical is fundamentally rooted in the affirmation of the otherness of the other (Other), as the essential move through which I define my self and my ethical responsibility" (p. 14). Patte bars making claims such as this universal, because universal moral claims deny the perspectivalism of moral arguments that keep us from becoming oppressive by asserting our moral beliefs against others, the prime mark of fundamentalism (p. 85).

Patte's effort is interesting for at least two reasons. First, his book is important in showing how wrestling with Scripture is a practice of being transformed, and that this stands in polar opposition to the expert mentality. The expert already has knowledge that he or she can use, but believers are on a transformative journey with Scripture that can include their hermeneutical frameworks. In recounting his struggles to be less oppressive by becoming more aware of his interpretative frameworks, Patte corroborates Schüssler Fiorenza's claim that our hermeneutical frameworks have concrete ethical implications. It is important to note, in the second place, that this line of thought assumes that the community of critical exegetes depends on the existence of communities that are being liberated by Scripture, and who are reading it in rich and ethically generative ways. The fertility of such groups provides the material for Patte's critical work, as they do for Charles Cosgrove's development of his project.

Charles Cosgrove: Justice as Hermeneutical Consistency

We can now begin to see a line of development in this approach to the Bible and ethics. Schüssler Fiorenza has called for biblical scholars to promote justice by overturning structures of power and dominance through biblical criticism. For her, biblical scholars should be activists who take up the Bible to facilitate the formation of a truly democratic polity. Patte develops this view by defining justice as openness to the other, which he fleshes out by offering his critical skills to faith communities. In doing so he hopes to encourage and facilitate their becoming more reflective biblical exegetes and thus less susceptible to oppressive readings.

Cosgrove develops Patte's approach by trying to describe some of the general hermeneutical structures of all faith communities that appeal to the Bible as authoritative Scripture. He thus brings Patte's position to its logical conclusion. For Cosgrove, justice in biblical interpretation equals the structural coherence of one's argumentation from the Bible. Both Patte and Cosgrove stand self-consciously outside such faith communities, commenting on the coherence of their biblical interpretations in order to promote the vision of justice set out by Schüssler Fiorenza: hermeneutical transparency. All three fully agree that the task of ethical interpretation is to encourage people to use the Bible justly in rhetorical performances. Thus they also agree that the role of interpretative ethics is to set out a method that can distinguish between legitimate and illegitimate appeals to Scripture, facilitating the just use of Scripture in moral argument. Cosgrove's title succinctly summarizes their shared aims: *Appealing to Scripture in Moral Debate: Five Hermeneutical Rules.*

Cosgrove starts where Patte leaves off. If "critical biblical studies help believers confront the plurality of plausible interpretations and to take responsibility for the interpretations they choose," then it will be important to specify why some ordinary readings are illegitimate and others are legitimate. Cosgrove suggests three reasons. Interpreters must choose (1) between logically incompatible alternatives, (2) between alternatives that rely on completely different or incompatible basic images, and (3) between interpretations that demand practical impossibilities in the context of the interpreter's life. Cosgrove concludes:

> Choosing between these alternatives is a matter of finding the "most valuable" interpretation of one's own context. This most valuable interpretation must be contextually plausible and it must have a foundation in the text. Hence, any interpretation must be tested for epistemological-contextual fit and textual legitimacy. Moreover, confronting the plurality of legitimate

and plausible interpretations challenges believers to reconsider whether their own interpretations really are the most valuable for their respective contexts.[8]

Note that Cosgrove has fully reappropriated the role of expert repudiated by Schüssler Fiorenza, and so uncomfortably inhabited by Patte. The critical exegete is no longer conceived as an invested party; the exegete is now conceived as an impartial referee challenging ordinary readers to read in a consistent and therefore just manner. "Critical reading," which Patte wanted to protect from Schüssler Fiorenza's criticisms, has returned in a new and still-globalized form.

Justice, Cosgrove argues, is grounded in consistency (pp. 183-85, 192-93). "Hermeneutical rules are one way we promote consistency and fairness in the way we use Scripture. Their most basic *raison d'etre* is that fundamental moral principle of our existence, which says, 'Treat like things alike.' Formulating rules makes explicit the plausibility structures inherent in our discourse, so that those structures can be subjected to analysis and critique for coherence and consistency" (p. 8). Like Schüssler Fiorenza and Patte, Cosgrove is exclusively concerned with monitoring how Scripture is rhetorically used to justify moral positions (p. 7). His interest has been directed by Patte to faith communities who affirm the moral authority of Scripture, even though they differ in how they do so. This leads Cosgrove to undertake the project of describing the hermeneutical presuppositions of all those groups who do make arguments from Scripture. He discovers five rules among such interpreters: the rules of Purpose, Analogy, Countercultural Witness, Nonscientific Scope, and Moral-Theological Adjudication. His analysis of these presuppositions is intended to be descriptive rather than normative, and it aims only to help those for whom appeals to Scripture are persuasive to become more reflective readers and interpreters (pp. 11, 183). His "rules" are not binding; rather, they are guidelines offered to faith communities so that they can be more consistent, making them, in his account, more just.

Assessment

We need not go into the details of Cogrove's five rules to see that he and Patte have undercut their own ability to make moral claims from the Bible by re-

8. Charles Cosgrove, *Appealing to Scripture in Moral Debate: Five Hermeneutical Rules* (Grand Rapids: William B. Eerdmans, 2002), p. 171 (page references to this book hereafter cited parenthetically in text).

treating to a position of objective critical neutrality. Schüssler Fiorenza retained the ability to make moral claims in her refusal of scientific objectivity, which meant that her investment in political change could suggest that moral change was incumbent on the SBL. But Cosgrove has again taken up the mantle of the expert or technician, who, observing the landscape before him, offers only to point out the inconsistencies in others' positions, thus barring himself from moral exhortation. Hermeneutical clarification has become the sum total of Cosgrove's moral language.

This creates several problems. Most importantly, Cosgrove cannot appeal from the Bible (which would entail reading it as Scripture); he can only argue from the position of the expert against certain readings of Scripture. He can claim neither that his position is an interpretation of Scripture nor that it is justified by reference to Scripture. The upshot is that the Bible is unable to judge or question his moral presuppositions. Despite his desire to promote justice, he must define justice without any reference to Scripture, and so ends up chained to the profoundly hermeneutically and morally conservative stance of the impartial observer who can only offer suggestions to those faith communities who want to be more consistent about their exegesis and might choose to take advice from an "expert."

This makes it clear that, had Cosgrove written a book entitled *Appealing to Film in Moral Debate,* his approach would have been methodologically identical. The way he defines "moral debate" and "appeal" has no connection to the concept of Scripture in his methodology. He does not, for example, claim to learn his "fundamental moral principle" of "treating like things alike" from Scripture; rather, he is unconsciously expressing a watered-down version of the Enlightenment's concept of justice as mathematical equality *(Appealing to Scripture,* p. 111). Schüssler Fiorenza is more consistent in admitting this up front: she explicitly defines her biblical criticism as activism for a thoroughly modern vision of morality in which the Bible is one of many resources *(Rhetoric and Ethic,* pp. 51, 54). Because she already knows which aspects of the Bible are liberating and which ones are oppressive, she is free to critique both the Bible and its interpreters. To underscore her point, she quotes on the first page of her book what she considers the flagship texts oppressing women in the New Testament: the "women be silent" passages in 1 Corinthians 14:33-36 and 1 Timothy 2:11-15.[9] Her moral problematic is the

9. As a New Testament scholar, Schüssler Fiorenza is not as concerned to establish the unity of the Bible and thus does not deal with the complexities of Old Testament representations of marital and sexual relations (e.g., in Ezek. 16 and 23), which raise similar questions for a Christian sexual ethic.

classic Enlightenment moral chestnut in a new guise: How can we strip off the oppressive husk of this ancient text to discover its eternal truth? To be moral is to circumvent the oppressive effects the Bible has exerted on Western culture, at times by way of citing the Bible against itself. This accusation that the Bible promotes injustice is a critical one for Christian ethics, and so we will return to reconsider these passages from the viewpoints afforded by different approaches in the next few chapters.

These authors share the modern vision of scientific investigation in which divine agency is not susceptible to scholarly investigation. Only in Patte's book do we get the occasional glimmer that God may be at work in using Scripture to liberate people in "ordinary" faith communities. Patte leaves open the possibility that God is at work, but his approach to his discipline sharply emphasizes the human aspects of interpretation against what he considers the much more numerous interpreters who claim the name of God and marshal Scripture to oppress others. The result is that all three writers secularize familiar religious terminology. Schüssler Fiorenza, for instance, tries to recover the term *ekklesia* to describe not a confessional community but a public, democratic assembly of adult voices who share equal standing.[10] Cosgrove uses the familiar theological distinction of letter and spirit to denote a completely immanent reality, the moral rule and the reason for it (p. 12). Though he occasionally tries to resist the anthropomorphism of his position, Patte nevertheless often uses theological terminology in starkly anthropocentric ways, such as "overcoming the idolatrous character of my critical exegetical practices is something that I must first do for my own sake" (p. 27), or "the ethical is fundamentally rooted in the affirmation of the otherness of the other . . . through which I define my self and my ethical responsibility" (p. 14).

Marginalizing divine agency yields a definition of the Bible inimical to reading it as Scripture. The Bible becomes nothing more than a text produced by human agents constructing symbolic universes as they record perspectival discourses. The Bible becomes one of many texts and interpretations understood as political interventions designed to remake the way we live and think of ourselves (Schüssler Fiorenza, p. 27). This leads Patte to be suspicious of all universal moral claims. Anytime a universal moral claim is made, it is, by definition, an illegitimate reading of the Bible. All is process and politics; moral

---

10. Schüssler Fiorenza, *Rhetoric and Ethic*, pp. ix, 188. Richard Hays calls this a "wildly misleading interpretation of the New Testament's use of the term" (Hays, *The Moral Vision of the New Testament Community; Cross, New Creation: A Contemporary Introduction to New Testament Ethics* [San Francisco: HarperSanFrancisco, 1996], p. 274).

absolutes are nothing but rhetorical moves designed to shut down other people's voices (Patte, p. 5).

This position runs into several further problems of ethical methodology. It is clearly activist in its definition of morality: the only world we have is the world we make, and thus inaction is immoral by definition. Against such a position, it is important that Christian ethics in a modern technological age be able to specify why we might refuse to act rather than constantly urging action, a possibility methodologically foreclosed by these writers. Second, the reliance of all three positions on procedural method to solve all ethical problems leaves many questions unanswered. If justice equals democratic equality of adults, then what is the place of children and the handicapped who cannot take up this role? If justice is attention to the other, without holding any moral absolutes, what does this mean in concrete terms? How am I attentive to a suicide bomber? If justice equals hermeneutical transparency and consistency, then what happens when this suicide bomber has an utterly coherent set of reasons and interpretive principles? How does clarifying these for him or her promote justice? These are all serious questions that are invisible to the methodological proposals we have investigated so far. Without several more layers of specification, we simply do not know how to be just in many particular circumstances.[11]

Despite my substantial criticisms above, these proposals do advance our inquiry. They helpfully draw attention to the fact that the Bible is always read in historically particular contexts and thus for or against other readers. Exegesis is always "rhetorical" in using language to reshape social perceptions and behavior. Schüssler Fiorenza is right to criticize "scientific positivistic detached objectivity," whose insistence that New Testament interpretation is primarily about excavating first-century "meaning" is revealed as a ploy to silence dissenting biblical interpreters. All three writers' sensitivity to this point, and their calls for a more publicly responsible and politically aware biblical studies community, is therefore welcome. But it is important to note that they have insufficiently elucidated the way they make their point. All three writers are united in pursuing the modern quest for a single vision of truth (which grounds modern science), but Schüssler Fiorenza threatens to lose this truth by giving rhetoric (and thus power struggle) methodological pride of place. It is theologically important not to

---

11. John Rawls's influential procedural theory of justice has attracted a wide range of critiques of moralities that rely solely on such proceduralism. These are helpfully summed up in an early but still classic critique: George Grant, *English Speaking Justice* (Notre Dame: University of Notre Dame Press, 1974).

give up the affirmation of the unity of truth.[12] At the same time, I have tried to show in this chapter why it is so important to see how modern uses of ideas of the unity of truth have yielded oppression and thus demand from theology a more nuanced formulation (which I seek to develop in chapter 9 of this book).

In terms of method, these writers also help us see the intertwining of the "intellectual frameworks or lenses that make possible such a reading not only of the Bible but of other authoritative cultural and religious texts" (Schüssler Fiorenza, p. 14). Our biblical hermeneutics are inseparable from the meaning frameworks that order our moral perception. The writers discussed in this chapter are thus of great service in showing that behind familiar moral debates are questions of moral perception that color our moral deliberation and define with whom we will consider "persons" worthy of deliberating. The Bible is not self-evidently "historical data" or "evidence" for establishing truth claims; rather, it is an artifact that forces us to make explicit how our ethical and theological questions reveal the interpretative grid through which we perceive all reality. Finally, with varying degrees of success, the authors we have discussed in this chapter pursue an undeniably Christian impulse in struggling to find a place for the outsider and the powerless, and thus for a diversity of readings of the Bible.

Patte is perhaps most helpful in explicitly admitting the transformative power of Scripture (p. 4). Yet he makes this admission while defending a definition of biblical studies as a community keeping a critical distance from the faith communities generating full-bodied ethical interpretations of Scripture. Schüssler Fiorenza criticizes him (and Cosgrove implicitly) at just this point: they fail to see that they are also invested, that they also open Scripture with a hope of making some impact on the world, and thus are not simply "describing" the exegesis of others but are part of a community of readers with "interests, values, and visions" (p. 8, n. 23). Their community of critical scholars is itself a moral and interpretative community. It turns out that their adherence to Enlightenment canons of critical distance has rendered faith communities, Scripture, and especially God's living action a foreign land. The only thing they share as familiar territory is a modern sensibility about the importance of egalitarian tolerance and the moral value of hermeneutical transparency. I devote the next chapter to proposals that set out to describe "ordinary" faith communities, not criticallly, but from the inside. Unlike those by the writers represented in this chapter, these propos-

---

12. See Odo Marquard, *Apologie des Zufälligen: Philosophische studien* (Stuttgart: Philipp Reclam, 1986), pp. 11-32.

als also assume that one not only can, but should, orient one's moral claims on the basis of Scripture.

QUESTION FOR FURTHER STUDY: Is it possible to define the hermeneutical sensitivity of "ethical interpretation" without placing the faculty of criticism outside the faith community?

CHAPTER 2

Reading Together:
The Communitarian Solution

With this chapter our treatment of the topic takes an important turn. The authors discussed in chapter 1 all share the classic foundation of modern biblical scholarship, the presupposition that faith must be methodologically separated from scholarly exegesis in order to read Scripture ethically. Elisabeth Schüssler Fiorenza formulated a question about the communal and political location of biblical interpretation that makes assumptions questioned by the remaining thinkers of Part I. As Francis Watson puts it, "Modern biblical scholarship has devised a variety of strategies for concealing, evading or denying the simple fact that Christian faith has its own *distinctive* reasons for concern with the Bible. To reassert this fact, and to draw from it implications about how biblical interpretation should be practiced, is to break with the tacit consensus that this fact should on no account be mentioned."[1] Chapters 2–5 trace some of the most prominent lines of attack against the scholarly boundaries erected between exegesis and ethics. The authors represented in these chapters are agreed that distinctively Christian beliefs should be allowed a role in the formulation of Christian exegetical and ethical methodology. In chapter 1, it is morality that is certain, the Bible and church foreign by design; in chapter 2, the church and ethics are familiar, the Bible foreign and unfamiliar.

During the same decade that the biblical exegetes of chapter 1 were thinking about "ethical interpretation" (the 1980s), members of the guild of Christian ethicists were asking the same question from the other side: "At what points in the Christian moral life do biblical materials have an appropri-

---

1. Francis Watson, *Text and Truth: Redefining Biblical Theology* (Edinburgh: T&T Clark, 1997), p. viii.

ate impact? When and towards what ends do we employ Scripture? Do the kinds of biblical materials that are appropriate vary from one situation to another? What is the proper starting point?"[2] This chapter traces an early and still popular communitarian response that explicitly locates itself within the life of the church's "ordinary" practices of reading Scripture, yet still espousing some of the critical skills of the academy.

Their shared "communitarian," or "postliberal," presuppositions can be roughly characterized as follows. They are dissatisfied with what they see as the tendency of liberal theology to evacuate theological language of any substantive meaning, and the inability of traditional dogmatic theology to meet contemporary problems.[3] Their response draws heavily on virtue theory, with its focus on habits and performances as derived from the thought of Aristotle,[4] and a keen sense of the formation of these habits in traditions as developed in the neo-Aristotelianism of Alasdair MacIntyre.[5] This focus on the solidity and continuity of habits and traditions allows them to affirm that individual moral claims are always in flux, a flux regulated by the narratives and stories that shape Christian character (Birch and Rasmussen, p. 105). This formation of character takes place in communities. Where modern liberal society values independence, the communitarians see themselves as resisting the forces of capitalist, Enlightenment atomization by emphasizing our dependence on other humans and the role of community in making us the "individuals" moderns believe themselves to be (p. 54). A canonical decay narrative explains the predominance of this problem. The earliest church was deeply communal, but it soon imbibed Greek concepts that broke it up into dualisms, culminating in Constantine's disastrous decision to identify the community of the church with the whole empire. Individualism's victorious triumph was secured in the seventeenth- and eighteenth-century Enlightenment, which obliterated any vestigial appreciation of community and its goods (p. 27). And finally, over time, with the loss of community came the loss of moral virtue. Thus the writers represented in this chapter see their basic problematic as how to reinvigorate the community of character that is the church, and how to understand the role Scripture plays in this process.

2. Bruce Birch and Larry Rasmussen, *Bible and Ethics in the Christian Life* (Minneapolis: Augsburg Press, 1989), p. 16 (page references to this book hereafter cited parenthetically in text).

3. The classic statement of this position is that of George Lindbeck, *The Nature of Doctrine: Religion and Theology in a Postliberal Age* (Philadelphia: Westminster John Knox Press, 1984), pp. 7, 102.

4. Especially *Nichomachean Ethics*. See Birch and Rasmussen, *Bible and Ethics*, p. 42.

5. Developed primarily in *After Virtue: A Study in Moral Theory*.

Birch and Rasmussen:
Moral Deliberation as Communal Self-Definition

The revised version of *Bible and Ethics in the Christian Life* by Bruce Birch and Larry Rasmussen is an important text in inaugurating the current discussion of the role of the Bible within the discipline of Christian ethics. Therefore, it is necessary to clarify how they understand the task of criticism, especially as they have located themselves inside the church *and* the academy.

Their treatment begins by validating the results of historical criticism and its emphasis on the difference between "biblical ethics" and contemporary "Christian ethics," casting the translation of biblical ethics into Christian ethics as the main task of the discipline of Christian ethics (ch. 1). Unlike the authors represented in chapter 1, they place themselves under the Bible's power to reveal moral problems (p. 15), and they grant that it is "formative and normative" for Christian ethics (pp. 18-19). Criticism, therefore, plays at least the same role that it played in chapter 1, that is, there remains a historical gap that is maintained between the Bible and the present, and this gap is understood as primarily one of temporal distance.

Birch and Rasmussen are similarly clear about their ethical methodology. Christians are already engaged in moral deliberation even if they are unable to articulate the proper role of the Bible in shaping this activity (p. 16). In this the church is no different from any other community, because "in its most fundamental sense, community refers to any social grouping, any collection of people sharing something important. In this sense we all live in many communities . . . [this is] a fact of human existence" (pp. 18-19). Note the nontheological definition of community: all humans are communal beings, and the community of the church differs only in having a special understanding of the purpose of that formal unit (community): living out faith in God (p. 20).

To fulfill this task, the church must school its members to appreciate its basic moral commitments (p. 120). Here Scripture is important in supplying a fund of communal memories about what it means to be a faithful community. These images shape moral identity rather than function as a catalog of eternal moral commands (p. 32). The Bible thus plays a twofold role in the Christian community: it keeps the centrality of moral deliberation at the heart of the community's self-definition, and it supplies the content of that morality (pp. 34, 103). The Bible reminds the church that moral deliberation is where the church continually defines itself through moral deliberation according to the image of communal life that Scripture provides (p. 156).

Though contemporary Christians will wish to share the ethos of the faithful in Scripture, they may well dispute many specific *moral* claims made in the Bible.[6]

In this, character is the "chief architect of our decisions and actions," and "community the chief architect of character" (p. 81). The central task of Christian ethical thinking turns out to be negotiating the multiple communities that shape our character. The communities we inhabit bestow on us social roles that have a thick moral content. When at church, we do as expected, and when at work, we "are the effective moral agents of these roles, whether we heartily approve or not, and whether we even give it much thought" (p. 92). To realize this makes social criticism a central component of moral thinking. If we do not engage in criticism of the ethical presuppositions embedded in our social practices, we do not see how they shape our moral perception and action (p. 85). We turn out to be morally fragmented among the many communities we inhabit.

The narrative of Jesus in the Gospels frames Christian moral formation by providing a point of unity for all social criticism, identity formation, and moral deliberation. It brings order to our fragmented moral perception but does not freeze it by fixing it in specific moral claims. The Christ story orders Christians' lives as they tell their own stories through the lens of that story (p. 105). The basic form of this story is "(1) God is like that which is seen in Jesus, Jesus in the Spirit is a disclosure of God; (2) and God, the source of all being, is on the side of life and good." Christianity is the community "bound to this particular story . . . and is carried on among those who strive to make this life their own" (p. 107).[7]

This clarifies why Birch and Rasmussen believe that the community is formed as it deliberates about its life together under the unifying force of this narrative. The church's problem is that it is insufficiently claimed and formed by Scripture, and thus it needs to spend more time deliberating about its life

6. The claim that the Bible shows Christians the proper *process* of moral decision-making (rather than moral propositions, *Bible and Ethics*, p. 208), is also defended by historical critic J. Ian McDonald, in *The Crucible of Christian Morality* (London: Routledge, 1998). He defends this position by appealing to a reconstruction of the New Testament church's processes of synthesizing various secular and Jewish ethical conceptions. McDonald suggests that Christian moral decision-making should conform to this model in which Christians do not transform secular or pagan ethical conceptions in the light of Christ (see Yoder's account in ch. 2 of this book), or interpret their Scripture with and against their culture (as in Watson's account; see ch. 4), but synthesize various streams of moral tradition as one group of participants in the "moral quest of humankind" (p. 206). His treatment is a development of the similar approach of Wayne Meeks, *The Moral World of the First Christians* (London: SPCK, 1987).

7. We must leave aside the question of whether this is a story or a grammatical assertion.

together and the society in which it lives in the light of its guiding narratives. The authors offer several practical recommendations (which they summarize in *Bible and Ethics,* ch. 7). The church is to be a community carrying a vision of moral identity that it inculcates over the long term, nurturing in believers the character traits expressed in the biblical narrative. As such, the church is the bearer of tradition, "traditioning" people by actively introducing them to the fund of images and narratives that make moral deliberation possible. Having supplied these, it is also an arena within which public issues can be discussed and moral positions can be developed. Finally, as it acts to reform itself, it generates social activism, an outward movement of engagement in public democratic politics, with a primary interest in speaking up for the protection of the oppressed.

It is clear that this treatment has most of the features of mainline American liberal Protestantism, where the Bible is given a functional role, and conversation, moral deliberation, and self-conscious identity formation bear heavy methodological weight. One new methodological point, however, is worthy of further comment: Birch and Rasmussen give an important place to a critical principle that will be of interest in future chapters. Since the community is formed by the narrative of Scripture, it is protected from oversimplified moral judgments by the stipulation that "any person who seeks to do exegesis within and for the church must do it in the context of the total canon" (p. 176; cf. pp. 157-58, 162-63, 171-81). The simple outlines of the Jesus story must be defined in reference to the complex diversity of the whole biblical narrative. This amounts to a rule about communal deliberation: avoiding the moral complexity of the whole canon will yield oversimplified moral positions. Several authors discussed in the next chapters return to this point, offering more detailed accounts of how it might be used. But Birch and Rasmussen are satisfied with the pregnant stipulation that, when Christian moral deliberation appeals to the Bible, it should take account of the whole witness of the Old and New Testaments.

Fowl and Jones:
Practical Wisdom as the Continuity of Moral Traditions

In *Reading in Communion: Scripture and Ethics in the Christian Life,* Stephen Fowl and L. Gregory Jones present four sympathetic objections to or modifications of *Bible and Ethics.* Their most sweeping reorientation of Birch and Rasmussen's approach is to suggest that the problem of the Bible and ethics is not our temporal distance from the writers of the Bible and their moral prob-

lems, but our moral distance.[8] Our inability to imagine living with the seriousness in faith and morals that biblical characters portray is a much more serious
gap than our unfamiliarity with the cultural trappings of Bible times. Here
there should be no gap between the past and present communities of faith. But
sadly, in comparing it to biblical faith, Fowl and Jones see contemporary
Christianity as a fairly typical "lifestyle enclave" or club in which people gather
who share common interests, but not in moral formation (pp. 65-67).

In one sense, this only reiterates the centrality of the practices of moral
formation in the life of the Christian community. But it is also a sharpening
of the concept of criticism. For the church to be a community being separated from the world, it most desperately needs to learn the skills of moral
self-criticism rather than textual and historical biblical criticism. Historical-
critical methods may help Christian communities to withstand tendencies toward self-deception, but they are useful only in making supposedly easy texts
more difficult, thus helping Christians to read the Bible against themselves by
recognizing hard texts. The maturity of the Christian community is measured by its having formed its members as biblical exegetes who are critics of
their own moral lives and the moral trajectories of the other communities
within which they live (pp. 40-49). Here Fowl and Jones criticize Schüssler
Fiorenza as being insufficiently critical in her wholesale acceptance of the
early Enlightenment agenda by using concepts such as "*the* global discourse"
to criticize Scripture (pp. 18-19). By locating herself within the Enlightenment
narrative of global rationality and justice, she loses the ability to criticize the
world from the Bible. This critique is based on Fowl and Jones's fundamental
agreement with Birch and Rasmussen that the Bible's role in Christian ethics
is to provide the reservoir of narratives and images that sustains the critical
relationship of the Christian community to itself and the world.

Such critical skill must be paired with the ability to discern how our situations are analogous and disanalogous to those of the Bible, a project, they
say, that does not "begin by attempting to understand the past on its own
terms and then ask about the past's present relevance" (p. 58). They take the
early Christians' relationship to Scripture as the template for the contemporary hermeneutical relationship to Scripture. Those early Christians "did not
seem to be preoccupied by the historical discontinuities between their canon
and their particular contexts. Rather, they tried imaginatively to formulate
metaphors, draw analogies, and make connections between their canon and

8. Stephen Fowl and L. Gregory Jones, *Reading in Communion: Scripture and Ethics in the
Christian Life* (Grand Rapids: Wm. B. Eerdmans, 1991), pp. 57-61 (page references to this book
hereafter cited parenthetically in text).

their present situations to order and adapt their common life in a manner appropriate to that canon" (p. 59). There is no formula for this process of illuminating our present by linking it with Scripture: this will always be a skill of making a particular text shine light on unique situations in order to bring Christians into the story narrated in Scripture.

Fowl and Jones modify Birch and Rasmussen's *Bible and Ethics* in a second way: by emphasizing the continuity of tradition as the handing on of virtues and skills of interpreting Scripture. Here they draw heavily on Alasdair MacIntyre's definitions of tradition, character, virtues, and moral judgment (p. 10). Instead of framing the Christian community's relationship to Scripture by way of the problem of historical distance, they emphasize the continuity of community values over time. This modification, however, creates a strong methodological tension. If communities are held together by traditions, of how many communities are we a part? And if traditions are a force for continuity in moral life, how are the many idolatrous traditions of the world transformed into the faithful tradition of Israel and the church?

Fowl and Jones emphasize the claim that only a morally distinctive Christian community can read the Bible aright; but again this complicates answering the question of how the Christian community becomes morally distinctive. How are its habits, traditions, character, and virtues changed if, methodologically, they are designated as the way the Spirit transforms the community?[9] Given the force of inertia in communal traditions and practices, the methodological problem created is the overcoming of the appearance that the church is either already morally distinctive, and thus can read Scripture, or cannot become so. Fowl and Jones give several examples of communities (biblical and extrabiblical) whose moral existence had been so warped that, even though they had Scripture and read it, it could not criticize them but would simply reinforce their perverted habits and character.[10] At other points, they suggest that we can choose with which tradition we identify (pp. 71-73), or revert to voluntarist circumlocutions such as "we need to work towards eliminating the moral discontinuities between Scripture and our own social settings" (p. 67). This leads to the claim that we can and even should undertake periods of "living away from society" (pp. 75-76) in order to reorient our lives from one community to another (p. 69). The world and the church are sharply dichotomized, a problem that Fowl and Jones meet by em-

---

9. See John Webster, *Word and Church: Essays in Christian Dogmatics* (Edinburgh: T&T Clark, 2001), p. 109.

10. The communities in question are the Dutch Reformed Church in South Africa under apartheid and the community of false prophets that Jeremiah confronts in chapters 42–43 of Jeremiah. Fowl and Jones, *Reading in Communion*, p. 99.

phasizing hospitality. In place of an account of the mechanisms of transformation, they emphasize that a fundamental part of the church's moral tradition is its habit of inviting all in (ch. 5).

A third Fowl and Jones criticism of *Bible and Ethics* is that it is overfocused on moral decisions (p. 9). Fowl and Jones emphasize that the vocation of Christians is not to "use the Bible in moral deliberation" but to embody Scripture (p. 1). And they understand "embodying" as a much more holistic formation of all aspects of the person by Christian faith, rather than thinking of morality as essentially related to occasional "moral problems," about which we need to come up with a "moral position" or "decision." They replace the methodological focus on decision with an emphasis on the learning of the life of faith as an apprenticeship in the skill of practical wisdom. "Practical wisdom, a notion that goes back to Aristotle, is the virtue of knowing how appropriately to discern a situation and to enact that discernment. The need for practical wisdom arises with questions that do not admit of demonstration. Ethics is one of those areas, and so is interpretation" (p. 50). Christian communities teach us how to make judgments that are different in kind from more mathematical or predictable knowledge (pp. 35-36; cf. pp. 30-31, 48).

But, as in chapter 1, without specifying what kinds of conclusions we might expect from this wisdom on any given moral question, we are left with a procedural definition of morality whose basic axiom can be summarized as this: "Communities should develop wise readers who are capable of deploying practical judgment." Conformity to this method defines Christian ethics, not any given moral judgment by any given actor. A further problem with this approach is that it also tends to make Christian ethics anthropocentric. Though the presence of the Holy Spirit is "a crucial criterion of faithful interpretation and performance . . . it is often difficult to discern the presence of the Spirit," and therefore, "we are called to discern, to exercise practical wisdom" (p. 90). This displacement of the Spirit's work by human wisdom is paralleled elsewhere by the suggestion that being able to hear the Spirit is a quality of character (pp. 102-3). Again, human efforts come to the fore: "*We* need to reorient our lives toward God" (p. 69; italics added; cf. pp. 68, 56).

The fourth modification of the communitarianism of *Bible and Ethics* is the replacement of Birch and Rasmussen's decision-focused ethic with an emphasis on the pedagogic centrality of moral models, that is, saints. Because we need the community to teach us how to act and judge wisely, and to properly use practical wisdom, we need friendship with saintly people. Only as we learn from them how to perform Scripture "masterfully" do we become a part of the church (p. 80). Fowl and Jones encourage their readers to see Dietrich Bonhoeffer's life as exemplary in exhibiting a growing virtue that allowed an increasing appreciation of Scripture, leading in turn to an intensive engagement with Scripture that facilitated further growth in virtue. Following the three stages of Bethge's biography of Bonhoeffer,[11] they trace three stages in his relationship to the Bible. Though several of Bonhoeffer's theological works were written before 1931-32, it was only when he discovered the importance of reading the Bible *against* himself that he developed the skill to really understand it. The second phase of his journey was to withdraw from society into the seminary of Finkenwalde, where his "primary task was to help the students learn how to pray and how to read scripture" (p. 144).

This withdrawal period was the source of several of Bonhoeffer's books, and in them he is understood to be developing a theology that exhibited moral seriousness and a commitment to follow Christ, a central concern with the community and the formation of disciples, and an emphasis on the Christian virtue of nonviolence. Fowl and Jones read the last phase of Bonhoeffer's life as the loss of this clarity about Scripture and the betrayal of his nonviolence because of his participation in the plot to assassinate Hitler. In their view, it was as Bonhoeffer became involved in the resistance community that his character was subtly corrupted by their values, that his role in that community obscured his role in the church community, finally obscuring his former clarity about the centrality of nonviolence to the Christian life — and so, implicitly, the Bible (p. 158). These three phases are keyed to aspects of the biblical narrative at various places in *Reading in Communion*,[12] but nowhere are Fowl and Jones's presuppositions about the saintly embodiment of Scripture laid out as clearly as they are in their interpretation of Bonhoeffer's life.

This interpretation of Bonhoeffer's life through Bethge's biography may not, however, do justice to Bonhoeffer's life or his thinking on the Bible and ethics.[13] We will return to the question of whether he lost his critical relation-

11. Bethge refers to these stages as theologian, Christian, and contemporary Christian, stages that structure his biography of Bonhoeffer. Eberhard Bethge, *Dietrich Bonhoeffer: Theologian, Christian, Contemporary*, trans. E. Mosbacker, P. and B. Ross, F. Clarke, W. Glen-Doepel (London: Collins, 1970). It is fascinating to see how the literary structures of Bethge's biography are translated into a hermeneutical framework in *Reading in Communion*.

12. Isaiah's servant (Fowl and Jones, *Reading in Communion*, pp. 31-32) and Ben Sira of the apocryphal Ecclesiasticus (43) are listed as examples of escaping from society to a segregated faithful community to study Scripture. Paul is taken to be the prime biblical example of self-critical exegesis and the skill of making imaginative links between Scripture and the contemporary situation of his hearers.

13. Bethge's biographical interpretation is not without its critics. His account is an integrated interpretation of Bonhoeffer's life and work which did not begin to crystallize until twenty years after the latter's death (cf. John de Gruchy, "Eberhard Bethge: Interpreter

ship to the Bible in the last phase of his life in chapter 5. But we have raised several questions about the Fowl and Jones account that Fowl returns to address in his book *Engaging Scripture: A Model for Theological Interpretation.*

Stephen Fowl: Practicing the Spirit

Engaging Scripture develops but does not substantially alter the substance of the argument of *Reading in Communion.* Because it deals with criticisms of the earlier book, the more sophisticated reasoning of *Engaging Scripture* will help us to examine whether the charges of anthropocentrism, formalism, and pneumatological deficiency are warranted. In the book's fourth chapter, "How the Spirit Reads and How to Read the Spirit," Fowl returns to the central methodological components of hospitality, character, and communal reading in order to clarify how he understands the Spirit to work in and through them.

This chapter replaces what is taken to be a paradigmatic example of "reading the Spirit" from an Old Testament to a New Testament exemplar. In *Reading in Communion,* Jeremiah is the archetypal example of someone who can hear, discern, and act according to the leading of the Spirit. He does so amidst a community of faith that has been formed by a distorted picture of Yahweh, and thus cannot hear his voice. But because Jeremiah has a richer vision of God, a thicker faith, he also possesses a more appropriate hope, which shapes his action. "This faith, in turn, forms Jeremiah into someone capable of bearing a word from the Lord. . . . His interpretative conflicts with the 'lying prophets' and with Hananiah in particular illustrate that when the character, practices and habits of the people of God become distorted, there is little that a more refined interpretative method can do to enable them to hear the word of the Lord aright" (*Reading in Communion,* pp. 95-96).

Fowl has reason to revisit this judgment, if for no other reason than to give a clearer explanation of how members of a single interpretative commu-

---

Extraordinaire of Dietrich Bonhoeffer," paper presented at the American Academy of Religion, 2005). This interpretation is increasingly being investigated for its historical accuracy (Victoria Barnett, "The Quest for the Historical Bonhoeffer," and Stephen R. Haynes, "Bonhoeffer and the Jews: Bethge and Beyond," papers presented at the American Academy of Religion, 2005). Stephen R. Haynes, in *The Bonhoeffer Phenomenon: Portraits of a Protestant Saint* (Minneapolis: Fortress Press, 2004), p. 147, raises a more important theological and methodological question: What does it mean for Protestants to turn Bethge's interpretation into a hagiography with normative value, especially as the Lutheran Bethge rejected the suggestion? (Geffrey Kelly, in a review of the Haynes book, in *International Bonhoeffer Society Newsletter* 87 [Fall 2005]: 6).

nity can generate such radically different faiths, ethics, and readings of Scripture. This leads him to a New Testament narrative that features a community in conflict, the conflict that culminated in the Jerusalem Council debate about whether gentiles should be admitted into the church without circumcision (Acts 10–15). This narrative in Acts is also one in which "the central characters show a remarkable facility for recognizing, interpreting, and acting upon the work of the Holy Spirit."[14] This is because, Fowl suggests, "[t]here are several very practical social structures, practices, and habits at work which enable the characters to recognize, interpret, and enact the work of the Spirit" (p. 105).[15]

Here Fowl develops an idea nascent in *Reading in Communion* by adding the Johannine point that the Spirit facilitates communities abiding in Christ by causing them to remember his acts at appropriate times (*Engaging Scripture* p. 101). This is a pneumatological ontology of practical wisdom: when people recall the story of Christ in ways that have interpretive and moral force in the present, this can only be the work of the Spirit. "The Spirit's role is to guide and direct this process of continual change to enable communities to 'abide in the true vine' in the various contexts in which they find themselves" (p. 101). This may not suffice as an explanation of how the Christian community is wrested away from its old habits, character, and practices; but it is a more nuanced account in which divine action is a fundamental part of the human exercise of practical wisdom.

Yet the question remains whether this is simply a more subtle retroactive baptizing of human action. Christians, Fowl explains, cannot interpret Scripture without the prior experience of the Spirit, yet

> the Spirit's activity is no more self-interpreting than a passage of scripture is. Understanding and interpreting the Spirit's movement is a matter of communal debate and discernment over time. This debate and discernment is itself often shaped both by prior interpretations of scripture and by

14. Stephen Fowl, *Engaging Scripture: A Model for Theological Interpretation* (Oxford: Blackwell, 1998), p. 103 (page references to this book hereafter cited parenthetically in text).

15. One other reason why Fowl may have chosen to concentrate on this passage is that Richard Hays (discussed in the next chapter) calls it a paradigm case for the possibility that "the church as a whole might acknowledge some new experience as revelatory even against the apparent witness of scripture." Richard Hays, *The Moral Vision of the New Testament: Community, Cross, New Creation: A Contemporary Introduction to New Testament Ethics* (San Francisco: HarperSanFrancisco, 1996), p. 297. Fowl's discussion can thus be read as a preliminary to his refutation of Hays's conclusion that the "universal testimony of scripture and the Christian tradition" has called homosexuality "a tragic sign that we are broken people" (*Moral Vision of the New Testament*, pp. 399-400).

traditions of practice and belief. This means that it is probably difficult, if not impossible, to separate and determine clearly whether a community's scriptural interpretation is prior to or dependent upon a community's experience of the Spirit. (p. 114)[16]

Given this priority, "several practices, habits, and structures . . . appear to be crucial for [Christians'] abilities to discern what the Spirit is doing and to act upon this discernment" (p. 115).

The list of practices and habits Fowl offers amounts to a more sophisticated account of the role of saintliness developed in *Reading in Communion*. The skills are of two main kinds: skill in testifying or bearing witness to the work of the Spirit, and skill in listening wisely to such testimony. In Acts 10–15, we see Peter establishing himself in the community as a person of the Spirit through his skill in testifying to the Spirit's work. He testifies that God is working, and thus he is testifying to the Spirit rather than to his own skill, and he testifies accurately that God is working in the lives of *other people*. Fowl concludes: "To be able to read the Spirit well, Christians must not only become and learn from people of the Spirit, we must also become practiced at testifying about what the Spirit is doing in the lives of others" (p. 116).

This skill, however, depends on another habit, the habit of friendship, because "we will not be able to detect the Spirit's work in the lives of others unless we know them in more than superficial ways" (p. 117). Despite basing his example on the "friendship" developed between Peter and the "unclean" Cornelius during their one meal together, Fowl nonetheless insists that we cannot discern the Spirit's work in others immediately, because "simply forming the friendships needed to be able to detect, much less interpret, the Spirit's work in the life of another is time consuming" (p. 119). Only communities who take such time will find the communion in the Spirit that emerges in the Acts narrative.

Fowl illustrates the implications of this position by referring to the American church's conflict over homosexuality. He correctly emphasizes that this debate is not so much about *if* there are morally relevant biblical texts but about *which* texts appealed to are relevant. Fowl finds the lessons learned from the Jerusalem debate about including gentiles in the church most pertinent to this debate, and he suggests that, just as the testimony of gentiles who had experienced the work of the Spirit led to their acceptance into the church, so too should the testimonies of homosexuals showing their holiness lead to

16. The wording of this passage finds a surprising parallel in the work of Francis Watson (ch. 4 of this book).

their inclusion in the community of believers. Fowl then offers an undeniably formalist conclusion: "Christians have no reason to think they understand how the Holy Spirit weighs in on the issue of homosexuality until they welcome homosexuals into their homes and sit down to eat with them" (p. 122). Fowl is skeptical that such a church exists in America. "In short, most Christian communities lack the skills and resources to debate what a life marked by the Spirit might look like in the present" (p. 125). The unbiblical anthropocentrism of Fowl's proposal is evident in the tone of this assessment, which is not a lament over the church or a prophecy to it (compare Isaiah 1), but either a historical observation (of unknown relevance) or a dismissive condemnation of a church that has become so corrupted that it has lost Scripture.

Assessment

As I have noted at the outset, the writers under review in this chapter differ from those of chapter 1 in explicitly acknowledging the methodological place of divine action. For them the church discusses the Bible only because it is God's chosen community. Stephen Fowl works hardest to clarify the methodological problems raised by this starting point; yet he is ultimately thwarted in finding a methodologically significant place for divine action by his strong focus on communal virtues and practices. Fowl, like the other writers reviewed in this chapter, cannot help but conclude that "Christians' abilities and successes in reading with the Spirit and reading the Spirit *depend* on their participation in a particular set of practices" (p. 128; italics added). The centrality of human action in this ethic has become more subtle yet remains of a piece with the bald voluntarism of Birch and Rasmussen, in which Christians are encouraged to change and strive, to choose their identity, and to "have an effect."[17]

The pneumatological deficits I have noted are an effect of this anthropocentrism. In *Bible and Ethics,* Birch and Rasmussen replace the role of pneumatology as the work of the revealing God with an ecclesiology in which the community forges its own identity, in dialogue with Scripture, through group discussion (pp. 194-95). This in turn yields an anthropocentric definition of Scripture as the book whose authority is established by the church's need for it (pp. 142-43). Stephen Fowl's anthropocentric methodology yields a quest to judge who has the Spirit. Fowl focuses our attention on acquiring the skills to judge the Spirit's work in other people's lives rather than on how be-

---

17. Birch and Rasmussen, *Bible and Ethics,* pp. 107, 129, 95-97, 140.

lievers might invite, facilitate, and perceive the Spirit's transformation of their own lives. We are presumably to learn this from "people of the Spirit"; but, despite his intentions, his methodology unwittingly renders him an outsider to this community, along with the authors (discussed in ch. 1), who explicitly choose this outsider's vantage point.

Thus, despite the emphasis on learning how to read Scripture from the saints, one is left wondering precisely how this is to proceed. Fowl and Jones are well aware that Birch and Rasmussen's anthropocentric formulation leaves something to be desired, but they are in the end unable to transcend it. We might at this point wonder whether there is more wisdom than Protestants suppose in canonizing saints after their deaths. Though it is undoubtedly right that we must learn interpretation from living saints, it might be a circumvention of proper eschatological reserve to assume that the Christians we know are saints. Every Christian confesses to be a saint, and every saint mingles with the people of God; but not all who confess are saints. In terms of biblical interpretation, this suggests that dead saints, whose work has been preserved and handed down to us, carry a normative weight that live saints cannot. This would suggest that the role of live saints is to give us entry into the living conversation of dead saints. (The next chapter will explore this issue further, and Parts II and III will flesh out the implications of such claims.)

A final question asks about the knock-on effects of the strong emphasis on narrative. The emphasis on narrative in shaping identity in postliberalism can tend, in one direction, to marginalize some traditional questions about the historical truth of the biblical narrative,[18] and, in the other, to become an apologetic strategy seeking a connection between human experience (as "storied animals") and distinctively Christian claims.[19] Birch and Rasmussen are more vulnerable to both criticisms than are Fowl and Jones, whose emphasis on the continuity of tradition assumes a transtemporal community of faith stretching back to biblical times. The effect is a somewhat attenuated but nonetheless important attention to not only the distinctiveness but the realism of Scripture's narrative.

More problematic, however, is the way the strong focus on narrative

---

18. For these charges, see Francis Watson, *Text, Church and World: Biblical Interpretation in Theological Perspective* (Grand Rapids: Eerdmans, 1994), ch. 7. For a nuanced account of Hans Frei's attempts to avoid this charge, see Mike Higton, *Christ, Providence and History: Hans W. Frei's Public Theology* (London: T&T Clark Intl., 2004), ch. 5. For the most persuasive theological rebuttal of this charge, see Robert Jenson, *Systematic Theology: Vol. 2, The Works of God* (Oxford: Oxford University Press, 1999), ch. 29.

19. Stanley Hauerwas, *Performing the Faith: Bonhoeffer and the Practice of Nonviolence* (Grand Rapids: Baker Books, 2004), ch. 5, "The Narrative Turn: Thirty Years Later."

yields a *de facto* ethical canon within the canon, in which narrative texts are seen as having primary or sole ethical force.[20] We have seen the authors of this chapter drawing exclusively on biblical narratives. Bruce Birch's otherwise fine survey of Old Testament ethics illustrates this problem more explicitly in giving space to non-narrative texts only on the grounds that "non-narrative materials are given narrative context."[21] Thus the Psalms, for instance, are morally relevant only as they flesh out the narrative of Israel's worship, or as simple denotative comments on the character traits of God. The problem lies not in this specification of one biblical genre as the most appropriate place to begin reading Scripture for Christian ethics, but in a lack of clarity about the theological effects of beginning in one genre rather than another, and an insufficient awareness of the problems created by limiting Scripture's ethical relevance to texts in a single genre.

In effect, the communitarians have replaced the analytic reading of Scripture, which looks to its "moral statements" as the only morally relevant part of Scripture, with a narrative schema in which only stories can shape our identity. Parts II and III of this book will suggest the importance of both kinds of biblical genres, exploring the implications for Christian ethics of having to take all biblical genres as morally binding Scripture. Hauerwas is certainly right that "the Psalms, the wisdom literature, and the more discursive books of the New Testament — are unintelligible apart from the story of God's call and care of Israel and the life, death and resurrection of Christ,"[22] though he does not go so far as to state the necessary corollary: the composition of the canon tells us that the intelligibility of Scripture's narratives is also theologically dependent on its non-narrative sections.

Despite these reservations, the writers reviewed in this chapter offer some important insights concerning the role of Scripture in Christian ethics. Perhaps most important is their agreement in beginning from the claim that "the Bible is the church's book. It has no special status outside the faith community."[23] The movement from ethics as part of a general ethical project to understanding it as a specific practice of the church is essential if we are to have any contact with the pre-Enlightenment Christian exegetical and ethical tradition. All the writers represented in this chapter encourage their readers to approach the Bible as Christian *Scripture*, as normative for Christian faith and morals and thus to be read together prayerfully and with moral seriousness.

20. Hauerwas, *Performing the Faith*, pp. 138-39.
21. Bruce Birch, *Let Justice Roll Down: The Old Testament, Ethics, and Christian Life* (Louisville: Westminster/John Knox Press, 1991), p. 40.
22. Hauerwas, *Performing the Faith*, p. 139.
23. Birch and Rasmussen, *Bible and Ethics*, p. 151.

The intercommunitarian debate about the proper methodological shape of ethics has also been instructive. Whereas Birch and Rasmussen define ethics through a more punctiliar, individualist emphasis on ethical decisions, Fowl and Jones suggest that much of importance for the moral life happens far outside the purview of what we think of as "moral deliberation," in the sphere of the daily habits and quiet virtues and vices that constitute the bulk of our waking activity. This understanding of ethics requires a much more interesting and subtle ethical methodology, in which ethical criticism of the world and ourselves are constant features. It is appropriate that Fowl calls this mode of critical engagement with ourselves and culture in the light of Scripture "word care" (*Engaging Scripture*, pp. 163-65). Since we have been born into a world saturated with moral judgments and practices embedded in language,[24] the reading of Scripture in Christian ethics includes an essential and continual component of self-criticism intertwined with social analysis of the many communities of which we are a part. This suggests that the words of Scripture are the focal point from which we can begin to enter into the more fine-grained and nuanced ethical critiques of the languages, and thus the habits, of the many different communities in which we live.

This proposal amounts to a relocation of criticism, away from its focus on the text and its interpretations, and toward ourselves, our readings of Scripture, and our societies. Fowl and Jones have properly emphasized that the Bible is a morally powerful book because it is different from us; yet the gap it creates is not cultural or temporal but moral. Though Christian moral thinking will take place in innumerable cultural contexts, Christians cannot afford to be estranged from the ways of living with God and the neighbor that are recalled in Scripture. A provocative alternative is highlighted in their emphasis on practical wisdom that questions the modern belief that the purpose of moral deliberation is the generation or application of universal moral claims. Their account raises the question of whether ethical and interpretive judgments are in a special category whose "fittingness" is inextricably linked with the particular circumstances within which they are ventured.

QUESTIONS FOR FURTHER STUDY: How are we to understand the relationship of human and divine action in Christian ethics? Would more clarity on this point elucidate *how* the ethos of the world's many different communities is transformed into a coherent and distinctive Christian ethos corresponding to Scripture?

---

24. Birch and Rasmussen, *Bible and Ethics*, p. 72.

CHAPTER 3

Focusing Reading:
The Biblical Ethics Solution

This chapter traces the development of the most familiar approach to the problem of the Bible's place in Christian ethics. Broadly put, its authors survey and synthesize the Bible's ethical teachings and suggest how they ought to be applied. Here we see a turn from procedural ethics to approaches focused on describing the Bible's explicit moral claims. The authors represented in this chapter are all aware of the crass ways in which biblical injunctions have often been singled out as eternally binding, and they attempt to develop more sophisticated approaches to such claims. The first two authors, Frank Matera and Richard Hays, are biblical scholars; the third, John Howard Yoder, is a moral theologian who leans heavily and explicitly on the historical-critical biblical method. The primary interest of all three is to work from the biblical text to develop Christian moral claims, principles, and guiding images. Here the church and specific parts of the Bible seem familiar, but the Bible's unity and the morality it demands often appear more difficult and distant — even foreign.

Frank Matera: Summarizing Scripture's Moral Claims

Frank Matera locates *New Testament Ethics: The Legacies of Jesus and Paul* both within the Christian community and within the guild of biblical scholarship. He holds a traditional Roman Catholic understanding of the place of the Bible in Christian ethics: "[T]he church holds that these writings . . . are a sure and reliable guide to the Christian life."[1] His questions about what these

---

1. Frank Matera, *New Testament Ethics: The Legacies of Jesus and Paul* (Louisville: Westminster John Knox Press, 1996), p. 1 (page references to this book hereafter cited parenthetically in text).

writings say are firmly rooted in the methodology of biblical studies. He is concerned that the diversity between forms and within forms of New Testament texts is honored, and that the location of the texts in their historical contexts not forgotten. In addition, the moral claims of the New Testament are not to be abstracted from the "religious message that proclaims salvation" within which it is embedded and to which it is oriented (pp. 1-2).

Unlike Birch and Rasmussen, for whom the diversity of the biblical canon was considered a stimulant to properly complex moral thinking, Matera expresses the view common in biblical studies that the diversity of Scripture is the central problem in understanding its contemporary moral relevance. His response is to keep his description close to the ground, taking as his goal only to describe "the moral and ethical vision that a given writing proposes" (p. 7), leaving the development of a synthesis of the entire Bible's moral teaching to others. By dealing with the biblical books as discrete units, Matera hopes to avoid running roughshod over textual features while preparing the ground for a future appreciation of the New Testament's moral teaching that would take its full diversity into account.

The problem with moving too quickly to synthesis is that most of the work of interpretation is done when we place texts in interpretative hierarchies. Matera feels that in some models of the intratextual relationships (such as the theological model), Romans and Galatians become too prominent, obscuring the distinctiveness of the other New Testament books, while in other models (that of historical-redaction criticism, for example) the Deutero-Paulines simply fall away as "not authentic" (p. 121). He hopes to flank these problems by providing a "fair" canon of the New Testament, and especially Paul, so that we can value each letter's distinctive contribution to our understanding of the New Testament's moral teaching.

In Matera's view, therefore, the fairest way to establish the relative weight of the New Testament books is indicated by archaeology. Archaeologists begin a study not by working the deepest and most difficult layers to decipher, but with surface layers, which give context to the deepest layers. Many works of New Testament ethics begin the other way around. "Should they not have proceeded instead by considering these writings in their present literary form, moved back by means of form criticism to the early church, and only then speculated about the ethical teaching of the historical Jesus?" (p. 8). Matera apparently believes that his archaeological metaphor yields a fair biblical topography, that is, it is descriptive rather than imposed. He thus surveys the New Testament following a reconstructed chronological order rather than reading the books in their canonical order, though he inexplicably breaks the logic of this approach by beginning with the Gospels.

36

The archaeological metaphor also plainly reveals where Matera understands the moral authority of the New Testament to lie. "This book proceeds on the assumption that the *primary* object of New Testament ethics should be the writings of the New Testament rather than a historical reconstruction of the ethical teachings of Jesus, the early church, Paul, and so on" (p. 7). Yet the force of his archaeological metaphor overwhelms this designation of his primary object. When asked how he knows the Bible presents a unified moral teaching, and why it should be normative for Christians, Matera inverts the historical critical method: the different books only *mediate* the ethical teaching of Jesus (p. 9) or Paul (p. 120). The teachings of Jesus and of Paul are normative in different ways, but it is the Jesus and Paul of history who ultimately provide the unity of the New Testament.

Matera's treatment of Galatians illustrates his approach. He develops the claim that the Paul of Galatians thought of "doing" and "fulfilling" the law as different approaches to the moral life, which he called the life of the flesh and the life of the spirit. "Flesh" *(sarx)* is taken to be a metaphor for all that is opposed to Christ's Spirit. Matera calls the works of the flesh "acts which destroy the fabric of communal life": sexual immorality, enmities, strife, jealousy, anger, quarrels, dissentions, factions, and envy (Gal. 5:19-21). To these the works of the Spirit are opposed: love, joy, peace, patience, kindness, generosity, faithfulness, gentleness, and self-control (Gal. 5:22-23). This yields the following summary of the ethical teaching of Galatians:

> [I]f the Galatians want to be under the law (4:21) and justified by it (5:4) after having known Christ, they are still in the realm of the flesh. In light of the Christ event, the ethical life has been redefined for them. If they walk by the Spirit and are guided by the Spirit, the Spirit will produce its fruit within them, allowing them to fulfill the law. But lest they think that such a moral life is automatically produced in the believer, Paul reminds them that those who belong to Christ have crucified the flesh with its passions and desires (5:26), a vivid image recalling his self-description as crucified with Christ (2:19). Because it is a cruciform existence, the moral life of believers is both a gift and a task . . . summarized in yet another exhortation: "Bear one another's burdens, and in this way you will fulfill the law of Christ" (6:2). (p. 172)

While undoubtedly an insightful account of the ethical message of Galatians, this summary does raise several important methodological questions. First, is this summary of the ethical teaching of Galatians really moral teaching as distinguishable from theological exposition? Given this summary's high level of generality, it is probably more accurately called an instruction in the grammar of Christian faith and life. The whole book, including its account of Christ's work, appears to be setting up parameters to which all Christian thinking must be conformed, including, but not limited to, "moral" judgments about what acts constitute "sexual immorality" or "bearing one another's burden."

Second, the summary's strong focus on the way of the cross rests in part on Matera bringing in a "synthetic" Paul at sensitive points. In what sense is Matera reading each text on its own terms when he makes comments such as, "Ethics, for Paul, are eschatological ethics; that is, they are rooted in the cross of Christ where God's eschatological future already breaks into the present through the power of the Spirit" (p. 166)? However interesting and important this observation might be, it undermines any claim that it is describing each book's message on its own terms.

We are left wondering what Matera means when he concludes his survey of the Gospels and Paul's writings by offering what he calls "provisional theses for a future synthesis of the New Testament's ethical teaching" (p. 248). His seven theses are general indeed, again reading like theological descriptions that methodologically situate all Christian thinking rather than setting out particular ethical judgments or claims.[2] That these are Matera's conclusions about the New Testament's moral claims suggests that, if the description-application model is correct, developing descriptions of Scripture constitutes the most straightforward and preliminary tasks of Christian ethics before Scripture. This impression is only strengthened when we note that Matera has surveyed only the Gospels and the writings of Paul, leaving out Acts, Hebrews, James, Peter, Philemon, John, Jude, and Revelation. Provocatively, Matera even hints that his methodology might not be able to handle all of these books.[3]

---

2. The moral life of believers: (1) is a response to God's work of salvation; (2) is lived in the light of God's coming salvation and judgment; (3) is lived in and with a community of disciples who form the church; (4) is instructed and sustained by the personal example of Jesus and Paul; (5) consists in doing God's will; (6) expresses itself in love for God, love for neighbor, and love for one's enemy; (7) is an expression of faith. Matera, *New Testament Ethics*, pp. 248-55.

3. With regard to these criticisms, Allen Verhey's *The Great Reversal: Ethics and the New Testament* (Grand Rapids: Eerdmans, 1984) represents an older but more sophisticated and satisfying use of this general approach. Unlike Matera, he does not seek a complete synthesis of the New Testament material, which allows him to complete a survey of the whole New Testament. Like the writers of chapter 1, however, he concludes not with a content-rich ethic, but with a biblically derived set of deliberative rules about how Scripture is to be used when the Christian community appeals to it in moral argument. William Brown's *The Ethos of the Cosmos: The Genesis of Moral Imagination in the Bible* (Grand Rapids: Eerdmans, 1999) presents a similar approach to

Richard Hays's survey of New Testament ethics also begins by summarizing the teaching of New Testament books, but it rests on the altogether more bold claim that Christian ethics demands not "provisional theses for future syntheses of the New Testament's ethical teaching," but must develop a robust synthetic account of the moral claim of Scripture's providing contemporary Christians access to its teachings.

Richard Hays: Summaries as Lenses for Life and Scripture

Hays's main interest is in clarifying how Christians reason from Scripture to moral questions, and, like Matera, he explicitly does so as a church member and critical biblical scholar.[4] He also begins with a survey of the New Testament's moral teaching beginning with Paul, moving through the Gospels, and ending with Revelation (with an excursus on the historical Jesus). A second brief section sets out and defends a synthetic description of the moral unity of the New Testament, and this will receive our most direct attention. A third part clarifies how this summary of the New Testament's teachings generates contemporary ethical claims by surveying how five theologians have used Scripture for Christian ethics. The book's final part undertakes the "pragmatic task" of applying his ethical method to test cases: Christians and violence, divorce, homosexuality, anti-Judaism and ethnic conflict, and abortion. Like the thinkers discussed in chapter 2, Hays aims to provide a full beginning-to-end introduction to the use of the Bible in Christian ethics; but rather than focusing on the character of the Bible's readers, he gives sustained attention to the New Testament texts.

The most interesting part of Hays's project is the concept he calls "focal images," which bears the traffic between contemporary moral questions and a description of the Bible's moral teaching (p. 10). Christians' understanding of Scripture's moral teaching must not be limited to its yielding moral principles or a list of prohibited acts, but must also allow the Bible to provide paradigms

---

the Old Testament, concentrating on describing the moral implications of the various creation accounts. Rather than seeking a single synthesis of their moral implications, he concludes that the various strands demand a broad plurality of moral imagination. In the context of this book, it is interesting that Brown forgoes describing the ethical claims of the Psalms. "Notably missing from this programmatic study, however, is any discussion of the creation psalms and their moral implications, a topic that well deserves an extended study in its own right" (p. 32).

4. Richard Hays, *The Moral Vision of the New Testament: Community, Cross, New Creation: A Contemporary Introduction to New Testament Ethics* (San Francisco: HarperSanFrancisco, 1996), p. 296 (page references to this book hereafter cited parenthetically in text).

and symbolic worlds to guide more analogical forms of biblical reasoning. This affirmation of the importance of reading the whole Bible emerges in his last chapter, but Hays sees the diversity of the canon as demanding that a diversity of *methodologies* be used in Christian moral thinking. Despite this espousal of methodological diversity, he gives analogical modes of moral reasoning priority because they are driven by narratives, paralleling the New Testament, which "presents itself to us in the form of story" (p. 295).

As a biblical scholar, Hays is careful to protect the differences between texts when seeking their unity; he insists that tensions between passages properly keep us from moving too quickly to synthesize. The unity of the whole exists, but

> is the looser unity of a collection of documents that, in various ways, retell and comment on a single foundational story. . . . The God of Israel, the creator of the world, has acted (astoundingly) to rescue a lost and broken world through the death and resurrection of Jesus; the full scope of that rescue is not yet apparent, but God has created a community of witnesses to this good news, the church. While awaiting the grand conclusion of the story, the church, empowered by the Holy Spirit, is called to re-enact the loving obedience of Jesus Christ and thus to serve as a sign of God's redemptive purposes for the world. (p. 193)

This is clearly a more biblically informed defense of the primacy of narrative in Christian moral reasoning than was developed in the last chapter.

Because the Bible is most fundamentally narrative, its unity, Hays continues, is not at the level of concepts *(Begriffe)* but of images *(Vorstellungen)*. Images that recur in this story focus our attention on the common ground its authors share and thus properly encapsulate the story of Scripture (pp. 194-95). Hays finds three images to encapsulate the New Testament's narrative coherence, even as he stipulates that the narratives themselves are nonreducible. (1) Community: the community of faith is the primary addressee of God's speech and is called to be a countercultural community of discipleship. (2) Cross: Jesus' death is the paradigm for human right action. Right action is judged not by efficiency or some other criterion but by correspondence to Jesus' example. (3) New creation: the community is the embodiment of the Resurrection in the midst of a not-yet-redeemed world (pp. 169-99).[5] The content of this synthetic account almost precisely parallels Matera's, though it is

---

5. These focal images are probably best understood as a pidgin systematics. The Marcionite tendencies inherent in beginning with a "New Testament ethic" become visible in Hays's rather too brisk account of how his focal images are visible in the Old Testament (pp. 307-8).

not framed as description but as synthesis formulated to serve in contemporary ethical formation.

One of Hays's basic claims is that all reading is an exercise in discovering analogies between the text and our experience. To call a text Scripture is to extend this process by committing ourselves to "form — and reform — our communal lives in such a way that the analogies will be made more clearly visible" (p. 298). Where interpreters discover fresh imaginative links between the biblical story and our contexts, we may suppose that the Spirit is inspiring such reading (p. 299). Because every text is culturally conditioned, only our imaginations and the Spirit can make them relevant for the believer's particular present (p. 302). Like Birch and Rasmussen, Hays takes the temporal gap between us and Scripture to be a key part of the problem of the Bible and ethics; but, like Fowl, he understands the work of the Spirit to be necessary if the biblical narrative is transposed to become part of our lives.

The role of Scripture in Christian ethics, therefore, is the "restructuring of meaning relationships." Having emphasized the irreducibility of biblical narrative, Hays finds that it is nevertheless the "focal images" that become methodologically essential in the project of "mapping" our lives onto the biblical narrative. Hays describes this basic task of Christian ethics as "relocat[ing] our contemporary experience on the pattern of the New Testament's story of Jesus" (p. 302). If and when this relocation of our experience, this "metaphorical transfer," successfully happens, the Word leaps from the past into the present, and the church becomes a "*living* metaphor for the power of God to which the text bears witness" (p. 304).

Again, the cross-pollination with some of the thinking represented in the last chapter is evident. Moral deliberation plays a critical role in the formation of the community for Hays, as it does for Birch and Rasmussen; but, like Fowl and Jones, Hays shows that the church deliberates not to make a decision but to embody Scripture (p. 305).[6] In contrast to Fowl and Jones, Hays allows deliberation to displace the methodological centrality of saints and practices in communal formation. This may explain why Hays is more positive than Fowl about the power of Scripture to change lives: "[T]here is a hermeneutical feedback loop that generates fresh readings of the New Testament as the community grows in maturity and as it confronts changing situations" (p. 304). Though Hays is happy to say that moral formation happens in moments of communal deliberation, "deliberation" is a much thicker concept in his work than in that of Birch and Rasmussen. The task of Christian ethics is not merely analysis of cultural conditions and biblical content, because "to

---

6. Here Hays and Fowl and Jones quote the same text from Nicholas Lash.

interpret a text rightly is to put it to work, to perform it in a way that is self-involving so that our interpretations become acts of 'commitment at risk'" (p. 305). Something happens in the act of committing ourselves to such performance that "transcends the experience of private rehearsal." Hays does admit that we learn how to perform Scripture from the saints, but by this he means not only the saints we live with but the whole biblical history and Christian exegetical tradition (p. 305).

Having laid out this methodological approach to interpretation, Hays seems to agree with the thinkers discussed in chapter 1, for whom exegetical method ensures some form of coherence and justice in biblical interpretation. The church's process of moral discernment is "most fruitfully pursued by the community within the framework of some synthetic account of the canonical witness" (p. 191). This leads Hays to claim that ad hoc interpretation either leads to "incoherent moral vision" or belies a coherence that "rests on norms external to scripture." It is worth noting the way Hays thereby emphasizes the centrality of hermeneutical theorizing for defining skill in Christian ethics. In effect, Hays demands that all Christians develop a facility in a complex metadiscourse so that they can grasp the ethical relevance of a given scriptural passage.

However, we might imagine or simply recall a community of believers who have never set out to develop the sort of synthetic account Hays suggests, and yet who have been deeply shaped by Scripture. Another counter-example is the community in the midst of having their synthetic frameworks broken down and reformulated. Hays would no doubt respond that both communities have an implicit synthetic account, or will need one to mature, and he might well be right. Yet the question remains of whether the performance of Scripture is ensured by the systematicity that a synthetic account promises, or whether it might be possible that, in the course of a serious communal wrestling with Scripture and moral issues, some moral judgments can emerge that will only retroactively appear to have been correct for their synthetic accuracy or otherwise. These moral judgments, *ex post facto*, might have been valid, or even prophetic, even though they appeared *ad hoc* when ventured. John Howard Yoder's account of Jesus' political ethic allows us to think a little further into the implications of this line of inquiry.

John Howard Yoder:
Are Summaries of Scripture's Ethical Teachings Necessary?

Like Hays's *Moral Vision*, John Howard Yoder's *The Politics of Jesus* is a hermeneutically complex work attentive to the details of Scripture. We will look at only one of its chapters to see some methodological contrast with the works of Matera and Hays. Yoder does not think it necessary to produce a general survey of the New Testament's teaching before developing a synthetic view of the whole. Instead, his "synthesizing" procedure explicitly works from difficult passages, assuming that the unity of Scripture will be visible in those most difficult of texts, and in more ethically interesting ways.[7] Yoder is similar to Hays in significant ways, especially when he emphasizes the importance of analogical moral reasoning and that "communal moral process" is a central means of determining God's will, when he understands the Spirit to be enlivening exegesis via the presence of Jesus, and when he emphasizes that the community maintains its moral orientation by retelling and celebrating the narrative of God's work (pp. 249-53).

In tracing their methodological differences, we may find it illuminating to look at Yoder's chapter 9, "Revolutionary Subordination," in which he considers the moral normativeness of the contested New Testament passages Luther dubbed the *Haustafeln*.

> Be subject to one another out of reverence for Christ.
> Wives, be subject to your husbands, as to the Lord.
> Husbands, love your wives, as Christ loved the church and gave himself up for her. . . .
> Children, obey your parents in the Lord, for this is right. . . .
> Fathers, do not provoke your children to anger, but bring them up in the discipline and instruction of the Lord.
> Slaves, be obedient to those who are your earthly masters, as to Christ. . . .
> Masters, do the same to them . . . knowing that he was both their Master and yours. (Eph. 5:21–6:9; see also Col. 3:18–4:1; 1 Pet. 2:13–3:7)

An examination of Yoder's approach to such difficult passages will give us critical purchase on the positions of both Schüssler Fiorenza, who calls these paradigmatic passages of oppression, and Hays, who says that Yoder's more appreciative interpretation "leans toward apologetic wishful thinking."[8]

---

7. John Howard Yoder, *The Politics of Jesus: Behold the Man! Our Victorious Lamb,* 2nd ed. (Grand Rapids: Eerdmans, 1994), pp. 12-13, 59 (page references to this book hereafter cited parenthetically in text). This approach came to prominence in modernity with the work of Albert Schweitzer.

8. Hays, *Moral Vision of the New Testament*, p. 246. If appropriate anywhere, such a dismissal would more properly be indicated by Yoder's attempt to establish that Jesus' cleansing of the temple with a whip was nonviolent. Cf. Yoder, *Politics of Jesus*, pp. 41-42.

Yoder begins by noting that the appearance of this list in several writings attributed to different authors is evidence of a church thinking through how Christ's lowering himself to humanity and servanthood should impact all social relationships. Yoder believes that an appreciation of the cross marks the single point focusing this broad and disparate process of moral rethinking (p. 131). From this Yoder concludes that Christians in all ages are to be like Christ only in joining with the first Christians in seeking out his socially revolutionary way of the cross (p. 53). Yoder's use of the cross focuses his analogical reasoning in a very similar fashion to Hays's broader and arguably more complete set of focal images; yet his use of a single image significantly reduces the meta-ethical machinery necessary to balance multiple images in relationship to one another.

We can see this in the way the image of the cross gives Yoder purchase on the *Haustafeln*. The early form critics, such as Martin Dibelius, read the embedded moral frameworks of the *Haustafeln* as attempts by the early church to translate the nomadic lifestyle and parabolic teaching of Jesus into something more concrete and practical. This case rests on the observation that the *Haustafeln* show a remarkable similarity to Stoic formulas, which also address men and women, parents and children, slaves and masters, and rulers and subjects.[9] Digging beneath surface resemblances, Yoder finds that, though Christians might well have been working with a Stoic (or other) template, their beliefs about the ethos of Christ led to sweeping revisions.

For instance, Stoic morality demands that I live up to my own individual nature by rising above the vicissitudes of sociality. The moral instruction of Stoicism is always addressed to the individual male and is essentially antisocial. But, says Yoder, "in the *Haustafeln* the listing occurs in *pairs:* both the woman and her husband are spoken to; both the slave and the master. Not only does this reciprocity of relationship show in the literary structure of the listing; it is also part of the imperative. The call to be 'subject' or to 'love' or to 'respect' always uses a verb which relates this person not to herself or himself, or to one's image of oneself, or to one's nature or role, but to the other member of the pair" (p. 169). A relational view of reality based on the priorities of Jesus' praxis displaces the Greek focus on the perfecting and purifying of materiality and essences.

Yoder continues that the Stoic ideal of the strong and free man is thus

9. It makes little substantive difference for our analysis, but it is nevertheless worth noting that scholarly consensus (as summarized by John Fitzgerald in "Haustafeln," *Anchor Bible Dictionary*, vol. 3, H-J [New York: Doubleday, 1992], pp. 80-81) now contends that the *Haustafeln* are more reliant on Aristotelian formulations than Stoic. See *Nichomachean Ethics*, bk. 8.1160b-1161a.

44

displaced by a vision of social relationship attuned to the power of the humble, the "lesser partner." This, in turn, revolutionizes the category of the lesser partner.

> Here begins the revolutionary innovation in the early Christian style of ethical thinking for which there is no explanation in borrowing from other contemporary cultural sources. The *subordinate* person in the social order is *addressed as a moral agent.* . . . Here we have a faith that assigns *personal moral responsibility to those who had no legal or moral status* in their culture, and makes of them decision makers. It gives them responsibility for viewing their status in society not as a simple meaningless decree of fate but as their own meaningful witness and ministry, as an issue about which they can make a moral choice. (pp. 171-72)

Thus, whereas Stoicism aimed to free men (alone) from the impingements of social relationships and understood obligation as a bondage and fetter, now, in the light of Christ, social bonds in all their fallen finitude are celebrated as the locus of liberation from self-destructive and impoverishing selfishness. When "everyone does what is right in his own eyes" (Judg. 21:25), neither society nor freedom exists, only chaos. Where modern interpreters have decreed that the early church quashed the revolution that Jesus set in motion, Yoder claims that it properly grasped the much more subtle and demanding revolution Christ set in motion. This revolution works through invested participation in the social order in the belief that the conventions of social order are not eternal truths but divine creatures that are given for this age but doomed to oblivion in eternity.[10] Social roles are a divine gift that serves human welfare under the conditions of finite creaturehood, constituting the fitting, indeed essential, context for human social freedom and actualization.

Yoder concludes that such difficult passages testify to a collision between the messianic liberation of Jesus' message and a patriarchal culture (p. 189). "In none of the three settings would there have had to be a warning against overdoing enfranchisement, if there had not in the first place been good news pointing in that direction. . . . The one thing the *Haustafeln* cannot

---

10. The insight was almost certainly learned at the feet of Karl Barth, who was deeply shaped by the point as often made by Luther: "Thus real citizenship, when carried on in a Christian manner, is ten times as hard as a Carthusian routine, except that it does not shine the way a monk does when he wears a cowl and lives in isolation from society." Martin Luther, "The Sermon on the Mount," *Luther's Works, Vol 21: The Sermon on the Mount and The Magnificat,* ed. Jaroslav Pelikan (St. Louis: Concordia, 1956), p. 256.

have meant originally is what they have mostly been used for since the second century, namely to reinforce extant authority structures as divinely willed for their own sake" (p. 190). This revolution is difficult, and thus often subverted, because it is always easier to solidify and ontologize social structures. But the innovation of Jesus' teaching and life was his willingness to accept all the strictures and restrictions of human existence, including social orders, but in a way that at every turn revealed them to be orders passing away (p. 172).[11]

Yoder challenges the modern church to once again reconsider this message. He emphasizes the ineradicably Christological grammar of the *Haustafeln* and directly challenges Schüssler Fiorenza's definition of equality:

> What if, e.g., the sweeping, doctrinaire egalitarianism of our culture, which makes the concept of "the place of women" seem either laughable or boorish, and makes that of "subordination" seem insulting, should turn out . . . to be demonic, uncharitable, destructive of personality, disrespectful of creation, and unworkable? Must we still assume that in order properly to "play twentieth-century occidentals" we must let this modern myth keep us from hearing what the Apostle says about the christological basis of mutual subordination? . . . It should be noted that the point of Gal. 3:28 is not *equality*, in the sense of overruling all variety of roles and rights, but unity. The reference to "slave and free, man and woman" simply reinforces the "Jew and Greek" concern which is the topic of the whole book. Jew remains Jew, Greek Greek in this unity. Equality of *worth* is not identity of *role*. To make of Gal. 3:28 a "modern" statement on women's liberation, from which one can then look down on the rest of Paul's thought, not only misplaces this text logically . . . ; it also misreads the text itself. (p. 174, nn. 25, 26)

The passage illustrates that Yoder finds in morally hard texts an accusation against contemporary biblical interpreters, suggesting not that their morals are faulty, but that they have failed to think Christ all the way through and into the New Testament.

Because Hays does not explain why he thinks Yoder's position is wishful thinking, it is a difficult criticism to assess. What we can do is show how his

---

11. This is an insight Yoder almost certainly learned from his teacher, Karl Barth, who, commenting on Rom. 13:1, says: "State, Church, Society, Positive Right, Family, Organized Research, &c., &c., live of the credulity of those who have been nurtured upon vigorous sermons — delivered-on-the-field-of-battle — and upon other suchlike solemn humbug. Deprive them of their pathos and they will be starved out. . . . To *be in subjection* is, when it is rightly understood, an action void of purpose. . . . Its meaning is that men have encountered God, and are thereby compelled to leave the judgment to him." Karl Barth, *The Epistle to the Romans,* trans. Edwyn Hoskyns (London: Oxford University Press, 1953), pp. 484-85.

chapter on the ethics of divorce and remarriage, in which he illustrates the use of his "focal images," exhibits striking similarities to Yoder's position. For instance, Hays notes that Ephesians 5:24 equates the church's submission to Christ with the submission of wives to husbands, and he agrees with Yoder that this "begins a revision of patriarchy" (Hays, p. 363). But nowhere does he explain whether this means that the revision downplays or reinforces the modern understanding of equality of roles in sexual relationships. Some passages seem to suggest that he is prepared to critique modern sexual egalitarianism. Drawing on Mark 10:42-45, which emphasizes the cruciform nature of mutual service, Hays says that this is a costly path, "especially for husbands who are summoned to follow Jesus' example of servanthood" (p. 365). All Christian spouses are called to the life of mutual service, but Hays later repeats that "husbands in particular are to give themselves up, surrendering power and prerogatives for the sake of their wives, just as Christ did for the church" (p. 365). If there is a difference between the positions of Yoder and Hays on sexual roles, it is not readily evident in their normative conclusions.

Hays's "new creation" focal image generates questions about how the church can embody an eschatological witness to an age of rampant divorce through its embodiment of marriage. Perhaps this question could have been put more helpfully by asking how Christian married couples are to live revolutionary subordination in the face of both the denial of social roles of modern egalitarianism and the latent patriarchalism that has learned to clothe itself in egalitarian rhetoric. Putting the question this way shows that Hays's concern with the dynamics of the end of relationships rather than the dynamics of life within is insufficiently concerned with the "symbolic construction" of married life (p. 368). While Hays concludes that Christians "must recover the New Testament vision of marriage as discipleship" (p. 372), Yoder is already confronting the hard exegetical questions this entails by linking questions of social roles to the narrative of Christ's work. In doing so, Yoder suggests a range of ways married believers might develop the "practice of love" (p. 372), to which Hays urges believers without indicating its content.

This point has relevance for our assessment of Hays's emphasis on the synthetic project. Though Hays's synthetic account is much more developed and explicit than Yoder's, they nevertheless arrive at strikingly similar moral recommendations. In the case of marriage, our expectation would be that Hays's more developed synthetic account would yield concomitantly thicker moral conclusions. Yet, to take one example, despite giving prominence to the focal image of "community" not present in Yoder, Hays does not suggest any surprising connections about *how* the church is to live out marriage.

He might have said, for instance, that the claim "as Christ loved the

Church" demands that we also say, in a qualified way — and because of Christ's priestly role — "as the priests loved Israel." When the Old Testament recounts episodes of priestly sin, they are ascribed a different gravity than the sin of the people, and receive different punishments.[12] Yet sin on either side yields breakdown in the lives of priests and people as a social organism. Nor does the subordination of the congregation to the priesthood mean that the congregation is denied the prophetic initiative of calling the priests back to faithfulness, to the benefit of both parties. When Jesus sighs over Israel because it has no shepherds (Matt. 9:36; Mark 6:34), he is lamenting the decadence of the whole but ascribing blame for the whole mess on people bearing a certain social role.

The point is that the Old Testament at least suggests that "subordination" names an ethical grammar in which blame for failures of relationship will be leveled in an asymmetrical way; but, for success, the faithfulness of both parties is required. Such an account would ultimately need coordination with Christian doctrine along lines suggested by Karl Barth: "Does subordination in God necessarily involve an inferiority and therefore a deprivation, a lack? Why not rather a particular being in the glory of the one equal Godhead. . . . Why should not our way of finding a lesser dignity and significance in what takes the second and subordinate place (the wife to her husband) need to be corrected in the light of the *homoousius* of the modes of divine being?"[13]

Therefore, we might put the issue as follows: it is a marker of the provisional nature of the relationships between the roles of priest and congregation and of husband and wife that, when the pair is united in faith and spirit, it is not equality but unity that results. Such couples live the life of the eternal Godhead, in which equal persons with different roles are united in harmony. In such a harmony each party will "lead" by calling the other party to repentance and faithfulness. The Greek for "to submit" *(hupotassai)* can carry the connotation of bending the knee to a ruler, as in Romans 13:1, but can also connote joyfully joining in with someone, as in 2 Corinthians 9:13. At the limits of this harmony is the specter of God's judgment in which the dissolution of the unity is the punishment itself, meted out and experienced in different ways by the different partners. On these grounds we can read the admonition to be submissive as a warning about what to expect punishment to look like when we are not Christ-like.

On such an account, for a marriage to function as a place for "joyful

---

12. A classic example is 1 Sam. 2:12-36. See the discussion in ch. 6.

13. Karl Barth, *Church Dogmatics*, Vol. IV.I, *The Doctrine of Reconciliation*, trans. G. W. Bromiley (Edinburgh: T&T Clark, 1956), p. 202.

joining in," the Spirit's leading and softening of human hearts will be required at critical junctures. To say this is to admit that Scripture suggests that God's regular self-bestowal is necessary for there to be any enduring marriage and begetting at all. To remain married requires a constancy of will and openness to hearing and being transformed that lies beyond the realm of ethics and in the realm of the continual seeking of God's presence and renewing of hearts. These observations are intended to illustrate that, as helpful as focal images might be, the imperative for Christian ethics is not to arrive at a definitive summary of Scripture but to encourage going deeper into it, a point that I develop at greater length in chapter 5. Our discussion has revealed that, in terms of metaphor and content, neither Hays nor Yoder has "gotten to the bottom" of what Scripture says about how Christian marriage is to witness to its age, nor how Christian practices of marriage are to express the hope that God's arrival will continually renew that union.

Methodologically, Yoder's account is important because it is an example of an exploration of the Bible's grammar that works comfortably without a prior survey of the whole Bible's moral witness. It relies on a grasp of the whole of Scripture, but in a way that challenges the belief that Christian ethics can most properly pursue its work by using this knowledge as a description or synthetic account. He begins not by summarizing Scripture but with moral problems taken to Scripture. In doing so, Yoder reveals the importance of recognizing that what makes texts "hard" can be defined in many ways. The *Haustafeln* are not difficult because the text is degraded or unintelligible — just the opposite: they are difficult because they clash with deeply held contemporary moral presuppositions. Yoder suggests that exegetical maturity in Christian ethics consists in engaging one's efforts to examine claims that a text is morally hard, or that swaths of the Bible are morally irrelevant. For Yoder, the point of going to Scripture is to let it burrow into and confront our moral presuppositions. This means that the interesting exegetical work is not summarizing Scripture but becoming aware when Scripture threatens our moral presuppositions, a view he shares with Fowl and Jones (chapter 2).

Assessment

This chapter has highlighted the methodological problem of how to understand the role of a summary of the Bible's moral teaching for Christian ethics. The problem is focused by asking how the different thinkers understand the New and Old Testaments to fit together. Matera is most problematic in that he simply admits the incompleteness of his integration of the moral teaching of the New Testament, setting aside the much more difficult process of summarizing the whole Bible. Hays takes a broader sample of the New Testament and suggests the connection of this material to the Old Testament, while complaining that a proper survey of the whole Bible's moral teaching is "too complicated" (Hays, p. 306). Yoder offers a way beyond this difficulty by drawing from the whole biblical canon to explain specific New Testament passages. He considers an interaction with the Old Testament to be essential — and Christ as its unity — but eschews the development of a complete survey of the whole Bible's ethical teaching. We also get the distinct impression that these analyses disproportionately favor the New Testament, with the implication that Christians, in their actual use of the Bible, should look for moral guidance to the New Testament, which, in Marcionite fashion, they treat *de facto* as more important and accessible to Christian ethical inquiry. We are left wondering whether a complete survey of the ethical teaching of Scripture is possible, or even desirable, as Matera and Hays suggest, but then do not undertake.

Again, important insights have emerged. The writers represented in this chapter display a refreshing familiarity with the content of the Bible, placing a premium on wrestling with specific texts, which they do in a much more sophisticated way (Hays, p. 291). All are aware that moral arguments from Scripture often turn on what passage is considered relevant in a given case, highlighting the fact that much moral argument from Scripture is decided on the basis of one's biblical topography (Matera, p. 8). Matera approaches this problem by emphasizing the importance of reading each book for its unique contribution, while Yoder has simply gone to passages that seem relevant, not referring to the bulk of Scripture. We are left wondering whether we ought to seek a complete biblical topography or to grasp some essential unity from which to address specific moral questions and problem passages. Is it sufficient for Christian moral reasoning to know which passages stand near the "peak" of the scriptural landscape, or is it necessary to know where every passage lies in relationship to this peak?

Hays's and Yoder's works are especially important because they draw in many of the insights of the last chapter, combining them with the fine-grained textual knowledge of biblical studies. Most important is their agreement that ethical interpretation is not complete until we risk it as action: they understand Christian action as the proper confession of an interpretation of Scripture.

Finally, Yoder has suggested that what is important in a biblically engaged Christian ethic is not the development of a hermeneutical theory but a perseverance in taking our ethical questions to the content of Scripture.

When our moral sensibilities clash with the apparent meaning of passages of Scripture, rather than discarding them, we need to continue reading them until we think we can understand and live even Scripture's difficult passages, a process that we cannot complete before the eschaton. We may never finally know what "subordination" means in marriage, but Yoder is most suggestive in hinting that the key is not to have a final moral answer but to find a plausible way to begin exploring in life the moral challenge Scripture presents.

QUESTIONS FOR FURTHER STUDY: What is the appropriate role of systematicity in biblical interpretation? Does it generate or ensure accuracy in ethical interpretation?

CHAPTER 4

Reading Doctrinally:
The Biblical Theology Solution

When we investigate the role of Scripture in Christian theology, it is impossible to overlook the impact of Karl Barth's work on the contemporary discussion. This chapter will not develop an account of Barth's hermeneutics,[1] about which we need only observe that his thinking on the subject was rich enough to nourish two closely related but visibly distinct approaches to the question of the role of Scripture in Christian ethics. Few recall that Barth was a professor of both dogmatics and New Testament exegesis,[2] and he lectured on a remarkable range of New Testament books throughout his career.[3] These last two survey chapters reveal that, in the eyes of his interpreters, the Barth who thinks about the doctrinal location of the church's reading of Scripture has drifted away from the Barth concerned with the details of theological exegesis, though the subjects are side by side in Barth.[4] The thinkers surveyed in

1. Cf. Richard Burnett, *Karl Barth's Theological Exegesis: The Hermeneutical Principles of the Römerbrief Period* (Grand Rapids: Eerdmans, 2004); Mary Kathleen Cunningham, *What Is Theological Exegesis? Interpretation and Use of Scripture in Barth's Doctrine of Election* (London: Continuum, 1995); David Demson, *Hans Frei and Karl Barth: Different Ways of Reading Scripture* (Grand Rapids: Eerdmans, 1997).

2. Eberhard Busch, *Karl Barth: His Life from Letters and Autobiographical Texts,* trans. John Bowden (Grand Rapids: Eerdmans, 1994), pp. 162-63.

3. For a list of these lectures, with dates and places delivered, see Bruce McCormack's essay in Karl Barth, *The Epistle to the Philippians: 40th Anniversary Edition,* with introductory essays by Bruce McCormack and Francis Watson (Louisville: Westminster John Knox, 2002), pp. v-vi.

4. This claim is disputed by Paul McGlasson, in *Jesus and Judas: Biblical Exegesis in Barth* (Atlanta: Scholars Press, 1991), who argues that Barth's practice of exegesis is so eclectic that it is not readily correlated with his explicit hermeneutical discussions. I take the view that the discontinuities McGlasson draws out are also visible in, for instance, the work of Luther and Au-

this chapter learn a range of theological moves from Barth the dogmatician, most obviously his use of Christian doctrine to define Christian exegesis, ethics, and their relationship.[5] The writers represented in chapters 4 and 5 learn from Barth that God's life is foreign to all human designs, rendering all we think and know foreign to us in order to introduce us to God's form of life. Only God can make us true participants in his story and thus at home in creation.

Brevard Childs: Canon as Prism for the Church's Present

Some of the basic parameters of what is referred to as biblical theology are rooted in a set of conceptual moves developed by Barth and used, most famously and successfully, by the Old Testament scholar Gerhard von Rad.[6] One of Barth's basic strategies was firmly to locate the doctrine of creation within God's redemptive work, relocating concepts of time and space within theological rather than general philosophical terms. This is most famously put in this statement: "Creation is the external basis of the covenant, and the covenant is the internal basis of creation."[7] Ultimately, Barth's definition of Scripture and the proper approach to its study were based on trinitarian affirmations,[8] which Barth continued to develop throughout his career.[9] While

---

gustine, but they do not sufficiently account for the fact that these three thinkers, especially the latter two, understood their practice and reflections on practice to be mutually illuminating. Arguments for the unity of Barth's hermeneutical reflection and exegetical practice are found in Helmut Kirschstein, *Der souveräne Gott und die heilige Schrift: Einführung in die Biblische Hermeneutik Karl Barths* (Aachen: Shaker Verlag, 1998); Richard Burnett, *Karl Barth's Theological Exegesis;* McCormack's essay in *Epistle to the Philippians,* pp. xxii-xxv; and Nathan MacDonald's "The *Imago Dei* and Election: Reading Gen 1:26-28 and Old Testament Scholarship with Karl Barth" (unpublished paper).

5. Space precludes discussing the interesting and related project of Friedrich Mildenberger, which is organized around the idea of theology as preached doctrine. Mildenberger, *Biblische Dogmatik: Eine Biblische Theologie in dogmatischer Perspecktive,* 3 vols. (Stuttgart: W. Kohlhammer, 1997).

6. Walter Brueggemann gives one popular (but cursory) account of their relationship in *Old Testament Theology: Testimony, Dispute, Advocacy* (Minneapolis: Fortress, 1997), pp. 159-60.

7. This is argued at length in Karl Barth, *Church Dogmatics,* III.1, trans. J. W. Edwards, O. Bussey, and H. Knight (Edinburgh: T&T Clark, 1958), para. 40.

8. The earliest and most influential statement of this conception is found in Karl Barth, *Church Dogmatics,* I.1, ed. G. W. Bromiley and T. F. Torrance, trans. G. W. Bromiley (Edinburgh: T&T Clark, 1995), para. 4; also *Church Dogmatics,* I.2, paras. 19-21.

9. In *Church Dogmatics* II.2, ed. G. W. Bromiley and T. F. Torrance, trans. G. W. Bromiley, J. C. Campbell, Iain Wilson, J. Strathearn McNab, Harold Knight and R. A. Stewart (Edinburgh:

these presuppositions have all been challenged,[10] they still exert enormous influence on biblical theology. The mature Brevard Childs can simply state that Barth's analysis "has not been superseded in its basic insight."[11]

Childs is referring to Barth's claim that the Bible is the history of God's speaking. Its genre is Scripture for the community formed by God's Word. These presuppositions frame von Rad's survey of the divine history recorded in the Old Testament, which he concludes points to the New Testament.[12] Childs extends this project by surveying the whole Bible in order to suggest that it points to and validates the development of Christian doctrine.

Childs's reliance on Barth's understanding of God is explicit and admitted. God can be no other than a being in communion with himself and creation.[13] Biblical theology, therefore, interprets Scripture as a collection of diverse witnesses to a single subject, the trinitarian God. It is to this God that both Old and New Testaments point, and the aim of biblical theology is to develop an account of the evolution of views of this God in Israel's history (p. 85). Biblical theology is theological because "by faith seeking understanding in relation to the divine reality, the divine imperatives are no longer moored in the past, but continue to confront the present as truth" (p. 86). As such, its descriptions of biblical content become normative for interpreters in their concrete historical settings through the agency of the Holy Spirit, who "makes understanding of God possible" (p. 87).[14]

From this theological starting point Childs affirms the exegetical problematic of biblical studies, with its focus on the diversity of the different biblical texts and their historical contexts. He responds to the set of problems this

---

T&T Clark, 1997), para. 15, "The Mystery of Revelation," Barth gives his account of why faith in a divine man, born of a virgin and resurrected from death, cannot possibly be the subject of historical records, given the methodological presuppositions of modern historiography. He develops this discussion in terms of the relationship between "worldly" and "covenant" history in *Church Dogmatics* III.3, ed. G. W. Bromiley and T. F. Torrance, trans. G. W. Bromiley and R. J. Ehrlich (Edinburgh: T&T Clark, 1996), para. 48.3, pp. 33-57, and applies it to Scripture in more detail in *Church Dogmatics* II.2, para. 19, "The Word of God for the Church." This latter discussion unpacks how these Christological reflections locate the theologian's appreciation for various forms of critical biblical method.

10. Cf. Brueggemann, *Theology of the Old Testament*, pp. 160-62.

11. Brevard Childs, *Biblical Theology of the Old and New Testaments: Theological Reflections on the Christian Bible* (Minneapolis: Fortress, 1993), p. 679.

12. Gerhard von Rad, *Old Testament Theology, Vol. II: The Theology of Israel's Prophetic Traditions*, trans. D. M. G. Stalker (New York: Harper and Row, 1965), pp. 428-29.

13. Childs, *Biblical Theology of the Old and New Testaments*, p. 82 (page references to this book hereafter cited parenthetically in text).

14. Cf. Barth, *Church Dogmatics*, I.2, pp. 797-843.

raises in separating the Bible from contemporary theology with the concept of "canon-consciousness." The Bible recounts a community's journey of faith, the growth over generations of its self-awareness under God. The continuity of this community's dialogue with itself explains the Bible's formation as a piece of literature. This frames the exegetical task in terms of secular history, as the correlation of "elements of diversity with those of stability within the history of the growth of the Jewish canon without falling prey to the danger of extrapolating beyond the evidence in order to fill in the many gaps in our knowledge" (p. 57). At the same time, this approach affirms the validity of the contemporary faith community in relationship to Scripture, because the church is the community that "identifies religiously with the faith community of the original tradents" (p. 71).

When we examine Childs's presuppositions, it is easy to see that Hays's more complex conception of focal images rests on Childs's relatively undifferentiated use of the canon as "a prism through which light from the different aspects of the Christian life is refracted" (p. 672).[15] Childs is also the originator of the insights visible in earlier chapters that it is a divine work to make Scripture real and present to the living church, and that the diversity of the Bible revealed by historical criticism is not a liability but a resource for Christian theology. The fact that the Bible was not reordered in the course of its writing and editing to form moral tractates, to set out autonomous moral rules, or to establish a normative moral system becomes a positive argument for the claim that the church's ethical methodology must parallel this "great diversity as a theological witness to life under the rule of God" (p. 679).[16]

Such a biblical theology conceives of itself as a bridge discipline to systematic theology, locating itself within the living community of faith that once closed the canon and has continually interpreted it to the present. It differs from systematic theology only in that it begins with a descriptive task.[17] One need not take up a position of faith to ask about Israel's faith; thus bibli-

---

15. Given the clear reliance of Hays's work on Childs, he might have been included in this chapter rather than chapter 3. Hays was placed in chapter 3 because of his primary interest in developing a moral schema, while the writers represented in this chapter concentrate on doctrinally locating hermeneutics.

16. Childs overstates his case. In regard to the Old Testament, there is arguably a development toward the emphasizing of statutes or commands as the focus of Israel's moral identity. Cf. Frank Crüzemann, *The Torah: Theology and Social History of the Old Testament Law*, trans. Allan Mahnke (Edinburgh: T&T Clark, 1996), ch. 8. Bonhoeffer picks up this point (ch. 5), which Childs denies with his insistence that the various strands of the Old Testament witness must be given equal weight in determining moral methodology.

17. Childs, *Introduction to the Old Testament as Scripture* (Minneapolis: Fortress, 1979), pp. 72-73.

cal theology begins by asking only about "the biblical text in relation to a community of faith and practice for whom it served a particular theological role as possessing divine authority."[18] Childs's material treatment is thus devoted to describing the "discrete witness" of the two testaments, with the aim of exposing the growth and change in the record of Israel's history, and the church's reception of it in the New Testament. Here the secular understanding of history, and sacred history as the history of God's action, are understood to have a complex relationship that allows the past to be both an object of secular historical research and the normative witness for the Christian community. Childs affirms von Rad's hermeneutical presuppositions while criticizing the latter's use of them, which he feels yields two histories rather than one divine history with two legitimate aspects (p. 103). It is a problem that also concerns Watson, as we shall see.

Because there is one diachronically developing faith community that understands itself as hearing from and pointing to God through Scripture, Childs continues, we can trace the development of that community as it appropriates and synthesizes its reading of Scripture to form doctrines. This leads Childs to emphasize that doctrines should be tested against the content of Scripture to ensure that theological claims stay true to the trajectory developing in the historical witness of Scripture (p. 336). His biblical theology culminates in an analysis of how ten familiar Christian doctrines (God, creation, reconciliation, faith, etc.) do indeed properly continue the trajectory of Scripture. The final "doctrine" is ethics, where Childs leans especially heavily on one reading of Barth. He sets as his task to understand "the role of scripture in theological reflection on the human response to the imperatives of the gospel"(p. 658). Childs avoids the trap of thinking there are "moral teachings" distinguishable from the general content of Scripture by affirming Scripture as the community's reflection on God's will for all creation, expressed in different literary forms (legal, prophetic, etc.), all of which unambiguously communicate God's command to "keep my commandments and live" (Prov. 7:2). Therefore, Childs considers some form of "command ethics" the best way forward for a biblical ethic (p. 713), in which believers enter the "strange new world of God's action" rather than a moral rule system (p. 679) by means of Scripture, the unique and indispensable vehicle bringing us face to face with the commanding God (p. 714).[19]

Childs's treatment faces several insoluble problems at this point, which parallel those faced by Matera in chapter 3. Having undertaken a description-

---

18. Childs, *Introduction to the Old Testament*, p. 74.
19. Here he cites Barth, *Church Dogmatics* II.2, pp. 564ff.

synthesis project when asking about ethics, Childs must embark yet again on a summary of the ethical teachings of the different biblical books. Despite claiming that ethics is not a separate part of the whole Bible's witness to God's working, he nevertheless undertakes to supplement his 287-page description of the witness of the Old and New Testaments with a brief treatment of the "ethical witness" of this same material (organized by genre). The result is that Childs finds himself stranded between the claim that Scripture's witness is inherently moral and his critical impulse to say that all Christian doctrine must be defended by recourse to historical analysis of the text. Though Childs laments that there has been no "full blown treatment of Old Testament ethics within its canonical context"(p. 678), [20] and several times expresses shock that "there has been almost no attention directed to the nature of the faithful Christian life in light of the two testaments," his own attempt's grinding to a halt seems rather to suggest the impossibility of the task as he conceives it. It appears that the project of describing the Bible's moral content and its development in successive stages of Israel's and the church's history in order to "extend" it into "contemporary ethical application"(p. 672) is one doomed to suffocate under its own bulk.

This is clearly the conclusion of Francis Watson, who explicitly locates himself within this tradition of biblical theology (he subtitled one of his books *Redefining Biblical Theology*)[21] yet does not feel compelled to begin biblical ethics with a summary of the Bible's ethical witness.[22]

---

20. Childs might have moderated this judgment had he been aware of an older and more elegant treatment, which takes its bearings from an older biblical theology but organizes its treatment around the development of themes or ethical mandates in Scripture, John Murray's *Principles of Conduct: Aspects of Biblical Ethics* (London: Tyndale Press, 1957).

21. Francis Watson, *Text and Truth: Redefining Biblical Theology* (Grand Rapids: Eerdmans, 1997) (page references to this book hereafter cited parenthetically in text).

22. Some might suspect that the impulse to produce a comprehensive survey has been transposed from an ethical to a hermeneutical key in Francis Watson, *Paul and the Hermeneutics of Faith* (London: T&T Clark International, 2004). Here Watson surveys the hermeneutical approaches of Paul to the Old Testament. If his attempt suggested the limitation of contemporary hermeneutical approaches to those displayed in Scripture, the problems would arise that face attempts to generate a complete survey of the Bible's ethical teachings. This fear seems misplaced, however, as his intent appears to be the opening up or enlivening of theological hermeneutics (p. 528, n. 7). Thus the work intends to open up new hermeneutical options, rather than list the methods that are given an imprimatur by their use by New Testament authors, much as this work does by examining the exegetical approaches of contemporary authors and the Christian tradition.

Francis Watson:
Defining Hermeneutics and Ethics Christologically

Watson believes that Childs's methodologically prominent notions of canon, history, and progress deserve critique: "A further step must be taken at this point, which is to recognize that theology may itself constitute a hermeneutic" (p. 241). Agreeing with Childs that Christian doctrine is an interpretation of Scripture leads Watson to replace a canon-hermeneutics with a doctrine-framed hermeneutics.

The effect of that is to endorse but strictly limit historical-critical hermeneutical presuppositions based on nontheological concepts of history. While the Bible does remain a "text," a human artifact read by many people who are not part of the Christian community, the church also learns from the perspective of faith that this interpretative community is the "world." Watson emphasizes that this knowledge does not elevate the church to another plane from that of the world, and thus "there seems no valid reason why one should not practice a mode of interpretation responsive both to the traditions of the ecclesial community and to the demands of the world beyond the community, for the church is itself related diachronically to its own past and synchronically to the wider world, and must be faithful to the requirements imposed by both dimensions of its location" (p. 229). [23] Without compromising its beliefs, the church can agree with the world that not all events in Scripture happened as narrated if the criteria are those of secular history, while radically disagreeing about the importance of this fact (p. 231).

This yields a significant critique of Childs, who claims that the community of faith can criticize but not learn from the world. Such a position is insufficiently theological, contends Watson: God can and has used the traditions of the world to challenge the church to a more faithful reading of Scripture (pp. 236-37). The observation is an important one for Christian ethics because Watson presses the point that even if one is in the church, fully desiring to submit to Scripture, this is not easily done or cleanly separated from the "secular" ethical categories that one brings to the text.

Therefore, Watson emphasizes that an ethical reading of Scripture is a constant interpretative engagement. It is a process of discerning the gospel in our culture to enliven our grasp of Scripture, and the gospel in Scripture that

---

23. Watson's use of the term "wider world" is a telltale sign that the center of gravity in his hermeneutics is not as deep in theology as the previous paragraphs of his analysis suggest. In Christian theology the church is the widest possible human reality, the world its dark and ephemeral margin.

confronts and critiques our familiar moral notions. We cannot specify in advance which way we will be pushed, toward a more faithful rereading of Scripture or toward more acute criticism of ourselves and our culture. Though contemporary Christians may affirm the New Testament's exhortations to be like Christ, they can only do so as members of modern (Western) culture. That this culture now places a moral premium on the contribution of female voices to public discourse helps us, for instance, to take Scripture's sayings about men and women more seriously by pressing for clarification of the many judgments of intertextual weighting on which ethical interpretation necessarily rests. Watson thus believes it important to listen closely to feminist (and other) critiques of modern society and exegesis.[24] The same questions are raised by contemporary moral certainties about democracy, multiculturalism, inclusivism, the free-market economy, and so on. Clashes of ethical sensibility with the plain meaning of biblical texts force a closer reading of Scripture and a more developed view of Christology, soteriology, and ethics, a process within which Watson does not foreclose radical rereadings of parts of Scripture. This is not a denial that the church submits to Scripture but a confession that it is God's speaking to the church that is morally determinative, and that this speaking happens in the midst of a complex relationship between the traditions of the church and other traditions, all of which are open to criticism (*Agape*, p. 89).

Only one full-length study sees Watson using his hermeneutic to generate content-rich ethical claims: *Agape, Eros, Gender: Towards a Pauline Ethic.* Here he displays his hermeneutics to full effect by integrating an extensive exploration of several strands of feminist philosophy and literature and a wide-ranging engagement with the Christian tradition. The investigation orbits around three pivotal Pauline passages relating to the role of women: 1 Corinthians 11, Romans 7, and Ephesians 5. Watson takes Scripture to be ethically normative in a way that Schüssler Fiorenza rejects, while he resists and makes more complex Yoder's stark appeal to submit to Scripture *against* the ethical presuppositions of culture. This allows Watson to explain, for instance, how Christian beliefs about Christ can simultaneously be based on Scripture and critique parts of its witness regarding the role of women. Watson squarely faces the fact that Christian culture no longer asks women to veil their heads or to have long hair (despite clear biblical statements to this effect, such as 1 Cor. 11:5, 14-15); and he seeks Christologically and exegetically grounded reasons why the passages that seem to demand it should be read otherwise.

24. Francis Watson, *Agape, Eros, Gender: Towards a Pauline Ethic* (Cambridge: Cambridge University Press, 2000), p. 2.

Christological premises also undergird Watson's affirmation that Christians inhabit both secular and theological ethical traditions. Christian ethics is an expression of a doctrine of the person and work of Christ that must be simultaneously ethical, ecclesiological, and eschatological (*Agape*, pp. ix-x). This means that Christian hermeneutics (at least of the New Testament) is framed by the confession that Christ discloses the divine commitment to and affirmation of humankind. Therefore, the church is called to the practice of participating in this commitment to and affirmation of humankind. It is a calling not yet fulfilled, but it is definitive for the community of faith at which God's working aims. Watson sees Barth as exemplary in placing the primacy of the divine commitment to humanity in the foreground, thus theologically grounding the *diachronic* unity of the faith community. This divine commitment is the source of the long tradition of faith recorded in and sustaining the community of faith. In *Text, Church and World,* Watson also applauds Yoder's emphasis on the political and social impact of Jesus Christ's work within his first-century context, because it emphasizes that God's love for the world must always have a *synchronic* referent (p. 243). Jesus' actions call the whole world to participate in his divine love by entering conversation with past saints, being attuned to the present world, and thus "oriented to the restoration of authentic human community in situations where it is distorted or absent" (p. 247).

This is a tightly integrated understanding of the relationship between theology and ethics as grounded in the divine-human person and work of Christ. Because the one gospel of Christ is the proclamation of the liberation of human action, the love of God must be understood in its inextricable linkage with the love of neighbor. And because all are liberated in Christ, Christian ethical responsibility is limited only by our particularity, because "a generalized practice of universal love is in itself impossible, [but] a particular, localized praxis may nevertheless concretize an orientation of love towards humankind as such, as in the case of Jesus' own praxis" (p. 268). Watson's theological hermeneutics helps us to see that, though there are counter-voices in the New Testament, Christians' love should be the same expansive love as Christ's, directed to all, and not just the "brothers." Love of the neighbor so defined, then, emerges as the Christian hermeneutical criterion of the Old Testament. Jesus' own interpretation of the Torah (Mark 12:29-30) is exemplary in not adding to or subtracting from it but reading it from within itself, thus implicitly critiquing strands of the Old Testament that move in other directions.

Christian ethics is the discipline of understanding how Christ's being and work define human love of the neighbor and the perfection of human community by "comprehending within itself a new human interrelatedness, and abolishing the alienating dichotomy between vertical and horizontal dimensions which leads to a construal of love of God and of neighbour as separate claims upon us which may even be played off against one another" (p. 280). The position of the church as worldly and within the world thus promises to move toward a resolution, Watson continues, because in Christ the divine image is restored, perfecting all the limited and imperfect forms of community we presently inhabit. This perfecting is not wholly other than the activities of human solidarity that are always present in various forms, but it differs enough from them that Christian love is inevitably drawn into conflict (p. 282).

The point is illustrated from the book of Ecclesiastes, which Watson reads as an anti-gospel to the gospel of Christian love. Qoheleth's sentimental agnosticism takes a sanguine approach to justice, the view of a jaded and indolent "realist" ruler.

> Its basic dogma, that there is nothing new under the sun, conflicts fundamentally with the prophetic and early Christian orientation towards the future, which culminates in the vision of the one who is the Omega as well as the Alpha, the end as well as the beginning, who announces: 'Behold, I make all things new!' (Rev. 21:5-6; cf. 22:13). Whereas for Qoheleth the tears of the oppressed will not cease to flow, John the Seer envisages a consummation of the covenant relation between God and his people in which God 'will wipe away every tear from their eyes, and death shall be no more, neither shall there be mourning nor crying nor pain any more, for there former things have passed away' (21:4). (pp. 284-85)

Only Christian hope for a "new thing" can sustain the love for others that makes political reformation possible, concludes Watson. The Bible is a "text" to the world, despite witnessing to the divine work beyond human expectations. Scripture's story is of a Jesus Christ who takes human form, and whose resurrection is mediated to us through a text written by humans, but who transcends the limits of both to meet his disciples (pp. 290-92). Scripture shapes the Christian hope that orients Christian ethical action, primarily by pointing to the praxis of this historical yet living Jesus Christ. This focusing of Christian ethics on the role of hope and eschatology in orienting Christian ethics is welcome, and it shapes Watson's treatment of sexual ethics (*Agape*, pp. 217-18).

Despite ending on this eschatological note, the pneumatology of Watson's account remains ambiguous. The Spirit, who is "redemptively present in all goodness, justice and truth" *(Text,* p. 240), seems at its most active in guiding "individuals to comprehend and to communicate possibilities of truth and praxis that are appropriate for a determinate situation, which are already present in the discourse of the community" (p. 120). Watson seems uncomfortable with the introduction of novelty by the Spirit, submitting that prophecy "becomes the divine word only as it is accredited as such in the course of the dialogue that it initiates" (p. 121).[25] This leaves the impression that Watson is happier to admit that the Spirit speaks to the church through the world than he is with prophetic speech within the church itself. The reverse is true of John Webster.

John Webster: Listening to God and Not Just Ourselves

In the work of John Webster we see a further movement of doctrine toward methodological center stage. Though not part of the biblical theology interpretive tradition, Webster shares many of its Barthian presuppositions. We have seen how Childs traces Israel's history as culminating in the doctrines of the church, and how Watson critiques Childs's canon-critical hermeneutics by means of a doctrinal hermeneutics. Webster shifts the discussion further toward doctrine, setting out to describe what doctrine tells us about what is happening when Christians read Scripture. Thus this chapter, like the last, moves from proposals that take a more descriptive, or "outside," methodological stance to proposals seeking to discern the inner dynamics of the church's reading of Scripture.

The writers represented in this and the preceding two chapters have given greater or lesser prominence to the idea that Christians learn to read Scripture from the saints, or with the community of faith. Fowl and Jones gave learning from the saints a central hermeneutical role, suggesting that the saints we learn from are the saints we live with; but Hays has intimated that we can also learn from the writings of dead saints. Biblical theology has constantly emphasized that God speaks, but through humans and the communal memories they collect in Scripture. Webster's inquiry tries to clarify what is meant by "learning from the saints" in yet another direction, an investigation he says is only properly undertaken "with the expectation that

25. Compare Stephen Fowl's formulation: "Understanding and interpreting the Spirit's movement is a matter of communal debate and discernment over time. . . . It is probably difficult, if not impossible, to separate and determine clearly whether a community's scriptural interpretation is prior to or dependent upon a community's experience of the Spirit." *Engaging Scripture,* p. 114.

in what we find hard or unpalatable we may discover a rendering of Christian truth."[26]

He begins by pointing out that, from the perspective of Christian doctrine, the confusions of modern theology about biblical exegesis are based on its having bought into the widespread erosion of belief in the eschatological presence of Jesus Christ. Once the work of the risen Christ has been lost, other doctrines expand to do the work once attributed to Christ as prophet, priest, and king. At root, most postcritical biblical interpretation proceeds on the basis of elaborate philosophical and hermeneutical machinery in which doctrinal considerations play a minor or nonexistent role. Concepts are almost absent from the discussion that once linked exegesis with theology, such as the perfection, perspicuity, sufficiency, and inspiration of Scripture. This dogmatic underdevelopment leads to the confusion of church and general concepts of sociality in ways that obscure an adequate theory of God's revelatory grace. The confusion of ecclesiology and revelation is exacerbated by the loss of pneumatology and eschatology. In sum, contemporary approaches to the question of the role of Scripture in Christian ethics are unclear about how they learn from the saints because they (1) dispense with the frameworks of Christian doctrine, and (2) thus they do not have the conceptual categories to keep from confusing the saints' words with the Spirit's.

Before outlining his own position, Webster investigates the approaches of Barth and Bonhoeffer to biblical exegesis. He first notes that for both theologians (as inherited by biblical theology) the subject of all Scripture is Christ present to humans. The church's reading of Scripture is not "a spontaneous human action performed towards a passive and mute textual object, but . . . an episode in the communicative history of God with us."[27] The point emphasized by Barth, says Webster, is that we must not assume that philosophical hermeneutics can simply be "adapted" for use in scriptural exegesis. As the Bible is the human word caught up in God's revelatory activity, it is properly heard only by those who also affirm an antecedent mastery by its Lord (pp. 96-97). Thus, in the second place, the proper reading of Scripture depends on a repentant self-effacement before the converting power of God and his Word. Scripture is the "textual ingredient of a process of divine self-manifestation" (p. 94), demanding an attitude of ready submission and compliance. Therefore, Scripture is not identical to revelation but is the paradig-

---

26. John Webster, Editorial, *International Journal of Systematic Theology* 5, no. 2 (July 2003): 131. See also Webster, *Barth's Moral Theology: Human Action in Barth's Thought* (Grand Rapids: Eerdmans, 1998), p. 7.

27. John Webster, *Word and Church: Essays in Christian Dogmatics* (Edinburgh: T&T Clark, 2001), p. 93 (page references to this book hereafter cited parenthetically in text).

matic testimony of humans to the efficacy of divine self-revelation, a testimony that is equipped effectively to serve Christ's work of catching its readers up in his self-revelation (p. 95). *"[E]xegesis is an aspect of sanctification"* (p. 95; italics in original).

Bonhoeffer's practice of reading Scripture leads Webster to a third dogmatic specification. Salvation is a matter of discovering ourselves within the divine action narrated by Scripture, the irreducible fundament and orienting point for Christian thinking (p. 100). By providing such an account of reading Scripture, says Webster, Barth and Bonhoeffer assume that the Bible is God's chosen tool for overturning our perceptions of what we once took to be the "present." We do not need to make the Bible or Christ present; Jesus Christ in the Bible announces his presence, and this happens when we come to see our perception of the present as standing before Christ's claim and judgment (p. 102).

This chain of logic leads to a warning that reducing reading to technique is a spiritually perilous procedure. Here Webster endorses Bonhoeffer's claim that reading Scripture is not a technique that can be learned but is something that waxes or wanes according to one's spiritual condition. Rather than personalizing or immanentizing Scripture, Bonhoeffer argues, such a move acknowledges the dogmatic implications of Christian doctrines of revelation: I have no choice but to seek God in my own experience and insights, or learn about him as he speaks from outside my horizon of possibility (pp. 105-6).

Webster comes to three conclusions as he reflects on Barth and Bonhoeffer's exegetical practices. His first is that sophisticated contemporary biblical hermeneutics often fail because they ask the wrong questions, leaving the real problem of reading Scripture in Christian ethics untouched. That difficulty is spiritual and moral: we refuse as sinners to be spoken to, resist the divine address, and desire to live from our own word. It is a dogmatic task to reveal this problem and to depict the proper context within which we might meet Scripture, or rather allow God through it to meet us.

Second, Webster agrees with Fowl and Jones that a proper reading of Scripture requires the transformation of character appropriate to Christian discipleship. Yet he warns that "character," like "hermeneutics," is easily reduced to a set of techniques, collapsing the role of openness to God's Word into the learning of practices or virtues. He applauds recent works on ecclesial hermeneutics for correctly situating the reading of Scripture within the life of the church. But he sharply criticizes them for lacking the eschatological resources to resist the reductionist hermeneutics built not on the positivist foundations of historical criticism but a praxologically oriented postmodern hermeneutical method. Webster emphasizes that there is no sub-stitute for repentance in the reading of Scripture, a repentance at once meth-odological, moral, and praxological, because God not only works through community but is also its Lord and judge.

His third conclusion is that theology is exegesis, or exegesis theology. This is because Christian theology is interested in "Jesus Christ *as he is at-tested to us in Holy Scripture*" (p. 110; italics in original). With this move Web-ster wishes to combat the trend in modern theology that has steadily reduced the status of Scripture from clear and sufficient for faith to merely necessary (p. 110). Exegesis is too important to be made a technical discipline, and bibli-cal scholars are not to blame for the severing of theology and exegesis; rather, dogmaticians have too often contented themselves with modes of argument that make exegesis a secondary (or tertiary) exercise.

Relying on dogmatic conceptualizations developed in his previous studies of Barth's moral theology,[28] Webster goes on to flesh out this criticism by offering a competing account of Christian conscience in which the doc-trines of Christology, pneumatology, creation, ecclesiology, Scripture, escha-tology, and the-anthropology play more integrated roles. The treatment is in-tended to highlight the difference between a doctrinal approach and contemporary accounts of Scripture in which essential Christian terms such as "conscience," "humanity," and "character" become detached from language of God's acts in history through Christ and the Spirit, and become harnessed to essentially philosophical, or immanent, concepts.

Webster contends, as a counter to this trend, that we can adequately de-fine the Christian conscience and humanity as an eschatologically deter-mined creature only within a theological concept of "moral space." The gos-pel, understood as the history of the "encounter between the God who graciously creates, saves and perfects, and the creatures who receive these graces and respond to them with grateful action" (*Word and Church*, p. 234), delimits this space and locates moral reasoning and action. As we shall see, this language of moral space draws on conceptions of ethics with strong Au-gustinian roots.[29] Webster conceives of theological reflection on that space as having four necessary features.

First, a gospel-driven moral theology will begin with the confession that God's works of creating, reconciling, and perfecting the creation are the "de-termining environment" for all human agency. It will thus understand God as

---

28. John Webster, *Barth's Moral Theology*; and Webster, *Barth's Ethics of Reconciliation* (Cambridge: Cambridge University Press, 1995).

29. Cf. ch. 6, "Metaphysics, Epistemology, and the Primacy of the Moral," esp. pp. 125-29.

a self-manifesting agent who counters all threats to his self-revelation and his sustenance of creation. Second, it will define humanity by referring to this God rather than to terms of qualities existing without this relationship, such as reason, will, or consciousness. A Christian theology of the moral field will, third, try to spell out how the episodes recounted in Scripture of the encounter between God and humanity are not just sub-acts in a more basic narrative but in fact constitute all human destiny. Finally, it will give particular attention to the church of Jesus Christ as the provisional but real reconciling and perfecting work of God, and thus an anticipation and provisional pointer to the shape of redeemed human moral culture (*Word and Church*, p. 234). In sum,

> the contours of the moral field can be mapped by asking four questions: Who is the God who commands? Who is the human subject responsible to this commanding God? What is the situation in which these two subjects encounter one another? What is the command that God gives to the human subject in this situation so depicted? (p. 236)

The concept of conscience is thus properly defined in Christian theology as "an aspect of our fellowship with this [trinitarian] God; it is what it is in the history of that fellowship, destroyed by human wickedness and restored by divine mercy" (p. 251). This allows Webster dogmatically to elucidate the concept of conscience. As a work of the Creator, conscience must be understood as limited, possessed within the definite limits of finitude and creaturely dependence. In light of the work of the Redeemer, Christian definitions of conscience will give a special prominence to the work of Christ as judge, shaping human life by accusing, exposing, and acquitting the pronouncements of our conscience. Finally, Christian theology will also define conscience by talking of the work of the Holy Spirit, who realizes and perfects in humanity the Father's verdict in the Son.

Defining conscience in this way replaces common anthropocentric understandings of conscience such as "hearing from my inner self" with conscience as "the amazed acknowledgment of moral and theological truth before it is an awareness of obligation" (p. 255). In conscience I attend to the call of my self as perfected in Christ, who both reveals my distance from perfection and urges and guides the closing of that gap. In this way the "good chooses me; it annexes my projects to itself; it binds me, and thereby sets me free. . . . Both moral and pastoral theology must not allow themselves to be trapped by the competing alternatives of either heteronomy (conscience as the internalization of moral codes or prohibitions of the social order overseen by guardians of communal values) or autonomy (conscience as a necessarily undetermined centre of judgement)" (p. 260).[30]

Thus construed, the concept of conscience is properly subsumed in Christian dogmatics within the heading of faith, Webster continues. Conscience is faith's repeating and affirming God's judgment and clinging to it by God's help,

> not simply an extension of antecedent subjectivity but rather that in which I first become subject. Faith defines my being; it does not modulate a being which I already have or am. In faith I am not my own. If this is so, then human being as such is not a core element of subjectivity to which we attribute certain activities or characteristics in a straightforward way. (p. 260)

The context of conscience language is thus properly within Christian speech and action that seeks to affirm God's actions; in the words of John Milbank, it exists as "a bad conscience but a good *confidence*."[31] Baptism is an appeal to God for a good conscience. Christian faith lives in the confession of eschatological hope, a knowing and a learning that is always under way, becoming self-contradictory only when becoming too sure of having captured a complete picture of God's work in time. Christian eschatology is positively promissory but never possessive in character.

Webster's account of the interrelationship of Scripture, God's self-revelation, faith, conscience, and eschatology raises sharp questions about claims, such as that of Birch and Rasmussen that we must actively constitute our identities through our moral decisions, or the emphasis of Fowl and Jones on the Spirit's mediation through practices. For Webster, the heart of Christian moral deliberation is not decisions, character, hermeneutical sophistication or moral practices, but the "amazed acknowledgment of [the] moral and theological truth" that "the 'field' or 'space' of moral selfhood and action" is "the drama of human nature, origin and destiny, a drama presided over by the triune God who will bring it to its consummation at the appearing of the Lord Jesus" (p. 283). Such Christian conscience is immersed in reading and learning to read Scripture and in living in the world, but always in readiness to have all it has learned and loved overturned by the Spirit's speaking.

---

30. Webster picks up the shift of nomenclature from *God* choosing me to "the good" from Barth, who, in his *Ethics*, is trying to reunite the concept of God with the conceptions of the good that bear much weight in Catholic and Kantian moral theology.

31. Quoted in Webster, *Word and Church*, p. 261.

Assessment

In responding to the contemporary crisis of ethics and Scripture, Webster re-emphasizes how Christian doctrine helps hold open a methodological space for God's speaking in Christian ethics and biblical exegesis. Among the authors examined so far, the theological support provided by Christian doctrine gives his work the clearest grasp of the ecclesiological, eschatological, and pneumatological issues at stake, allowing all the moments of God's work to be understood as determining human action and thinking, yet admitting the limitation of human knowledge by the eschaton.

But, in arriving at the conclusion that theology is exegesis, Webster leaves undone what he asks his readers to do. Having said that theologians should not make exegesis a secondary or tertiary part of theology, he nevertheless takes as his primary texts the writings of Barth and Bonhoeffer on theological hermeneutics. He explains that a theological synthesis of the biblical witness in the form of a description of moral space should shape Christian conscience, but this statement rests not directly on biblical texts but on a doctrinal reconstruction of the unity of Scripture's narrative. Here Watson's *Agape, Eros, Gender* shines, with its focus on particular ethical questions and biblical texts, as well as its bringing together of the tools and concepts of biblical criticism, Christian dogmatics, and cultural sensitivity. The strength of Webster's proposal is the way it clarifies how a firm and primary belief in Jesus' eschatological presence turns the "problem" of Christian access to Scripture into the presumption that robust and Christian biblical interpretation (such as Watson's) is an artifact of God's work to create in Christ a redeemed community.

We might also ask whether Webster's definition of conscience would be sharpened by asking, "How do I read the Bible with a bad conscience?" rather than, "What is the doctrinally correct concept of conscience?" The former question is interested in the much more concrete question of *how* to meet God in the text today. Webster's "what" question ratchets up the pressure placed on readers by clarifying *why* attentive and repentant scriptural exegesis is critical, but provides few clues about how to proceed to the gift of Scripture with a smitten conscience, or even a clear one. Exactly how do we "attend to the call of my perfected self" *(Word and Church*, p. 251) in front of Scripture?

The underlying problem is that even a thick description of the moral space within which we ask and deliberate about moral questions may not be sufficient to flesh out the many fine-grained judgments we must make in order to act. This narrow focus on the importance of cognitive processes in the transformation of human action is a problem Webster shares with Watson, for whom interpretation aims to "discern the truth mediated in the texts of holy scripture."[32] Properly clarified concepts and descriptions assume a high level of rationalized and explicit theological knowledge that we have rarely fully clarified amid the myriad specific questions about proper action that we confront daily. The focus on concepts makes it difficult to conceive of learning the good by acting or performing it, in order to think it, and thus complicates our ability to explain how we actually come to know many of the moral truths we learn from the church and world.

Several previous chapters have pressed the question of whether, for instance, I should consider myself, as a husband, to be confronted by the biblical statements about the headship of husbands. Having a clear view of the Christian *concept* of conscience does not necessarily tell me whether the biblical passages that suggest it, read today, demand my repentance or not, or whether the patterns of behavior I may have inherited from Christian or non-Christian parents are embodiments or repudiations of Scripture. The skill of judgment in the present may be sharpened by a clear concept of Christian conscience, yet not teach what it means to judge the present circumstances and to hear the Spirit. Having a general description of right action, or its "space," must be paired with a skill of "judging the time" that amounts to a form of prayerful attentiveness to the divine voice and present social dynamics. This attentiveness has many forms, which may not emerge first as conceptual insights but through conversations with others, hunches, feelings, or shadings of conscience that are only later clarified into conceptual formulations.

Watson has ventured interpretative judgments about gender relations that suggest this experimentation in life, but his treatment systematically downplays its hermeneutical role and pneumatological basis, thus leaving some basic ethical questions unanswered. Though we might have expected Watson to clarify, for instance, what exactly is meant by the headship of husbands in *Agape, Eros, Gender*, his treatment is studiously ambiguous and hence of limited ethical content.[33] He admits that the New Testament frames the relationship of husband and wife in terms of the asymmetrical relationship of Christ and the church (*Agape*, pp. 245-46), making it legitimate for a wife to acknowledge her husband as head. He then immediately suggests that

32. Watson, *Text, Church and World*, p. 293. Both Watson and Webster inherit this focus from Barth, who is clearly indebted to German Idealism at this point. "This transformation of thought is the key to the problem of ethics, for it is the place where the turning about takes place by which men are directed to a new behaviour." Karl Barth, *The Epistle to the Romans*, 6th ed., trans. Edwyn Hoskyns (London: Oxford University Press, 1953), p. 436.

33. See the discussion of this question in ch. 3, "John Howard Yoder: Are Summaries of Scripture's Ethical Teachings Necessary?" especially pp. 47-49.

the earthly pedestal this assumes for husbands is so far beneath the headship of Christ that it "looks ridiculous, and it is a relief to be rid of it and to live the truly human life of mutual agape and subjection" (p. 248).

Again, important insights have emerged. Webster, Childs, and Watson have clarified the hermeneutical and ethical implications of Scripture's role in revealing the identity in Christ that orients Christian moral thinking. On their models, faith is living into an identity that is not yet fully possessed. That Christian identity is externally constituted makes prayer and repentance central, as Webster emphasizes, and in a way that we will find is congruent with the Christian tradition as represented by Augustine and Luther.

Finally, Watson has done us a service with his reminder of how deeply the church's interpretative practices and moral sensibilities are shaped by the world's knowledge. The world is not as "other" to the church as the church often supposes. Watson thus retains an important corollary to Webster's (and Yoder's) emphasis on the church's repentance of its worldliness. At the same time, Webster's strong pneumatology balances Watson's squeamishness about the role of the Spirit to do a truly new thing by overturning the certainties of both the church and world.

QUESTION FOR FURTHER STUDY: What is the appropriate relative weighting of the text of Scripture and the synthetic or doctrinal summaries that spring from and allow us to read and apply it?

CHAPTER 5

Reading as Meditation:
The Exegetical Theology Solution

It is striking that Barth's theological career began with something most contemporary theologians and ethicists would never attempt: a biblical commentary. Barth's second edition of the *Epistle to the Romans* (1922) is a studied attempt to do theology face to face with the actual text of Scripture in a postcritical intellectual environment. This chapter traces how the start Barth made in this direction was continued by one of his interpreters: Dietrich Bonhoeffer. And it departs from the previous four chapters in focusing on a single thinker for three reasons. First, a significant, possibly even dominant, stream of Christian theologizing has taken place through direct exegesis of Scripture, a fact that has been lost to our contemporary view, given the divisions in modern academia. By ignoring these divisions, Bonhoeffer paves the way to hear the Christian tradition in which these divisions did not exist. Second, tracing the exegetical theologies of Bonhoeffer (and Barth) shows that the form of the last chapter of this book, which proceeds exegetically, is not unprecedented in modern theology. Third, reading Bonhoeffer's commentary on the Psalms will begin to familiarize us with some of the contours of the biblical book that will be the steady focus of the rest of this book's analysis.

Modern Exegetical Theology and the Psalms

The form of Barth's *Romans* was not unprecedented, but it was inspired by an engagement with several trends, including Søren Kierkegaard's exegetical theologizing in *Fear and Trembling*. As in his *Edifying Discourses,* Kierkegaard does theology as a genuine and intense wrestling with theologically problematic, or ethically revealing, biblical texts. Barth goes to the book of Romans with similar impulses: he engages it because a range of theological problems and debates has crystallized around it, which he tries to resolve by interpreting the text directly, and afresh. These debates explain his engagement with Romans[1] and later 1 Corinthians 15 and Philippians.[2] It also makes it clear that his main target in writing theology in a commentary style is not biblical scholars and certainly not exegetical method. He exegetes these biblical books to enter theological and philosophical debates already in motion, and often crystallized around contentious biblical passages.

Barth's approach drew on and influenced other continental intellectual currents. There is a tradition within Jewish thought of engaging in similar projects, as evidenced by Martin Buber's commentaries on the Torah and the Psalms,[3] and the Talmud commentaries of Emmanuel Levinas.[4] Both were exploring responses to the subversion of scriptural traditions by the interjection of foreign conceptual and hermeneutical structures between readers in particular traditions and their seminal texts. Such commentaries queried the force of the dominant Idealist-inspired Enlightenment frameworks that strove to excavate the universal content of particular historical texts on scriptural reading. In commenting directly on texts, Barth, Bonhoeffer, Levinas, and Buber shared an attempt to resist the reduction of Judaism and Christianity to being only *part* of a universal history that transcends them and their texts. Their interpretive practices suggest that a close reading of Scripture is basic in a serious post-Enlightenment Christian ethic, within which discussions of hermeneutical method are only one part of the primary task of discovering the import of particular texts.

As the preceding chapter has indicated, Barth's early exegetical theologizing in *Romans* soon developed into a more sustained inquiry into

1. Karl Barth, *The Epistle to the Romans,* 6th ed., trans. Edwyn Hoskyns (London: Oxford University Press, 1953); Barth, *A Shorter Commentary on Romans,* trans. D. H. van Daalen (London: SCM Press, 1959).

2. Barth, *The Resurrection of the Dead,* trans. H. J. Stenning (London: Hodder and Stoughton, 1933). See also Barth, *The Epistle to the Philippians,* trans. James Leitch (London: SCM Press, 1962), which, interestingly, has been rereleased with an introductory essay by Francis Watson: Barth, *The Epistle to the Philippians: 40th Anniversary Edition,* with introductory essays by Bruce McCormack and Francis Watson (Louisville: Westminster John Knox, 2002). The only other exegetical lectures published to date are the 1925-26 lectures on John 1–8: Barth, *Erklärung des Johannes Evangelium (Kapital 1–8),* ed. Walther Fürst (Zurich: TVZ, 1976).

3. Martin Buber, *Right and Wrong: An Interpretation of Some Psalms,* trans. Ronald Smith (London: SCM, 1952).

4. Emmanuel Levinas, *Beyond the Verse: Talmudic Readings and Lectures,* trans. Gary Mole (London: Athalone, 1994); *Nine Talmudic Readings,* intro. and trans. Annette Aronowicz (Bloomington: Indiana University Press, 1990).

the *structure* of the revelatory act in volume 1 of *Church Dogmatics*, while Bonhoeffer, on the other hand, continued the direct exploration of Scripture's *content* exemplified in *Romans*. Bonhoeffer's *Creation and Fall*[5] takes up Barth's exegetical style and applies it to the first chapters of Genesis; in *Discipleship*[6] he continues the experiment by commenting on the Sermon on the Mount. Remarkably, Bonhoeffer's efforts almost certainly stimulated Barth to return to exegetical theology focused on these same passages, as marked by the structural role of his exegetical engagement with the opening chapters of Genesis in *Church Dogmatics* III.1,[7] and his treatment of ethics as a commentary on the Lord's Prayer in *The Christian Life*.[8]

However, Barth was not the only influence on Bonhoeffer's exegetical theology, especially regarding the Psalms. The influence of Luther's commentaries on the Psalms is also regularly visible. Bonhoeffer follows Luther in understanding the book as a "children's primer" for learning to talk to God, in assuming that only one book in the Bible is devoted to training our speech and affections toward God, and in his Christological approach to the Psalms.[9] There are striking parallels between Bonhoeffer's exegesis of Psalm 119 and Luther's treatment in his first lecture series, especially regarding the central place of the undivided heart, the primacy of the petition for grace, and the centrality of relying on God's Word rather than our own interpretations of Scripture.[10] Bonhoeffer was also familiar with Augustine's commentary on Psalm 119, though his exegesis shows less direct evidence of Augustinian influence.[11]

It is well known that Bonhoeffer equated his "discovery of the Bible" with his "conversion to Christianity."[12] It is perhaps appropriate that his hand-

---

5. Dietrich Bonhoeffer, *Creation and Fall: A Theological Exposition of Genesis 1–3, Dietrich Bonhoeffer Works* 3, ed. Martin Rüter, Ilse Tödt, John W. de Gruchy, trans. Douglas Stephen Bax (Minneapolis: Fortress, 1997).

6. Dietrich Bonhoeffer, *Discipleship*, Dietrich Bonhoeffer Works 4, ed. Martin Kuske, Ilse Tödt, Barbara Green, and Reinhard Kraus, trans. Barbara Green and Reinhard Krauss (Minneapolis: Fortress, 2001).

7. Barth, *Church Dogmatics, III.1, The Doctrine of Creation*, ed. G. W. Bromiley and T. F. Torrance, trans. J. W. Edwards, O. Bussey, and H. Knight (Edinburgh: T&T Clark, 1958).

8. Barth, *The Christian Life: Church Dogmatics IV.4, Lecture Fragments*, ed. G. W. Bromiley and T. F. Torrance, trans. Geoffrey Bromiley (Edinburgh: T&T Clark, 1981).

9. See Dietrich Bonhoeffer, *Life Together and Prayerbook of the Bible*, Dietrich Bonhoeffer Works 5, ed. Gerhard Müller, Albrecht Schönherr, and Geffrey Kelley, trans. Daniel Bloesch and James Burtness (Minneapolis: Fortress, 1996), p. 156.

10. See Luther, *Luther's Works, First Lectures on the Psalms II, Psalms 76–126*, pp. 417-19.

11. Bonhoeffer, *Life Together*, p. 180.

12. "For the first time I discovered the Bible. . . . I had often preached, I had seen a great deal of the Church, and talked and preached about it — but I had not yet become a Chris-

book for praying the Psalms, *The Prayerbook of the Bible,* was the last book published during his lifetime.[13] It is less often recalled that at the end of his life Bonhoeffer could write, "I read the Psalms every day, as I have done for years; I know them and love them more than any other book," and that he chose Psalm 103 as the text for his wedding sermon.[14] One easily misreads some of the central moves in his ethical writings without understanding how his love of the Psalms and his daily meditation on them shaped his mature method in Christian ethics. Reading Bonhoeffer as a biblical theologian will reveal the accuracy of John Webster's charge that contemporary readings of Bonhoeffer have largely overlooked his exegetical works and emphases in favor of his ethical and sociological texts and concepts—thus misunderstanding both.[15]

My treatment of Bonhoeffer will trace his concept of ethics as a way in his *Ethics,* but will do so through the lens of the unfinished 1939-40 exegesis of Psalm 119 that he was simultaneously writing.[16] Though it has been almost completely overlooked by moral theologians, Bonhoeffer considered this commentary on his favorite psalm the climax of his theological life, and he quoted Psalm 119 more than any other biblical passage in his late works.[17] Here he develops a concept of "ethics as a way" in which Scripture is accorded a central role in the divine transformation of humanity.

Bonhoeffer has been roundly criticized for his use of the concept of

---

tian." Eberhard Bethge, *Dietrich Bonhoeffer: Theologian, Christian, Contemporary,* trans. E. Mosbacker, P. and B. Ross, F. Clarke, and W. Glen-Doepel (London: Collins, 1970), p. 154.

13. Dietrich Bonhoeffer, *Dietrich Bonhoeffer's Meditations on the Psalms,* ed. and trans. Edwin Robertson (Grand Rapids: Zondervan, 2002), p. 83.

14. Dietrich Bonhoeffer, *Letters and Papers from Prison,* enlarged edition, ed. Eberhard Bethge (London: SCM Press, 1971), pp. 40, 415.

15. John Webster, *Word and Church: Essays in Christian Dogmatics* (Edinburgh: T&T Clark, 2001), p. 90.

16. The fragment is translated in Dietrich Bonhoeffer, *Meditating on the Word,* trans. and ed. David McI. Gracie (Cambridge: Cowley Publications, 1986), pp. 101-45. I will occasionally refer to the other versions and overlapping fragments of this meditation that were written during this period. A comment on verses 17-20 is found in Bonhoeffer, *Dietrich Bonhoeffer's Meditations on the Psalms,* pp. 81-97, and on verses 10-19 in Bonhoeffer, *Reflections on the Bible: Human Word and the Word of God,* trans. Eugene Boring (Peabody: Hendrickson, 2004), pp. 69-78.

17. Bethge, *Dietrich Bonhoeffer,* pp. 335, 571. Even less well known is the fact that Bonhoeffer learned to love the psalm from the experience of English monastic life. Bonhoeffer, *Life Together,* p. 120. This experience was so formative that he could later write from a German monastery that "a day without morning and evening prayers and personal intercessions was a day without meaning or importance." Bonhoeffer, *Life Together,* p. 145. I am told that Bonhoeffer even wrote back from Germany to Father Bull of Moorfield to request a copy of Richard Meux Benson's *The Way of Holiness: An Exposition of Psalm 119, Analytical and Devotional* (London: Methuen, 1901).

mandates to organize his discussion of material questions in Christian ethics, not least because he constantly rethought his use of the term.[18] To my knowledge, no moral theologian has explored the implications of Bonhoeffer's derivation of the important term "mandates," and the way it focuses Christian ethical thinking, from Luther's discussion of Psalm 119:168.[19] Bonhoeffer's choice of the term intertwines the methodological questions of his mature ethical thinking and the conceptual structures of the Psalms. The term's development in his thought traces a search for a concept that would emphasize the reliability and continuity of the moral claim of Christ through Scripture while disallowing any final solidification of our descriptions of its content. To approach these questions through his concept of theology as a *path* will yield insights into the architectonic of Bonhoeffer's moral theology, the role of Scripture within it, and, as he meditates on the "instruction" psalm par excellence, a view of his understanding of the role the mandates play in God's commanding activity.

As an introduction to Bonhoeffer's theological emphases, it will be helpful to sketch three major psalm thought structures that played an important role in his ethical thought. Psalms 1 and 2, generally accepted as an introduction to the Psalter, set out a polarity that runs throughout the book: the blessed "delights in the law of Yahweh and murmurs [meditates on] his law day and night" (1:2), while the nations, powers, and sinners are marked by "impotent muttering. . . . 'Now let us break their fetters! Now let us throw off their bonds!'" (2:1, 3).[20] The critical difference between the blessed and sinners is whether they murmur (הָגָה, *hagah*) the Torah or against it. This parallelism is obscured by most English translations, which use different words to translate *hagah*.

It is important to see how, in his exegesis of Psalm 119, Bonhoeffer is trying to reintroduce this focus on verbal meditation on Scripture into the method of Christian ethics by replacing the philosophical concept of ethics dominant in many Christian ethics with the biblical concept of Torah and defining the blessed in terms of a *verbal* relationship.[21] If philosophical ethics

---

18. Cf. the German editors' survey of this discussion in Dietrich Bonhoeffer, *Ethics*, Dietrich Bonhoeffer Works 6, ed. Ilse Tödt, Heinz Eduard Tödt, Ernst Feil, and Clifford Green, trans. Reinhard Krauss, Charles West, and Douglas Scott (Minneapolis: Fortress, 2005), p. 204, n. 115.

19. Samuel James Preuss, *From Shadow to Promise: Old Testament Interpretation from Augustine to the Young Luther* (Eugene, OR: Wipf and Stock, 1999), p. 186.

20. Quote from the New Jerusalem translation, which is one of the few in which the Hebrew parallel is retained in the English.

21. Cf. Dietrich Bonhoeffer, *Ethics*, p. 387, n. 80.

asks about good acts, the Torah asks to be explored physically, with desire, thus shaping our moral sensitivity. Exploring something with our mouth is a sensual affair, as Psalm 119 often emphasizes (Ps. 119:97, 103, 131; cf. John 14:24; 15:10), an affair of love described via metaphors that remind us of

> caressing, tapping, trying, testing, probing, delineating its contours . . . although it is always the one same body, it is always fresh and exciting when looked at, approached and taken from different angles, in different positions, and so on. As for the materiality of the law that is put in front of the psalmist, it is not 'text' but 'scroll,' with a distinct surface, look, smell, not something to be scanned by the eyes alone so as to sink immediately into the inner dark of the brain's activity, but something to move the lips accordingly in the practice of murmuring or meditating: something to be voiced, heard, proclaimed.[22]

Second, Bonhoeffer felt that the concept of "statutes" was indispensable to Christian ethics because it is prominent in the Psalms, especially Psalm 119, with its conspicuous enumeration in verses 41-48 of the seven main synonyms for the Torah of the Lord that structure the whole psalm.

> The central theme of Psalm 119 is the *Torah* (NRSV = "law") of the Lord. In all, eight synonyms for "law" are used in the Psalm, namely, *Torah, dabar* ("word"), *mishpatim* ("ordinances"), *'edut* ("decrees"), *piqqudim* ("precepts"), *chuqqim* ("statutes"), *mitswah* [*sic*] ("commandments"), and *'imrah* ("promise"). With two exceptions (vv. 90 and 122), each of the 176 lines contains one of the synonyms for "law."[23]

The way the Torah claims us cannot be pinned down in one term (such as "command"). The diversity of the nomenclature emphasizes the erotic, ongoing relationship with the Torah to which Psalm 119 calls us, says Bernd Wannenwetsch.

> The richness and variety of the semantic concepts again seems to resemble the inventiveness of lovers who usually have a whole arsenal of pet names in stock. In the cosmos of loving encounter, a "cat" is not just a cat, but equally well a "mouse," and only this plurality of names is capable of doing justice to the complexity of the encounter — a complexity that would be

---

22. Bernd Wannenwetsch, "Walking the Ten Words: Exploring the Moral Universe Through the Decalogue" (unpublished paper), p. 16.

23. Willem Prinsloo, "The Psalms," in James Dunn and John Rogerson, eds., *Eerdmans Commentary on the Bible* (Grand Rapids: Eerdmans, 2003), p. 422.

inevitably hampered by the use of any monolithic vocabulary and its tendency to "pin down" the other to the particularity of one role.[24]

Third, the Psalter sets the concept of instruction or command with a dynamic understanding of human behavior. The statutes mark out a path, stand alongside something continuous and ongoing. This emphasis on continuity sharply delineates the biblical idea of the divine decreeing from modern understandings of divine commanding as occasional interventions in the normal course of affairs, or as a synonym for the pronouncements of the conscience or analytical self-observation. At this point a decision about the genre of biblical command language radically shapes how we understand them to function in Christian ethics. Bonhoeffer stays quite close to the thought structures of the Psalms by interpreting commands within a dynamic view of human life and moral deliberation. Psalm 119 is rife with this imagery, as marked by the regular occurrence of terms such as "walk,"[25] "way,"[26] "paths,"[27] "to restrain/turn back my feet,"[28] "let my steps be established by your word,"[29] "your word is a lamp to my feet,"[30] "to wander,"[31] and "to make haste, come quickly."[32] These terms are set beside many other verbs to yield dynamic conceptions, such as "to observe" (v. 168), "to turn aside" (v. 102), "diverted/perverted" (v. 157), and "stray" (v. 67). All of these yield a picture of the Torah as the opposite of a stumbling block (v. 165).

Bonhoeffer's aim is to discover how verbal meditation on Scripture facilitates the embodiment of faith.

Bonhoeffer: Exegesis as Meditation on the Torah of the Lord

We turn now to Bonhoeffer's exegesis of Psalm 119, with special interest in the passages where his understanding of the role Scripture plays in Christian ethical deliberation is most clearly illuminated. This will entail a verse-by-verse analysis of the first six verses and a summary of the main points of the remaining commentary.

---

24. Wannenwetsch, "Walking the Ten Words," p. 15.
25. The term הָלַךְ is centrally placed in vv. 1, 3, also 45.
26. דֶּרֶךְ vv. 1, 3, 5, 14, 26, 27, 29, 30, 32, 33, 37, 59, 168.
27. אֹרַח vv. 15, 101, 104, 128; נָתִיב vv. 35, 105.
28. אָשִׁיבָה רַגְלַי vv. 59, 101.
29. פְּעָמַי הָכֵן בְּאִמְרָתֶךָ v. 133.
30. נֵר־לְרַגְלִי דְבָרֶךָ v. 105.
31. תָּעִיתִי v. 110, 176.
32. חַשְׁתִּי v. 60.

119:1   How blessed are those whose way is blameless, who walk in the Law of the LORD![33]

Bonhoeffer opens by dispatching the accusation that God's commanding is only an occasional interjection into the normal course of affairs: "Life with God is not essentially a matter of ever new beginnings. . . . God has made the beginning; that is the happy certainty of faith."[34] The community of faith does not, therefore, need to constantly urge one another to make a new effort of faith, but to "know they are together on this way," "under the Word of God in all its many shapes and forms, its richness, its inexhaustible wealth of knowledge and experience" (p. 106). The faithful have been placed on this way and must not try to go behind God's Word, but "learn to understand ourselves now as those who have been placed on the way and no longer can do anything other than walk in it" (p. 106).

What, then, is the law in which the blessed so walk? Bonhoeffer answers by quoting the *Shema* (Deut. 6:20-25) in full, which he interprets in terms that are familiar to us from our discussion of Webster in the last chapter. The law is God's deeds, commandments, and promise. Jesus Christ encapsulates the deliverance from death and the new beginning that Torah promises. "In answer to the question about the law of God we are not presented with moral teaching or an ethical norm, instead, we hear about a completed action of God" (pp. 107-8). For Bonhoeffer, the law is a space created by God's judgments, which humans truly inhabit only in the acknowledgment that it is God who acts and decides in the fullest sense of the words, but who makes humans into real actors. Creation is thus conceived as a location *within* the law conveyed to us by Scripture. God's redeeming is the context of his creative work.

Bonhoeffer continues to define the main terms of verse 1 by explaining how this theological affirmation of the primacy of God's work locates the Psalms' chief descriptor of human wholeness: happiness or blessedness. Here he links the psalmist's giving a central place to meditation on the law with the Pauline and Reformation emphasis on the undivided heart. This yields a theological interpretation of the polarity between acceptance and rejection of the law. Human happiness is found by those who "have been freed from the

33. I will occasionally modify the NRSV translation by inserting phrases from the New Jerusalem Bible, as it clarifies the nuances of the Luther Bible from which Bonhoeffer is working.

34. Dietrich Bonhoeffer, "On Psalm 119," in *Meditating on the Word*, trans. and ed. David McI. Gracie (Cambridge: Cowley Publications, 1986), p. 105 (page references to this book hereafter cited parenthetically in text).

torment of their own beginnings; happy are they, because they have overcome the inner divisions which result when we oppose our own beginnings to the beginning of God; they are complete, whole, undivided, blameless" (p. 109).

This is not simply a spiritual or inner happiness, Bonhoeffer continues, but a real earthly prosperity. Those who walk in the Torah of the Lord are "not blessed because you lack nothing, but because you receive everything you have from the hand of God" (p. 111). Bonhoeffer soon elucidated this point in a letter to Eberhard Bethge: "It would be natural to suppose that, as usual, the New Testament spiritualizes the teaching of the Old Testament here, and therefore to regard the Old Testament blessing as superseded in the New. . . . The only difference between the Old and New Testaments in this respect is that in the Old the blessing includes the cross, and in the New the cross includes the blessing."[35] In a poignant reflection on his own approaching death (and in contrast to Yoder's emphasis on the way of the cross), Bonhoeffer says martyrdom is not inevitably the Christian lot in life, but it is a special task for which God will provide special preparation and ensure its witness.[36] In a final note, Bonhoeffer points out that, because God rules the world, this construal of human blessedness is not merely a prescription for the personal faith of the individual but is the way of blessedness for the family, a people *(volk),* a nation — in short, the whole world ("On Psalm 119," p. 112).

119:2 Blessed are those who observe his decrees, who seek him with all their hearts.

If the blessedness of verse 1 is the promise of the undivided heart, the blessing of verse 2 is that "the decrees are the warning signs which God has set up on the way of his people, so that they do not go astray" (p. 112). Here Bonhoeffer asks about the inner dynamics of meditation. How can the confession of the all-encompassing nature of God's judgments make space for,

---

35. Bonhoeffer, *Letters and Papers from Prison*, p. 374.

36. "Should God require this of any, he will certainly so prepare their hearts beforehand that they will be the very ones who by their strong faith testify anew and with authority: 'Happy are they who walk in the law of the Lord.'" Bonhoeffer, "On Psalm 119," p. 112. It again illuminates Bonhoeffer's exegetical suppleness that it was another psalm that comforted him and clarified the meaning of his period of imprisonment, Psalm 30:5: "For his anger is but for a moment; his favour is for a lifetime. Weeping may linger for the night, but joy comes with the morning." Bonhoeffer, *Dietrich Bonhoeffer's Meditations on the Psalms*, p. 12. For purposes of comparison, it is worth noting the proximity and distance of Bonhoeffer at this point from Calvin's cruciform definition of happiness as best known in the circumstance of utter earthly loss. *Institutes of the Christian Religion*, Book III.II.7

rather than stifle, human action? Bonhoeffer finds the link in one of the synonyms for Torah, עֵדוּת (edut), "testimony." Testimony points away from itself to an object, thus continually uniting the heart and engaging the lips and hands in seeking the One to whom Scripture testifies (p. 113). The Torah creates space for human action by making it possible to prepare to hear the Creator's voice. Thus the divine provision of a form for seeking to hear is inseparable from the provision of a form through which God guides human action.[37]

119:3 who also do no wrong, but walk in his ways.

The law, then, is God's own revelation of his ways, the "ways which he himself has gone and which we are now to go with him" (p. 114). This brings Bonhoeffer to an important first formulation of the concept "way" as a theological framework for conceiving Christian ethics:

> With God one does not arrive at a fixed position; rather, one walks along a way. One moves ahead or one is not with God. God knows the whole way; we only know the next step and the final goal. . . . The Gospel and the faith are not timeless ideas, but the action of God with human beings in history. . . . The way of God is his way to the human being, and only thus the way of the human being to him. The way is Jesus Christ (John 14:6). (pp. 114-16)

Because Christian ethics is only part of walking with God, the divine statutes are not properly understood as eternal moral commands: this is to misunderstand how they function as divine revelation. But how, then, are they to be "kept" if not as moral maxims?

119:4 You lay down your commandments to be carefully kept.

Having thus interrelated the terms "law," "blessedness," and "way," Bonhoeffer has firmly situated the "commandments" as the place where we meet the God who rules all reality and who wishes to guide us into Christ in our daily lives. Bonhoeffer draws on the Hebrew etymology of מִצְוֹת (mitsvot), "commandments," to explain that the commandments function as a meeting place for God and humans, and thus to provide humans with a heuristic to understand God's presence. The term "commandments," he writes, is derived from

---

37. Cf. Bonhoeffer, *Ethics*, p. 330.

seeking, visiting, paying attention to. Hence, the commandments are what God looks at, pays attention to, and the means by which he seeks and visits the human being. The commandments then reflect God's way toward the human being. They have a definite purpose and goal for me. They are not given for their own sake, but for our sake, that we "should fully keep them." We ought to keep them in the sense of holding fast to them; indeed we should do so fully, with all our might, so that we do not lose them or let them be torn away from us. (p. 116)

We "keep" the commandments by attempting to inhabit them through the confession of changed action. To put the case this way is to affirm that the statutes are fixed and our interpretations constantly seek their meaning in hope and faith, rather than in final definitive claims that replace the statutes with our interpretations.

119:5 O that my ways may be steadfast in keeping thy statutes!

If the commandments are God's designated way to us, then prayer is our way to hold fast to them and so to God. My ways must be directed to the statutes, and thus the prayer of repentance is not a promethean hoping or a wishful begging but a "prayer that has promise. . . . This prayer leads straight to action, and just where it is most needed — in what concerns myself. But clearly this action can only proceed from prayer, or else it too will be lost" (p. 118). The law is God's chosen means of drawing us into conversation, the processes of prayer whereby a single goal for our existence emerges from the many divergent desires and aspirations that mark the sinful condition. Only because Scripture "instructs" does repentance become a possibility, *the* possibility of human renewal.

119:6 Then I shall not be put to shame, if my gaze is fixed on your commandments.

Shame, Bonhoeffer continues, is the opposite of happiness and consists of the collapse of justification for my existence.[38] All justifications of life and action not growing from regard for God's commandments stand on shifting sand. This includes my own most devout experiences, highest human thoughts, and, of course, hermeneutical concepts. The Psalms teach us to expect continual growth and rearrangement of our exegetical frameworks. My gaze is fixed on the commandments when I continually turn to

---

38. See Bonhoeffer, *Ethics*, pp. 303-7, where Bonhoeffer defines shame as the "irrepressible memory of disunity from their origin."

them and ask what God commands me to do. Bonhoeffer is developing a justification of the constant study of Scripture as the proper context of Christian ethical deliberation.

This claim rests on four points. First, the false roads we face in life are so varied that we need the whole diverse treasure of God's commands to guide us through them. Second, faith can rest secure that God's commandments are equal to this task, and that through them God will make our way visible in time of decision. Third, hearing this divine Word depends, however, on earnest and tireless questioning of the commands in order to perceive the statute that illuminates the salient features of the context I face. When I make the connection between specific commands and my concrete situation, I can recognize anew the depth, breadth, and goodness of the Torah's ability to comprehend all possible realities. Fourth, such discernment becomes more pressing and difficult on issues where the world has no regard at all for the commands, where the structures of its self-understanding run in diametrically opposed paths. Bonhoeffer's response parallels that of Yoder and Webster at this point: Christians must not give up the hope of God meeting them on the way, but must redouble their resistance to the temptation to discard some of the statutes by insisting on keeping all of God's commandments open and in play (p. 120).[39]

With this emphasis on the multifaceted nature of Scripture, Bonhoeffer develops a strikingly greater complexity of the creation-reconciliation-redemption schema, or the incarnation-crucifixion-resurrection structures that oriented the theological ethics with which he was in dialogue. He does not give up the idea that we can and must group the commands under broad headings such as these; but he realizes that such orderings must not solidify to produce blind spots in our own attention to all of God's commands. The confusing complexity of the whole is necessary if the processes of the sanctification of our conceptual schemas are not to be arrested. The aim of constructing such ordering schemas is not complete conceptual coherence, because only the law itself and Christ as its source exhibit true and complete coherence. All human interpretative schemas are necessary yet provisional, partially illuminating and partially obscuring.[40]

Making the path metaphor methodologically central yields another insight: there is only one path, and the commands, in their whole range, find their ultimate coherence only in Christ, their source and aim. Thus the be-

---

39. Bonhoeffer clearly resists the moves we saw by Schüssler Fiorenza and Fowl to reject or heavily reinterpret the biblical witness and Christian tradition.

40. See Bonhoeffer, *Ethics*, p. 74.

liever who clings to the commands is not obeying them as moral maxims but is constantly being trained through them to listen to God in new and historically unique contexts. Continuous listening allows new connections within Scripture to emerge as we put new questions to it. This is what is meant by understanding the law as a "space" within which we discover ourselves within the gift of grace through the practice of prayerfully bringing questions about faithful living to the law of the Lord.

119:7 I will praise you with a sincere heart for teaching me your upright
      judgments.
8   I will observe your statutes, O forsake me not utterly!

The essence of paganism, Bonhoeffer continues, is to receive the gifts of creation but refuse honor to God (Rom. 1:21). "The thanksgiving of the world refers always to the self; one seeks through giving thanks only a higher confirmation and consecration of one's own good fortune (Nietzsche)" (p. 121).[41] The blessed, conversely, are learning what God gives and humans are not capable of giving, and "these are necessarily united when I give thanks 'with a sincere heart'" (p. 121; cf. Ps. 147:19-20). The psalmist thanks as one still learning to thank, and so experiences the law as judgment as well as gift. To say, then, that "I will observe your statutes" is not an assertion of human constancy but a word of retrospective thanks and hopeful praise for God's freeing of his children to will what they formerly hated.

> So the circle is complete. God's grace is at the beginning; grace makes the beginning for us, so that we may be freed from our own beginnings; grace puts us on the way; and it is grace for which we pray from step to step. Note how in these verses and in all that follow we find over and over again: *your* law, *your* commandments, *your* statutes, and so forth. Human beings are not being praised here, but God and his revelation. (p. 124)

With this summary Bonhoeffer has sketched the main lines of his account of Christian ethical deliberation in relocating the place of exegetical methods and "synthetic" accounts. Such a framing of moral theology dispenses with the usual focus on ethics as analysis of the virtuous actor, of rules for action, or of the teasing out of the different features of problem cases. In its place, the indispensability of God's being present with us and revealing to us the meaning of the way of Christ is given a new prominence.

---

41. This is the theme of the poem "Christians and Pagans," written during this period; cf. Bonhoeffer, *Letters and Papers from Prison*, pp. 348-49.

119:9 How can a young man keep his way spotless? By keeping your words.
10   With all my heart I seek you, do not let me stray from your
         commandments.

A clearly autobiographical note is again evident as Bonhoeffer continues by contrasting his theology of advent from "ethics."[42] "A young man here
asks the question of his life, and he asks it not because of flaming idealism or
enthusiasm for the good and noble in general, but because he has experienced
the power of the Word of God and his own weakness" (p. 124).[43] A theology
of advent demands a biblical hermeneutic in which sanctification as a journey is given a serious exegetical role.

> Whoever has received God's Word has to seek God; she can do no other.
> The more clearly and deeply God's Word shows itself to her, the more
> lively will be her desire for the total clarity and the unfathomable depth of
> God himself. . . .[44] God wants to fully glorify himself and make himself
> known to us in his complete richness. Of course we can only seek God in
> his Word, but this Word is lively and inexhaustible, for God himself lives
> in it. (p. 126)

This hermeneutics must (1) define us as embedded within Scripture as we are
within no other "texts," (2) clarify how constant attention to Scripture inter-
faces with more general moral schemas, including those drawn from Scripture, and (3) give us some hints about what kind of exegetical practices this
concept of Christian ethics might entail.

119:11 Thy word have I hid in my heart, that I might not sin against you.

Building on the Hebrew notion of "hiding in the heart" (בְּלִבִּי צָפַנְתִּי),
Bonhoeffer again emphasizes that Christ and the human lives claimed for
him are the concrete unity that binds together all God's commands. To be
transformed into Christ is thus to be a concrete example of their unity, a living interpretation of their unity (p. 127). Here Bonhoeffer is not claiming that
we must have a naive relationship to Scripture,[45] but emphasizing that the Bi-

---

42. This distinction is conceptually elaborated in a chapter in *Ethics*, "The Ethical and
Christian as a Topic."

43. This passage is referred to in *Ethics* on p. 187, n. 60.

44. In another draft, he cites Matthew 13:12 at this point: "For to those who have, more
will be given, and they will have an abundance; but from those who have nothing, even what
they have will be taken away." Bonhoeffer, *Reflections on the Bible*, p. 69.

45. Contra Webster, *Word and Church*, p. 99. "Psychologically speaking, it is possible for

ble is not a repository of moral guidelines to be mined and systematized as a conceptually finalized "biblical ethic" possessed in the intellect as a conceptual construct. The whole Bible claims our whole being, or rather, God uses the space and diversity of the scriptural commands to make us aware that we exist only within the sphere of his rule. We come to possess Scripture as we develop knowledge of Christ in the form of lived certainty.[46]

God's Word is thus not an ethical program but a heuristic, and a negative heuristic at that: it strips away our divergent self-referential hermeneutics to reveal our total dependence on God's presence, and so to direct us to his real (as opposed to imagined) presence. That is why a catalog approach to the moral passages of Scripture is doomed to failure: only when Scripture is "treasured in the heart" in all its bewildering complexity will its true unity in Christ begin to emerge. This unity, again, cannot be in the first instance conceptual, though it will have conceptual content; it will be in Christ and in his meeting us in the course of making us real humans as we take real steps of faith in our historical context.

119:15   I will ponder your precepts and fix my gaze on your paths.

Here Bonhoeffer raises a point that is often noted, but its methodological implications are rarely wrestled with in biblical scholarship.[47] "How could I go through the length of this psalm and begin it ever anew, how should I not grow weary of this incessant repetition, if God should not enable me to see that each of his words is full of undiscovered, unfathomable wonder?" (p. 136).[48] Wonder emerges only in meditation on Scripture, and meditation takes time: "There is no standing still. Every gift we receive,

---

someone who, in following Jesus, has become single-minded and free to be a person engaged in very complex reflection." Bonhoeffer, *Ethics*, p. 320.

46. See Bonhoeffer, *Ethics*, pp. 342-44.

47. In *A Theological Introduction to the Book of Psalms: The Psalms as Torah* (Nashville: Abingdon Press, 1993), J. Clinton McCann helpfully traces why historical and form critical approaches have flirted with, but not dealt directly with, the question (see pp. 16-21). Though McCann discerns the methodological importance of the Torah's claim to contain all that is (ch. 1), he nevertheless does not explicitly ask what this means for our definitions of biblical scholarship and how we construe what we think words "mean."

48. Bonhoeffer also develops this theme with explicit reference to Psalm 119 in Bonhoeffer, *Life Together*, pp. 57-58, 156: "[T]he apparent repetitions are in fact always new variations on one theme, the love of God's word. As this love can have no end, so also the words that confess it have no end. They want to accompany us through all of life, and in their simplicity they become the prayer of the child, the adult, and the elderly."

every new understanding, drives us still deeper into the Word of God" (p. 132).[49] Because Scripture tells us we must meditate on it, Christian ethics is fundamentally questioned about its reliance on modern ethical (Kantian) conceptualities: "God's Word is not a collection of eternally valid general principles that we can have at our disposal any time we wish" (p. 132). Nor is it "the sum of a few general statements that I can call to memory anytime I want but is the word of God directed to me, new every day, in the inexhaustibly rich process of interpretation."[50]

Again, this should not be understood as an espousal of *ad hoc* proof-texting, because we have seen that Bonhoeffer has already emphasized the continuity of God's grace and thus the reliability of his statutes. What Bonhoeffer is emphasizing, almost single-handedly in contemporary discussions of the role of the Bible in Christian ethics, is that the Bible can never be replaced in concrete moral deliberation by summaries of its moral content to which we turn in time of moral decision. To put his claim in the strongest possible terms: only when we are faced with apparently insoluble life decisions do we really penetrate more deeply into the richness of God as accessed through Scripture, thus discovering new possibilities for living as we discover implications of Scripture never before noticed. This possibility is cut off if we refuse to spend time with the actual text of Scripture, or if we set meditation on Scripture aside because we believe we possess an adequate summary of its "moral content."

119:16 I find my delight in your statutes, I do not forget your words.

This verse is a confession of the ethical centrality of recalling the works of God that happened "in the world outside of my psyche."[51] Because our identity comes to us from outside of us, such remembering is the condition for being caught up in God's working. Here Bonhoeffer clarifies the role of verbalization in "meditation on the law," the "muttering of the Torah" that marks out the blessed. Recounting God's deeds gives us a future by showing

---

49. The closest contemporary academic theology comes to this insight appears in the literature on homiletic preparation, where we still find statements such as the following from John Goldingay: "Our task as preachers is to enable people to make the Psalms their own living speech. We may most plausibly do that by making them our own speech in such a way as to draw others into them. . . . The style of preaching into which it invites us is an expository approach to the Psalms that preaches them by praying them and letting the congregation overhear what we are saying to God." Goldingay, *Models for Interpretation of Scripture* (Grand Rapids: Eerdmans, 1995), pp. 264-65.

50. Bonhoeffer, *Reflections on the Bible*, p. 72.

51. Bonhoeffer, *Reflections on the Bible*, p. 74.

us how to identify with God's saving deeds and not our own damning deeds. Justification entails our sanctification in Christ's meeting us and remaking our memory. In this way our self in Christ is constructed through remembering.[52] "We must return every day to the saving acts of God in order to be able to go forward . . . because my righteousness is the righteousness of Jesus Christ alone, because that can only be proclaimed to me in the Word, remembering and repeating are necessary for blessedness, and forgetting is equivalent to falling away from the faith" ("On Psalm 119," p. 132). But only love keeps us from forgetting.

> Why is it that my thoughts so quickly wander away from God's word and that the word I need is often not there when I need it? Do I ever forget to eat or drink or sleep? Why then do I forget God's word? Because I am not yet able to say with the psalmist, "I will delight in your statutes." I do not forget that in which I delight. Whether or not I forget something is (not) a matter (of my intellect but) of the whole person, a matter of the heart. That on which I depend, body and soul, is something I cannot forget. The more I begin to love God's statutes written in creation and Scripture, the more they will be present to me in every moment. Only love keeps one from forgetting. (*Reflections*, p. 73)

To have an identity, and so to be able to act, is to love the One in whom our true self is hidden, because he loved us from all eternity (Is. 49:14-16) (*Reflections*, p. 74).

119:17   Deal bountifully with your servant, that I may live and keep your words.

19   Wayfarer though I am on the earth, do not hide your commandments from me.

The result of these meditations is a strong affirmation by Bonhoeffer that *lived* life is the place where God aims to unite and re-create humanity in Christ. Before God broke in on us, "we were haters and despisers of life, and lovers and worshipers of ideas" ("On Psalm 119," p. 135), but the command is God's means of creating a unity in lived life.[53] The command opposes our faith being organized by an idealist emphasis on truth as conceptual clarity or completeness, which Bonhoeffer sees as inevitably "ideological" in displacing, rather than fostering, a primary attentiveness to the neighbors we face in daily

---

52. Bonhoeffer, *Ethics*, pp. 146-47. The point is made in relation to Ps. 119:16, and tied to Ps. 103:2, Deut. 6:2, and 2 Tim. 2:8 in Bonhoeffer, *Reflections on the Bible*, p. 73.

53. Bonhoeffer, *Ethics*, "God's Love and the Disintegration of the World."

life.[54] In a striking divergence from contemporary sensibilities, the psalmists do not think to worry where to find God's commands, or that they will confront a moral dilemma that is outside the biblical writers' purview. Only one nemesis fills the psalmists with dread: that they will take up God's statutes but God will no longer reveal what is required for living today. The solutions for our personal decisions and God's actions in history are often hidden, and no cause for anxiety (*Reflections,* p. 76). Bonhoeffer fears only that the synthetic schemas we use to organize the moral content of Scripture would themselves become a false god, so that "I would continue to live by my own principles, but God's law would no longer be by me."[55] Cursed are those who stray from thy commandments (Deut. 27:26).[56] "The psalmist, praying, speaks of 'straying.' He no longer thinks of willful, intentional violation of the divine commands. But how easily we go astray" (*Reflections,* p. 70).

It is all too easy to endlessly circle within the love of our distinctions and concepts, our angst about ethical conflicts, and a tragic view of our lives. Yet God's commands stand as an inviolate invitation to fellowship: "Things are much simpler here than we would prefer. It is not that we do not know God's commandments, but that we do not keep them. And then, of course, as a result of such disobedience, we also gradually stop recognizing them. That is our situation."[57] Thus Bonhoeffer concludes:

> It makes all the difference whether I obey God or my principles. If I am content with my principles, then I cannot understand the prayer of the psalmist. But if I allow myself to be shown the way by God, then I will depend entirely on the grace that is revealed or denied to me; then I will trem-

---

54. This polarity is probably too baldly put, given Bonhoeffer's obvious debts to idealism and idealism's awareness of the problem as Bonhoeffer puts it. Indeed, one way to read the methodological development in Bonhoeffer's work is as the movement of a representative of theological idealism toward phenomenology, a movement paralleling the development of thinkers such as Martin Heidegger. Though Bonhoeffer is clearly aware of, and trying to overcome, this philosophical problematic (explicitly in the *Act and Being* chapter, Part A, "The Problem of Act and Being, Portrayed in a Preparatory Manner as the Epistemological Problem of an Autonomous Understanding of Dasein in Philosophy"), my suggestion is that he did not effectively do so until he committed himself to exegetical theology. This is why it is important to pay attention to the methodological innovations of his Psalms exegesis, which are clearly distinguishable from the trajectories of these philosophical trends. Bonhoeffer may have arrived at this questioning of the terms of the philosophical debate in his meditations on Psalm 119; cf. v. 96: "I have seen a limit to all perfection, but thy commandment is exceedingly broad."

55. Bonhoeffer, *Dietrich Bonhoeffer's Meditations,* p. 92. Substantially the same point is made in Bonhoeffer, "On Psalm 119," p. 140.

56. Bonhoeffer, *Dietrich Bonhoeffer's Meditations,* p. 96.

57. See the linkage with this passage in Bonhoeffer, *Ethics,* p. 58, n. 42.

ble as I receive each word from the mouth of God, because of my need for the next word and for his continuing grace. Thus I will remain in all my ways and my decisions totally bound to grace, and no false security will be able to lure me away from this living fellowship with God. ("On Psalm 119," p. 141)

Bonhoeffer: Ethics as a Path

Despite this broadside on synthetic ethical frameworks, Bonhoeffer does not shy away from developing his conception of the mandates of work, marriage, government, and church. The problem that came to shape his mature thinking on ethics was how to place the doctrines of reconciliation and Scripture in the foreground in such a way that historical, experiential, and creaturely knowledge were not simply invalidated in Christian ethics but allowed a subsidiary and precisely delineated role. Bonhoeffer says that Barth's writing on ethics provided an essential template for his developing thought in relating these aspects of creaturely life to God's work in Christ.[58] Both Barth and Bonhoeffer had been alerted to the importance of any discussions of the ethical claim of creation or experience being set within the reconciling work of Christ by their neo-Lutheran opponents' emphasis on the ethical claim of family, people, land, and race, framed in terms all but impervious to theological critique.

Bonhoeffer's growing emphasis on Christian life as a path is an important part of his solution to this dilemma and is central to the rhetorical structure of *Ethics,* where Bonhoeffer says: "The issue is the *process* by which Christ takes form among us" (p. 134; italics added). Bonhoeffer conceives this path as Christ's way to us, who stimulates human action to respond by preparing a highway *(Bahn)* to "make straight the way of the Lord" (Luke 3:4-6). This concept grew so much in importance to the late Bonhoeffer that he considered it for the title of the whole work (p. 161, n. 64). As a result, Bonhoeffer comes to understand that at the heart of Christian ethics is the desire to prepare a way for Christ through a continual process of theological exegesis of Scripture and cultural and material orders. Scripture provides essential hints about how we are to discover what God accepts, rejects, and is renewing in our historical and creaturely realm, and thus "Christian life neither destroys nor sanctions the penultimate. In Christ the reality of God encounters the re-

---

58. Correspondence, quoted in Bonhoeffer, *Ethics,* p. 414 (page references to this book hereafter cited parenthetically in text).

ality of the world and allows us to take part in this real encounter" (p. 159). Bonhoeffer thus firmly establishes the Christological focus of the doctrine of reconciliation.

The result is that Bonhoeffer is keen to emphasize that ethical judgments are made "in the middle," in contexts where the criterion of the good we have at hand is not directly applicable to the situation we face. Here he is making what is now fashionably called a postmodern distinction, that in our daily lives we do not face good and evil in "pure" forms between which ethical theory helps us to choose, but in historically particular constellations in which good and evil aspects and trajectories are hopelessly intermixed. Christian moral judgment aims not at discerning the "absolute good act" but only the next step in a path of obedience, a path whose end is clear while the middle distance is not. Only in this way is Christian ethics a journey of faith and hope, and not of sight.

> No one has the responsibility of turning the world into the kingdom of God, but only of taking the next necessary step that corresponds to God's becoming human in Christ. . . . The task is not to turn the world upside down but in a given place to do what, from the perspective of reality, is necessarily objective [*sachlich*] and to really carry it out. But even in a given place, responsible action cannot always immediately do what is ultimately right. It has to proceed step-by-step, ask what is possible, and entrust the ultimate step, and thus the ultimate responsibility, to another hand. (pp. 224-25)[59]

These observations reveal that in the chapter in *Ethics* entitled "Ultimate and Penultimate Things," Bonhoeffer is laying out the doctrinal structure of a theological hermeneutics of culture drawn from and linked to his hermeneutics of Scripture. The mandates are thus not properly understood as metaphysical axioms, ethical blueprints, or programs; they are Christologically keyed signposts indicating the features of reality that allow us to encounter Christ (p. 388). The Torah/divine Word delimits the concrete domain within which responsibility is possible, and by living into the divine

---

59. "To turn the world upside down" is a reference to Barth's *Epistle to the Romans.* The aim of Bonhoeffer's reflections on Psalm 119 is perhaps most clearly visible when we understand them as part of an attempt, paralleling Barth's, to retain the strong emphasis of *Romans* on the primacy of God's grace, but to mitigate the appearance that this grace is only experienced in punctuated interventions. On the phrase and its implications for Christian ethics, see Michael Banner, "Turning the World Upside Down — and Some Other Tasks for Dogmatic Christian Ethics," in *Christian Ethics and Contemporary Moral Problems* (Cambridge: Cambridge University Press, 1999), esp. pp. 1-13.

command we have creation's nature and character revealed to us (p. 267). Here Bonhoeffer exhibits a deep continuity with the thought world of the psalmists, in which the law is a heuristic, understood and used only as lived into, and so epistemically productive only as it is "confessed in word and life" (p. 256).

In order to minimize the danger of the subheadings under which we organize discussions of the various topics in Christian ethics displacing Scripture, Bonhoeffer shifts traditional sensibilities about where theological systems ought to exhibit their highest levels of conceptual clarity. Here he makes explicit the ethical implications of his insistence that we not allow a focus on conceptual coherence to displace a central role for attentiveness to situation and relational considerations. If we insist on defending our subheadings on the grounds that they exhibit a watertight conceptual clarity, says Bonhoeffer, we no longer direct our attention to the origin and aim of Christian ethics as a lived encounter with Christ, replacing it with the moralizing application of universal moral concepts (p. 263).

This innovation yields an all-important ethical conclusion, says Bonhoeffer: "The attention of responsible people is directed to concrete neighbors in their concrete reality. Their behavior is not fixed in advance once and for all by a principle, but develops together with the given situation . . . they seek to understand and do what is necessary, or 'commanded' in a given situation" (p. 261). The command thus understood is not divine fiat but attentive meditation on the law (a general but not primarily diachronic referent), which attunes us to hear the command of Christ in the neighbor (a specific but spatially rather than temporally conceived referent) amid the static and obscurities of sinful human historical existence. Spouses, for instance, face claims of their mates and Scripture that cannot be displaced by any ethical schema.

Bonhoeffer provides one example of how the close reading of Scripture returns as a fundamental part of post-Enlightenment Christian ethics. His reassertion of the indispensability of concrete and ongoing biblical interpretation for Christian ethics attacked its deadening tendency to rely on moral categories only *derived* from Scripture, which render a continuing attention to God's Word superfluous. At the same time, however, he could see that Christian ethics also needs a way of establishing how the ethically relevant aspects of human life and the creaturely world are distinguished for purposes of moral judgment. Luther made these distinctions via his doctrine of the three *Stände* (estates, i.e., political, economic/family, ecclesial), to which Bonhoeffer responds with a critical revision: "The Lutheran doctrine of the three estates [*Stände*] . . . must be replaced by a doctrine which is drawn from the Bible, the doctrine of the four divine mandates, marriage and family, work, government, and church" (p. 389, n. 2). Bonhoeffer's doctrine of the mandates is as clearly an attempt at a Christological reworking of the doctrine of the *Stände* as it is a thorough attack on the version circulating among his contemporaries.

These observations make possible an analytic summary of Bonhoeffer's understanding of the mandates, the main categories through which he approaches particular moral questions.

1. They are concept clusters that name regions of human existence through summarizing steady scriptural emphases of ethical relevance.
2. Thus they indicate the features of our creaturely existence (the penultimate) through which God sustains all creatures, and within which God rejuvenates the brokenness of creation (pp. 158-59).
3. As such they constitute the theological heuristic, the path on which Christian faith in God's eternal judgment of justification in Christ (the ultimate) prayerfully, through continuous engagement with Scripture and daily life, discovers the real in itself, the neighbor, human sociality, and creation.

Therefore, the mandates should be understood as a naming in faith of the main contours of God's saving work within a fallen world. They are not a synthetic account, because their claim to legitimacy is not grounded in the completeness of a survey of Scripture but on a theologically described biblical topography. They function like "focal images" in guiding analogical reasoning, but are more concrete than Hays's cross, community, and new creation, yet more flexible in assuming the necessity of their being constantly reconfigured and debated. Nor are the mandates an exegetical "method" that will reliably produce results, nor a "virtue" that the reader can claim to possess. Finally, they also have the virtue of distinguishing between ethics as *imitating* God and *obeying* God.

The mandates have no salvific value, or even ultimate conceptual worth, but they pedagogically indicate basic aspects of creaturely existence, which Scripture suggests are necessary for the continued existence of all creation, including the unregenerate. In themselves they are inconsequential; what matters is the "obedience of faith rendered within them" (p. 358). Only as so construed do they provide a measure for moral deliberation that is not consequentialist or procedural but full of content and richly theological (pp. 165-66). Bonhoeffer finds the journey of faith described in Psalm 119 powerful from the point of view of the one who clings to God's words, trusting God's presence and working, while not yet seeing all that this entails for one's personal destiny or that of the world. The details of that history lie in God's ultimate Word, to which the Christian clings in an attempt to discern how God's Word leads on a way to God that is clear only in its nature as Scripture, but not yet in terms of the many judgments about the world that the path of faith will demand.

At various points we can see Bonhoeffer clarifying how the mandates were to be derived and were to function in relationship to material questions. When talking about marriage in *Ethics,* for example, Bonhoeffer clearly structures his account of the mandate of family on his exegesis of the Genesis account (pp. 203-4). Perhaps more instructive is a comment he made in a 1944 letter to Eberhard Bethge, in which Bonhoeffer explains that friendship is not a mandate but belongs with them. Though he cannot find it in the Bible, and thus cannot call it a command, his experience of its richness drives him to look for its place within Scripture.[60] Bonhoeffer wants to call friendship important, but he does not want to put words in Scripture's mouth. He believes that his term "mandates" grasps the strands of Scripture most relevant for Christian moral thinking, but he is vigilant in stating this in terms that do not imply that the mandates exhaust the ways that obedience follows. Mandates are constantly revised descriptions of Scripture that help the faithful distinguish essential aspects of the many ways of humanity so that we can learn to discern between them. In so doing they provide a topography of moral priority that serves as a heuristic for the steps of faith of human decision-making. Friendship stands somehow below marriage in importance because it is so in Scripture, yet this observation does not exhaust or limit the possibilities for faithful human action, but opens up the main features of God's acts by recalling his commands, and is a signpost on a way that we might fruitfully explore.

Assessment

In conclusion, I will make a few brief comments on the implications of this reading of Bonhoeffer's ethics. We can dismiss Fowl and Jones's contention that Bonhoeffer's involvement in the plot against Hitler caused him to lose

---

60. See Bonhoeffer's comment in a letter to Bethge about friendship being a "cornflower that belongs to the [mandates] as a cornflower to the cornfield." In Bonhoeffer, *Letters and Papers from Prison,* pp. 192-93. The metaphor and thought are developed in more detail in Bonhoeffer's prison poem "Der Freund — The Friend." See the poem and commentary in Bonhoeffer, *Voices in the Night: The Prison Poems of Dietrich Bonhoeffer,* ed. and trans. Edwin Robertson (Grand Rapids: Zondervan, 1999), pp. 83-94.

touch with Scripture (ch. 2). More constructively, Bonhoeffer has suggested that we must be prepared to understand Christian ethics as a structured facilitation of human cooperation with the divine sanctification of humanity. This substantially shifts the remit of Christian ethics. Such an ethic would be devoted to theological thinking about problem areas, and within those areas to seeking the resources for indicating some clear avenues within which Christians may in good faith discover the implications of the confession of Christ. The desire to offer theologically informed and biblically meditative judgments of historical trends and conceptual trajectories would displace moral reasoning as devoted solely to the development of moral rules or axioms (however derived) on the grounds that obedience must remain obedience in *faith*. On such a view, moral claims would be understood as confessions of faith, lack of faith, or counter-faith, to be "muttered" in word and life. Moral theology thus construed is not a program but a theologically attuned ear that directs the constant rediscovery of — and reorientation within — our place in creation (*Ethics*, p. 55). Ethics thus serves human salvation as the processes of hearing, repentance, and sanctification. Like Webster, Bonhoeffer emphasizes the centrality of prayer and repentance, but he does not fully flesh out their roles. It is at this point that Bonhoeffer's palpable lack of pneumatology is a liability that cries out for further articulation. The Christian confession is that we are within the law of the Spirit, the evangelical form of the law. This deficit may pair with another, noted by Barth, that Bonhoeffer, in his material filling out of his conception of the mandates, betrays his best insights by putting too much weight on created order and thus experience, interpreted without adequate recourse to reconciliation and redemption.[61]

Is Bonhoeffer susceptible to the accusation of proceduralism that was leveled at the writers represented in the first two chapters? Is he defining justice as a method when he says that we meet God and are reformed by continual utterance of God's past acts? To heavily weight "utterance" as a practice or method of obedience would certainly make him liable to this accusation. But Bonhoeffer says that it is the formed utterance of *Scripture*, and not just "utterance"alone, by which God transforms Christians. Form and content are intertwined in a way not apparent in the method represented in the first two chapters. Bonhoeffer's approach also leads to a sharpening of Webster's approach. Webster conceives of the events of God's action as the "space" of moral deliberation, but Bonhoeffer points out that Scripture tells us that God's commands and statutes are the only proper points of access to that space.

---

61. See Nigel Biggar's excellent account of Barth's critique in *The Hastening That Waits: Karl Barth's Ethics* (Oxford: Clarendon Press, 1993), p. 59.

Furthermore, Bonhoeffer has substantiated our worries that summaries of the Bible's ethical content are methodologically problematic. Such summaries turn Scripture into a book that contains moral claims rather than being the point at which meditation on God's Word can become even richer. This allows him to restate in slightly different terms Watson's important observation that the church always reads Scripture "in the middle" of immersion in the world.

QUESTION FOR FURTHER STUDY: How does Scripture conceive of itself as shaping Christian prayer, praise, repentance, and transformed behavior?

Listening to the Saints
Encountering the Ethos of Scripture

CHAPTER 6

Augustine's Ethos of Salvific Confession

Introduction to Part II

"Developing a Hermeneutics" vs. "Immersion in a Tradition"

One of the most important criticisms I have leveled at the contemporary Bible-and-ethics discussion is that, by and large, it assumes that one of the basic conceptual problems, if not *the* basic problem, to be resolved is the estrangement of the disciplines of biblical studies or hermeneutics from Christian ethics. From whatever side of the disciplinary chasm theologians or biblical scholars approach it, questions about how to read the Bible (hermeneutics) and about the Bible's role in God's claiming of Christian behavior (ethics) are thus severed by those traditions' self-identification with various strands of the late-modern philosophical tradition. It is not our purpose here to recount the familiar history of the processes of that identification and the resulting separation of ethics and exegesis.[1] My approach will be to explore parts of the Christian exegetical tradition in the hope, as Brevard Childs puts it, of being "made aware of the many different models of interpretation which have all too frequently been disparaged through ignorance."[2]

The task of Part II is to experience for ourselves life on the other side of the ugly ditch between biblical hermeneutics and ethics. Such an approach resists the contemporary tendency to pay lip service to the idea that all read-

1. Cf. Stanley Hauerwas and Samuel Wells, "Why Christian Ethics Was Invented" and "How the Church Managed Before There Was Ethics," in Stanley Hauerwas and Samuel Wells, eds., *The Blackwell Companion to Christian Ethics* (Oxford: Blackwell, 2004).

2. Brevard Childs, *Introduction to the Old Testament as Scripture* (Philadelphia: Fortress, 1979), p. 523.

ing is tradition-bound yet allowing the modern disciplines of ethics, systematic theology, or academic biblical hermeneutics to remain unaffected by the deep challenges presented by the "hermeneutical" stance of premodern biblical interpretation. In so doing, contemporary exegetes and ethicists further entrench the divide they set out to cross. When we make forays into the Christian tradition only to recover some "resources," the most important questions remain untouched. Immersion in our own, though now unfamiliar, tradition helps to shed light on why — and, more importantly, how — Christian ethics and hermeneutics might begin, not to cross the divide, but to recapture the integral relationship of ethics and exegesis in the Christian life.

The Ethos of Participation in Tradition

This approach, best understood as an ethos of tradition, recasts what we take to be a valid hermeneutics. I understand tradition as an enacted form of agreement. This agreement has limits, which make disagreement possible and productive, while themselves standing under an eschatological caveat, thus remaining open to development. Tradition is a form of agreement into which we can introduce people; and we can hand it on as those who possess it, yet must do so as those possessed by it. Therefore, it is not best understood as a single line of descent, as a stream in which forces and influences coalesce and dissipate, parallel one another, are constantly in motion, and constantly influencing and being influenced by neighboring discourses. Nor are exegetical traditions sharply divided from one another. The Christian tradition is open to other traditions, and it has maintained its integrity by at times designating certain strands within itself to be illegitimate. Thus, one way of naming the current crisis of Christian ethical exegesis is to say that it is a manifestation of the church's confusion about whether it is part of the historical Christian tradition, the modern tradition, or some of each. Polemics against modernity do not resolve this problem, which can only be addressed by carefully teasing out how both traditions make Christians better servants of the God of Scripture.

The story of the interaction between the Christian and modern exegetical traditions is a familiar one. By the nineteenth century, the gradual loosening of ties between the universities, churches, and synagogues begun in the eighteenth century allowed a stable academic exegetical tradition to form that distanced itself from the Christian faith tradition. Questions not previously asked by Christian interpreters of Scripture came to dominate this discourse. The effect on Psalms exegesis was that a text-critical inquiry into the historicity of Psalms headings developed into a wholesale questioning of the ascription of Psalms to the named authors, and culminated in the widely held opinion that the Psalms were a haphazardly arranged collection used as a songbook in a late period of Israel's history.[3]

The emphases of today's academic Psalm criticism express a reaction to this deconstruction. Hermann Gunkel developed a form-critical apparatus that gave some unified shape to the Psalter by defining Psalms according to literary genres. These genre designations developed out of a search for a *Sitz im Leben* for the composition of individual psalms and by comparison with other ancient Near Eastern poetry.[4] Gunkel's student Sigmund Mowinckel elaborated on this method by asking how the Psalms give hints of use in a reconstructed temple cultus, most notably its festal calendar.[5] A relatively new approach (1960-80) draws on literary criticism or Brevard Childs's canonical criticism to reconstruct the redactional principles behind the current arrangement of the Psalter.[6]

It would be worth tracing how this academic tradition, with its explicit bracketing of faith commitments, has nevertheless paralleled the Christian exegetical tradition in a range of obvious and more subtle ways. In practice, form critics and historical critics were rarely as free from the influence of Christian concepts of God and worship as they claimed to be. Mowinckel, for example, whose whole method of Psalms exegesis rests on locating individual psalms within a definition of cultus, which he claims is generalizable to all religions,[7] goes on to define worship using remarkably Christian categories.[8]

---

3. This account is influenced by the excellent chapter-length summary of Psalm exegesis that begins with the interpretive decisions of the earliest extant Jewish commentaries and translations, and continues to the present, in David Mitchell, *The Message of the Psalter: An Eschatological Programme in the Book of Psalms* (Sheffield: Sheffield Academic Press, 1997), ch. 1.

4. Hermann Gunkel, *Die Psalmen* (Göttingen: Vandenhoeck & Ruprecht, 1926); translated by T. H. Horner as *The Psalms*, intro. by J. Muilenburg (Philadelphia: Fortress, 1967); also Hermann Gunkel and J. Begrich, *Einleitung in die Psalmen: De Gattungen der religiösen Lyrik Israels*, Göttinger Handkommentar zum AT (Göttingen: Vandenhoeck & Ruprecht, 1933).

5. Sigmund Mowinckel, *The Psalms in Israel's Worship*, 2 vols. (Oxford: Basil Blackwell, 1962). Though this text is a translation of the original Norwegian edition, *Offersang og Sangoffer*, published in 1951, it is heavily revised and is considered by author and translator to be the more mature text.

6. Childs, *Introduction to the Old Testament.* Important Psalms commentaries in this form are Walther Zimmerli's "Zwillingspsalmen," in J. Schreiner, ed., *Wort, Leid, und Gottesspruch: Beiträge zu Psalmen und Propheten* (Würzburg: Echter Verlag, 1972), pp. 105-13, and Claus Westermann's "The Formation of the Psalter," in *Praise and Lament in the Psalms*, trans. K. R. Crim and R. N. Soulen (Atlanta: John Knox, 1981), pp. 250-58.

7. Mowinckel, *The Psalms*, vol. I (Oxford: Oxford University Press, 1962), p. 15.

8. One place where this influence is blatant is his understanding of the relationship between prayer and worship, prayer being the "primary expression of religion": "[P]rayer is a peti-

Despite their supposed methodological distance from faith claims, historical and form critics can still reach surprising agreements with theological readings on specific passages. In order to be clear about the tradition that contemporary theologians and biblical scholars share (modernity), in the next few chapters I will on occasion indicate points where the Christian and "secular" academic exegetical discourses come into close proximity and where they differ in ways that illuminate the role being played by modern presuppositions. This should yield more clarity regarding the implications of the claim that we are placed before specific biblical passages not as members of one tradition but of many, as those who desire to become Christians.

Here the question of what a "meaningful" interpretation might be takes center stage. Traditions, including the many strands of Jewish and Christian exegesis, define "fidelity to the text" via their own canons of acceptability and on the basis of commitments that may or may not be defended by reference to the text itself. Thus the question of a "meaningful" interpretation is the field in which any new proposal must take its stand. Therefore, it might be more accurate, rather than asking about how traditions understand an interpretation to be meaningful, to ask about the form of rationality that they seek in the text.

As a test case, let us consider Psalm 119:33-36 as a definition of sanctified knowledge: "Teach me, Yahweh, the *way* of your will, and I will observe it. Give me *understanding* and I will observe your Law, and keep it wholeheartedly. Guide me in the way of your commandments, for my *delight* is there. *Bend my heart* to your instructions, not to selfish gain."[9] The psalmist seeks here to be remade, to become holy, not only or first of all by learning understanding (not exactly an equivalent to reason or assent to true statements), but also by learning to walk a way, or a path, and to be given a delight, a redirection of the affections. The psalmist's breadth of expression allows us to query the extent to which contemporary theology and exegesis can handle the various aspects of the psalmist's rounded definition of rationality. Within the scope of the Old Testament, the faithful are depicted as being redeemed in their perception, action, and desire in an interrelated, reciprocally defining form.

This biblical definition of knowing presents a much broader conceptual field than most modern conceptions, challenging any hermeneutics or ethics

---

tion to a powerful, willing and personally acting God, and is intended consciously to support, underline and express what the acts in their way express and effect. What is performed is accompanied by prayer and praise." Mowinckel, *The Psalms*, vol. I, p. 15.

9. The New Jerusalem translation emphasizes the simultaneity of singing and obedience better than the NRSV does (italics added).

that has no substantive role for all the aspects of sanctified rationality depicted in Psalm 119. My suggestion is that modern traditions have lost the ability to handle this breadth. As members of the modern tradition, in order to gain access to the whole Christian tradition, we must set aside familiar ideas of the tradition as something that progresses in a linear fashion like a train leaving the past behind forever, or a building block model in which our knowledge rests on pilings long ago driven into the swamp of precivilized ignorance. We must be prepared to listen attentively to the saints, whether from early, middle, or late points in the discourse of faith, an approach that has several further implications.

First and foremost, it is based on a conception of the tradition not as a repository of settled ontological truths but as a broad, multifaceted, and somehow unified and unbroken wrestling with specific texts. It thus stands as an invitation not only to repeat it but to become interpreters within it. Its value is not in its antiquity but in its ability to shape us as those who can read. Chapter 9 of this book is thus "traditional" in joining in and inviting others to join in interpreting Scripture with the saints. Such wrestling with Scripture exhibits a range of obvious divergences from the contemporary Bible-and-ethics discussion. Part I surveyed a contemporary discussion more engrossed in methodological questions about hermeneutics than the much less generalizable skill of developing a content-rich reading of the Bible that responds to the questions of today. My hope is that, in turning now to precisely such content-rich treatments, our approach to Scripture will be shaped in unexpected ways as we are shown how to read and comment on particular texts rather than hermeneutical theory.

Empathetically entering methodologically unfamiliar readings gives us different and complementary but not necessarily methodologically commensurable ways of discovering meaning in texts. More importantly, such readings may challenge at its roots our modern predisposition to begin all study with discussions of method. Just as the parallel Gospels provide multiple accounts of one event whose unity cannot be established at the level of historical chronology, so too may the placing of modern conceptual sensibilities within the whole sweep of the Christian tradition reveal important unities amid methodological incommensurability. By reading Augustine and Luther together, we see how Scripture is resistant to and productive for them in different ways, and what they share is therefore not susceptible to definitive location in hermeneutical method.

This is, as I have said, to conceive tradition as a set of practices or, more precisely, as an ethos giving priority to attentiveness in intellectual, moral, and affective forms. This approach stands in contrast to early Enlightenment biblical criticism, which took its stand on the claim that all previous forms of attentiveness obscured Scripture's meaning; they were to be set aside and a new practice was to be developed. As late modern philosophy realized, this was terribly corrosive of any notion of tradition. Yet what continued to unite modern biblical criticism with the tradition it repudiated was a central focus on attentiveness to the details of Scripture. This continuity reveals that what the Enlightenment properly questioned was not attention to Scripture but allowing it to be submerged within a synthesizing exegesis by the faith community. Yet, as the writers surveyed in Part I have regularly pointed out, the modern claim to be surmounting this problem by stepping outside the influence of reading traditions altogether is a blatant self-deception. This criticism opens the way for a fresh appreciation of the Christian exegetical tradition.

The final result of this chain of logic is the claim that we begin to see anew the basic texts that founded a tradition not by asking what these texts are, or what they tell us, but in joining a reading tradition by practicing reading that is attentive, moral, and communal. We enter a tradition not by grasping its theoretical underpinnings but by learning its ethos and the skills that make it function. This parallels the approaches of Augustine and Luther: they had such an ethos because they understood the Christian tradition to have its center in a people's experiences of the one God, an experience itself shaped by what has been handed on to them. For them, the existence of Scripture is the proof that it is through Scripture that God creates his people. In the course of the discussion we will also give more theological clarity to what it means for a tradition to be a set of skills with which we approach Scripture.

This commitment to the primacy of particular activities of reading in community grounds my decision to re-engage with the genre of biblical commentary. Born in the Patristic period, this genre's strong theological focus and method were disrupted by modern historicist interests only within the last 200 years. As a result, modern biblical commentators, who are highly trained in the skills of translation, are nevertheless oriented by nontheological exegetical traditions in a manner that often obscures the *theological* importance of the translation and commentary. While modern biblical commentaries take the actual text of Scripture more seriously than does much modern theology, their methodological presuppositions preclude the broad readings of the theological, ontological, and moral implications of specific biblical texts necessary in Christian ethics. In short, their methodological presuppositions place a barrier in the way of the Bible's being read as Scripture. Christian theology has only recently rediscovered the relevance of this point, as evidenced by a groundswell of interest in theological commentaries.[10] That these observations are of immense importance in the interpretation of the moral import of a book such as the Psalms will shortly become apparent as we enter the interpretive worlds of Augustine and Luther.

Scriptural Exegesis as Praise: Comparing Augustine and Luther

This chapter and the next reveal that Augustine and Luther both conceive of the reading of Scripture as an action of praise facilitating the entry of the church into its new life in Christ. This is an important agreement, and Part III builds on it. At the same time, they have very different understandings of what one is doing when praising God through exegesis, and how this is morally transformative. For Augustine, one takes up Scripture in praise to *teach* doctrine for *salvation*, while Luther's aim is to *preach* doctrine for *consolation*. Augustine conceives of the church he addresses as a material body moving in time and space, and he encourages its members to embrace being changed on the journey. Luther thinks of the church as a space opened by God's Word, a word that transforms the world. The church of all times partakes of God's calling people out of the crowd and remaking them into a community. Augustine's church is made of concrete bodies whose action he seeks to change by exegetical teaching: his is an ethics of the church. Luther's church is made up of those who worship and pray: his is an ethics of worship. Augustine's ethos of *peregrinatio* and Luther's of conformation to Christ will be revealed to have different semantics, not easily synthesized. But before we can make any comparison, it is important to read each thinker on his own terms. We shall see that one important and sympathetic philosophical reader of Augustine, Charles Taylor, while deeply influenced by his moral conceptualities, misreads Augustine at critical points but in a way that gives us better access to his moral theology and its relationship to the exegesis of Scripture.

---

10. Three massive commentary projects mark this swell. The *Ancient Christian Commentary on Scripture* (ed. Thomas C. Odin, InterVarsity Press) series resurrects patristic commentaries in a digest form; the *Brazos Theological Commentary on the Bible* (R. R. Reno, ed., Brazos Press) enlists theologians to write commentaries on biblical books without special reference to biblical criticism; the *Two Horizons* commentary series (Wm. B. Eerdmans) attempts a more conscientious and thorough integration of biblical criticism and theology. See the manifesto for this project in Joel B. Green and Max Turner, eds., *Between Two Horizons: Spanning New Testament Studies and Systematic Theology* (Grand Rapids: Eerdmans, 1999).

Doctrine as Hermeneutics in Augustine

A familiar misreading of Augustine's exegesis of the Psalms is based on two intertwining misapprehensions. The first is that Augustine constantly uses an arcane typological or allegorical method to uncover the Christ symbolically foretold in the Old Testament.[11] This misreading is based on a half-truth: Augustine does see Christ in the Old Testament and thus in the Psalms, but this is not because he thinks that the authors of the Psalms explicitly knew Christ, or because he thinks the true meaning of the Psalms was primarily to foretell Christ. In recovering what he actually did think, we will discover that Augustine has a quite sophisticated account of the unity of the two testaments in the Christ event, one only recently rediscovered in biblical hermeneutics. Augustine's position is quite close to many of the better contemporary exegetical proposals at this point: he thinks that the unity of the two testaments can and must be established on the basis of theological arguments that take into account as many of the Bible's different facets as possible.

The obscuring of this theological and exegetical sophistication is due to a second pervasive misapprehension: that Augustine's biblical exegesis is a direct application of the biblical hermeneutics he develops in *De Doctrina Christiana*.[12] He was not entirely satisfied with this work when he began it

11. Adolph von Harnack presents a caricature of Augustine's exegesis, born of the Enlightenment distaste for allegory, which still survives in some strands of biblical studies. "Exegesis became a kind of black art, and Augustine was not the only man who was delivered from Manichean, by Biblical, Alchemy." *History of Dogma*, vol. III, trans. Neil Buchanan (New York: Dover Publications, 1961), p. 199. John Rist correctly observes that "when in the Enlightenment the rebellion against Christianity broke out, its fury was often directed at Augustine in particular, and often fuelled by contempt for Calvinist and Jansenist 'restatements' of his positions. The resulting criticisms of Augustine were launched with a mindless and undiscriminating hostility which often persists today, while the power and persuasiveness of many of Augustine's ideas, and the perspicacity of many of his observations, were ignored in the flood of emotional condemnations let loose on his (and his followers') excesses in theory and practice." John Rist, *Augustine: Ancient Thought Baptised* (Cambridge: Cambridge University Press, 1996), p. 292.

12. Though both show some awareness of this problem, Brevard Childs's *Biblical Theology of the Old and New Testaments: Theological Reflections on the Christian Bible* (Minneapolis: Fortress, 1993), pp. 36-39, and Beryl Smalley's *The Study of the Bible in the Middle Ages* (Notre Dame: University of Notre Dame Press, 1978), pp. 23-24, passim, nevertheless sharply focus their account of Augustine's hermeneutics on *De Doctrina Christiana*. James Preuss's otherwise excellent history of biblical hermeneutics, *From Shadow to Promise: Old Testament Interpretation from Augustine to the Young Luther* (Eugene, OR: Wipf and Stock, 1999), has a slightly wider focus, which includes both *De Doctrina* and *On the Spirit and Letter*. Yet in not analyzing Augustine's actual exegesis, Preuss also misses that he is more subtle in practice than in theory. His treatment of Luther is far more satisfying precisely because he turns from exposition of his writ-

early in his career; thus he set it aside and forgot about it until rediscovering it late in his life.[13] Augustine's difficulties in prescribing a Christian hermeneutical method are perfectly understandable within the presuppositions of this study — that people are often better at doing things than explaining what they have done. In addition, his interest in finishing the book must not be taken to mean that it described his own exegesis, especially since his stated aim in writing is to teach others to read Scripture and to preach.[14] The illusion that they can be taken as a description of his own practice rests not on a detailed comparison of his theory and practice but on the wide influence *De Doctrina* exerted on the subsequent exegetical tradition and, in turn, on the way his exegetical work was read. The work shows Augustine at his most neo-Platonic, displaying the techniques of ancient rhetorical method and suggesting their use for biblical exegesis. This leads interpreters such as Alasdair MacIntyre and J. Ian McDonald to praise Augustine's use of Greek philosophical concepts, because in so doing he paves the way for the medieval reappropriation of Greek learning.[15] I will suggest that such accounts of Augustine's exegesis are less appreciative of his exegetical practice than were the medieval interpreters who put his exegesis to use, and thus they misconstrue its basic contours. In their haste to portray Augustine as a forerunner of the synthesis of biblical and Greek thought, such interpretations repeat the contemporary tendency to pay insufficient attention to the way Augustine executed his exegetical craft. They concentrate on the philosophical concepts displayed in his early theorizing, which I will suggest were eclipsed in his most ambitious and mature exegesis.

Close examination of Augustine's mature exegetical practice, especially in his sermons, renders the claim that he is "applying" the hermeneutics of *De Doctrina* implausible. Augustine's expositions increasingly draw their interpretive principles not from Greek rhetoric but from Scripture itself. This is due in large part to his commitment to the Bible as Scripture, that is, to the Bible as a "methodically" unique book playing a special role between God

---

ings on hermeneutics to a close study of his Psalm exegesis, which he finds, unsurprisingly, to be theologically complex in ways that illumine Luther's prefatory writings on hermeneutics (cf. pp. 153f.). For a defense of the integral relationship of Luther's exegesis and hermeneutical writings, see Heinz Bluhm, *Martin Luther: Creative Translator* (St. Louis: Concordia, 1965), ch. 5.

13. Augustine, *The Retractions, The Fathers of the Church: A New Translation*, vol. 60, trans. Mary Bogan (Washington, D.C.: Catholic University of America Press, 1968), ch. 30.

14. Discussed and defended in the preface.

15. Alasdair MacIntyre, *Three Rival Versions of Moral Inquiry* (London: Gerald Duckworth and Co., 1990), pp. 86, 96. J. Ian McDonald, *The Crucible of Christian Morality* (London: Routledge, 1998), p. 204.

and humanity. Augustine locates his activity of reading in relation to this larger story, a relationship that yields a reading strategy very different from the general hermeneutical strategies of Greek (and modern) philosophy. As we follow his actual practice of exegesis in motion, we become aware that the general hermeneutical tools laid out in *De Doctrina* have been stripped from their original location in an ancient rhetorical metaphysic and dismembered — to be brought out only occasionally and in an *ad hoc* way.

An *ad hoc* hermeneutical procedure is to be differentiated from one that is inconsistent. As we shall see, in his best exegetical work Augustine is most accurately described as formally consistent in a nongeneralizable way. His reading is grounded in certain biblical images and metaphors that he uses to illuminate the flow of the larger text, even as they are themselves under constant revision and clarification. One of the best examples of this nonmethodological Augustine at work trying to understand Scripture is found in the sprawling biblical and cultural exegesis that is the *City of God* (written between 413 and 426). One of Augustine's main aims in this work is to understand the continuity of the biblical narrative by tracing the story of God through the entire Bible. This story, he finds, is best understood from the vantage point of membership in a community: God is redeeming humanity by choosing a people whom he leads on an exodus from captivity in this sinful world. From here Augustine undertakes a narration of the state of that conflict in his own age; he does so in order to guide the ethic of the church of his day by showing Christians how they are in a *story* that frames their moral transformation as they learn about and pursue their *telos.*

The best view of the contours of the mature exegesis of the *City of God* comes in Book 17, where Augustine deals with the Psalms. The book's argument can be seen in highly compressed form in chapter 4 of Book 17, which focuses on Hannah's Song (1 Sam. 2:1-11), linking it with two other central events of the Samuel-Kings narrative complex.[16] The first is the divine rejection of the high priest Eli for Samuel, and the second is the divine rejection of Saul for David. Hannah sings her song of praise as she delivers her son, the child Samuel, into the care of the high priest, Eli, whom Samuel will one day replace, as the narrative soon tells us. Augustine wants to emphasize that the song reveals the deep structure of the narrative: Hannah sings a song of God's

---

16. It is instructive to note that Augustine's inclusion of Hannah's Song in his investigation of the meaning of the Psalms makes use of an assumption common in modern form-criticism, but put to different use. "There are psalms outside the Psalter, and whether these have been composed for the same purpose as the others, or are only literary imitations, they are nevertheless dependent on the traditional style and thus contribute to the explanation of the types." Mowinckel, *The Psalms,* vol. I, p. 40.

power from the vantage point of one involved in the transformation from barrenness to fertility that is sweeping God's people. The son she bears will be a central part of God's faithfulness as he cares for and renews a priesthood rendered barren by its wickedness.[17] Samuel, as a participant in this divine renewal and as the new high priest, will challenge and then curse Saul, who, like the priests Samuel has replaced, has grown proud and corrupt. And again, Samuel will be the agent of God's revivification of Israel when he discerns and anoints David as the new and faithful king of God's provision.[18]

For Augustine, these transitional events display the surprising rationality of God's care in tending Israel's religious and political traditions of descent. The biblical passages portraying God's breaking into the proper lines of descent for priest and king are thus particularly meaningful: they are interruptions revealing God's form of rule. God's raising up a new priest and king "foreshadowed the change which was to take place in the future with respect to the two covenants, the old and the new: The transformation of priesthood and kingship brought about by the new and everlasting priest-king Who is Christ Jesus."[19] The deposing of Saul and Eli, and their replacement by David and Samuel, prefigure the replacement of the kingship and priesthood as a whole by Christ, only because they reveal the ways of a God who is committed to showing his holiness in the world by creating and maintaining his people in holiness.

Hannah, as the mother of Samuel, inaugurates a biblical age in which the people of God are for the first time able to understand and articulate this divine dynamic in sung prayer, making her the herald and first representative of the age of the prophets: "Hannah, who had formerly been barren but rejoiced in her fruitfulness, seems to *prophesy* exactly the same transformation, when, exulting, she pours forth her gratitude to the Lord" (Book XVII.4, p. 770; italics added).[20] Augustine sees in her song the characteristic marks of the whole age of biblical prophecy. By placing her song at a critical point in the building of the narrative momentum, the authors (redactors) of Samuel indicate that it represents the essence of the narrative that follows, an essence

---

17. The text recording this transition (1 Sam. 2:27ff.) is examined in Augustine, *The City of God against the Pagans*, ed. and trans. R. W. Dyson (Cambridge: Cambridge University Press, 1998), Book XVII.5.

18. Augustine examines this rejection (1 Sam. 13:13ff.) in *City of God*, Book XVII.6.

19. Augustine, *City of God*, Book XVII.4, p. 770 (references to this work hereafter cited parenthetically in text).

20. The biblical topography Augustine is narrating has a forward momentum for the theological reasons indicated. Though not mentioned in the *City of God*, the logic of his position would no doubt have been able to accommodate earlier biblical singers, such as Moses' Song of Exodus 15.

not visible without the flesh of the narratives.[21] Hannah's pregnancy and the role of her child in the renewal of the priestly and kingly lines (like that of Mary, whom Luke the evangelist models on her) represent moments in which God's way of caring for his people is made particularly evident. The renewal of the prophetic, priestly, and kingly lines in the person of Christ is in no way a new feature of the story of God with his people, Augustine contends, because God has previously and regularly undertaken similar renewals.

It is worth noting that Augustine also assumes the importance of the Torah. These narratives do not undermine the law; rather, they assume its importance as the condition for perceiving God's interventions. Without the law, the dispossession of Eli and Saul would have been no surprise, nor would it have so apparently been a gracious renewal of Israel. Augustine exploits a tension between narrative and non-narrative biblical texts, not to take up a position on one side or the other (as do the authors discussed in ch. 2), but to find Scripture's message in their interrelationship. The genre tensions within Scripture are taken to be communicative, to be suffered conscientiously rather than closed down by interpretation that stands on one side or the other of the genre divide. This is a technique that Augustine regularly and skillfully exploits in his Psalms exegesis and that leads him, for example, to defend the exegetical value of Psalm titles (Book XVII.14).[22]

21. The development of interpretation of Hannah's song recapitulates the development of Psalm criticism discussed above (J. Wellhausen's *Der Text der Bücher Samuelis untersucht* consolidating the multisource reading of 1-2 Samuel). The approach has been so dominant in shaping interpretations of Hannah's song that contemporary conservative historical critics only venture that the song is "consistent with" the subsequent chapters (Ralph Klein, *Word Biblical Commentary: 1 Samuel*, vol. 10 [Waco: Word Books, 1983], pp. 19-20). Given the modern biblical studies climate, it is striking that, via canonical criticism, Brevard Childs arrives at an Augustinian reading of the passage, but without naming him. "Chapter 2 then interrupts the narrative. . . . The focus of this chapter is not on history in the abstract; rather it falls specifically on the history which unfolds in the books of Samuel. The God who 'brings low and also exalts', who 'judges the end of the earth', who 'will give strength to his king' reveals his nature in the stories which follow. Chapter 2 offers an interpretative key for this history which is, above all, to be understood from a theocentric perspective. The focus on God's chosen king, his anointed one, David, appears right at the outset, and reveals the stance from which the whole narrative is being viewed." Childs, *Introduction to the Old Testament*, p. 273. Jan Fokkelman draws similar conclusions on the grounds of the compositional centrality of the songs in Samuel, in *Narrative Art and Poetry in the Books of Samuel: A Full Interpretation Based on Stylistic and Structural Analyses*, 4 vols: 1. King David (2 Sam. 9–20; 1 Kings 1–2 [1981]); 2. The Crossing Fates (1 Sam. 13–31; 2 Sam. 1 [1986]); 3. Throne and City (2 Sam. 2–8; 21–24 [1990]); 4. Vow and Desire (1 Sam. 1–12 [1993]) (Assen, Netherlands: van Gorcum, 1981-1993).

22. As noted above, it was skepticism about the historical accuracy of these titles that led to the most deconstructive phase of modern historical criticism. It is now clear, however, that

Augustine has drawn our attention to a narrative complex centered in the royal histories to develop the claim that the Psalms play a unique role in expressing the rationality of biblical narratives, because the Psalms set the form of grace described in both the Old Testament and Gospel narratives into words. We may paraphrase his view by saying that, if we read the Old Testament chronologically, the whole community, including Christ and the church, comes clearly into view for the first time in the Psalms, of which Hannah's song is the first.

The uniqueness of the Psalms is further developed in Augustine's rendition of the ages of salvation history. Augustine notes that Matthew 1:17 establishes eras of the history of Israel: "So all the generations from Abraham to David are fourteen generations; and from David to the deportation to Babylon, fourteen generations; and from the deportation to Babylon to the Messiah, fourteen generations." Augustine does not read these as *chronological* but as *theological* groupings, which yields the following interpretation in XVI.43. The infancy of the people of God who lived before Noah is sunk in oblivion. Between Noah and Abraham is Israel's childhood, in which the Hebrew language was established. With Abraham the adolescence of Israel is inaugurated, a biological designation that allows Augustine to highlight the central role that begetting plays in the Abraham narrative. David marks the coming of age of the people of God, because here, for the first time, Israel's speech is harnessed to the praise of God, transcending the local so as to include future generations, and so Christ. Solomon's apostasy causes this moment of clarity to be submerged for a time (Book XVII.21), which reappears in the form of the Minor Prophets, John the Baptist, and Jesus himself (Book XVII.24).

The centrality of the Psalms in Augustine's definition of Christian faith is especially apparent in his account of the final maturity of the city of God. This is achieved in the Sabbath age, in which the saints rest in God and are "filled up and made new by His blessing and sanctification." In order for the songs of eternity to be real songs, the saints will not totally forget the sins for which they have been forgiven, "for if they were not to know that they had been miserable, how could they, as the Psalm says (89:2), forever sing the mercies of God? Nothing will give more joy to that city than this song of the glory of the grace of Christ, by Whose blood we are redeemed" (Book XXII.30). Again, the important point is to note Augustine's biblical topography, its location of the different biblical books in reference to one another and to Christ, and the central place this lends the Psalms.

Augustine defends their relevance on grounds that would differ from, but be intelligible to, a redaction-, literary-, or canonical-critical exegete.

Clearly, for Augustine there is a logical continuity bordering on synonymity between the terms "prophecy" and "prefiguring." He intends to elucidate how the same truth is expressed in complementary forms, with a shared trajectory, through narrative "prefiguring" and hymnic "prophecy." His reading of the biblical narrative takes it to be less like a linear narrative with the punch line at the end, and more like a musical score. A melody is built up and successively elaborated, which continues and climaxes in the Christ-moment. Neither "prophecy" nor "prefiguring" are terms Augustine intends to refer to future-telling; his point is that the Christ-moment is not something other than these many events but integral to them. His "finding Christ" in the Old Testament is revealed not to be obscure allegorizing but a sophisticated theological exegetical practice oriented around faith in the praxological continuity of Christ with all God's works.

Following from this, we begin to see that the promises of God to Abraham and his descendants are a linchpin in Augustine's construal of the biblical narrative. The promise of God to Abraham, "I will make you exceedingly fruitful; and I will make nations of you, and kings shall come from you" (Gen. 17:6), is the primal promise of the new covenant. Augustine is not reinterpreting the Old Testament: he is reading the Old Testament as fully binding and relevant for Christians, and he finds within its pages the necessity of the New Covenant. The church is here, too: "By the fact that God commands the circumcisions not only of all the sons, but of the house-born slaves and the purchased slaves also, it is attested that this grace pertains to all men" (Book XVI.26). God's promise to Abraham looks to Christ but is not a "figure" of Jesus. So Augustine precedes canonical criticism: if we take the text seriously, the story of God's people it tells must be followed beyond the pages of the Old Testament to find out if God's promise to Abraham was upheld or not (Book XVII.1; see ch. 4). The continuity of the divine narrative is this: "[N]ewness resounds throughout the story" (Book XVI.26).

For Augustine, then, the cross and resurrection are anything but "a distinctly new contribution to the New Testament."[23] God is always putting to death and raising up. Note that the newness to which Augustine believes Scripture is directing our attention does not excite him because in it we see acts that display a "perfect performance of scripture" for us to emulate, nor does it display in exemplary ways the performance of moral acts: Scripture prepares believers to discern God's particular interventions in human affairs.

---

23. Richard Hays, *The Moral Vision of the New Testament: Community, Cross, New Creation: A Contemporary Introduction to New Testament Ethics* (San Francisco: HarperSanFrancisco, 1996), p. 308.

These divine interventions have a describable grammar but cannot be humanly performed, only seen and cooperated with or not looked for and hence not seen.

In yet another way, this move foreshadows the best of modern biblical hermeneutics. The main lines of Augustine's exegesis of the Old Testament have recently been paralleled in Francis Watson's work: he finds similar dynamics in the Gospels' portrayal of Jesus' interpretation of the Torah.[24] Watson emphasizes that reading the Bible as a single unit is an intertextual exercise in which the various texts are related with the aim of drawing out features conducive to a unity. Jesus' upholding of the Torah by using its narrative sections to question the interpretive priority of non-narrative texts is suggestive of some very practical exegetical techniques. Augustine has been shown not only to have been aware of them but proficient in using them. Watson concludes with a call for a new biblical hermeneutics:

> To see Jesus Christ as the centre of a single Christian canon, comprising an Old and a New Testament, is not necessarily to impose an artificial unity on an irreducibly heterogeneous body of writings. It is to refuse the insidious Marcionite temptation to think of the law, the prophets and the writings as the holy scripture of the Jewish community alone. It is to suggest that hermeneutical criteria might be found which would help to make some sense of the heterogeneity of these writings: criteria such as the privileging of the "prophetic" over the "priestly" perspective in the light of the praxis and teaching of Jesus. Such criteria would have to be formulated, developed and corrected in the course of an interpretative practice in which one would again seek and expect to find substantive links between the writings of the two testaments.[25]

Augustine has showed us that such a criterion need not be developed from scratch but may be learned from the saints.

Hannah's Song: Singing vs. Reading

After this prefatory explanation of his approach to Hannah's Song, Augustine quotes the text of 1 Samuel 2:1-10 in full. Before proceeding with a verse-by-verse exegesis, he makes two revealing remarks, the first one on the song's sur-

---

24. Francis Watson, *Text, Church and World: Biblical Interpretation in Theological Perspective* (Grand Rapids: Eerdmans, 1994), pp. 275-79.

25. Watson, *Text, Church and World*, p. 279.

plus meaning. According to the immediately surrounding narrative, this is the song of a woman thanking God for a son given in answer to her prayer. What then, Augustine asks,

> did she intend to express when she said, 'The bows of the mighty men are broken, and they that stumbled are girded with strength. They that were full of bread have been reduced to want, and the hungry have passed over the earth. The barren hath borne seven; and she that hath many children is waxed feeble'? For had she herself borne seven, though she was barren? She had only one child when she spoke these words; and even afterwards she did not bear seven — or six, with whom Samuel would have made the seventh — but three sons and two daughters. Moreover, her closing words were as follows, spoken at a time when no one yet reigned over that people: 'He shall give strength unto our kings, and exalt the horn of His anointed.' (Book XVII.4, p. 772)

Having come to a better appreciation of his definition of prophecy, we can better appreciate his conclusion: "Why should she say this, if not by way of prophecy?"

Augustine is pressing the textual observation that this song is set within a narrative that it does not exhaustively interpret and from which it cannot be abstracted. Hannah's Song demands what the Psalms demand from us: a struggle to identify its referent. Augustine's interpretive strategy is to draw out a dilemma of interpretation, not by applying a "typological" method but by insisting on the importance of the historical referents indicated by the narrative. Far from flattening the text out into so many unidimensional prefigurings of Christ, Augustine insists that the passage demands an integrated account of both its historical and theological references. The foundation of any such reading is its local narrative setting, which Augustine emphasizes by leveling a strong warning: "Certainly, it seems to me that he errs greatly who thinks that none of the events recorded in writings of this kind has any significance beyond the merely historical; but, then again, he is just as rash who contends that every statement found there is wrapped in allegorical meaning. . . . However, I do not condemn those who have been able to arrive at a spiritual meaning for every historical episode: provided, of course, that they have preserved the *primary* historical truth" (Book XVII.3, pp. 769-70; italics added).

This exegetical commitment to the primacy of the local narrative context as accurately conveying historical truth is developed out of the song itself. Augustine has no independent grounds on which to base his claim that the local narrative context is to be primary other than that Hannah really does sing praise to God for including her in his work of founding a transtemporal community of followers. As he reads her prayer, Augustine refines the approach to the text, which he tells us draws out the heart of the prayer. "[T]hrough this woman (whose very name, Hannah, means 'God's grace') there speaks the Christian religion itself, the City of God itself, whose King and Founder is Christ" (Book XVII.4, p. 771). And if this is so, then in order to properly read it, we must speak the words she speaks in acknowledgment that these words were written of us. "Let the Church of Christ speak, therefore: the 'City of the great King', full of grace and fruitful of offspring. Let the church speak the words which, as she acknowledges, were spoken of her long ago by the mouth of this pious mother, 'My heart rejoiceth in the Lord, mine horn is exalted in the Lord.' Her heart indeed rejoices, and her horn is exalted indeed; not in herself, however, but in the Lord her God" (Book XVII.4, p. 772).

2:1 וַתִּתְפַּלֵּל חַנָּה וַתֹּאמַר עָלַץ לִבִּי בַּיהוָה רָמָה קַרְנִי בַּיהוָה רָחַב פִּי
עַל־אוֹיְבַי כִּי שָׂמַחְתִּי בִּישׁוּעָתֶךָ

2:2 אֵין־קָדוֹשׁ כַּיהוָה כִּי אֵין בִּלְתֶּךָ וְאֵין צוּר כֵּאלֹהֵינוּ

2:1 exultavit cor meum in Domino exaltatum est cornu meum in Domino dilatatum est os meum super inimicos meos quia laetata sum in salutari tuo

2 non est sanctus ut est Dominus neque enim est alius extra te et non est fortis sicut Deus noster[26]

26. It is difficult to establish precisely which Latin translation of the Bible Augustine was using at any one time. I have chosen to include the Vulgate, the dominance of which he was to be so (inadvertently) influential in establishing. However, where Augustine quotes the text he is discussing in full, as he does in this passage, I will clarify where his translation differs from ours and the Vulgate. Augustine acutely felt the lack of a good and uniform Latin translation, as Latin translations first proliferated in his native North Africa. These apparently were translated from a range of sources, including the Septuagint and several eastern translations. The Septuagint was Augustine's favored translation, which he took to be as inspired as the Hebrew (cf. Augustine, *City of God*, Book XVIII.43; *De Doctrina*, Book 2, XV.22), though he had direct access to neither, having no knowledge of Hebrew (*Confessions* xi. 3), and for at least the early part of his career only a superficial knowledge of Greek. With some chagrin he was forced to rely on various Latin translations, including Jerome's Vulgate (*De Doctrina*, Book 4, VII.15), to whom he wrote in desperation, "You would therefore confer upon us a much greater boon if you gave an exact Latin translation of the Greek Septuagint version: for the variations found in the different codices of the Latin text are intolerably numerous; and it is so justly open to suspicion as possibly different from what is to be found in the Greek, that one has no confidence in either quoting it or proving anything by its help" (Augustine, *St. Augustin: Prolegomena: St. Augustine's Life and Work, Confessions, Letters: Nicene and Post-Nicene Fathers: Vol. I*, ed. Philip Schaff [Edinburgh: T&T Clark, 1996], letter 71). Jerome's response also tells us much about the early popularity of

2:1   My heart exults in the Lord; my strength is exalted in my God.
      My mouth derides my enemies, because I rejoice in my victory.
2   There is no Holy One like the Lord, no one besides you; there is no Rock
      like our God.

Having seen that Augustine understands Hannah's Song to have sprung from her appreciation of the newness that is God's salvation of his people, and having seen that, though this knowledge of newness is not of Christ directly but of his grammar, we can understand why he immediately links her song with that of Simeon. Simeon, too, has awaited the newness of God's redemption through a barren period of his people, and he, too, breaks forth in song at the sight of a young child brought into the temple to be presented to the Lord: "Master, now you are dismissing your servant in peace, according to your word; for my eyes have seen your salvation, which you have prepared in the presence of all the peoples, a light for revelation to the Gentiles, and for glory to your people Israel" (Luke 2:29-32).

Augustine now raises the question of whether, for Christian readers, the parallel between Hannah and Simeon can be ignored.[27] Finding that it can-

---

the Psalms. He tries to persuade Augustine not to write a commentary on the Psalms on the grounds that they had already been exhaustively interpreted in the commentaries widely available in the fourth century, citing those by Origen, Eusebius of Caesarea, Theodorus of Heraclea, Asterius of Scythopolis, Apollinaris of Laodicea, and Didymus of Alexandria, pointedly noting that these are only the complete commentaries, *and* that some were already available in Latin translation (*St. Augustin: Prolegomena: Vol. I,* letter 112).

27. The ways contemporary biblical scholars skirt the theological force of Augustine's question are methodologically illuminating against the backdrop of criticisms raised of contemporary conceptual frameworks in Part I. The commentaries of Schweizer, C. F. Evans, and Bock do not mention the connection (Eduard Schweizer, *The Good News according to Luke,* trans. David Green [London: SPCK, 1984], pp. 32-36; C. F. Evans, *Saint Luke* [London: SCM, 1990], pp. 167-77; Darrell Bock, *Luke: Vol. 1: 1:1–9:50* [Grand Rapids: Baker Books, 1994], pp. 142-62). Fitzmeyer urges special vigilance *against* the canticle's bewitching invitation to "introduce considerations from other standpoints," by which he means interpretive approaches making reference to considerations from outside a historical-critical framework. Joseph Fitzmyer, *Luke the Theologian: Aspects of His Teaching* (London: Geoffrey Chapman, 1989), p. 27. Marshall allows that Hannah's Song is the one suitable model for Luke's composition, but on the criterion that the canticle's sentiments are "Jewish rather than characteristically Christian." I. Howard Marshall, *The Gospel according to Luke: A Commentary on the Greek Text* (Exeter: Paternoster Press, 1978), p. 79. Somewhat enigmatically, John Nolland notes links between the songs of Hannah and Mary and concludes that Luke is suggesting that both women exhibit paradigmatic responses to the presence of God, which Luke has "artistically carried through by treating the presence of Mary (or the unborn Jesus) as equivalent to the presence of the ark of the covenant." Nolland, *Word Biblical Commentary: Vol. 35a, Luke 1–9:20* (Dallas: Word Books, 1989), p. 74.

not, he concludes that no Christian can read the "salvation" praised in Hannah's song as anything other than the salvation wrought in Christ, despite Hannah's having no way of being aware of the details of that event. To recognize this unity is to be invited to sing with Hannah and Simeon of God's newness. "Thus, let the church say, 'I rejoice in Thy salvation. There is none holy as the Lord: for there is none beside Thee. For He is holy, and He sanctifies; He is just, and He justifies.' 'There is none holy as the Lord,' for no one is made holy without Him" (Book XVII.4, p. 772).

אַל־תַּרְבּוּ תְדַבְּרוּ גְּבֹהָה גְבֹהָה יֵצֵא עָתָק מִפִּיכֶם כִּי אֵל דֵּעוֹת יְהוָה   2:3
וְלוֹ נִתְכְּנוּ עֲלִלוֹת

קֶשֶׁת גִּבֹּרִים חַתִּים וְנִכְשָׁלִים אָזְרוּ חָיִל   4

שְׂבֵעִים בַּלֶּחֶם נִשְׂכָּרוּ וּרְעֵבִים חָדֵלּוּ עַד־עֲקָרָה יָלְדָה שִׁבְעָה וְרַבַּת   5
בָּנִים אֻמְלָלָה

2:3   nolite multiplicare loqui sublimia gloriantes recedant vetera de ore vestro quoniam Deus scientiarum Dominus est et ipsi praeparantur cogitationes

4   arcus fortium superatus est et infirmi accincti sunt robore

5   saturati prius pro pane se locaverunt et famelici saturati sunt donec sterilis peperit plurimos et quae multos habebat filios infirmata est

2:3   Talk no more so very proudly, let not arrogance come from your mouth; for the Lord is a God of knowledge, and by him actions are weighed.

4   The bows of the mighty are broken, but the feeble gird on strength.

5   Those who were full have hired themselves out for bread, but those who were hungry are fat with spoil.
The barren has borne seven, but she who has many children is forlorn.

Hannah's Song now turns to describe those who refuse to join in this song of praise, a refusal marking the great division Augustine sees between those who live by faith in God and those who prefer self-reliance, he says, drawing on a Pauline connection: "These, as the apostle says, are 'ignorant of God's righteousness' (that is, of that which God, Who alone is just and justifies us, gives to men); and they are 'going about to establish their own righteousness' (that is, as if it were something achieved by themselves instead of given by God); and so 'they have not submitted themselves unto the righteousness of God'" (Book XVII.4, p. 773).[28] For them God "prepares His own designs." This clause is rendered in the NRSV as "by him actions are weighed," but the point is the same. God will raise up the humble and lay low those who

---

28. Quoting from Rom. 3:2.

rely on their own superiority. This, Augustine says, is what is meant by "'The bows of the mighty men are broken, and they that stumbled are girded with strength.' The bow has been broken: that is, the intention of those who seem to themselves mighty enough to fulfill the divine commands by human sufficiency alone, without the gift of God and without His aid. And men gird themselves with strength when their inner voice says, 'Have mercy upon me, O Lord; for I am weak'" (Book XVII.4, p. 773).[29]

Despite saying with great clarity that Christ is the glory of Israel, Augustine does not shy away from paralleling Hannah's barrenness and the dispossession of Saul and Eli with the implied barrenness of Israel before the coming of Christ. In the next chapter I will discuss whether this ought to be taken to have any supersessionist implications. Here we are concerned with Augustine's diagnosis of the cause of this spiritual withering. Again, as with Jesus' response to the accusation that he was breaking the Sabbath, Augustine builds a textual argument for understanding how people read Scripture to have a bearing on their state of spiritual barrenness. Material, earthly Jerusalem, who "hath many children, is waxed feeble" (Book XVII.4, p. 772).[30] Barrenness results when humans have faith in the causative importance of the human and temporal rather than awaiting and singing the praises of the newness of God's salvation. Such a preference is marked by a paradoxical possession of and estrangement from Scripture. "They have been reduced because, though they had bread — that is, the divine oracles, which of all the nations at that time, only the Israelites received — they tasted only earthly things" (Book XVII.4, p. 774).

"By contrast," Augustine continues, "nations to whom the Law had not been given, after they had come to those oracles through the new covenant, passed over the earth in great hunger, because they tasted in those oracles the heavenly meaning, not the earthly" (Book XVII.4, p. 774). The earthly people of Israel, the agent of God's salvation, have borne many earthly children, but the barren has borne seven, meaning completion. Augustine picks up on the Old Testament usage of the number seven to signal completion, and as this completion here refers to the completion of offspring, he has no trouble connecting this passage with other biblical allusions, such as Proverbs 9:1: "Wisdom has built her house, she has hewn her seven pillars," and John the Seer's writing to the seven churches, signifying "the perfection of the whole church." Again, Augustine does not impart a typological meaning; rather, he concentrates on understanding the biblical passage before him. Does not this praise

29. The last reference is to Ps. 6:2.
30. Referring to the spirit-letter distinction of 2 Cor. 3:6ff.

of God for bringing his people to the number of completion point beyond the boundaries of the Old Testament? Having decided that it does, Augustine is glad to say that Hannah, therefore, "prophesies" about a church whose divine rationality she knows by participation, but whose earthly completion she cannot have fully grasped. What she knows is that God was at work, and that God will continue to work until his designs are accomplished.

2:6   יְהוָה מֵמִית וּמְחַיֶּה מוֹרִיד שְׁאוֹל וַיָּעַל

7   יְהוָה מוֹרִישׁ וּמַעֲשִׁיר מַשְׁפִּיל אַף־מְרוֹמֵם

8   מֵקִים מֵעָפָר דָּל מֵאַשְׁפֹּת יָרִים אֶבְיוֹן עִם־נְדִיבִים וְכִסֵּא
כָבוֹד יַנְחִלֵם כִּי לַיהוָה מְצֻקֵי אֶרֶץ וַיָּשֶׁת עֲלֵיהֶם תֵּבֵל

2:6   Dominus mortificat et vivificat deducit ad infernum et reducit

7   Dominus pauperem facit et ditat humiliat et sublevat

8   suscitat de pulvere egenum et de stercore elevat pauperem ut sedeat cum principibus et solium gloriae teneat Domini enim sunt cardines terrae et posuit super eos orbem

2:6   The Lord kills and brings to life; he brings down to Sheol and raises up.

7   The Lord makes poor and makes rich; he brings low, he also exalts.

8   He raises up the poor from the dust; he lifts the needy from the ash heap, to make them sit with princes and inherit a seat of honor.
[He gives strength to him that makes a vow.][31]

This raises a question: In what sense did Hannah know she was a participant in God's work? Her song of praise indicates that it was through experience that she learned of the divine rationality. God humbles the proud but lifts up the weak. Augustine is aware that, taken on its own, this maxim is susceptible to misinterpretation. It is another mode of human self-reliance if applied as a method for achieving the good life without humility before God: the more I abase myself, the more I will be exalted. But this, he says, is only to humble myself before myself. The maxim is applicable only if the acting agent of these verses is properly understood: "The *Lord* kills and brings to life," an interpretation drawing on Colossians 3:1: "So if you have been raised with Christ, seek the things that are above, where Christ is, seated at the right hand of God." The humility-exaltation maxim is not a method for self-improvement but a description of God's killing of humans by denuding them of their sense of self-reliance to raise

---

31. Here Augustine's Latin translation tracks the Septuagint, which varies considerably from the Hebrew and our modern critical translations. Luckily, Augustine includes his translation in his text, which I have put in brackets in verses 8 and 9. More accurately translated, verse 9 reads, "For the pillars of the earth are the Lord's, and on them he has set the world."

them in Christ by the power of God. Augustine's interpretive maxim is thus not a moral program but a Christology with moral implications.

The grammar of this Christology is the subject of Hannah's song.

> By His poverty we are made rich; for 'the Lord makes men poor and enriches them.' Now to understand the significance of this, we must give ear to the following: 'He humbles, and He exalts' — that is, He humbles the proud and exalts the humble. For in another place we read, 'God resisteth the proud, but giveth grace unto the humble.' And this is the whole meaning of what she says, whose name means 'God's Grace.' (Book XVII.4, p. 775)

Because and only because Jesus was lifted up from among his persecutors, and because and only because "for your sakes he became poor so that by his poverty you might become rich" (2 Cor. 8:9), are we able to find meaning in being severed from our self-reliance and self-knowledge. Otherwise, it would be self-mutilation.

It is Christ, then, who is "raised up from the dust," and Christ who is needy and "lifted from the ash heap." But because it is only in Christ that the poor and needy are lifted up, it is in Christ that Hannah is given a child in her barrenness. Hannah is part of a community whose life is in Christ, and as she pledges her firstborn to God, so too do those others who participate in this community make the pledge of Peter: "Look, we have left everything and followed you" (Matt. 19:27). Augustine raises this point in commenting on the additional line in his translation, which reads, "He grants the vow of the one who vows, and blesses the years of the just." The community that is raised up with Christ is the City of God, here represented by Hannah. Augustine wants to hammer home the point that the vow of faithfulness to God she and Peter make, as members of that community, cannot be from their own strength. "Otherwise they would be like those mighty men whose bow He has broken . . . for no one who makes a righteous vow to the Lord can do so unless he receives from Him the power to make such a vow. Only those who sing praises in this way will 'sit with princes and inherit seats of honor,' in the gospel's words, will 'sit upon twelve thrones'" (Matt. 19:28).

רַגְלֵי חֲסִידָיו יִשְׁמֹר וּרְשָׁעִים בַּחֹשֶׁךְ יִדָּמּוּ כִּי־לֹא בְכֹחַ יִגְבַּר־אִישׁ   2:9

יְהוָה יֵחַתּוּ מְרִיבָיו עָלָיו בַּשָּׁמַיִם יַרְעֵם   10a

2:9   pedes sanctorum suorum servabit et impii in tenebris conticescent quia non in fortitudine roborabitur vir

10a   Dominum formidabunt adversarii eius super ipsos in caelis tonabit

2:9   [He has blessed the years of the righteous,][32] but the wicked shall be cut off in darkness;
for not by might does one prevail.

10a   The Lord! His adversaries shall be shattered; the Most High will thunder in heaven.

Here Augustine's reliance on translations affects his interpretation. Where the English has a more literal rendering of the Hebrew, "He will guard the feet of his faithful ones," the Septuagint translation, on which Augustine's Latin translation is based, interprets the metaphor's meaning as: "He has blessed the years of the righteous." This Augustine reads in the light of the addition to verse 8: "Now of the two statements — that is, 'He giveth strength to him that maketh a vow' and 'He hath blessed the years of the righteous' — the former has reference to something that we do, and the latter to something that we receive. But the blessing is not received through the generosity of God, unless the vow has been performed with His aid; 'for by strength shall no man prevail'" (Book XVII.4, p. 776). To sing of God's praises is to be caught up in a twofold movement. The first aspect of this movement, interpreting the idea that God gives the strength to make a vow, Augustine understands as an awareness of being under a radical epistemological questioning by God. "If a man understands and knows that his very capacity to know and understand is given to him by God, then it is in no small degree that such a man understands and knows God Himself." Second, this yields the movement of righteousness that is pure love, conceived as both acts and rightly directed desire.

> Now the man who lives rightly does justice and righteousness; and he who lives rightly is he who obeys God's commandment. And 'the end of the commandment', that is, that towards which the commandment is directed, 'is love out of a pure heart, and of a good conscience, and of faith unfeigned'. Moreover, as the apostle John attests, 'love is of God.' Thus, the capacity 'to do justice and righteousness,' is of God. (Book XVII.4, p. 777, quoting 1 Tim. 1:5 and 1 John 4:7, respectively)

God judges the world, scattering his foes to form his church, whose desires and actions are oriented by this divine act.

יְהוָה יָדִין אַפְסֵי־אָרֶץ וְיִתֶּן־עֹז לְמַלְכּוֹ וְיָרֵם קֶרֶן מְשִׁיחוֹ   2:10b

2:10b   Dominus iudicabit fines terrae et dabit imperium regi suo et sublimabit cornu christi sui

32. NRSV, "He will guard the feet of his faithful ones."

2:10b   The Lord will judge the ends of the earth; he will give strength to his king, and exalt the power of his anointed.

Augustine understands the final section of the song to expose the theological roots of this linkage of the City of God with Christ, what he calls the *totus Christus*. For him, to sing of God's giving "strength to his king, and exalting the power of his anointed" is to confess and thus express the unity of Christ and of his kingdom (a connection suggested by the Septuagint formulation taken up in Augustine's translation). Christ's humiliation and exaltation are understood as taking place in God's raising up the poor and needy to "make them sit with princes" (v. 8).

> It is Christ Himself, as is said here, who will 'exalt the horn of His anointed'. Who, therefore, is Christ's anointed? Will He exalt the horn of everyone who believes in Him, just as Hannah herself says at the beginning of her hymn, 'Mine horn is exalted in the Lord'? Indeed, we can rightly say that all who have been anointed with the oil of Christ are His anointed; and yet it is the whole body, with its Head, which is the one Christ. (Book XVII.4, p. 779)

Augustine developed his doctrine of the *totus Christus* in reading the Psalms. It is no accident that the powerhouse metaphor of his mature political theology, the "city of God," is an expression that this doctrine describes, nor that his mature theology of the two cities finds its most succinct expression in the book devoted to the Psalms, Book XVII. Augustine finds it impossible to comprehend the Psalms without understanding their authors as part of the body of Christ, and this leads him both to a Christological and ecclesiological hermeneutics of the Psalms. His church is the material body of Christ, made up of human materiality reordered. Praying for the exaltation of God's anointed is inseparable from praying to exalt his followers. The Psalms are to David and of David, because David exists only as a participant in Christ's body.

In Book XVII.12, Augustine explains how the singing of praises is the pathway into the promises of God to Israel via an interpretation of Psalm 89:49-51: "Lord, where is your steadfast love of old, which by your faithfulness you swore to David? Remember, O Lord, how your servant is taunted; how I bear in my bosom the insults of the peoples, with which your enemies taunt, O Lord, with which they taunted the footsteps of your anointed." This psalm's title, Augustine notes, asks us to read it as having been written during David's reign. Redaction criticism takes the title every bit as seriously as does Augustine, who also picks up on the title's reference to the narrative of the royal history. The problem that this creates is that a poem ostensibly written during David's lifetime describes David as being "ancient." Historical criticism would call this a joint between collected materials and thus cause for a discussion of redactional activity. Augustine prefers to ascribe an intellectual and spiritual ingenuity to the author, which demands further consideration. The prophet, he says, may well have "taken upon himself the person of those who were to come in the far future, to whom the time when these things were promised to King David was 'ancient'" (Book XVII.12).

This leads Augustine to clarify his threefold interpretation of Old Testament prophecy. These are, first, words that might have been written at any point before the exile and thus have a level of reference within the temporal horizon of the Old Testament narrative. "For such words could have been spoken by those servants of God who, after the sack of the earthly Jerusalem, before Jesus Christ was born in human form, were led away captive." But there is another community within the temporal horizon of Christian Scripture, which is the church of the New Testament. Second, these words, therefore, fit "those who, when they suffered great humiliations through persecution for Christ's name, could remember that an exalted kingdom had been promised to the seed of David: to those who, desiring such a kingdom, could say — not in despair, but as seeking, knocking — 'Lord where are thine ancient lovingkindnesses, which thou swore to David in thy truth?'" (Book XVII.12).

Third, if within the textual horizon of the Christian Bible we see this correspondence, it is clear, says Augustine, that "these words apply appropriately to the whole people of God who belong to the Heavenly Jerusalem: both to those who were concealed during the time of the old covenant, before the revelation of the new, and to those who, after the revelation of the new covenant, are clearly revealed as belonging to Christ." The Old Testament ground for this claim is the promise to David's seed that it will endure for all eternity, a foundation that demands the full-flesh moral ontology of the *totus Christus* concept. The eternal house of David's seed

> is called the house of God because of the temple of God, made of men, not of stones. In that temple, the people shall dwell eternally with their God and in their God, and God shall dwell with His people and in His people, so that God may fill His people, and the people be filled with their God, while God shall be all in all. . . . For this house is built both by us, by living well, and by God, by helping us to live well; for 'except the Lord build the house, they labour in vain that build it.' (Book XVII.12, p. 800)[33]

---

33. Quoting 1 Cor. 15:28; 2 Sam. 7:11; 7:27; and Ps. 127:1, respectively.

Augustine's ethic calls the church to live well in cooperation with Christ's building of his body on earth.

In addition to these ecclesiological arguments, Augustine also defends the possibility that the psalmists were writing for a different community beyond their contemporaries by referring to Jesus' quotation from the Psalms. It was Jesus' custom both to identify himself with his persecuted followers, and to speak words, such as those of Psalm 89, that might be understood as the expression of another community spoken through him. "[I]t was His custom to transfer to Himself what is true of His members, and to attribute to Himself what belongs to them, for Head and Body are one Christ. Hence what is said in the Gospel: 'For I was an hungered, and ye gave me meat', which He explains by saying, 'Inasmuch as ye have done it unto one of the least of these my brethren, ye have done it unto me' [Matt. 25:40]" (Book XVII.18, p. 810). Augustine often summarizes these points by referring to Acts 9:4, where Jesus completely identifies himself with the church that Paul persecutes. "Saul, Saul, why do you persecute me?" The centrality of the *totus Christus* in Augustine's Psalms exegesis is marked by the regular recurrence of this citation.[34] Further examination of Augustine's Psalms exegesis will reveal that the Israel-Jesus-church interpretive schema that serves to link and intertwine the testaments also yields a single account of the present community of faith and the authors of Scripture.

Augustine's *totus Christus* concept is not best described as a mystical union but as a real and material forepresence of God's renewal of all things in Christ. The Israel that knows God's newness partakes of Christ: the church that knows Christ is unified with this true Israel. *Totus Christus* is thus essentially a hermeneutical theory with ontological import, not simply an ontology. The metaphor allows for a Christological ecclesiology to shape and anchor the reading of Scripture. This suggests that in his mature work Augustine moved far beyond his theory of meaning and general hermeneutics outlined in *De Doctrina*. If his *totus Christus* doctrine is read as a "theory of meaning," one misses that he is first explicating Scripture through an ecclesiology shaped by Scripture.

By way of review, Hannah's Song is paradigmatic for Augustine for understanding the Psalms because it is a text that, because of its narrative location, tells us something essential about biblical Psalms — that they cannot be "read." Therefore, there is no such thing as a "reader" for Augustine, unless

---

34. Cf. sermons on Psalms: 26 (11); 30 (3); 32 (2); 34 (1); 37 (6); 39 (5); 44 (20); 52 (1); 54 (3); 55 (3); 69 (3); 75 (14); 86 (3); 88 (3); 90 (5); 90 (9); 91 (11). See also commentaries on Psalms: 67 (25); 67 (36); 87 (15).

this describes the activity of those who make this song an "objective" text devoid of any personal claim because they see human strength as determining of world events. This distancing stands in contrast to those who affirm Hannah's praise of God by singing with her. We have traced the arguments Augustine adduces for this claim, but the important point to note is that the form of Scripture that is called a psalm, and the interpretive ontological claims Augustine brings to this form, work together to question a basic commitment of contemporary hermeneutics: that we can describe a *general* hermeneutical strategy that is appropriately applied to the biblical texts. Because this is not simply a text, but Scripture, to read the Psalms as a text is to consolidate our self-emasculation in deciding in advance that they point only to human activities. The psalm form is thus correctly understood only when it appears as an invitation to the community of faith to sing God's praises.

I will devote the remainder of this chapter to explicating the ontological commitments Augustine finds in the Psalms and their linkage with moral theology.

Metaphysics, Epistemology, and the Primacy of the Moral

Charles Taylor's *Sources of the Self* gives Augustine a starring role in shaping the way Westerners conceive of the "self," going so far as to say that Augustine is "responsible for the invention of the Western concept of the self."[35] But as we shall see, Taylor brings a definition of "the self" to Augustine that masks Augustine's own way of thinking of the self as an artifact of God's work. Taylor platonizes Augustine in his misguided contention that Augustine's main concerns are "the good" and by implication the "self's" relationship to it. Nevertheless, Taylor helps us to ease ourselves out of common contemporary ways of thinking about ethics and morality.

Augustine's use of the concepts of the city of God and the *totus Christus* is what Taylor calls an "ontological account." Ontological accounts, he says, "attribute predicates to human beings — like being creatures of God, or emanations of divine fire, or agents of rational choice — which seem rather analogous to theoretical predicates in natural science, in that they (a) are rather remote from our everyday descriptions by which we deal with people around us and ourselves, and (b) make reference to our conceptions of the universe

---

35. Cf. Charles Taylor, *Sources of the Self: The Making of the Modern Identity* (Cambridge: Harvard University Press, 1989), p. 31 (page references to this book hereafter cited parenthetically in text).

and the place we occupy in it" *(Sources,* p. 7). As Thomas Kuhn so famously argued, such accounts (or paradigms, as he called them) frame the way we interpret the world and thus cannot be argued about from an independent standpoint. Taylor is emphasizing a point Kuhn did not: that such ontological accounts underlie not only scientific experimentation but also the way we live our lives. They are rationalities whereby we test and probe reality to see how it is. This does not mean that moral ontology is a pure fiction, says Taylor, but that it is our mode of rational access to the world and can therefore be argued about and sifted.

An excursus on Taylor's reading of Augustine will help us grasp the full relevance of Augustine's thought by showing how Taylor uses it to develop a concept of the moral realm with a range far wider than contemporary usage. He contends that moral ontologies have two main axes that frame our moral judgments about ourselves and others: first, what makes a good human life? What do we believe makes for human flourishing and its opposite, wasted human life? Second, how do I locate myself as an individual in relationship to myself as a part of a community? How do I make judgments about legitimate and illegitimate ways of understanding and practicing this relationship? Exploring the implications of this conceptual map will set the stage for a return to Augustine's reading of the Psalms and illuminate his understanding of moral deliberation within his account of the flourishing human life.

Taylor's account of modern moral philosophy begins with a complex and intriguing genealogy of contemporary moral thinking that we need not recount in detail here. He concludes that contemporary modes of moral deliberation are heavily marked by the impact of Kantian metaphysics and scientific naturalism. Based on these background commitments, contemporary moral philosophy tends to ask only about what it is good to do, leaving out questions of what it is good to be. Framing the question in this way allows the intellectual landscape to be dominated by procedural forms of moral thinking that avoid making any thick (or ontological) truth claims in a modern pluralist context, and thus they are conceived of as mechanisms for reaching a pragmatic decision about how to *act.* Within this wider commitment to action, moral theory comes to serve the project of defining the content of obligation rather than the nature of the good life. "In other words," concludes Taylor, "morals concern what we *ought* to do; this excludes both what it is good to do, even though we aren't *obliged* (which is why supererogation is such a problem for some contemporary moral philosophy), and also what it may be good (or even obligatory) to *be* or *love,* as irrelevant to ethics" (p. 79). If, on the other hand, says Taylor, we think that what it is good to be and to love are integrally part of thinking about how we act, then we begin to grasp that metaphysical, epistemological, and moral considerations must be addressed simultaneously, or not at all.

Taylor's contention is that all humans do, in fact, believe in some truths, and so love some things that determine the form of their actions, even if they explicitly hold moral doctrines that deny the relevance of these loves for the formation of duties. He bases this claim on the following definition of human selfhood, which he conceives as a three-dimensional diagram mapping the main ways in which people find meaning by having "strong evaluations" about where they personally reside in an imagined moral space. The first axis is based on images or pictures of what makes a full life. Here we ask what makes life worth living, what constitutes a rich, meaningful life, as opposed to one devoted to trivialities or one that is simply wasted. A second axis is made up of images and ideas about how and why we should respect others, which includes answers to questions about the relationship of freedom and self-control, and the place of our work and family life in a competitive environment. A third axis is constituted by our assessment of where we lie on the other two axes. Taylor calls this our sense of personal dignity, which he understands to be constituted in our own, or others', assessment of how successfully we have lived up to our vision of the good life and our definition of respect for others.

Our ideas about respect and the good life, Taylor emphasizes, are not formed in abstraction but in the mundane daily social contexts of life. "The very way we walk, move, gesture, speak is shaped from the earliest moments by our awareness that we appear before others, that we stand in public space, and that this space is potentially one of respect or contempt, of pride or shame. Our style of movement expresses how we see ourselves as enjoying respect or lacking it, as commanding it or failing to do so" (p. 15). The implication is that we should expect each age to have its characteristic ways of filling each axis with content and valuing axes in relation to one another.

The influence of the Kantian heritage has been to define the axis of respect for others in terms of duty, and to make it the only serious axis, while visions of what makes a full life have been completely subjectivized. The result is a largely nonmoral contemporary definition of selfhood and personal respect. This does not imply that the search for meaning is no longer on the agenda, but only that meaning is no longer conceived of as having an ontological referent, any real value beyond the subjective. The meaning axis is one we construct *de novo*. Duty to others impinges on us from outside, but meaning is something for which we search. Searching requires articulation, and thus "moderns have become acutely aware of how much sense being there for us depends on our own powers of expression. Discovering here depends on, is interwoven with, inventing. Finding a sense to life depends on framing meaningful expressions which are adequate" (p. 18).

Taylor's essential point is that all human existence takes place in a giant "space of questions."[36] Without developing strong ideas about what makes up the good life and respect for others, we cannot make decisions or evaluations about anything, and we become paralyzed, unable to form a hypothesis about what to do. Believing in something provides parameters for a hypothesis about how to find meaning. Taylor understands his axes as a general account of the types of hypotheses we must have in order to begin to function as selves, capable of making decisions and responding to the events of our lives. Without them, we have no way of determining what things have meaning for us; but with them, we have the possibility of conceiving one path or evaluation as superior or inferior to another. Those who are unable to speak a truth worth believing become empty and devoid of desire, love, or orienting schema (p. 18).[37]

Because in contemporary society each person is expected to define his or her own vision of the good life, the most widespread fear of our modern secularized age is meaninglessness: the inability to articulate a vision of the good life that seems worth aspiring to. Being without meaning, or not having a firm identity, can take two forms, says Taylor. He uses the image of a hiker on a mountain to illustrate his point. A hiker may have been deposited on a mountain by helicopter; she may thus be looking at the mountain without knowing its wider context, including, for instance, what continent it is on. In this case the hiker would know about an important feature of the space she inhabited, but she would not be able to find herself on a map. Conversely, a hiker who was familiar with the mountain and its geographical location, but could not find her way back to the car after her hike, would be lost in a different way. If both hikers were given a map, they would still be helpless, but for different reasons. The first would not be able to extract any orienting sense from it, and the second would be unable to say where she was on a familiar map. Taylor concludes: "By analogy, our orientation in relation to the good requires not only some framework(s) which defines the shape of the qualitatively higher but also a sense of where we stand in relation to this" (p. 42).

---

36. The insight coheres with the diagnosis of Genesis, which reveals that what is lost in the modern account of this space is that we no longer speak to God and expect no answers. Gen. 3:10: "I heard the sound of you in the garden, and I was afraid, because I was naked; and I hid myself."

37. This general observation holds as a description of the majority, says Taylor, despite the strong evaluations of some minority groups, such as evangelicals, who see damnation for instance as a primary negative possibility to be avoided, which orients the definition of the good life.

The aspiration to have a full life can be met, Taylor continues, by embracing some pattern of higher meaning, by embracing some narrative as true, or some secular or religious combination of the two. This "suggests a connection between four terms: not just (a) our notions of the good and (b) our understandings of the self, but also (c) the kinds of narrative in which we make sense of our lives, and (d) conceptions of society, that is, conceptions of what it is to be a human agent among human agents" (p. 105). Having already argued that epistemology, metaphysics, and morals must be understood as a package, Taylor has now linked this claim to another about the way our understandings of each question are held together by ideas and narratives. This whole complex of relationships, by serving as hypothesis about meaning within the "space of questions" that is human existence, defines the shape of our identity.

Taylor's basic contention is that human life cannot exist without moral intuitions, even if these are of the kind that "those who talk about moral intuitions are confused." Taylor's next move is crucial: all thinking about truth and meaning is inescapably linked with the frameworks of evaluation, the hypotheses about what makes the good life that give our own lives meaning. We cannot and do not conceive of our ideas about the good and meaningful in an abstract space but in a social one. This is as true for the politician, for whom public opinion is truth, as it is for the natural scientist, for whom the subjective is untrue in principle. Each has a set of beliefs about the truth that gives his life meaning, which necessarily leads him to general evaluations about other ways of life. To deny this, says Taylor, is to claim that we are able to step outside of our moral intuitions, which is tantamount to saying that we can set aside the frameworks that establish our sense of purchase on reality (pp. 75, 78).

This brings us back to the problem of contemporary moral theory. These integral relationships between our ideas of the good and what makes up a good life, between what it is good to be and how I, personally, should act to have a meaningful life, have

> been suppressed by these strange cramped theories of modern moral philosophy, which have the paradoxical effect of making us inarticulate on some of the most important issues of morality. Impelled by the strongest metaphysical, epistemological, and moral ideas of the modern age, these theories narrow our focus to the determinants of action, and then restrict our understanding of these determinants still further by defining practical reason as exclusively procedural. They utterly mystify the *priority of the moral* by identifying it not with substance but with a form of reasoning, around which they draw a firm boundary. They then are led to defend this

boundary all the more fiercely in that it is their only way of doing justice to the hypergoods which move them although they cannot acknowledge them. (p. 89; italics added)

This amounts to an accusation that modernity can be characterized by the widespread and illegitimate presumption that the "moral realm" is only a small part of a larger description of reality that is thereby conceived as essentially nonmoral. It is an assessment with which Taylor strongly disagrees, despite its being defended on the grounds of the so-called naturalistic fallacy that "ought can not be derived solely from what is." But descriptions of what is are deeply and inescapably laden with moral aspects, argues Taylor. To describe the world is to think about how to act in it and how to comport oneself toward it, and to imply that some "facts" have no moral implications is simply to be deluded about what we do when we describe what is.

My suggestion is that, by exposing these particular weaknesses of contemporary philosophy and moral thinking, Taylor has highlighted three sets of issues that will help us appreciate new aspects of Augustine's Psalms exegesis. First, Taylor follows Augustine by making spatial metaphors his main means of conceptualizing the moral life.[38] He also follows Augustine in claiming that, without some understanding of the respect due to others and a vision of the good life, we are doomed to expend our energies and loves in self-destructive ways. Second, because Taylor follows Augustine in emphasizing that our descriptions of the world do most of the work of deciding how to live in it, he alerts us to the moral implications of Augustine's ontological descriptions, such as the definition of the good life he finds in Psalm 31. Third, Taylor concurs with Augustine's contention that we cannot and do not think our ideas about the good and meaningful in an abstract space, but in a social space. The last part of this chapter will follow Augustine as he preaches on Psalm 21, as he elucidates the connections between the individual and communal aspects of flourishing human life. Yet behind Taylor's agreement with Augustine regarding the interrelationship of metaphysics, epistemology (hermeneutics), and morality lies a more fundamental disagreement about how a moral community, or a moral actor, is generated and maintained.

Despite Taylor's helpful elucidation of some of the larger structures of

---

38. "Augustine's picture of the universe shows us one who is the source and goal of being, value, and activity, himself in the center of the universe and at rest; and it shows us the remainder of the universe in constant movement, which, while it may tend toward or away from the center, is yet held in relation to it, so that all other beings lean, in a multiplicity of ways, toward the source and goal of being." Oliver O'Donovan, *The Problem of Self-Love in St. Augustine* (New Haven: Yale University Press, 1980), p. 157.

Augustine's moral theology, Augustine nevertheless undermines some of Taylor's most important presuppositions. Taylor's main contribution to our inquiry is his critique of popular notions of morality—as well as his suggestion that we cannot do without a thicker account. At the same time, he reads Augustine as having shaped the Western development of the self by placing the longing self at the heart of identity. We will see that this focus on the shape of my longing, what happens *in* me, contradicts Augustine's clear focus on the primacy of God's work, and thus what happens *to* me.[39] Taylor has no sense for the way Augustine situates and thus defines human longing within the divine narrative.

The upshot is that Taylor appears to violate his own universal prescription: his theory of the axes on which all of us must find ourselves is developed by a philosopher who, to all appearances, is a detached observer. Thus a problem is generated at the boundary of Taylor's project that he does not have the resources to resolve: Do we choose meaning, or does it choose us by, for instance, its "narrative power"? Here Augustine's formulation is starkly different from modern accounts: the Psalms teach him that Christians understand themselves as chosen for a community in which they become those able to make right choices. Taylor shares with the modern thought he has critiqued the belief that verbal expression is the preferred mode of finding personal meaning. Augustine discovers that the Psalms give humanity words and thus a self within God's life as we participate in taking them up. Because Taylor is consciously doing philosophy, he cannot acknowledge Augustine's insistence that God is the primary actor of history and thus the effective generator of the living body of people who inhabit the Christian ethos. Taylor can only say that (1) we inherit our axes, values, or stories from communities, and (2) we more or less choose to adhere explicitly to these horizons or choose others. But having strongly argued that our evaluations structure all perception, he leaves aside the problem of their transformation. The question is, what does it do to Taylor's framing of the questions to say that we are chosen — given stories and prayers — and that we did not choose the stories that give our lives meaning?

One answer is that such an affirmation, while cohering with Taylor's claim that we cannot exist without moral intuitions, denies a basic moral intuition on which Taylor's project is built: that there is such a thing as a "self" that must exist for there to be individuals as we understand them. Here Augustine disagrees. The "self" has no meaning and, indeed, no reality outside of God's sustained assault on our belief that we define ourselves without ref-

---

39. Cf. Hans G. Ulrich, *Wie Geschöpfe leben: Konturen evangelischer Ethik* (Münster: Lit Verlag, 2005), ch. A3.5: "Der 'innere Mensch' oder die 'Quellen des Selbst.'"

erence to him. The "self" is always an elusive being, always on a journey — *peregrinatio*. A close examination of Augustine's exegesis of the Psalms will raise questions about Taylor's claim that Augustine was the first modern because he turned Western theology and philosophy toward the first-person standpoint (p. 131). As we have seen in his account of Jesus' prayer on the cross as an expression of the church, if there is a definitive first-person account for Augustine, it is Christ's. To take this approach is to insist that statements that were later emphasized in abstraction by modernity, such as *De Trinitate*'s proto-Cartesian "I know because I doubt,"[40] be kept in contact with Augustine's biblical and theological conceptions. This inverts Taylor's decision to follow modernity's attenuation of Augustine's and the Christian tradition's displacement of the primacy of the self.

Still, a basic question remains: What, then, are selves, and how important is having one in a Christian account of reality? Augustine and Luther agree that the Psalms teach that we do not choose to enter God's story, and we can only be told that we are already inside it. Augustine agrees with Taylor that speaking is a mode of self-discovery; but, unlike moderns, he says it is not words that we construct but words that we are given that orient us in moral space, in claiming and reshaping our self-identifications, our desires, and our sense of the beautiful. Having said that, Augustine would have agreed with Taylor that "orientation in moral space turns out to be similar to orientation in physical space. We know where we are through a mixture of recognition of landmarks before us and a sense of how we have traveled to get here" (p. 48). The Psalms, for Augustine, play an essential role in telling us where we are and settling into the place in Christ where we find ourselves. However, in making such an affirmation, Augustine contradicts Taylor's basic assumption that we can talk about temporal and moral space with no reference to the work of Christ. Augustine's exegesis of Psalm 32 shows him using a thoroughly Christological account of the time and space within which human life discovers its true flourishing.

Psalm 32: Fulfilled Life as Attentiveness to God

In his exegesis of Psalm 32 (tentatively dated 412-413), Augustine displays his vision of the fulfilled life, which is developing as he wrestles with the details

---

40. "Nobody surely doubts, however, that he lives and remembers and understands and wills and thinks and knows and judges." Augustine, *The Trinity*, ed. John Rotelle, trans. Edmund Hill (New York: New City Press, 1991), Book X.14, p. 296.

of specific psalms.[41] He begins by framing his ethical thought within the Greek framework, conceived as the search for the happy life *(eudaimonia)*,[42] a framework that, in the end, has been heavily modified. His mature ethical thought is framed by the metaphor of the good life as a road on which God sets Christians by his work of forgiveness. Because this journey into the fulfilled life continues to develop beyond the boundaries of this temporal life, it is not finally achieved within time. In this life, the good life is a dynamic progression of faith, overseen by God, in which we progress only as we keep our eyes on God. Augustine stretches the familiar Greek metaphor of the "good life" as a narrow path of virtue beyond anything in Greek thought by contending that its *telos* and fulfillment is life in the presence of God, complete only in the afterlife.[43] His decision to define the ethical importance of eternal life through the earthy "good life" trope suggests the possibility that he may, in fact, be developing a more nuanced position than allowed by those who accuse him of illegitimate otherworldliness. His joining of the good life with eternal life rests on an interlocking system of distinctions he finds in Psalm 32: good and evil, strength and weakness, folly and wisdom, straight and crooked hearts, which together define a moral, epistemic, and metaphysical topography that Taylor has called the "fulfilled life" axis.

"This is a psalm about God's grace, and about our being justified by no merits whatever on our own part, but only by the mercy of the Lord our God, which forestalls anything we may do."[44] In his sermon on Psalm 32, Augustine deals with the question of what constitutes a life rich in meaning by relating the question to a central Christian doctrine, the doctrine of justification by faith.

---

41. For a general discussion of how attention to Scripture continually reshaped Augustine's categories, see Rist, *Augustine*, pp. 15-16, 19-21.

42. The centrality of the eudaemonist framework in Augustine's moral thought, and the range of ways he protected the content of Christian faith by modifying it, is documented in detail by Oliver O'Donovan in *Self Love in St. Augustine,* ch. 1, esp. pp. 56-59, and ch. 6, esp. pp. 152-59. While one can hardly disagree with O'Donovan's claim that in places Augustine allows or even emphasizes that immanent teleology (the creature's created desire for God) is "the metaphysical root of his eudaemonist ethics" (p. 157), by focusing on Augustine's exegesis of the Psalms (with their focus on the redemptive moment) we see more clearly that eudaemonism has faded so far into the conceptual background that it becomes a protological and teleological *presupposition* rather than defining any ethical *content*, as it clearly does in Aristotelian and modern consequentialist eudaemonisms.

43. Cf. Rist, *Augustine*, pp. 168-73.

44. St. Augustine, *Expositions of the Psalms 1–32; Vol. 1,* trans. Maria Boulding, ed. John E. Rotelle, O.S.A. (New York: New City Press, 2000), Exposition 2.1 of Psalm 31.

אַשְׁרֵי נְשׂוּי־פֶּשַׁע כְּסוּי חֲטָאָה 32:1

אַשְׁרֵי אָדָם לֹא יַחְשֹׁב יְהוָה לוֹ עָוֹן וְאֵין בְּרוּחוֹ רְמִיָּה 2

31:1 intellectus beati quorum remissae sunt iniquitates et quorum tecta sunt peccata

2 beatus vir cui non inputabit Dominus peccatum nec est in spiritu eius dolus

32:1[45] Happy are those whose transgression is forgiven, whose sin is covered.

2 Happy are those to whom the LORD imputes no iniquity, and in whose spirit there is no deceit.

Happiness, or blessedness, is a central rubric of the Psalms, as indicated by its regular repetition and prominent placement as the first word of the Psalter.[46] The Psalms continually elucidate the contrast between the blessed and the wicked, a contrast heavily freighted with moral implications. Augustine is aware of this, and he immediately understands the statement of verse 1 to be the key to Psalm 32: "Happy are those . . ." Not having access to the Hebrew semantic of blessedness, Augustine fills it out using the Greek concept of *eudaimonia.* In both Greek and Hebrew thought, moral questions are decided by referring to a description of the happy or blessed life. By drawing on his inherited Greek concepts to interpret the Psalms, Augustine subverts the Hebrew language and thought complex at the level of etymology, only to subvert the Greek conceptuality in turn by his commitment to the project of reading the Old and New Testaments together.

It is this commitment to the unity of the biblical witness that leads Augustine to interpret verses 1 and 2 through Paul's Romans 4:3 comment on Abraham's faith: "Abraham believed in God, and it was reckoned to him as righteousness." Abraham, he knows, is the prototypical happy — or, more properly, divinely blessed — biblical exemplar, and Augustine clarifies the happiness that is the key to this psalm by examining Abraham's exemplary faith. Was Abraham blessed because he obeyed God's command to sacrifice Isaac? Or was he blessed because he had faith? Admiring Abraham's action, Augustine concludes that it was good only because it sprang from faith. "I

45. Augustine uses the chapter and verse numbering of the LXX and Vulgate, but for ease of reference, I will refer to the English verse numbers in the discussion. Augustine comments on the Latin Psalm 31, and the following commentaries on Psalms 21 and 27 are on the Latin Psalms 20 and 26, respectively.

46. The deeper meaning of this central term has been perceptively and succinctly discussed by Martin Buber, *Right and Wrong: An Interpretation of Some Psalms,* trans. Ronald Smith (London: SCM, 1952), ch. V, "The Ways."

have nothing but praise for the superstructure of action, but I see the foundation of faith; I admire the good work as fruit, but I recognize that it springs from the root of faith."[47] Unlike the ancient view of the good life, Augustine is insisting that faith's desire for God hallows behavior; behavior does not hallow wrong desire. For Augustine, then, a happy life is one in which right desire shapes action, not one characterized only by supposed, or "mere," moral purity.

This framing of faith in terms of desire is obviously influenced by the ancient concentration of moral thinking on right love.

> After all, what is it in any one of us that prompts action, if not some kind of love [*amor*]? Show me even the basest love that does not prove itself in action. Shameful deeds, adulteries, villainies, murders, all kinds of lust — aren't they all the work of some sort of love? Purify this love, then, divert onto your garden the water that is going down the drain, let the current that drove you into the arms of the world be redirected to the world's Maker. Do you want people to ask you, 'Don't you love anything, then?' Of course not. If you loved nothing you would be sluggish, dead, loathsome and unhappy. Love [*amate*] as much as you like, but take care what you love. Love of God and love of your neighbor are called charity; but love of the world, this passing world, is called greed or lust. Lust must be reined in, charity spurred on. (Exp. 2.3 of Ps. 31, p. 367)

The point at stake for Augustine is not so much the ancient problematic in which we find happiness when we correctly attach our desires, because this assumes that ethics is part of a rational and a self-referential search to find the proper object for our desires. Augustine knows that Abraham's obedience was pleasing to God because he obeyed not for his own advantage, nor because he was searching for personal happiness, but in order to continue life with God. Faith as the core aspect of happiness is in tension with and deeply modifies the ancient view that questions of virtue are, in Taylor's words, part of my search to articulate a vision of that which will give my life meaning.

Having thus modified the Platonic concept of eros-love as the driving force of human action, Augustine further specifies it, thus distinguishing it

---

47. Augustine, *Expositions*, Exp. 2.3 of Psalm 31 (references to these Expositions hereafter cited parenthetically in text). It is illustrative of the difference between ancient and modern emphases that Augustine focuses on Abraham's right *desire* defining faith (affect), while Kierkegaard, in *Fear and Trembling*, is interested in how faith defines all *knowledge* and *communicability* (epistemology and linguistic theory). For a closely observed discussion of the linkages Augustine draws here, see Bernd Wannenwetsch, "Caritas fide formata. 'Herz und Affekte' als Schlüssel zu 'Glaube und Liebe,'" *Kerygma and Dogma* 45 (2000): 205-24.

from traditional desire-ethics. The commands of God are obeyed not only in well-directed love, Paul says in 1 Timothy 1:5, but in "love that comes from a pure heart, a good conscience, and sincere faith" (cf. 1 Cor. 13:3). Here Augustine develops the Pauline triad of faith, hope, and love by interpreting it as faith, a clear conscience, and love, and explains the equation by saying, "Anyone who wants to have good hope needs to have a good conscience, and to have a good conscience we must both believe and work. So from this middle term, hope, we can work backward to the beginning, that is, to faith; and forward to the end, which is charity" (Exp. 2.5 of Ps. 31, p. 368). There is an integral and dynamic relationship between the state of faith as properly directed desire, the clarity of the conscience as reflection on that desire's instantiation in action, and charity as the criterion of Christ's love for others as applicable to directing our action.

The action of love for neighbor, Augustine is arguing, is not the application of a moral rule in order to reach what is hoped for (eternal life). It is, rather, a rational response of appreciation for God's love for us as a Good Samaritan (Luke 10). We love our neighbor because God has been a good neighbor to us. "So it is through being forgiven that you begin to live in faith; that faith gathers to itself hope and the decision to love [*dilectione*] and begins to express itself in good actions; but not even after that may you boast and preen yourself. Remember who planted you on the right road; remember how even with your strong, swift feet you were wandering off it; remember how even when you were sick and lying half-dead by the wayside you were lifted onto a mount and taken to the inn" (Exp. 2.7 of Ps. 31, p. 370). Augustine's use here of the term *delectatio* for love indicates the drawing of human rationality into God's work, which the believer rationally appreciates, as one might a painting. Oliver O'Donovan explains: "His reason is engaged with the object's goodness; but this engagement is not a force drawing him toward it nor a hand reached out to possess it but a relation which allows the contemplative distance to remain. Love is neither 'appetite' nor 'movement' but estimation, appreciation, and approval."[48]

The Christian has been set by God's grace on the right road and given the task of remaining on it by letting faith orient love as guided by the hopeful conscience. Here Augustine uses spatial metaphors to convey moral coordinates in a way that Taylor emulates. The way of Christian love is to "not turn aside, to the right or to the left" (Prov. 4:7). "Do not presume on your virtue to get you into the kingdom; but do not presume on God's mercy and go on sinning. The divine command calls you back from both: from trying to climb

---

48. O'Donovan, *Self Love in St. Augustine*, p. 29.

the steep bank on the one hand, and from sliding down on the other" (Exp. 2.1 of Ps. 31, p. 363). This concern not only to clarify how we establish landmarks in moral space but also how we continue to be oriented and move within moral space goes well beyond Taylor. Only right faith and sure desire for God can keep a person on the narrow road. Those who do good works without faith are skillfully enacting a wrong vision of the good life, and are "like someone running with great power and at high speed, but off course." Augustine advises that an assessment of works is thus of secondary importance to taking care with the object of faith, because wrong faith cannot reach the harbor of eternal life. "You should not pay too much attention to what a person does, but consider where he is aiming as he does it, and whether he is directing his efforts toward the right harbor, like a skilled pilot" (Exp. 2.4 of Ps. 31). Again, we see that, as Augustine defines it, the fulfilled life is not a possibility that human action can generate.

Augustine understands these verses to show that the fulfilled life is the received gift of faith as love for God. It is not the living that defines the good life but the faith that, either well or poorly, directs that living. The essential ethical task is to attend to rightly directing our desires, and to be continually on the move in moral space toward God, the fulfillment and consummation of human life. The next verses indicate that, on this journey, the Christian conscience plays an essential role by orienting and shaping our love.

כִּי־הֶחֱרַשְׁתִּי בָּלוּ עֲצָמָי בְּשַׁאֲגָתִי כָּל־הַיּוֹם 32:3
כִּי יוֹמָם וָלַיְלָה תִּכְבַּד עָלַי יָדֶךָ נֶהְפַּךְ לְשַׁדִּי בְּחַרְבֹנֵי קַיִץ סֶלָה 4
חַטָּאתִי אוֹדִיעֲךָ וַעֲוֹנִי לֹא־כִסִּיתִי אָמַרְתִּי אוֹדֶה עֲלֵי פְשָׁעַי לַיהוָה 5
וְאַתָּה נָשָׂאתָ עֲוֹן חַטָּאתִי סֶלָה

31:3 quoniam tacui inveteraverunt ossa mea dum clamarem tota die
4 quoniam die ac nocte gravata est super me manus tua conversus sum in aerumna mea dum configitur mihi spina diapsalma
5 delictum meum cognitum tibi feci et iniustitiam meam non abscondi dixi confitebor adversus me iniustitiam meam Domino et tu remisisti impietatem peccati mei diapsalma

32:3 While I kept silence, my body wasted away through my groaning all day long.
4 For day and night your hand was heavy upon me; my strength was dried up as by the heat of summer.
5 Then I acknowledged my sin to you, and I did not hide my iniquity; I said, 'I will confess my transgressions to the LORD,' and you forgave the guilt of my sin.

Augustine understands these verses to specify the role the confession of sin plays in maintaining the believer in the faith that determines human blessedness. In Taylor's terms, Augustine believes that this psalm orients the self-understanding of the believer in Christ by plotting his or her relationship to God and neighbor. He explains the progression this way: "The first stage of understanding is to recognize that you are a sinner. The second stage of understanding is that when, having received the gift of faith, you begin to do good by choosing to love, you attribute this not to your own powers but to the grace of God. Then there will be no guile in your heart, which means in your inward mouth, for you will not have one thing on your lips and something different in your thoughts" (Exp. 2.9 of Ps. 31, p. 371).[49] In singing this psalm of human blessedness, the singer is provided with a potent tool for self-analysis, a standard by which her desires and actions can be oriented.

Augustine is developing a definition of eschatological knowledge that is not complete, grasped as a form as in his early neo-Platonic thought, but constantly being refined by the conscience. Refinement yields true knowledge but does not assume a God's-eye perspective on the whole of creation's workings.[50] God's words are provided for self-measurement by the enlightening of the Spirit, and this measurement is an unending project. Augustine makes this point by reiterating that the foundation for any true human knowledge is God's decision to look away from our sins in forgiveness and instead to see us as we were created to be. Human knowledge is the artifact of faith in the God who is not possessed by faith but possesses and so remakes us. Augustine sees this definition of knowledge vividly portrayed in the parable of the Pharisee and the tax collector in Luke 18:10-14.

> Any who aspire to be strong, relying on themselves and displaying their own merits, whatever these may be, will be kin to that Pharisee who managed to boast even about what he admitted was the gift of God, saying, *O God, I thank you.* . . . By repeating, *I thank you,* he was avowing that he had received what he had from God, for *what have you that you did not receive?* (1 Cor. 4:7). . . . Why was this a proud attitude? Not because he thanked God for the gifts he had, but because he was exalting himself above his neighbor on the strength of those gifts. (Exp. 2.10 of Ps. 31)

49. Martin Luther develops this line in "Psalm Thirty Four," in *Luther's Works, Vol. 10, First Lectures on the Psalms I, Psalms 1–75,* ed. Hinton Oswald (St. Louis: Concordia Publishing House, 1974), pp. 162-63.

50. "The man who cannot view the whole is offended by what he takes to be the deformity of a part; but this is because he does not know how it is adapted or related to the whole." Augustine, *City of God,* Book XVI.8.

The equity of God's law is that "Anyone who exalts himself will be humbled, but the one who humbles himself will be exalted" (Exp. 2.11 of Ps. 31).

If knowledge is knowledge "on the way," Augustine interprets these verses and the narrative of the Pharisee and the tax collector to place the confession of sin as an essential component sustaining us in this way. Speaking of our sin instead of our merit keeps our eyes on Christ's merits, allowing them to remedy our weaknesses. "Who can boast of having a pure heart, or of being clean from sin in all respects? The Pharisee was indeed guilty of sin; but he was looking the wrong way, and failed to realize where he was standing. He was like someone in need of healing who had come to a doctor's surgery, but presented only his sound limbs and covered up his wounds" (Exp. 2.12 of Ps. 31, p. 375). The tax collector provides the model for the Christian confession of Christ's knowledge of our true being: "He took the role of judge over himself so that the Lord might be the intercessor; he was punishing himself so that another might set him free; he was accusing himself so that the other might defend him" (Exp. 2.12 of Ps. 31, p. 374).

Augustine's contention is that specific forms of speaking are essential in maintaining the believer in the path of blessedness. In Taylor's terms, responsibility to others and the good life are tied together by formed speech. Speaking and singing God's words prepare singers to confess being incompletely possessed by their song. Taylor has argued that moderns feel obliged to speak in order to fabricate some vision of the good life worth pursuing. We thereby construct a speculative hope to remedy a perceived deficit. But Augustine finds the articulation of psalms to form Christian living, not by creating something in which we can hope but by learning to live the hopes God has for us. God's being in Christ serves to re-create our perspective, exposing the failures and hopelessness of which we were previously unaware. By calling out our sins to God, we rejuvenate our bones — our virtues.

32:6 עַל־זֹאת יִתְפַּלֵּל כָּל־חָסִיד אֵלֶיךָ לְעֵת מְצֹא רַק לְשֵׁטֶף מַיִם רַבִּים אֵלָיו לֹא יַגִּיעוּ

7 אַתָּה סֵתֶר לִי מִצַּר תִּצְּרֵנִי רָנֵּי פַלֵּט תְּסוֹבְבֵנִי סֶלָה

31:6 pro hac orabit ad te omnis sanctus in tempore oportuno verumtamen in diluvio aquarum multarum ad eum non adproximabunt

7 tu es refugium meum a tribulatione quae circumdedit me exultatio mea erue me a circumdantibus me diapsalma

32:6 Therefore let all who are faithful offer prayer to you;
at a time of distress, the rush of mighty waters shall not reach them.

7   You are a hiding place for me; you preserve me from trouble; you surround me with glad cries of deliverance.

These verses describe what Taylor would call the primal ontological truth claim of Augustine's account of Psalm 32: the possibility of human confession rests on exemplary and efficacious self-humiliation of God in Christ. Verses 6 and 7, says Augustine, are a confession from the side of human subjectivity that Christ is a hiding place for me, Christ preserves me from trouble, and it is Christ who surrounds me with glad cries of deliverance. "Let those others take refuge with their gods, or with their demons, or in their own strength, or in defending their sins. As for me, I have no refuge in this flood except yourself, my refuge from the distress that besets me" (Exp. 2.19 of Ps. 31). Christ alone can urge the cry of confession, humbling our hearts so that we can say with the psalmist, "It is good to confess the LORD" (Ps. 92:1). There are many other faiths, and many other philosophies, a "multiplicity of variegated teachings," each of which propounds "excellent precepts of morality and self-improvement, but nowhere humility like this. The way of humility comes from no other source; it comes only from Christ. It is the way originated by him who, though most high, came in humility" (Exp. 2.18 of Ps. 31). Reality is known in and through Christ, and the first lesson of the journey into this reality is that the search to construct one's own self or identity on anything other than Christ is futile.

32:8   אַשְׂכִּילְךָ וְאוֹרְךָ בְּדֶרֶךְ־זוּ תֵלֵךְ אִיעֲצָה עָלֶיךָ עֵינִי

9   אַל־תִּהְיוּ כְּסוּס כְּפֶרֶד אֵין הָבִין בְּמֶתֶג־וָרֶסֶן עֶדְיוֹ לִבְלוֹם בַּל קְרֹב אֵלֶיךָ

10   רַבִּים מַכְאוֹבִים לָרָשָׁע וְהַבּוֹטֵחַ בַּיהוָה חֶסֶד יְסוֹבְבֶנּוּ

31:8   intellectum tibi dabo et instruam te in via hac qua gradieris firmabo super te oculos meos

9   nolite fieri sicut equus et mulus quibus non est intellectus in camo et freno maxillas eorum constringe qui non adproximant ad te

10   multa flagella peccatoris sperantem autem in Domino misericordia circumdabit

32:8   I will instruct you and teach you the way you should go; I will counsel you with my eye upon you.

9   Do not be like a horse or a mule, without understanding, whose temper must be curbed with bit and bridle, else it will not stay near you.

10   Many are the torments of the wicked, but steadfast love surrounds those who trust in the LORD.

The use of spatial metaphors to describe the moral life in these verses allows Augustine to elaborate his moral ontology. In verse 8, a metaphor of path and guide is central; in verse 9, the metaphor is of horse and rider. The first emphasizes the narrowness of the path and God's responsibility of guiding us on it; the second, the importance of nearness and attentiveness to the master. Augustine begins by drawing out the moral implications of what he takes as a path image: "I will instruct you and teach you the way you should go."

> He does not mean to set you there so that you stay put, but so that you do not stray off it. I will give you understanding so that you may always truly know yourself, and always rejoice in hope toward God, until you arrive in your heavenly homeland, where there will be no place for hope, but only the reality. *I will keep a firm eye on you.* I will not take my eyes off you, because you will not take yours off me either. (Exp. 2.21 of Ps. 31)

To keep our eyes on Christ is to leave the responsibility to God to "pluck my feet from the snare" (Ps. 25:15), and "God has promised to this one who prays both understanding and protection" (Exp. 2.22 of Ps. 31). Because Augustine has given responsibility for the avoidance of unpleasant events to God, he must now say that unpleasant events cannot vitiate the fulfilled human life. Nor is fulfillment a specification of human action, a moral category: it is solely a quality of the human-divine relationship.

Human love must be remade to sustain this relationship, and Augustine concludes with a typology of the loves that are subject to God's discipline:

> So the people with crooked, twisted hearts propose three opinions. Either God does not exist; so the fool says in his heart, 'There is no God' . . . which is the opinion of the impious person who is angry about anything unpleasant that happens to him or her, but does not happen to someone else deemed to be less deserving; or, secondly, 'God is unjust, since he enjoys this sort of thing, and acts like this'; or, thirdly, 'God is not in control of human affairs, and does not concern himself with any of them.' All three of these opinions entail grave impiety, whether it is denial of God's existence, or charging him with injustice, or doubting his governance of the world. Why does anyone hold such views? Because they are crooked of heart. God is straight and true, and therefore a crooked heart is not at peace with him. (Exp. 2.25 of Ps. 31, p. 385)

This exegesis further clarifies how Augustine, like Taylor, assumes the interpenetration of metaphysics, epistemology, and ethics. That Augustine does not understand this metaphysics in terms of complete or systematic knowledge, but as a conceptualization of truth that orients our action, is emphasized by his reading of these verses. Here knowledge is not the possession of human actors but a quality of living and desiring in which knowledge is built up by remaining in the reciprocal gaze of human and divine vision. Humans are oriented in moral and temporal space, and thus fulfilled, in undertaking the steps necessary to live within this reciprocal gaze, steps that orient human action conformed to Christ's love for humanity. Augustine's conclusion is that life within this reciprocal gaze is characterized by and sustained in the singing of praises.

32:11 שִׂמְחוּ בַיהוָה וְגִילוּ צַדִּיקִים וְהַרְנִינוּ כָּל־יִשְׁרֵי־לֵב

31:11 laetamini in Domino et exultate iusti et gloriamini omnes recti corde

32:11 Be glad in the LORD and rejoice, O righteous, and shout for joy, all you upright in heart.

Such praise, concludes Augustine, is the flowering of the one metaphysical, epistemic, and moral truth of the universe. The crooked in heart believe in the power of the devil, or of the stars, or other created things, thus violating the first commandment to "have no other gods before me." Conversely, the psalmist trusts in faith that the only power who makes us glad is the Lord, our only righteousness a share of his. As Job confesses, "The LORD gave and the LORD has taken away; blessed be the name of the LORD" (Job 1:21).

For Augustine, the triune God has undertaken the project of straightening crooked human hearts, using the Son as the ruler. This shifts the definition of the good life away from a search or quest for the good life.

> [Y]ou were wanting to live, and not wanting any calamity to fall upon you; but God willed otherwise. There are two wills, then; but your will must be straightened to fit the will of God, not God's will twisted out of shape to fit yours. Yours is crooked, his is the ruler. The ruler must stand steady so that the crooked thing may be conformed to it. (Exp. 2.26 of Ps. 31, p. 387)

This thought was so comforting and challenging to Augustine that this became his favorite psalm, which he had inscribed above his bed so that he might see it each morning upon waking, as well as on the wall beside his deathbed.[51]

A close reading of Augustine's sermon on Psalm 32 has shown that Tay-

---

51. Rowland Prothero, *The Psalms in Human Life* (London: John Murray, 1909), p. 38.

lor has followed Augustine in using the image of moral space to indicate the interconnections between metaphysics, epistemology, and ethics. Yet Taylor reveals his modern presuppositions by framing his search in terms of identity and self-formation. This makes it difficult for him to give proper weight to Augustine's insistence that a fulfilled life is not in one's interiority but is found only outside of a person, in the person of Christ. An emphasis on forming the self or identity is always inward focused, even when an outer world is named as its basis, as it is in Taylor. Conversely, an ethos of ordered desire is fully focused on and determined by what is outside us, which is for Augustine God and neighbor.

This difference between the internal and external constitution of the actor has sweeping import for moral theology. While both approaches give a central role to articulation in orienting the actor in moral space, we have discovered that they take sharply different positions about what is to be articulated. For Augustine, praise makes confession of my difference from Christ — and thus my moral reorientation — possible. Here Taylor is correct to criticize modern moral articulation as vacuous in its disconnection from any ontological reality. Yet he leaves us only with hints about how we should properly articulate the good.[52] Taylor thinks of persons as constructing their identity or inheriting it, while Augustine is not at all concerned with the formation of identity, only with how to love others properly — "love" being defined as the medium through which the self-humbling God confronts and reorders human selfishness by forgiving and creating new desires.

Psalm 22: Political Unity as a Theological Concern

If Augustine's exegesis of Psalm 32 gives us a sense of what he would put on Taylor's "meaningful life" axis, in Psalm 22 we see him outlining the content of the "communal worth" axis. Recall that Taylor placed visions of community and communal respect, as well as the ideas and images that describe and evoke such community, on this axis. If we keep firmly in view that Augustine is not writing and preaching to form selves understood in the modern sense, we will find clear evidence that he is both describing a form of communal life

---

52. When he does, preaching seems to be his original example. "Indeed, the most powerful case is where the speaker, the formulation, and the act of delivering the message all line up together to reveal the good, as the immense and continuing force of the gospel illustrates. A formulation has power when it brings the source close, when it makes it plain and evident, in all its inherent force, its capacity to inspire our love, respect or allegiance. An effective articulation releases this force, and this is how words have power." Taylor, *Sources of the Self*, p. 96.

in which the individual is meaningfully distinguished and integrated into the whole, and using this image to call the church to its proper sociality.

However often Augustine might have espoused the idea of timeless truths in his mature work, the main concern of his biblical exposition is with bringing Scripture to bear on the particularities of place and communal life. This is biographically marked by his movement from written commentaries on the Psalms to the oral and communal commentary of the sermon. He regularly reminds his congregation that he is preaching the words they have just sung, implicitly calling them to exercise the formed conscience of Psalm 32. In his sermon on Psalm 22, his aim is to show how the Psalms situate his congregation's particular obedience. He does so by pointing out that they have sung the psalm in the context of a Good Friday service,[53] and he undertakes to explain what it means for (1) them to sing, (2) today, (3) this psalm. Throughout the sermon he addresses individuals in order to emphasize that their primary location is not in a building listening to a lecture, and so forth, but within the story of Christ taking place here and now. He says of verse 1, for instance, "Beyond doubt, he [Christ] was speaking of me, of you, of him over there, of her, for he was acting as his own body, the church" (Exp. 2.4 of Ps. 21).

Reading Augustine alongside contemporary communitarian discourses outlined in chapter 2 suggests that he is thinking of "community" not as a general concept applicable to various social groupings, but as the body of Christ. Its uniqueness is indicated by his usual mode of address to the congregation as *caritas vestra,* or *sanctitas vestra* ("you who are love" or "you who are holiness"). On the basis of Psalm 22, Augustine explains that the congregation before him is not an "assembly," a general term, but the physical presence of the love and holiness of Christ.

Unlike the thinkers represented in chapter 2, Augustine understands that the biblical witness refuses to define the Christian community by way of a general concept applicable to various social groupings. And unlike Taylor, he also does not lecture on the general ideals toward which individuals might aspire, or which will give their life meaning. Taylor plays the role of the university professor who dispenses wisdom to society at large about how they should form their identities; Augustine stands in the middle of the congregation and points to the wisdom of Christ within which he and the congregation are already involved. Taylor wants to display something before his

---

53. The year of delivery is unknown, but we do know that he is here exercised about the Donatist controversy that drew his attention from 401 onward. The relative development of the position and the absence of references to Pelagian issues makes it less likely that it was delivered after 411.

thoughtful and reflective constituency; Augustine (and Luther) sings and encourages songs of praise to Christ from within that community whose unity is solely in the unity of worship expressed in such songs.

In addition to explicitly responding to the congregation's location in time on Good Friday, Augustine also addresses a question raised by their spatial, social, and thus ecclesial location in relation to the schismatic claims of the Donatists. This rival church was actively tempting his congregants to abandon the church for their sect. Their grievance rested primarily on what was by then a century-old claim that the rest of the church had fallen away from Christ because of its capitulation to the demand to hand over sacred books during the persecution of Christians by the emperor Diocletian in CE 303. The struggle had nationalist overtones because the Donatists were an African church, and they accused the Catholics of sympathy with the (Roman) oppressor. It also had ecclesiological and sacramental aspects because of the Donatists' claim, denied by Augustine, that the validity of the sacraments depended on the validity of the priest. We see Augustine dealing with each of these issues in the course of his sermon on Psalm 22.

The heart of that psalm, he says, is found in verses 27 and 28:

22:28 יִזְכְּרוּ וְיָשֻׁבוּ אֶל־יְהוָה כָּל־אַפְסֵי־אָרֶץ וְיִשְׁתַּחֲווּ לְפָנֶיךָ כָּל־מִשְׁפְּחוֹת גּוֹיִם׃

29 כִּי לַיהוָה הַמְּלוּכָה וּמֹשֵׁל בַּגּוֹיִם

21:28 reminiscentur et convertentur ad Dominum universi fines terrae et adorabunt in conspectu eius universae familiae gentium

29 quoniam Dei est regnum et ipse dominabitur gentium

22:27 All the ends of the earth shall remember and turn to the LORD; and all the families of the nations shall worship before him.

28 For dominion belongs to the LORD, and he rules over the nations.

This passage evokes Augustine's most passionate eloquence. It bears quoting at length, both to get a feel for his preaching at its best and in order to display the central theological point of his exegesis of the psalm.

> Look at the psalm, this same psalm that is read here today and is being read among them as well. Let us write it on our foreheads! Forward march, everyone! Let not our tongues fall silent, let us shout, 'Look, Christ suffered, the merchant offered his price. The money he handed over was his blood, the blood he shed. He carried our ransom-money in a purse; he was pierced with a spear, the purse spilled out, and the price of the whole world gushed out.' What have you to say to me, you heretic? That it was not the ransom-

price of the whole world? That Africa alone was redeemed? You dare not say, 'The whole world was redeemed, but perished later.' Who attacked Christ, and robbed him of what was his own? . . . But *all the ends of the earth* is what he said, you heretic; *all* is the word he used. Where are you off to, to hide from further questioning? You have no way out, only a way in. (Exp. 2.28 of Ps. 21, pp. 238-39)

Augustine meets the Donatists' claim that they comprised the sum total of the wheat of the kingdom — the Catholic church and the world being chaff — with the astounding claim that the whole world is Christ's possession: all people belong to God and are thus the church![54] If it is true that Augustine often "envisages fallen man as locked or glued together in a chaotic and evil lump from which individuals can be prized free in joining a different kind of body, that of the Incarnation,"[55] it is also true that the Psalms and the Donatist controversy sometimes led him to the less familiar point that this whole "lump" of humanity is first and basically ensnared in Christ's rule, if not yet fully transformed into his body. At the 411 conference where Augustine debated the Donatists face to face, they immediately sensed the implications of this claim and accused him of calling the world what Jesus had called the church, thus inverting the parable of the wheat and the tares (Matt. 13:24-30). Augustine's reply was that, in terms of the gospel, *mundus* and *ecclesia* are interchangeable terms, because Jesus himself said that he came "not to judge the world but to save it" (John 12:47).[56] "'World' and 'church' are coextensive," says R. A. Markus. "There is a real distinction to be drawn between them, but it is eschatological rather than sociological or historical. . . . So in the last resort the Church *is* the world, the world reconciled in Christ."[57]

This move significantly shifts the vantage point from which Augustine develops his ethical theory. In effect, he has extended the Old Testament logic of the people of God to the whole world. In the Old Testament the whole people of Israel were God's possession, God's flock, even if some chose to stray. Those who avowed their possession by God remained in God's path, to walk

54. Stephen Fowl insightfully suggests that, despite the polemical language of passages like these, Augustine's responses to the Donatists are examples of interpretive charity precisely in taking their theological claims seriously, and not simply unmasking them as political threats veiled in theological language. Stephen Fowl, *Engaging Scripture: A Model for Theological Interpretation* (Oxford: Blackwell, 1998), pp. 91-95.

55. Rist, *Augustine*, p. 287; cf. pp. 283-87.

56. This interchange is sensitively discussed in R. A. Markus, *Saeculum: History and Society in the Theology of St. Augustine*, rev. ed. (Cambridge: Cambridge University Press, 1988), pp. 121-23.

57. Markus, *Saeculum*, p. 123.

with God and be sanctified. Those who reject Christ's lordship do not thereby escape being God's possession; but they fight it, to their own destruction. Augustine's suggestion is that one can be a conforming or selfish possession of Christ, but one cannot escape being a possession. More importantly, he argues that to be a good possession is not only an ecclesial trait in the way the Donatists formulated it, but is a feature of all human life. *All* people find their fulfillment in God. This means that the only ethical question is this: Will God's people consent to life as the people of God?

This presses a further question: If the *ecclesia* is the whole world, what is the meaning of baptism, of preaching, of the whole range of Christian practices? The answer to this question Augustine finds in the inclusion of a partial quotation of this psalm in the passion account.

22:2 אֵלִי אֵלִי לָמָה עֲזַבְתָּנִי רָחוֹק מִישׁוּעָתִי דִּבְרֵי שַׁאֲגָתִי

3 אֱלֹהַי אֶקְרָא יוֹמָם וְלֹא תַעֲנֶה וְלַיְלָה וְלֹא־דוּמִיָּה לִי

4 וְאַתָּה קָדוֹשׁ יוֹשֵׁב תְּהִלּוֹת יִשְׂרָאֵל

21:2 Deus Deus meus respice me quare me dereliquisti longe a salute mea verba delictorum meorum

3 Deus meus clamabo per diem et non exaudies et nocte et non ad insipientiam mihi

4 tu autem in sancto habitas Laus Israhel

22:1 My God, my God, why have you forsaken me? Why are you so far from helping me, from the words of my groaning?

2 O my God, I cry by day, but you do not answer; and by night, but find no rest.

3 Yet you are holy, enthroned on the praises of Israel.

Why did Jesus quote these specific lines during his suffering, "unless he was somehow trying to catch our attention, to make us understand, 'This psalm is written about me'?" (Exp. 2.3 of Ps. 21). Augustine draws the attention of his congregation to Christ's utterance of these verses to explicate the meaning of their Good Friday service, a service designed to "make present what took place in time past, and in this way it moves us as if we were actually watching our Lord hanging on the Cross, but watching as believers, not mockers" (Exp. 2.1 of Ps. 21).[58] Christ's prayer on the cross continues today in the commemoration of the church. He emphasizes that the world and his

---

58. Compare Luther's comment on Ps. 31:13, where his use of the first person pronoun makes this point from the perspective of one who praises, rather than mocks, at the cross. Luther, "Psalm Thirty-One," p. 141.

congregation both stand before that cross, either as mockers or as those who groan with the sufferings of Christ. "[T]he chaff on his threshing-floor mocks him, and the wheat groans to hear its Lord derided" (Exp. 2.1 of Ps. 21).

Augustine is unpacking for his congregation what it means to sing this psalm, as Christ's body, part of the *totus Christus*. Why did Christ say these words on the cross? "For what other reason was this said than that we were there, for what other reason than that Christ's body is the Church" (Exp. 2.3 of Ps. 21). Christ was praying the prayer of his church, presenting their fear and trial as he carried their sin, and quoting the very words that they, too, sing today as a memorial of his passion. The words of the psalm thus form the basis of a reciprocal identification: they are at once the lament of Christ to God as a mediator for his church and the words of lament sung by a church undergoing the travails of Christ in the world. These words present an opportunity for the church to groan with the mistreatment of Christ as he groaned for them. "This is what I mean to groan over now, together with you, for this is the time to lament. The Lord's passion is being commemorated: it is time for groaning, a time for weeping, a time for confessing and imploring God's help" (Exp. 2.1 of Ps. 21).[59]

For Augustine, the psalm is an opportunity to raise our voice in harmony with Christ's suffering. This is not a repetition of a scene that happened long ago and far away. The drama of the cross is not over, for humanity stands before the cross today and always. In these verses humanity is reminded of its place in the unfolding of this drama of the cross, either to mock or to cry out with God's sufferings at the hands of a godless world.[60] The world lamenting with Christ is a godless world redeemed. This use of the *totus Christus* con-

59. The different approaches of Augustine and Luther are evident in their interpretation of this passage: in Augustine the diachronic sense is ascendant; in Luther, the synchronic. Compare Luther's comment on Ps. 31:9: "[T]his is the role for tropological language: Wherever in the Psalms Christ complains and prays in bodily affliction according to the letter, there, in the same words, every faithful soul, born and trained in Christ, complains and prays, confessing that it has been tempted to sin or has fallen into sin. For to the present day Christ is spitted on, killed, scourged, crucified in us ourselves. Even now there lie in ambush for Him without ceasing the flesh with its feelings, the world with its pleasures, and the devil with his offers and temptations, just as the Jews did to Christ in his flesh." Luther, "Psalm Thirty-One," p. 139.

60. The phrase is from Bonhoeffer, whose much misunderstood "religionless Christianity" draws on this Augustinian point. "The poem about Christians and pagans contains an idea. . . . 'Christians stand by God in his hour of grieving'; that is what distinguishes Christians from pagans. Jesus asked in Gethsemane, 'Could you not watch with me one hour?' That is a reversal of what the religious man expects from God. Man is summoned to share in God's sufferings at the hands of a godless world." Dietrich Bonhoeffer, *Letters and Papers from Prison*, enlarged edition, ed. Eberhard Bethge (London: SCM Press, 1971), p. 361; cf. pp. 348-49.

cept may be understood to be a way of responding to one of Watson's central points: here a Christological doctrine is shaping hermeneutics in a way that pulls together ethical, ecclesiological, and eschatological concerns. The *totus Christus* concept links and yet distinguishes Christ's being and the being of the church, the church's regeneration and its ultimate end.

With this reading of verses 1-3, Augustine is doing two things: he first defines the whole world as God's possession, and then he specifies this claim by saying the city of God is that part of Christ's possession that laments and praises with Christ. This implies that, for Augustine, there is no such thing as anthropology, only ecclesiology. Augustine's formulation holds in tension the claims that the church *is* the whole world, and is *in the midst of* the world. The tension rests on a sharp but eschatologically conditioned differentiation between humanity that either exists in Christ or is, like chaff, subject to the threshing of God's fury. There are only mockers and praisers; and of the mockers, says the psalmist, "You will destroy their offspring from the earth, and their children from among humankind" (Ps. 21:10).

Those who mock seek to remove themselves from Christ's story and to become their own possession. This is not to imply that one can escape the realm of Christ's power by scoffing. Such an escape from Christ's power is impossible within the orbit of the question of human life as Augustine understood it, that is, "What is happening to Christ's possession?" Because all humans love something, they praise it, meaning that all human life inevitably assumes the form of praise, whether well directed or badly directed.[61] The church is thus a sung reality expressing a God-given desire for God. Conceptualizations of the body of Christ must steer between two extremes. They may so emphasize that we need the church to know Christ that the church *becomes* Christ. On the other hand, they can so emphasize Christ's freedom to be God apart from his creation that they lose the idea that we can depend on meeting Christ in the church. If I am right in saying that Augustine's *City of God* displays his mature view of the body of Christ, it is clear that he was careful to avoid both of these extremes.

Perhaps he was even more careful than is contemporary theology. As chapter 2 outlined, contemporary communitarian and ecclesiological ethics understand the church and its practices to be God's indispensable tools for giving shape to raw human life. This is a new version of the Donatist claim that Augustine attacked for not preserving the freedom of God. He inverts this definition of church by re-emphasizing the centrality of God's kingship, and his prior suffering in which the church participates. This approach em-

---

61. Cf. Rist, *Augustine*, pp. 173-85.

phasizes God's acting to include humans in Christ, but it retains a place for human agency by insisting that only the praising church will endure. Thus the central act of the church is not a mode of living that those outside the church also do, such as moral deliberation or pedagogy, but it is a mode of resonating with the reality of God's work.

By putting Christ and his church so close together, Augustine is not implying that the church itself is messianic, but that Christ is the Messiah sent to ensure that the world lives as church. "Christ died only once," says Augustine, but the words he uttered as he died live on in their repetition by the community being included in his death and resurrection. The world is saved in praising Jesus; the Messiah is "enthroned on the praises of Israel." Therefore, Psalm 22 is not talking about the church; rather, it makes up the words of the church spoken by Christ suffering on the cross. Christ knew our suffering: "Why did he make that prayer, then, except because he was bearing our weaknesses, and made it for those members of his body who still fear death?" (Exp. 2.4 of Ps. 21). He lamented because his life is the suffering humanity of the church, and the church's life is in this fellow suffering of Christ (Exp. 2.21 of Ps. 21).

The church is thus deeply identified in both directions with the suffering of Christ under his accusers. This is a theology of the cross functioning as an ecclesiological distinction. The condition of the church in a sinful world is as a participant in the suffering of Christ in the world; the praising church becomes aware of this participation precisely in its practice of singing.

22:15 כַּמַּיִם נִשְׁפַּכְתִּי וְהִתְפָּרְדוּ כָּל־עַצְמוֹתָי הָיָה לִבִּי כַּדּוֹנָג נָמֵס בְּתוֹךְ מֵעָי

16 יָבֵשׁ כַּחֶרֶשׂ כֹּחִי וּלְשׁוֹנִי מֻדְבָּק מַלְקוֹחָי וְלַעֲפַר־מָוֶת תִּשְׁפְּתֵנִי

17 כִּי סְבָבוּנִי כְּלָבִים עֲדַת מְרֵעִים הִקִּיפוּנִי כָּאֲרִי יָדַי וְרַגְלָי

18 אֲסַפֵּר כָּל־עַצְמוֹתָי הֵמָּה יַבִּיטוּ יִרְאוּ־בִי

21:15 sicut aqua effusus sum et dispersa sunt universa ossa mea factum est cor meum tamquam cera liquescens in medio ventris mei

16 aruit tamquam testa virtus mea et lingua mea adhesit faucibus meis et in limum mortis deduxisti me

17 quoniam circumdederunt me canes multi concilium malignantium obsedit me foderunt manus meas et pedes meos

18 dinumeraverunt omnia ossa mea ipsi vero consideraverunt et inspexerunt me

22:14 I am poured out like water, and all my bones are out of joint; my heart is like wax; it is melted within my breast;

15 my mouth is dried up like a potsherd, and my tongue sticks to my jaws; you lay me in the dust of death.

16   For dogs are all around me; a company of evildoers encircles me.
       My hands and feet have shriveled;
17   I can count all my bones.
       They stare and gloat over me;

Augustine continues by explaining the Christological mechanics of the relationship of Christ's suffering to his church, asking, "What did he suffer?" and "Why did he suffer?" He understands verses 14-17 to provide the answer to the first question. In verse 14, the speaker speaks of his suffering as a pouring out. Augustine interprets this speaker first as Christ, because the metaphor is spoken by his prophetic predecessor, David. Augustine seizes on the outward flowing aspect of the image: Christ's heart, he says, is Scripture, which before his death was closed, veiled. "When the Lord was crucified, it began to flow freely like wax, so that all the weak could understand scripture. As a result of the crucifixion even the veil of the temple was torn, because what had previously been veiled was now revealed" (Exp. 2.15 of Ps. 21, p. 233). Augustine associates the image of the potsherd with the tempering effect of fire. Christ is laid in the dust of death to bring other mouths to life; his mouth is dried up so that his wisdom will be spread by "preachers as his tongue." What he suffered was the crucifixion, the piercing of hands and feet, the staring and gloating of enemies, but this was so that the power of Scripture might be released, and, like a chain reaction, be carried by a church washed and propelled into the world by the force of his death.

Here, as elsewhere, Augustine describes the Bible as what the Protestant reformers would later refer to as the *verbum externum*. It is Christ's heart, the effective mediator of his person to humans. As a book, it is outside of the preacher. Yet this external book can be comprehended only by one already inside the orbit of Christ's power. He preaches as one inside of Christ's Word, and can thus include himself with his congregation by saying, "*We are the fragrance of Christ in every place*" (Exp. 2.2 of Ps. 21). As a preacher, Augustine continually reminds the congregation that he is subject to both Christ and his word. "[I]t is [not] my sermon that is important. Concentrate on the psalm, read the psalm. . . . Look at our Redeemer, look at the price of our ransom" (Exp. 2.29 of Ps. 21). Augustine continually reminds his hearers that Scripture claims them, not in his interpretation, but as Christ's heart. Two points are worth noting here. First, Augustine links Scripture and Christ by saying that Scripture is Christ's heart. Thus, to meditate on the Bible is to meditate on the heart of the divine Word. This is why he can say that each part of Scripture is not necessarily about Christ directly; but, as the plow is to its blade, each part serves to reveal Scripture's main theme, which is Christ.[62] Second, Augustine knows that he does not take up Scripture as an individual; he is only part of the "we" and can only say "we" in the address of the sermon if he has been taken up in the words of Christ to his church: "You are mine." This leads him to a further discussion of the attributes that unify Christ's body.

22:19 יְחַלְּקוּ בְגָדַי לָהֶם וְעַל־לְבוּשִׁי יַפִּילוּ גוֹרָל

21:19 diviserunt sibi vestimenta mea et super vestem meam miserunt sortem

22:18 they divide my clothes among themselves, and for my clothing they cast lots.

Augustine immediately refers this passage to John 19:23-24, which the evangelist explicitly states is an interpretation of this verse of Psalm 22: "[T]hey took his clothes and divided them into four parts. . . . Now the tunic was seamless, woven in one piece from the top. So they said, 'Let us not tear it, but cast lots for it to see who will get it.'" At this point Augustine follows John's Gospel, which understands this verse to have its essential truth only in relationship to Christ.

To press home his ecclesiological point about the unity of the church, Augustine interprets this verse — in combination with the Gospel account — as describing the nature of the church's unity. Remember that he is discussing *what* Christ suffered, and has repeatedly reminded his hearers that what Christ suffered on the cross is the expression of his church's (world's) sin.

> His garments are his sacraments. Now pay close attention, brothers and sisters. His garments, his sacraments, could be torn apart by heresies, but there was one garment that no one tore: *they cast lots for my tunic.* The evangelist tells us that *there was a tunic woven from the top* (Jn. 19:23) — down from heaven, then, from the Father, from the Holy Spirit. What is this tunic, which no one can tear apart? Charity. What is this tunic? Unity. Dice are thrown for it, but nobody tears it. The heretics have been able to tear apart the sacraments for their own use, but love they could not tear. And because they were not able to, they have taken themselves off, but love remains whole. Love falls to the lot of some people, and whoever has love is safe. Nobody ousts such a person from the Catholic Church, and if any begin to take hold of love from without, they are brought inside, as the olive branch was by the dove. (Exp. 2.19 of Ps. 21, p. 234)

---

62. Augustine, *City of God,* Book XVI.2.

The unity of the church is not a sacramental bestowal that can be torn by false teachings and improper priests. Defining the church's political unity in this way, says Augustine, is to conceive of the church as a governing body, with protocols that must be properly followed in order to mark off a small group as ritually kept separate from the damned masses. Instead, he says, the unity of the church is primarily a quality of action marking those possessed by Christ's love. In moral terms, the Donatists have violated a more basic moral requirement, the imperative of brotherly love to remain "eating the bread of unity," to protect a lesser moral claim. Augustine was of one mind with the Donatists, Bernd Wannenwetsch comments,

> that the church must have agreement about the central practices of its way of life and must separate itself from those who do not agree. His emphasis upon unity does not make it the single or highest moral concern, to which all other moral truths must be sacrificed. He means simply to note that the Church's moral discussions must be undertaken in the love of unity rather than the love of pride. Any handling of moral transgression or division that does not reflect Christ's love of unity will inevitably lead to moral corruption — a corruption that is all the more serious in kind if it comes (self-) deceptively wrapped in moral clothes.[63]

Christ suffered in the tearing of his clothes, the rending of the church by heresy; yet it preserves its essential unity in those who hold it dear, caring for and tending it (Eph. 2). Augustine will extend this definition of the church's unity in his comment on verse 22.

But before turning to that verse, we must deal with what feels to a modern interpreter like an impermissible promiscuity in making these interpretive linkages. We have already seen that, in the *City of God*, Augustine urges beginning interpretation from the historical sense of Old Testament passages. Nevertheless, with the New Testament, he is not interested in asking first about some allegedly primary historical meaning existing in a neutral space separate from Christ. With his intertextual relationship of the Gospels and Psalms, he deconstructs any general notion of metaphor or history that might render the preservation of Christ's tunic "only metaphorical," or symbolic, thus refusing a general concept of metaphor or symbol within which Christ is one in a series.

Augustine now explains *why* Christ suffered, when he asks, What is the fruit of that suffering?

63. Bernd Wannenwetsch, "Ecclesiology and Ethics," in Gilbert Meilaender and William Werpehowski, eds., *The Oxford Handbook of Theological Ethics* (Oxford: Oxford University Press, 2005), p. 70.

22:23 אֲסַפְּרָה שִׁמְךָ לְאֶחָי בְּתוֹךְ קָהָל אֲהַלְלֶךָ

21:23 narrabo nomen tuum fratribus meis in media ecclesia laudabo te

22:22 I will tell of your name to my brothers and sisters; in the midst of the congregation I will praise you:

He suffered, says verse 22, to create three things in the world. First, he suffered to create those who "tell of your name," the preachers who have been washed and sent out into the whole world. How do we know that it is the whole world? Because they praise in the congregation — in Augustine's Latin, *media ecclesia* — the "great assembly," which is the second creation of his suffering. Augustine repeats his question to the Donatists: "How could a tiny part of the world be the great assembly? The great assembly is the whole world" (Exp. 2.26 of Ps. 21). And third, he suffered to send out these representatives in the midst of the world to sing praise: "I will praise you." The fruit of the work of Christ on the cross was, in short, his church. Augustine continues, "Let us have a look at this assembly, this Church, for which he suffered" (Exp. 2.23 of Ps. 21).

22:24 יִרְאֵי יְהוָה הַלְלוּהוּ כָּל־זֶרַע יַעֲקֹב כַּבְּדוּהוּ וְגוּרוּ מִמֶּנּוּ כָּל־זֶרַע
יִשְׂרָאֵל

25 כִּי לֹא־בָזָה וְלֹא שִׁקַּץ עֱנוּת עָנִי וְלֹא־הִסְתִּיר פָּנָיו מִמֶּנּוּ וּבְשַׁוְּעוֹ אֵלָיו
שָׁמֵעַ

26 מֵאִתְּךָ תְהִלָּתִי בְּקָהָל רָב נְדָרַי אֲשַׁלֵּם נֶגֶד יְרֵאָיו

27 יֹאכְלוּ עֲנָוִים וְיִשְׂבָּעוּ יְהַלְלוּ יְהוָה דֹּרְשָׁיו יְחִי לְבַבְכֶם לָעַד

21:24 qui timetis Dominum laudate eum universum semen Iacob magnificate eum

25 timeat eum omne semen Israhel quoniam non sprevit neque dispexit deprecationem pauperis nec avertit faciem suam a me et cum clamarem ad eum exaudivit me

26 apud te laus mea in ecclesia magna vota mea reddam in conspectu timentium eum

27 edent pauperes et saturabuntur et laudabunt Dominum qui requirunt eum vivent corda eorum in saeculum saeculi

22:23 You who fear the Lord, praise him! All you offspring of Jacob, glorify him; stand in awe of him, all you offspring of Israel!

24 For he did not despise or abhor the affliction of the afflicted; he did not hide his face from me, but heard when I cried to him.

25   From you comes my praise in the great congregation; my vows I will pay
      before those who fear him.

26   The poor shall eat and be satisfied; those who seek him shall praise the
      LORD. May your hearts live forever!

Augustine has already described the unity in love of the church as a
quality created in it "from above" by the Spirit. This unity is describable in relationship to its love of neighbor, which Augustine understands as its participation in Christ's love. He now goes on to say that this unity is also characterized by the preaching of Christ's name — and the singing of praises.
Commenting on the linkage in verse 23 of fear and praise, Augustine again
strikes a blow against a clericalist church by suggesting that even within a he-
retical church there is true faith.

> Wherever God is feared and praised, there is the Church of Christ. Judge for
> yourselves, brothers and sisters, whether it is without good reason that
> 'Amen' and 'Alleluia' are sung today the world over. . . . Let us inquire
> whether the Donatists praise the Lord, whether the psalm is speaking of
> them, and whether Christ is praised in the middle of their assembly. They
> have a strange way of praising Christ, those people who say, 'He has lost the
> whole world, the devil has taken it all away from him, and he himself sur-
> vives only in one part.' (Exp. 2.24 of Ps. 21, p. 236)

"From you comes *my* praise," from the church comes Christ's praise,
meaning that those who participate by fear in Christ's vow to God will know
what sacrifice this entailed, and the church that is its fruit: they are the "poor
who eat and are satisfied." Augustine sees a multilayered eucharistic reference in
this phrase. At one level, poverty refers to the awareness of one's sinfulness and
spiritual lack. "Blessed are the poor, because they eat seeking to be satisfied, they
eat because they are poor; but the rich are not satisfied because they are not really hungry. In another way those who eat Christ's body and drink his cup share
in his work in the world, and have 'suffered like him on whom they fed.'"

In summary, Augustine finds that Psalm 22, in Taylor's terms, connects
his understanding of the good life as grounded in faith in God's forgiveness
with a thick theory of the social relationships within which this good life is
lived out. But to put things this way is to have turned the search for *my* good
life inside out by making it an ethic of service. This ethic of service is rooted
in an exegetically defended definition of community centered in Christ as its
head. It is a definition with quite different contours than community as it is
defined in contemporary communitarian discourse, and it yields a different
construal of the church's uniqueness. Augustine's "community" is first of all

humanity within which the church displays the true *telos* of the whole. The church is not a form of life that mechanically shapes faithful lives; rather, it is transformed by materially participating in Christ's suffering the rage of the nations. The church is the pinnacle of God's work of redeeming this generation, though he retains the right to judge and replace a church that becomes prideful in this status.

A look at one final psalm will help us draw together the concepts of the two cities, the blessed life, and the *totus Christus* that Augustine has so far developed. What is the essential unity binding these concepts together? We have seen how Augustine uses them to give content to Christian ethics, but we have not given a full account of the forces and processes that generate this ethos. We must make clear the essential point that whatever is generating and enlivening the Christian way of life is at the same time the *source* of its inner consistency. If we neglected this step, we would not move beyond the philosophy of Taylor. Here theology can say something more by giving full attention to the question of the generation of the Christian ethos.

Augustine's exegesis of Psalm 32 places love at the heart of Christian ethics and says that, for love to issue in the fulfilled life, it must not be attached to the material blessings of this life. How, then, does he understand this love to find its fulfillment — and thus the Christian ethos to constitute the fulfilled life? We can restate the point this way: What is the perfect object of love that fully satisfies human existence, making it complete and fulfilled even amidst material want in this life? Augustine's exegesis of Psalm 22 asks for a similar clarification. Having explained that the church is constituted by those who are grouped together by their status as mockers or cosufferers with Christ, the question remains: What brings that community of praisers together so that they may "stay on the path"? Having heard Augustine say that the whole world is the church, we must ask why some fall into darkness. Augustine's answer to both questions is that perfect human fulfillment is to find our joy in God's joy, and this is predicated on his bestowing his presence on us. Augustine finds this described in Psalm 27, a psalm in which our God is "speaking to us in a comforting way, to show us that he not only created us, but also dwells in us" (Exp. 2.1 of Ps. 26, p. 274).

Psalm 27: On the Generation of the Community of Faith

Augustine's commentary on Psalm 27, which internal hints suggest was delivered after the beginning of the Pelagian controversy in 411, begins by declaring a faith with wide-ranging practical implications.

27:1 לְדָוִד יְהוָה אוֹרִי וְיִשְׁעִי מִמִּי אִירָא יְהוָה מָעוֹז־חַיַּי מִמִּי אֶפְחָד

26:1 David priusquam liniretur Dominus inluminatio mea et salus mea quem
timebo Dominus protector vitae meae a quo trepidabo

Of David

1   The LORD is my light and my salvation; whom shall I fear?
The LORD is the stronghold of my life; of whom shall I be afraid?

Augustine understands this to be faith's denial of all intermediate spiritual forces in the universe. God, he says, is the donor of all good things that
humans enjoy, and if "what is given can be taken away, the donor is defeated.
Therefore my brothers and sisters, not even the gifts we receive in the temporal sphere can be taken away from us by anyone except the One who gave
them. The spiritual gifts he gives he does not take away" (Exp. 2.5 of Ps. 26,
p. 276). This succinct summary of the lesson of Job is intended to remind us
that Christian love must not be attached to earthly things. Fear, he says, results when our loves are attached to the perishable. Augustine here relies on
his neo-Platonic framework in a quite direct way, but again undermines its
foundations with his definition of the imperishable that is to be loved. His
question is, What is the one thing we must seek in order to have nothing to
fear?

27:4 אַחַת שָׁאַלְתִּי מֵאֵת־יְהוָה אוֹתָהּ אֲבַקֵּשׁ שִׁבְתִּי בְּבֵית־יְהוָה כָּל־יְמֵי חַיַּי
לַחֲזוֹת בְּנֹעַם־יְהוָה וּלְבַקֵּר בְּהֵיכָלוֹ

26:4 unam petii a Domino hanc requiram ut inhabitem in domo Domini omnes
dies vitae meae ut videam voluntatem Domini et visitem templum eius

27:4   One thing I asked of the LORD, that will I seek after:
to live in the house of the LORD all the days of my life,
to behold the beauty of the LORD, and to inquire in his temple.

Only here is the phrase "one thing I ask"[64] used in the Psalms, a singu-
larity exploited by Augustine. The church's present "house of the LORD," he
says, is rest in God, which means, "correctly speaking, the one we look forward to is our home, the one we live in now is a tent" (Exp. 2.7 of Ps. 26,
p. 278). The bodily, temporal church is *God's* tent in this world, says Augustine, which leads him to interpret verse 6 ("I will offer in his tent sacrifices
with shouts of joy") as speaking of believers' bodily praise. This joy in the

64. אַחַת שָׁאַלְתִּי

earthly tent is a real, though provisional, participation in the joy of eternal life in God's house. Here Augustine wrestles to overcome the implication that in heaven, once we have come to possess that which we love, time will begin to drag and boredom will set in. "You will not last long if you are not happy, but what will provide you with happiness?" (Exp. 2.7 of Ps. 26, p. 278).

Augustine's first answer to that question is again to deconstruct the claim that love is about the attainment of earthly comfort. "People love a wide variety of things, and when they are seen to have what they love, they are deemed happy. But the person who is truly happy is not so much the one who has what he or she loves, but the one who loves what is worthy of love; for there are many who are made more unhappy by having what they love than by being without it" (Exp. 2.7 of Ps. 26, p. 278). The only way to be truly happy, then, is to love the one thing that should be loved, and, says verse 4, that is to "behold [*contemplativa*] the beauty of the Lord."

However, he continues, referring to Psalm 5:5, "At present I do not contemplate you, because I have fallen over; in the course of time I shall stand up and gaze" (Exp. 2.9 of Ps. 26, p. 279). This is part of what it means to be living as God's tent in time, on a pilgrimage and so at a distance from the Lord (2 Cor. 5:6). We see only incompletely, but we will one day see face to face (1 Cor. 13:12) when we inhabit our true home, which replaces these tents. That house "offers something wonderful, the chance to contemplate the Lord's own joy . . . to be immovably established in God's light" (Exp. 2.9 of Ps. 26, p. 279). The fullness of human love that is the final source of true blessedness is to look on God's own joy. The consummation of this love is the *eudaimonia* of human life.

Such love is implanted in the inconstant human hearts that remain in a broken world. This places a strict demand on human prayer, a demand, we will find, that reveals what Augustine understands to be the primal source of the Christian ethos. The only prayer possible from an inconstant humanity in an age of brokenness is a very simple one.

שְׁמַע־יְהוָה קוֹלִי אֶקְרָא וְחָנֵּנִי וַעֲנֵנִי 27:7

26:7 exaudi Domine vocem meam qua clamavi miserere mei et exaudi me

27:7 Hear, O LORD, when I cry aloud, be gracious to me and answer me!

Such groaning is the only proper prayer of those in misery. Here Augustine comes upon the void left by neo-Platonic philosophy, which has stripped away the comfort possible in loving earthly things by emphasizing their inherent inconstancy and the inevitability of their disappointing our love. The psalmist has also reached this point of negating the fleeting, says Augustine: "He has made an end of all desires; that one plea alone is left" (Exp. 2.14 of Ps. 26).[65] Faith prays that one day weeping will be turned to praise; but in the meantime, says Augustine, unceasing pleas for God's ear are in order. "Let us not interrupt that petition until it is answered, by God's gift and through God's goodness" (Exp. 2.14 of Ps. 26, p. 283). Yet the question remains: What is essential about this specific plea? The psalmist has already asked for "one thing," to dwell in the house of the Lord, and Augustine argues that he has already defined the fulfillment of the Christian life as dwelling in God's joy eternally. Is this simply the neo-Platonic doctrine contemplation? If so, then there is nothing distinctive about the source of the Christian ethos.

27:8 לְךָ אָמַר לִבִּי בַּקְּשׁוּ פָנָי אֶת־פָּנֶיךָ יְהוָה אֲבַקֵּשׁ
9 אַל־תַּסְתֵּר פָּנֶיךָ מִמֶּנִּי אַל־תַּט־בְּאַף עַבְדֶּךָ עֶזְרָתִי הָיִיתָ אַל־תִּטְּשֵׁנִי
וְאַל־תַּעַזְבֵנִי אֱלֹהֵי יִשְׁעִי

26:8 tibi dixit cor meum exquisivit facies mea faciem tuam Domine requiram
9 ne avertas faciem tuam a me ne declines in ira a servo tuo adiutor meus esto ne derelinquas me neque dispicias me Deus salvator meus

27:8 "Come," my heart says, "seek his face!" Your face, LORD, do I seek.
9 Do not hide your face from me. Do not turn your servant away in anger, you who have been my help. Do not cast me off, do not forsake me, O God of my salvation!

"How wonderful it is," enthuses Augustine, "that nothing more consonant with God's being can be said" (Exp. 2.16 of Ps. 26, p. 284). Again, the Psalms divide humans between those who can utter this prayer and those who reject it. Augustine calls the worldly faith of those who think of God's anger in terms of their attaining, or not attaining, their desires for earthly goods "the city of man." "They would not want to lose gold, or silver, or some estate which caught their eye; they would not want their friends to die, or their children, or their wives, or their dependents, their wish would be to live forever amid these pleasures" (Exp. 2.16 of Ps. 26, p. 284). They live within the perennial logic of fertility and wealth religions, worshiping God so that he will guarantee them these things; the angry God is the God who denies them. The end result is that those with worldly faith struggle and fight for these material blessings, without which they believe they can never be happy.

But the psalmist has a very different fear, based on a completely differ-

---

65. This point will be taken up in ch. 9's exposition of Ps. 130:1.

159

ent desire. His fear is that God will give him precisely what the city of man desires, which is to live in abandonment to the reign of inchoate desire. His fear is that God will cease to comfort him with his rod and staff (Ps. 23), instead allowing his desire to become attached in quiet and peace to earthly things. He knows that, without the divine chastening, his eyes will fall and begin to love the temporal alone. Might it be better for God to overlook a few sins? No, comes the psalmist's reply: to so wish is to define God's punishment as an act of anger, when in fact "God's anger is nothing other than the turning away of his face." God's anger is to let me be me without him, which means that the city of God is constituted in the prayer of these verses, which Augustine summarizes thus: "Whatever my Lord may want to give me, let him take away the whole lot, if he will give me himself."[66]

Again, Augustine explores the metaphor of the church as Christ's tabernacle in the wilderness. The church collectively is God's tent in time, and Christ is the priest who takes us into the holy of holies of God's being. In the words of verse 5: "He will conceal me under the cover of his tent." "This was so that others of [Christ's] members, by believing in him, might be the tabernacle, and he its inner recesses. As the Apostle says, *You are dead, and your life is hidden with Christ in God* (Col. 3:3)" (Exp. 2.10 of Ps. 26, p. 281). The image explicates the prayer of the psalmist for God's presence through the concept of the *totus Christus,* bringing the most chilling words of the Old Testament narratives to bear on this psalm: "[A]nd the glory of the Lord departed from the tabernacle."[67] When the presence of the Lord was with Israel, the rise and fall of their fortunes had a hope and a future. But when the Lord removed his presence from the people, the faithful were afraid even though the hard of heart might be flourishing. This connection sustains the dynamism of Augustine's exegesis: happiness is not just static contemplation of God's beauty; life in all its vicissitudes is oriented by a love and an experience of God's presence with his people. This leads to the prayer of these verses, which Augustine paraphrases thus: "You who have made us also help us; you who have created us, do not leave us in the lurch" (Exp. 2.17 of Ps. 26, p. 285). The ethical implications of this prayer are made clear in verses 10 and 11.

---

66. Augustine, *Expositions*, p. 285. Contemporary Psalms criticism has validated Augustine's point in concluding that "the concept of the hidden face of God is a major one in the literature of the Psalms" (see Ps. 13:2; 27:9; 30:7-8; 44:25; 88:15; 89:47; 102:3; 104:29; also Gen. 4:14; Deut. 31:18; 32:20; Mic. 3:4; Job 13:24). Marvin Tate, *Word Biblical Commentary: Vol. 20, Psalms 51–100* (Waco: Word Books, 1990), p. 197. We have also seen in ch. 5 that Bonhoeffer draws out the hermeneutical implications of this turning away of the divine face.

67. 1 Sam. 4:21; Ezek. 10:18; from the individual, 1 Sam. 16:14.

27:10 כִּי־אָבִי וְאִמִּי עֲזָבוּנִי וַיהוָה יַאַסְפֵנִי

11 הוֹרֵנִי יְהוָה דַּרְכֶּךָ וּנְחֵנִי בְּאֹרַח מִישׁוֹר לְמַעַן שׁוֹרְרָי

26:10 quoniam pater meus et mater mea dereliquerunt me Dominus autem adsumpsit me

11 legem pone mihi Domine in via tua et dirige me in semita recta propter inimicos meos

27:10 If my father and mother forsake me, the LORD will take me up.

11 Teach me your way, O LORD, and lead me on a level path because of my enemies.

Augustine now returns to integrate the accounts of fulfilled individual and communal life that he developed in his exegesis of Psalms 32 and 22. He does this by interpreting the abandoning father and mother with the false loves and false community into which we are born. Who is the father who abandons us? Augustine quotes Jesus in John 8:44: "You are children of your father, the devil." And the mother? She is the false social rationality and ethos of a city called Babylon. But we know another father, says Augustine, God the Father; and we know a new mother, "the heavenly Jerusalem, holy Church, a part of which is on pilgrimage on earth; we have left Babylon behind. *My father and my mother abandoned me.* They no longer have anything to give me, and when they did seem to be giving me something, it was you who were giving it, though I attributed it to them" (Exp. 2.18 of Ps. 26, p. 286).

This is not a suggestion that Christians can somehow escape from contact with Babylon. Augustine's point is that the new life of the Christian is constituted in being given a truth beyond the schematizations of the age. God's turning his face to us is thus the condition for perceiving the lies that alienate us from God. The primal lie, of course, is that we think we must hedge our bets, mix our allegiances in order to ensure a safe and secure life. The futility of this hope, Augustine reminds us, is its reliance on there being intermediate gods. "Take all those who worship Neptune: are they immune from shipwreck? What about all those who scoff at Neptune: does that mean that they never reach harbor? And all those women who worship Juno: do they all give birth successfully? Or do all those who scoff at Juno miscarry?" (Exp. 2.19 of Ps. 26, p. 287).

This is a challenge of continuing relevance to Christians. To translate it into contemporary terms, the love of earthly goods without the love of their giver turns into a fear of losing them. And fear of losing them develops into a social rationality — an ethos. Augustine asks, Do all those who trust in technology live better lives? Do all those with comprehensive insurance coverage avoid disaster? Does ever-increasing investment in medicine stop untimely death? Augustine saw clearly that whole societies are structured around the avoidance of pain, embodying the escape from their primal fears. This fear, he says, is in itself obeisance to other gods, an obeisance based on the lie that threats to self-reliance are best met with more powerful forms of self-reliance. As a result of God's having turned his face and rod toward him, Augustine comes to see that these are the strategies of the blind ones who cope without the presence of God and whose loves are self-devouring. The prayer of the psalmist is to be recovered from those lies, and therefore to be drawn out of Babylon: Let Babylon "always lie to itself, but let it not lie to me" (Exp. 2.20 of Ps. 26, p. 288).

Do not remove your presence from me, the psalmist begs: "Give me a law, but do not take away your mercy" (Exp. 2.20 of Ps. 26, p. 288). My liberation is to have your hand on me, transforming me, revealing my sin, embarrassing me, giving me over to the hands of my oppressors; but to have you with me is my greatest peace, hope, and joy. Ellen Charry rightly concludes: "Augustine was psychologically astute enough to realize that motivation for change requires two insights: one must recognize that one has a problem, and one must not despair of success. The former requires humility, which has little to do with the extreme self-denigration seen in some forms of monasticism and later medieval piety. The latter requires trust, provided by a proper grasp of revelation and doctrine."[68] The psalmist cries out for the law of the goodness of the Lord, which Augustine understands as Christ, whose law is mercy, unlike that of "those who harass me."

This is Augustine's deep account of how the rift is opened up between the common conceptions of the good life in secular thought and the distinctive Christian ethos. The bestowal of God's presence on humanity is the force driving human moral renewal. As humanity is humbly receptive, a journey with God commences in which human patterns of faith and behavior are slowly remade, the society based on fear of material deprivation becoming a society of generosity that never fears want but only the loss of God's loving and chastening attention. The Psalms provide Augustine with a way to speak with proper doctrinal density of Christ's use of Scripture to generate saints with his ethos. If there is a question about the "use" of Scripture in Christian ethics, Augustine believes it to be how *Christ* uses it to shape us.

---

68. Ellen Charry, *By the Renewing of Your Minds: The Pastoral Function of Doctrine* (Oxford: Oxford University Press, 1997), p. 139.

Review

The following themes have emerged as we have listened to Augustine sing the Psalms. The details of his exegesis supply us with a generous range of practical hints about how the Bible can be read as one book. He has displayed a sophisticated understanding of Scripture within God's work in the world. When he looks at the Psalms, he sees evidence that God has successfully revealed himself, by which he means that he has brought to life the sound of human praise. Furthermore, Augustine has provided a suggestive account of the Psalms as standing divine invitations to enter that community of praise. This invitation is only part of their role in Christian regeneration. Augustine found in Psalm 32 a description of how the singing of God's praises orients the hopes and confessions that shape embodied practice. In his exegesis of Psalm 22, Augustine shows how this vision of the blessed life shapes the Christian understanding of the church, which is conceived not as a safe haven from the world but as the focal point of a praising people caught up in Christ's service to the world. The excursus on Taylor has made clear the moral resources that such a full-bodied description of moral ontology provides in a contemporary context. A description of the cursed and blessed life, of wasted and meaningful action, when teamed with a detailed description of the social nature of faith, provides the background from which we can develop the wide range of evaluative criteria necessary for moral deliberation about practical questions. Moral deliberation is always something that happens in a church that is not yet at its destination, a pilgrim church,[69] a *civitas peregrina* that cannot yet claim to know itself fully.[70]

At a deeper level, three basic themes emerge. First, Augustine accords a central role in the generation of the Christian ethos to the human address to God and God's reciprocal, or antecedent, attention. This leads to an ethos of salvific confession. Augustine understands his sermons to be Psalms commentaries that both call the congregation to confession and praise and train them in it. Second, this means that the Psalms facilitate our participation in Christ's speaking through his church. Despite moments of using an exegetical method that views the text "from above," we have seen that Augustine regularly emphasizes that theology and exegesis are always done from *within* the dynamics of God's working in the world. The Psalms uniquely encourage thinking from within the flow of God's work in speaking from the point of

---

69. *Etiam ista peregrina.* Augustine, *City of God,* Book XVIII.1.

70. For an explanation of this term and its centrality in Augustine's thought, see Peter Brown, *Augustine: A Biography* (London: Faber and Faber, 1975), ch. 27.

view of the participant in Christ's story. And finally, the Psalms represent a context for discovering the Christian form of life. What I discover is that my true being, or the truth of my being, constitutes me from the outside. The Psalms indicate the source and mechanics of this external constitution because they seek, from within the redemptive or soteriological moment, the God who is present to and in his people.

CHAPTER 7

Luther's Ethos of Consoling Doxology

Yearning for the Presence of God

Distinguishing Augustine and Luther

In turning from Augustine to Luther, we can immediately perceive the differences in their exegetical styles. Augustine builds up long and complex narrative arcs that situate and thus explicate large chunks of the Psalms. Luther's theological points grow from concentrated analyses of Hebrew etymologies, single verses and phrases. This is partly because Augustine did much of his exegesis in the pulpit; Luther's commentaries, on the other hand, began in the lecture hall or at the writing desk. But behind this rather superficial difference, one soon learns that their exegetical toolboxes are simply different, and this directly affects how they undertake interpretation of Scripture.

In one sense, this divergence is a surprise, given the regularity with which Luther explicitly draws on or debates with Augustine's exegesis. But we will see that the difference in exegetical approaches is paralleled by similar divergences in their ethical frameworks. Augustine follows ancient precedent in framing ethics as a search for and desire for the good life. Luther is less interested in developing an ontological account; instead, he focuses on an existential question: How does God become and remain present to me? The preoccupation of antique conceptions of ethics with individual flourishing is displaced in Luther by an inquiry into what it means to live with God, in which the dramatics of fellowship are emphasized. Luther's inquiry does include the ontological question "What does Christ do in the world?" But his inquiry is mainly interested in asking "What is God's will?" Luther's emphasis is on transformation into the form of Christ, understood in terms of

Nachfolge, the following of — or the discipleship by — a God who is leading in time. It is an inquiry with rather different contours than one focused on defining justice or fulfillment in terms of movement toward an essentially fixed *telos.*

In sum, Augustine's is a discursive ethic of knowing and speaking *about* God; Luther's is a dialogical ethic of hearing and speaking *with* God. This means that Luther is not looking for a physician, as Augustine is, to heal the wounds of sin, but (for a savior who leads back those who are lost), blinded by sin.[1] We have seen how Augustine undermines the antique idea of fulfillment by saying that (1) fulfillment is God's gift, and (2) it is related to God's drawing humans into a journey consummated beyond this life. But Augustine's reconfiguration of the ancient discourse is of a different order than Luther's wholesale resistance to it.

Luther continues Augustine's undermining of ethics as a discourse about the individual's fulfillment by taking as his subject of inquiry God and humanity together. For Luther, no human "self" exists outside of this pair. This leads him to eschew ethics as a quest for the fulfilled life in favor of ethics as a conception of dwelling in God's house in which the remaking of our affections plays a central role. Because Augustine's central category is humanity's *telos,* he often uses the language of pointing or signifying, and his journey metaphor emphasizes a time-structured conceptual framework. Luther's concern is not historical development but how Scripture alerts us to the dynamic of faith in all times and places. Becoming alert to this dynamic facilitates faith's correctly discerning what happens next in the divine working. Luther frames his discussion to highlight the constant drama entailed in keeping our eyes on Christ alone, while Augustine emphasizes Christ's protological character as the standard who reveals our defects so that we might be conformed to him.

In Luther the Augustinian definition of love via teleology is replaced by

---

1. It is clear, however, that this divergence rests on the young Augustinian monk having learned well many of the central themes we saw in the last chapter, including this emphasis on the salvific necessity of God's face shining on us. Compare the formulation of this comment to Augustine's interpretation of Psalm 27: "Indeed, he wants to arouse in us a desire for him, so that we may continue to cry out to him; he wants us to cry out to him in order that he may hear and answer us. He wants to hear us in order that he may save us, and thus he teaches us to distrust ourselves and put our confidence in him. And what he says is really true: 'I kill and I make alive' [Deut. 32:39], which means that here the words, 'woke him,' mean our deliverance." Luther, "Sermon on the Fourth Sunday after the Epiphany, Matt. 8:23-27, February 1, 1517," in *Luther's Works, Vol. 51, Sermons I, Psalms 1-75,* ed. and trans. John Doberstein (Philadelphia: Fortress, 1959), pp. 24-25.

a new polarity between *Anfechtung* ("testing") and *Trost* ("comfort"), with its close etymological associations with "trust." That we need comfort is Luther's way of saying that, for love to be rightly directed, we need "God with us." Humans are in need of consolation, not because they have difficult experiences, but because they have lost God and thus no longer know how to love aright. *Doxology* is the point where the lost meet God, suggests Luther, because doxology cries for and dares to enter God's presence. The Psalms are God's way of opening doxology to us, and thus they play a crucial role in Christian ethics: they are God's offer of himself to us, and the promise and form for our renewal. The new humanity has been renewed in order that they may be entirely given over to good works.

Luther: Theologian of the Psalms

One is left with the impression that, for all of Luther's admiration for and dependence on the exegesis of Augustine, his hermeneutics and ethics are structurally quite different. Yet the differences should not obscure the fact that Augustine and Luther belong together as theologians whose taproots formed in their struggles to interpret the Psalms. Scholarly opinion is largely agreed that "it was by studying and meditating on the Book of the Psalms that Luther was impelled to his remarkable discovery of justification: his movement was from the Psalms to Romans, Galatians and Hebrews, not vice versa."[2] Just as the challenge of interpreting the Psalms drove Augustine to develop his theory of the ontological relationship between Christ and his church, so Luther's struggles to interpret the Psalms yielded a revolution in his reading of the Old Testament. This led, among other insights, to new ideas about the theological import of the Old Testament's historical sense.[3] This recovery, we shall see,

2. Barth, *Church Dogmatics*, IV.1, ed. G. W. Bromiley and T. F. Torrance, trans. G. W. Bromiley (Edinburgh: T&T Clark, 1997), p. 605. Not that the point is without debate. For a more recent restatement of the point, see Lohse's cautious suggestion that Luther's breakthrough may have come as early as the fall of 1514 during his first Psalms lecture cycle. Luther's explanation of the righteousness of God in Psalm 71 finds a striking parallel in his own well-known 1545 account of this discovery. Bernhard Lohse, *Martin Luther's Theology: Its Historical and Systematic Development*, trans. Roy A. Harrisville (Edinburgh: T&T Clark, 1999), pp. 91-94. Cf. Luther, "Psalm Seventy-Two," in *Luther's Works, Vol. 10, First Lectures on the Psalms I, Psalms 1–75*, ed. Hinton Oswald (St. Louis: Concordia Publishing House, 1974), the comment on v. 19, pp. 401-2; see also the account of his "tower experience" in *Luther's Works, Vol. 54, Table Talk*, ed. and trans. Theodore Tappert (Philadelphia: Fortress, 1967), pp. 193-94.

3. In a characteristic formulation, Luther writes, "Faith must be built up on the basis of history, and we ought to stay with it alone and not so easily slip into allegories, unless by way of

rested on a renewed appreciation of the role that hope learned from Scripture plays in the shaping of the Christian life. Given the centrality of the Psalms in Luther's intellectual journey, the Lutheran theologian Oswald Bayer can conclude: "Luther's use of the Psalter is the key in general to the understanding of his use of language, his linguistic power, as well as his experience of his world and life."[4]

Luther chose the Psalms for his first lectures when he was a professor of Bible between 1513 and 1515. Several years later he began a second and much more detailed set of lectures on the Psalms. This increasing depth of investigation and understanding of the Psalms continued throughout his life, sustained by his constant turning to them as the basis for sermons, letters of exhortation, and edification. Most importantly, his translation of the Psalms deepened and improved over time in a truly remarkable way.[5] The introduction to the published version of his second set of Psalms lectures summarizes and explains his approach to the Psalms and so will serve to introduce us to his hermeneutics. Here he explains that his hermeneutics of the Psalter is based on the first psalm, which he understood as a summary of the whole Psalter. Four points frame his Psalms exegesis. The first is drawn directly from Psalm 1: Scripture is an indispensable part of our learning of the divine. The point rests on a sharp contrast between human and divine thought. He censures his fellow theologians who behave as though "Christ had said to Peter: 'command, order, teach' rather than (John 21:17): 'Feed my sheep'! This means: Bring out that by which they are fed. And they are fed only by the

---

metaphor we apply them to other things in accordance with the method of faith." *Luther's Works, Vol. 16, Lectures on Isaiah*, ed. Jaroslav Pelikan (St. Louis: Concordia, 1969), p. 327. Cf. Pelikan, *Luther's Works: Companion Volume: Luther the Expositor: Introduction to the Reformer's Exegetical Writings* (St. Louis: Concordia, 1959), ch. 5; see also Samuel James Preuss, *From Shadow to Promise: Old Testament Interpretation from Augustine to the Young Luther* (Eugene, OR: Wipf and Stock, 1999), chs. XIV–XV.

4. Oswald Bayer, "Luther as an Interpreter of Holy Scripture," in Donald McKim, ed., *The Cambridge Companion to Luther* (Cambridge: Cambridge University Press, 2003), p. 80.

5. Heinz Bluhm's closely researched study of Luther's biblical translation concludes: "Of all the books of the Bible, of the Old Testament at any rate, the Psalter was closest to his heart.... On no other part of the Bible did he lavish so much time, energy and sheer love. While it is perfectly true that he kept revising the Bible as a whole to the end of his all-too-short life, the Psalter was singled out for special attention and received two major revisions after the first edition of 1524. The 1528 revision moves on the same high level as the notable 1530 revision of the New Testament. But the third revision of the Psalter of 1531 is unique, utterly unique.... The consummate skill here demonstrated by Luther is without parallel in the long and distinguished history of the translation of the Bible into other tongues." Heinz Bluhm, *Martin Luther: Creative Translator* (St. Louis: Concordia, 1965), xi-xii.

Word of God, not by the opinions and traditions of men."[6] For Luther, this is no academic point-scoring, but a plea to cherish Scripture as the words that feed the Christian community.

Second, this leads him to admit that he cannot possibly have fully understood Scripture. We will see in more detail that Luther believes that the desire for comprehensiveness is futile because, on the one hand, the Psalms are the prayers of believers on a journey into God's infinite wisdom, and, on the other, because the search for accuracy assumes some third measure by which interpretations might be judged. Therefore, says Luther, "I must openly admit that I do not know whether I have the accurate interpretation of the psalms or not" (p. 285), a posture he maintained for the rest of his career. Despite his becoming ever more sure of his material, he claims only the certainty of familiarity, not comprehensiveness.[7] He wants to affirm that he has not learned all he can from Scripture, yet he does not doubt that his interpretations are orthodox. Understanding how this assurance of orthodoxy squares with this disavowal of "accuracy" and comprehensiveness will be a central concern of this chapter.

Happily, Luther's third point immediately gives a theological hint about how he understands this open-ended form of interpretation to work.

> The Spirit reserves much for Himself, so that we may always remain His pupils. There is much that He reveals only to lure us on, much that He gives only to stir us up. And, as Augustine has put it so clearly, if no human being has ever spoken in such a way that everyone understood him in all particulars, how much more is it true that the Holy Spirit alone has an understanding of all His own words! . . . I know that a person would be guilty of the most shameless boldness if he dared claim that he had understood even one book of the Scriptures in all its parts. In fact, who would even dare to assert that anyone has completely understood one single psalm? Our *life is one of beginning and of growth, not one of consummation.* That person is better who has come closer to the Spirit. (pp. 284-85; italics added)

This tight linkage of pneumatological, soteriological, and hermeneutical presuppositions will be teased out in the course of this chapter, most clearly in Luther's exegesis of Psalm 8.

---

6. Luther, "Psalms 1 and 2 from Works on the First Twenty-two Psalms, 1519 to 1521: A Composite Translation," in *Luther's Works, Vol. 14, Selected Psalms III*, ed. Jaroslav Pelikan (St. Louis: Concordia, 1958), pp. 283-84 (page references to this work hereafter cited parenthetically in text).

7. "There is no book in the Bible to which I have devoted as much labor as to the Psalter." *Luther's Works, Vol. 14*, p. 285.

That Luther understands believers to be praying and interpreting the Psalms from within the processes of transformation into the form of Christ[8] will be shown to have a wide range of important implications for ethical theory. What I take to be the most important of those implications shapes my approach in chapter 9: the church must interpret Scripture anew in each age. "I see some things that blessed Augustine did not see; on the other hand, I know that others will see many things that I do not see. What recourse do we have but to be of mutual help to one another and to forgive those who fall, since we ourselves have already fallen or are about to fall?" (p. 285). The essential point is that Luther addresses himself not to those who go to Scripture wishing it to yield comprehensive or accurate knowledge, but to those seeking to follow Christ. "There are degrees of living and working; then why not of understanding? The apostle says (2 Cor. 3:18) that we are being changed from one degree of clarity to another. To speak of the matter at hand, then, I am serving only those who do not know any of this and would like to" (pp. 285-86).

Luther's final introductory point indicates how the methodological fruitfulness of his exegesis of the Psalms is grounded in an observation about the region of life exposed in the Psalms genre. In all other biblical books, the narrator, as narrator, must assume a God's-eye view of events in order to tell us about the deeds of the saints. But Christian ethics cannot be a mimicking of the saints' deeds. What is required is a renewal of the heart, the affective dimension of human life, about which Luther concludes: "I would rather hear what a saint says than see the deeds he does, [and] would far rather see his heart, and the treasure in his soul, than hear his words. And this the Psalter gives us most abundantly concerning the saints. . . . There you look into the hearts of all the saints, as into fair and pleasant gardens, yes, as into heaven itself."[9]

Because the Psalms are words in the first person, they facilitate the individual's entry into God's presence, says Luther.

> In the other books we are taught by both precept and example what we ought to do. This book not only teaches but also gives the *means and method* by which we may keep the precept and follow the example. For it is not by our striving that we fulfill the Law of God or imitate Christ. But we are to pray and wish that we may fulfill it and imitate Him; when we do, we

8. See Luther, "Disputation concerning Man," in *Luther's Works, Vol. 34, Career of the Reformer IV,* ed. Lewis Spitz (St. Louis: Concordia, 1958), pp. 133-44.

9. Luther, "Preface to the Psalter, 1545 (1528)," in *Luther's Works, Vol. 35, Word and Sacrament I,* ed. Theodore Bachmann (Philadelphia: Muhlenberg Press, 1960), p. 255.

are to praise and give thanks. And what is the Psalter but prayer and praise to God, that is, a book of hymns? (p. 286; italics added)

The Psalms embody the love of God, whose Spirit is the "Father of orphans and the Teacher of the ignorant" (Rom. 8:26), who helps us to pray, to enjoy God, despite our weakness, our lack of desire for God and for good works, and our broken imagination. "As a teacher will compose letters or little speeches for his pupils to write to their parents, so by this book He prepares both the *language and the mood* in which we should address the Heavenly Father and pray for that which the other books have taught us to do and to imitate" (p. 286; italics added).[10]

To develop these points, we will look at three other psalms. Luther's exegesis of Psalm 1 explains how the performance of the Psalms reveals whether our faith is in ourselves or in God. Building on this distinction, Luther draws from Psalm 8 an account of the activity of praise as an action through which we discover our place in God's ongoing work. Only in praise are we given an identity and thus a framework for moral judgments. Finally, Luther's exegesis of Psalm 111 shows how he understands praise to be the purpose of the church, through which God builds humanity into a complex and discriminating community by giving new hearts. But before looking in detail at these three psalms, we will look briefly at a few verses that, Luther believes, teach how the Psalms should be read.

Luther often referred to Psalm 118 as his "own beloved psalm";[11] and verse 17 became his personal motto: "I shall not die, but live and recount the deeds of the Lord."[12] This leads to a larger claim in his 1529 treatise on Psalm

10. We have seen in ch. 5 that these ideas shaped Bonhoeffer's exegesis, and might have traced their sources in the tradition that preceded Luther. One such study concludes about the points made in this paragraph that "Luther thus has the same sensibility as did Athanasius twelve centuries earlier." William Holladay, *The Psalms through Three Thousand Years: Prayerbook of a Cloud of Witnesses* (Minneapolis: Fortress, 1996), p. 194.

11. Luther, "Psalm 118," in *Luther's Works, Vol. 14,* trans. George Beto, p. 45.

12. Luther's choice of this passage was perhaps inspired by Wycliffe's utterance of these verses as his last words, though his own last words (and those of Melanchthon) were those of Jan Hus and Jerome of Prague, Psalm 31:6: "Into thy hands I commend my spirit." Rowland Prothero, *The Psalms in Human Life* (London: John Murray, 1909), pp. 121-22.

As a case study of Luther's claim that he continually understood more of the Psalms and in different ways, it is interesting to observe that he does not even comment on these verses in his first lecture series on the Psalms (Luther, "Psalm One Hundred Eighteen," in *Luther's Works, Vol. 11, First Lectures on the Psalms II,* ed. Hinton Oswald [St. Louis: Concordia, 1976], pp. 410-13). Though the early influence of verse 16 is evident in his explanation of the 95 Theses (Luther, "Explanations of the Ninety-Five Theses or Explanations of the Disputation concerning the Value of Indulgences," in *Luther's Works, Vol. 31, Career of the Reformer I,* ed. Harold Grim [Phil-

118: that verses 15-18 comprise a unit of Scripture that is incapable of being read; it can only be sung — or otherwise it must be rejected.

Psalm 118: Talking to God as Learning His Language

118:15   קוֹל רִנָּה וִישׁוּעָה בְּאָהֳלֵי צַדִּיקִים יְמִין יְהוָה עֹשָׂה חָיִל
16   יְמִין יְהוָה רוֹמֵמָה יְמִין יְהוָה עֹשָׂה חָיִל
17   לֹא אָמוּת כִּי־אֶחְיֶה וַאֲסַפֵּר מַעֲשֵׂי יָהּ
18   יַסֹּר יִסְּרַנִּי יָּהּ וְלַמָּוֶת לֹא נְתָנָנִי

118:15   Man singt mit Freuden vom Sieg in den Hütten der Gerechten: "Die Rechte des HEERN behält den Sieg;
16   die Rechte des HEERN ist erhöht; die Rechte des HEERN behält den Sieg!"
17   Ich werde nicht sterben, sondern leben und des HEERN Werke verkündigen.
18   Der HEER züchtigt mich wohl; aber er gibt mich dem Tode nicht.

118:15   Shouts of joy and victory resound[13] in the tents of the righteous:
     "The right hand of the LORD does valiantly;
16   the right hand of the LORD is exalted;
     the right hand of the LORD does valiantly."
17   I shall not die, but I shall live,
     and recount the deeds of the LORD.
18   The LORD has punished me severely,
     but he did not give me over to death.

Luther's quite Augustinian basic claim is that these verses put us in the position of praising either ourselves or God; there is no middle position between the two. The claim rests on a proto-Wittgensteinian concept of the "happy performance," in which our understanding of the function of words begins not with metaphysical realities (such as atoms, ideal forms, or transcendentals) nor subjective states of consciousness (hunches, sensations, mental representations) but with beings in relationship, beings who share basic forms of life *(Lebensformen)*.[14] Beginning from such relationships, words are not un-

---

adelphia: Fortress, 1957], p. 243), he does not regularly use these favorite verses, Ps. 118:15-18, in his writings, nor does he ever "apply" or make ethical "use" of them. They crystallize a broader sense of the essence of his own experience of faith.

     13. I take this phrase from the NIV translation, as it captures the ring of Luther's German better than the more literal NRSV.

     14. Ludwig Wittgenstein, *Philosophical Investigations*, trans. G. E. M. Anscombe (Oxford: Basil Blackwell, 1968), pp. 225-26. For an excellent discussion of this idea and its implications,

derstood as "innately" meaning anything; they "mean" and "refer" in the context of communicative relationships. The meanings of words are thus defined in their usage by communities. When I speak, it is to take up words as packets of this communal meaning in order to reformulate my various relationships with some end in mind. Thus understood, the Psalms' meaning is not reducible to conceptual "content," though they do refer to reality. Their main role is in calling forth performances that cohere with them, and thus they function as condensed versions of the relationships out of which they were composed. As such, they are language constellations oriented by a formed dialogue and, if taken up, lead back into that same dialogue.[15] The psalm verses under discussion can thus be understood as conveying to us the relationship with God out of which they were born as they guide us into a similar relationship.

These verses, says Luther, train us to rely on God. Those who rely on human power perform them "unhappily," that is, in ways that do not seek to discover the form of communal life they demand, instead, cosmetically pasting them onto an unregenerate form of life. When such people take up the words "the right hand of the LORD is exalted," the connotative force of their words and works yields the meaning, "The right hand of man does valiantly; the right hand of princes is exalted."[16] Elsewhere, Luther is explicit that two kinds of false singing are possible. One is a singing that is built on the exchange mentality: these singers "will not praise him unless he does good to them." The more dangerous false singing, however, is the anti-song just paraphrased, the praise of self that takes the form of divine praise.[17]

According to Luther's account, any claim that a psalm has been misunderstood rests on a complex semantic judgment. This insight was to deeply mark modern philosophy. "Luther said that theology is the grammar of the word 'God,'" Wittgenstein famously wrote, continuing: "I interpret this to mean that an investigation of the word would be a grammatical one. For example, people might dispute about how many arms God had, and someone might enter the dispute by denying that one could talk about arms of God. This would throw light on the use of the word. What is ridiculous or blasphe-

---

see Fergus Kerr, *Theology after Wittgenstein* (Oxford: Basil Blackwell, 1986), especially pp. 69-76; see also Oswald Bayer, *Promissio: Geschichte der reformatorischen Wende in Luthers Theologie* (Göttingen: Vandenhoeck, 1971).

15. Wittgenstein, *Philosophical Investigations,* pp. 503-4.

16. Luther, "Psalm 118," p. 8 (page references to this work hereafter cited parenthetically in text).

17. Luther, "The Magnificat," in *Luther's Works, Vol. 21, The Sermon on the Mount (Sermons) and The Magnificat,* ed. Jaroslav Pelikan, trans. A. T. W. Steinheuser (St. Louis: Concordia, 1956), pp. 307-8.

mous also shows the grammar of the word."[18] Wittgenstein had picked up Luther's suggestion that Scripture reveals the grammar of the divine life, making theology a communal discussion about the proper interpretation of Scripture. Thus understood, the words of the Psalms do not force communal agreement automatically, by recitation, but provide access to and sustain a communal life of faith that is shaped by them.[19]

Luther has set up an important critical principle by defining wickedness as nonconforming psalm performance. In so doing he departs from the Augustinian hamartiology so prominent in the West, in which sin is the deprivation of the good. For Luther, sin is made up of concrete but aberrant responses to God's gifts, a filled-out and personified antidoxology. Conversely, wherever the saints gather, they sing these verses rightly in magnifying the "right hand of the LORD." Singing does not transform us in a mechanical way that is suggested by narrative theology or the Bulgarian proverb: "Who sings does not think evil." Singing is thus not defined in familiar terms but becomes a way of indicating how a certain way of speaking marks the Christian ethos. "Under 'singing,'" says Luther,

> I include not only making melody or shouting but also every sermon or public confession by which God's work, counsel, grace, help, comfort, victory, and salvation are glorified before the world. . . . As verse fourteen puts it: 'The Lord is my Strength and my Song; He has become my Salvation.' God wants to be praised, glorified, honored, and confessed by us in His works and wonders. Faith does this, for faith cannot be silent but must say and teach what it believes and knows about God, to the glory of God and the instruction of man, as Ps. 116:10 says: 'I believed, therefore have I spoken.' ("Psalm 118," p. 81)

---

18. Wittgenstein, *Wittgenstein's Lectures, Cambridge 1930-1932*, ed. Desmond Lee (Oxford: Basil Blackwell, 1980), p. 32. Elsewhere he says: "Grammar tells what kind of object anything is (Theology as grammar)." Wittgenstein, *Philosophical Investigations*, p. 373. Cf. Karl Barth, *Church Dogmatics*, I.1, ed. G. W. Bromiley and T. F. Torrance, trans. G. W. Bromiley (Edinburgh: T&T Clark, 1995), p. 86: "In the raw material of dogmatics, the first object is a series of expressions which, more or less constantly and emphatically, usually make up the spoken matter of proclamation in the whole church. . . . But here, as everywhere, these expressions acquire their meaning from the associations and contexts in which they are used."

19. Meaning is not in our *internal* state, but in our *communal interactions*, Wittgenstein explains. "Does it make sense to ask 'How do you know that you believe?' — and is the answer; 'I know it by introspection'?" "In some cases it will be possible to say some such thing, in most not. It makes sense to ask: 'Do I really love her, or am I only pretending to myself?' and the process of introspection is the calling up of memories; of imagined possible situations, and of the feeling that one would have if. . . ." Wittgenstein, *Philosophical Investigations*, p. 587.

Faith in human works produces and is produced by antidoxology; those caught up in God's work are made into those who are being taught to praise God in all things.

For praise to be congruent with the words sung, Luther continues, we must define the content that is praised with the phrase "right hand of the Lord." Christ himself is supremely this "right hand" because "the stone which the builders rejected has become the chief cornerstone" (Ps. 118:22).[20] This rejection by the world of God's mighty work of redemption is most visible at the point when God's conflict with death is at its final extreme: on the cross. "When the world hears, then, that its highest gifts are disapproved by the Gospel and that only this King is commended, it is not only offended, but even prepares weapons and strives with all its might to vindicate its own gifts against this affront. This is the occasion for the bitterest conflicts; thus the world and this King attack each other with hostile hearts."[21]

The good and bad performance of these verses from the Psalms is ultimately defined by referring to the conflict of the cross, where the deep grammar of God's redemption of humans is exposed. When Christians say that the right hand of the Lord is exalted, concludes Luther, they can mean only that Christ is exalted, in whom their own merits and eternal reward are found. Luther bases this interpretation of "the Lord's right hand" on 1 Corinthians 15:55-57 and Isaiah 9:4, concluding that God's power is first Christ, and as such the merits and rewards of those who participate in his life.[22]

20. Luther, "Psalm 118," p. 83. Some New Testament scholars concur in showing how various textual clues indicate that the writers of the New Testament understood this passage to speak of Jesus (cf. Acts 4:11). One of the most obvious is that the idiomatic Greek construction of verse 51 of the Magnificat (Luke 1: "He has shown strength with his arm; he has scattered the proud in the thoughts of their hearts") is clearly indebted to the Hebrew formulation of Ps. 118:15. See John Nolland, *Word Biblical Commentary, Luke 1–9:20*, vol. 35a (Dallas: Word Books, 1989), p. 71.

21. Luther, *Luther's Works, Vol. 22, Sermons on the Gospel of St. John, Chapters 1–4*, ed. Jaroslav Pelikan (St. Louis: Concordia, 1957), p. 62.

22. "The right hand is Christ, the Son of God, as Ps. 118:16 says: 'The right hand of the Lord has made strength,' for the Son of God is the strength, power, and wisdom of God, 1 Cor. 1:24, 30. Second, the right hand of God is the grace of faithfulness or work of God. Thus blessed Augustine correctly says by way of explanation that the right hand means God's propitiation and favor, according to Ps. 45:4: 'Thy right hand shall conduct Thee wonderfully.' The left hand, however, is God's rule or freely given grace, which is common to all. Third, the right hand is the awarding of glory in the future, as Matt. 25:33-34 says, 'He will place these on His right hand and those on His left, and then He will say, etc.' Therefore the right hand is, first, Christ; second, it is the merit of Christians, and third, it is their reward." Luther, "Psalm Seventeen," in *Luther's Works, Vol. 10*, p. 111. This definition of the right hand of God he develops in more detail in the later exposition of Psalm 118 (Luther, "Psalm 118," pp. 81-84), but for purposes of brevity I have used this earlier statement.

Reading Luther with Wittgenstein suggests that the meaning of Psalm 118:15-18 falls to pieces if severed from its glad performance as a song of Christ's victory. At the same time, the communitarian referent of happy performance is firmly set within the vertically oriented experience of divine deliverance that those songs describe. Luther correctly observes that the psalmists explain the genesis of their praise as the experience of rescue.[23] As a result, Luther considers 1 Peter 2:9 neither prescription nor command, but a description of conversion as the experience of rescue from death: "That you may declare the wonderful deeds of Him who has called you out of darkness into His marvelous light." This description of the experience of God is also an invitation, "For God does these wonders which are prefigured in the Red Sea to anyone."[24]

In this emphasis on the primacy of God's working, Luther goes far beyond Wittgenstein and the communitarians, who do not have the resources to describe how God generates the Christian ethos: praise as an epiphenomenon of human experience is inadequate to explain the texts themselves, which demand to be understood as emerging from the *experience* of God's work.[25] Thus it is not accidental that the form of the Psalms — poetry — is related to their content — praise. The poetic form (with its inherent linkage with music) expresses an immediacy before God via the text that is at root not critical and hence is destroyed by critical distance. This is similar to the understanding of poetry for which Paul Ricoeur is well known: "My deepest conviction is that poetic language alone restores to us that participation — in or belonging — to an order of things which precedes our capacity to oppose ourselves to things taken as objects opposed to a subject."[26] The point may also be illus-

---

23. Luther writes: "Ps. 51:13, 14, 15: 'I will teach transgressors Thy ways. . . . My tongue will sing aloud of Thy righteousness. . . . And my mouth will show forth Thy praise.' In Ps. 40, 'He brought me out of the pit, etc.' (v. 2), is followed by 'I have proclaimed Thy righteousness' (v. 9), and again, 'Thou hast made Thy wonderful works many, O Lord, my God.' Ps. 66:16: 'Come and see, all you who fear God, and I will tell you what great things He has done for my soul.' Ps. 46:8: 'Come and behold the works of the Lord, what wonders He has done.' Ps. 118:17: 'I shall not die but live and tell all His wonderful works.' Ps. 107:2: 'Let the redeemed of the Lord now say, etc.' Ps. 9:1, 4: 'I will tell of all Thy wonderful works. . . . For Thou hast maintained my judgment and my cause.'" Luther, "Psalm Seventeen," pp. 36-37.

24. Luther, "Psalm Seventeen," p. 37.

25. "How much more will such a lively inclination be awakened in us when we experience the favor of God, which is exceeding great in his works. All words and thoughts fail us, and our whole life and soul must be set in motion, as though all that lived within us wanted to break forth into praise and singing." Luther, "The Magnificat," p. 307. It is important to note that Luther says here that many, but not all, psalms originate in this way (p. 321).

26. Paul Ricoeur, "Toward a Hermeneutic of the Idea of Revelation," in Lewis S. Mudge, ed., *Essays on Biblical Interpretation* (Philadelphia: Fortress, 1980), p. 101.

trated by asking why Bonhoeffer, at the end of his life, wrote poetry. It is only in the last stages of his imprisonment, when death was imminent, that Bonhoeffer took up that genre of writing. Eberhard Bethge suggests — correctly, I think — that only poetry could achieve the combination of intimacy and decorum demanded by this relationship and the terrible demands being placed on it.[27] Luther's suggestion is that God has provided humans with poems that make intimate speaking with him possible in the dark and confined places, as well as in the green pastures of this life.

Giving architectonic roles to the metaphors of "singing" and "faith as a path" makes one's critical relationship to Scripture more complex and resituates it in establishing a theologically construed critical relationship to language itself. If God is a speaking God, then we are always in the midst of learning from him what our grammar is about. Language is not simply "there," but we are learning what it means, and thus what it is, by listening in the form of prayer. Language is the place God has given so that he can use it to claim us. In prayer and praise we take up God's words to expose our language and lives to divine remaking. Thus prayer is the dialogical relationship with God in which the regeneration of human life originates and is sustained.[28]

Because the theological location of prayer and praise is before God with the community of prayer, a togetherness is created through a multifaceted practice that we can describe (as Luther himself does not explicitly do) as the redemptive process. In Luther's final analysis, these verses' main function is to give access to an eschatologically open and thus dynamic state of walking with God. Luther calls this state of openness the "art of forgetting the self." "We must keep learning this lesson as long as we live, even as all the saints before us, with us, and after us must do." This tutelage

> works like this: I am nothing. The Lord is all my strength, as stated above. I am stripped of everything, of myself and all that is mine. I can say: 'Devil, what are you fighting? If you try to denounce my good works and my holiness before God, why, I have none. My strength is not my own; the Lord is my Strength. You can't squeeze blood out of a turnip! If you try to prosecute my sins, I have none of those either. Here is God's strength — prosecute it until you have had enough. I know absolutely nothing about either sins or holiness in me. I know nothing whatever except God's power in me.' ("Psalm 118," p. 85)

27. Dietrich Bonhoeffer, *Letters and Papers from Prison*, enlarged edition, ed. Eberhard Bethge (London: SCM Press, 1971), p. 386.

28. Gerhard Sauter, "Reden von Gott im Gebet," in Gerhard Caspar, ed., *Gott nennen: Phänomenologische Zugänge* (Freiburg im Breisgau: Alber Verlag, 1981), pp. 219-42.

To such a song of faith, "What can the devil do when he finds a soul so naked that it can respond neither to sin nor to holiness?" ("Psalm 118," p. 85).

Luther understands this art of forgetting the self through an active and verbal relationship to Scripture, God, and other humans to be the way that we embrace Christ's victory, won by God's right hand. Of verse 17, Luther says:

> We should recognize this verse as a masterpiece. How mightily the psalmist banishes death out of sight! He will know nothing of dying and sin. At the same time he visualizes life most vividly and will hear of nothing but life. But whoever will not see death, lives forever, as Christ says: 'If anyone keeps My Word, he will never see death' (John 8:51). He so immerses himself in life that death is swallowed up by life (1 Cor. 15:55) and disappears completely, because he clings with a firm faith to the right hand of God. Thus all the saints have sung this verse and will continue to sing it to the end. ("Psalm 118," p. 87)

Singing about God's power is thus the proper creaturely response to the experience of God's salvation and thus the salvation itself, the earthly form of eternal life. This means that prayer begins with the acknowledgment that we are unprepared to pray. Faith must flee to Christ's prayer and allow Christ to pray through it as it clings to God, as he has given himself in the content of the church's prayers. We can and must prepare to pray by learning how to begin, but this beginning is not by way of method, but by way of this particular performative clinging. We learn the grammar of life with God by taking these poems on our lips before God; that is, we learn this language by using it.[29]

A first result of our attention to Luther's exegesis of the Psalms is the discovery that, for him, faith is the central category of the Christian life — the famous *sola fide*. Prayer is the root activity of such faith: "Faith in [God's] promise is nothing other than prayer,"[30] a claim summarizing the tight set of conceptual connections just outlined. Faith is the effect of God's word and promise entering the heart, making it firm and certain. This certainty is not immobile, but active: "It bursts into action . . . impels him to compose beautiful and sweet psalms and to sing lovely and joyous songs, both to praise and to thank God in his happiness and to serve his fellowmen by stimulating and teaching them."[31] Because faith is trust in God's word and promise, its con-

---

29. This point is wonderfully and simply put in Luther's explanation to his barber about how to pray. Martin Luther, "A Simple Way to Pray," in *Luther's Works, Vol. 43, Devotional Writings II*, ed. Gustav Wiencke (Philadelphia: Fortress, 1968), pp. 193-211.

30. Bayer, "Luther as an Interpreter," p. 77.

31. Luther, "Treatise on the Last Words of David," in *Luther's Works, vol. 15: Notes on Eccle-*

stituent component is the acknowledgment that Christ is Lord, the most basic form of talking to God. All other Christian action takes place within this conversation, altering its shape in making it a response of appreciation for God's action. *Sola fide* means "let all your thinking and action be infiltrated by the truth that the crucified and resurrected Christ is still working and Lord of all things." The behavior this creates is no fixed aptitude or *habitus*, but a conversation, a "spirit that falls and rises."[32]

The Psalter is not superior to the rest of Scripture, but it is unique in being wholly devoted to teaching us this conversational faith. In beginning here, we also shift the methodological location of Christian ethics. Rather than being another discipline under the master discipline of hermeneutics or theology, it is redefined as reflection on the activity of praise and our life's coherence with it. The Psalter channels faith into a life of exploration of the divine bounty, in a world that praises its own glory and fights for what it sees as scarce resources to be secured by human efforts.

Psalm 1: Meditation as Formation by Living within Scripture

In Luther's 1519 treatment of Psalm 1, we see how he understands praise to frame Christian action as the exploration of the divine bounty. Having outlined how reliance on our own thoughts and power vitiates our psalm-singing, he now widens his focus to show how reliance on God alone shapes human desire, speech, and action, as well as to indicate the role Scripture plays in this determination.

1:1 אַשְׁרֵי־הָאִישׁ אֲשֶׁר לֹא הָלַךְ בַּעֲצַת רְשָׁעִים וּבְדֶרֶךְ חַטָּאִים לֹא עָמָד
וּבְמוֹשַׁב לֵצִים לֹא יָשָׁב

2 כִּי אִם בְּתוֹרַת יְהוָה חֶפְצוֹ וּבְתוֹרָתוֹ יֶהְגֶּה יוֹמָם וָלָיְלָה

1:1 Wohl dem, der nicht wandelt im Rat der Gottlosen, noch tritt auf den Weg der Sünder, noch sitzt, da die Spötter sitzen,

2 sondern hat Lust zum Gesetz des HErrn und redet von seinem Gesetz Tag und Nacht.

---

siastes, Lectures on the Song of Solomon, Treatise on the Last Words of David, ed. Jaroslav Pelikan (St. Louis: Concordia, 1972), pp. 272-73.

32. Luther, *Luther's Works*, Vol. 16, p. 321. Luther makes this comment as he examines Hezekiah's prayer to discover what it reveals about prayer in all times and places. We have seen the weight given to this insight by Bonhoeffer (ch. 5) and subsequently Webster (ch. 4).

1:1   Blessed is the man who walks not in the counsel of the wicked, nor stands in the way of sinners, nor sits in the seat of scoffers;

2   but his delight is in the law of the LORD, and on his law he meditates day and night.

Psalm 1 is taken by many, including Luther, to introduce the whole Psalter.[33] Luther finds in its first verse a close relationship between faith and human action that grounds his all-important understanding of ethics as sin. Verse 1 presents a negative contrast: blessedness is *not* to walk in the council of the wicked, nor to stand in the way of sinners, nor to sit in the seat of scoffers. This observation yields the following train of logic.

First, "the search for personal blessedness is common to all men." Yet all have strayed in their search, with the most honorable identifying blessedness with virtue or good works, an equation this verse rejects. Instead, the psalmist proposes a counterintuitive definition of blessedness unknown to human reason because it contradicts it: blessed is the one who loves the law of God. The first full sentence of the Psalter sets up this equation: blessedness equals delight in the law of the Lord. Having said that the activity of faith is prayer, Luther now interrogates the activity of faith as "walking in the Law of the Lord."

Luther is not content to leave the first verse as a simple set of negations that we are to hurry through to find out how to delight in God's law. Whatever further implications for human life this delight might have, they will be discernible as the mirror image of the negations of verse 1. His exegetical approach is to link the Hebrew words used with other citations in order to clarify the meaning here. First, he understands "man" to refer to all humanity, both sexes. All humanity, the Hebrew הָלַךְ (*halak*) suggests, must walk in, enter, or approach God's law. "It is well known that in the manner of the scriptures 'to walk' and 'to approach' are figures of speech, meaning 'to live' or 'to associate.'" What the blessed do not walk in is the counsel of the ungodly. "Here 'counsel' is undoubtedly used in place of 'principles' or 'doctrines,' since no human association exists unless it is constructed and maintained according to certain principles and laws" ("Psalms 1 and 2," p. 288).[34] Thus the

---

33. Text critical arguments for the point abound. See Hans-Joachim Kraus, *Psalms 1–59: A Continental Commentary,* trans. Hilton Oswald (Minneapolis: Fortress, 1993), pp. 112-14; see also Peter Craigie, *Word Biblical Commentary, Volume 19: Psalms 1–50* (Waco: Word Books, 1983), pp. 58-60. For a theologically sensitive discussion of how these literary clues suggest that we read Psalm 1 (and 2) as an introduction to the Psalter, see J. Clinton McCann, *A Theological Introduction to the Book of Psalms: The Psalms as Torah* (Nashville: Abingdon, 1993), pp. 30-42.

34. Luther cites Ps. 15:2 and 101:6, as well as Rom. 8:1, 4, to substantiate this point.

opposite of blessedness is to "disdain to walk in the Law of the Lord, but to follow their own counsel" (p. 288).

This analysis comes to serve Luther as a recurring tag for the polarity between human self-assertion and the "way of one's own will" elucidated above. This "counsel of the godless" is paradigmatically enacted in the Israelites' worship of the golden calf at Sinai. While Moses was receiving the words of the law of blessedness, the Israelites constructed a surrogate god: one has faith in the true God (Yahweh) through Christ, or one casts about on the grounds of confidence in the worth of human virtue or works (Rom. 3).[35] "Thus you must always have these two opposites in mind: faith in God and godlessness, just as the Law of God and the council of man. For when we deal with piety and impiety we are dealing, not with behavior but with attitudes, that is, with the source of behavior" (p. 289).

Ungodliness is at its root a desire to make one's own law, or to live according to the human laws of others. This has several implications. It means that outward virtue always tends to slide toward doing good for the sake of accolades. Luther understands that the behavior that this inner division produces is revealed in the phrase "standing in the way of sinners." Citing Romans 14:4, Luther argues: "'To stand' means, in Scriptural metaphor, 'to be steadfast' . . . this is the fixation of the ungodly, that to themselves they seem to live a righteous life and shine before others with their beautiful works." Such a desire to be praised for good works leads to the behavior of "sitting," that is, "to instruct, to be a master or teacher." The "counsel of the ungodly" is all who propagate teachings setting up standards other than God's judgments.[36]

Anticipating Nietzsche's understanding of the role of speech in power struggles, Luther thus finds that Psalm 1 defines ungodliness as (1) setting up one's own definition of blessedness in abstraction from Scripture, and (2) to propagate that definition by persuading others that this particular form of sin is admirable. Sin, therefore, is Janus-faced: "They not only fail to recognize themselves as ungodly, but besides this, devise a council in which they might move and give their wickedness a bright coloring" ("Psalms 1 and 2," p. 292). In the first lectures Luther sums up this complex of metaphors by referring to

---

35. Luther, "Psalm Fifty Nine," in *Luther's Works, Vol. 10.,* p. 274; Luther, "Chapter Three," in *Luther's Works, Vol. 25, Lectures on Romans, Glosses and Scholia,* ed. Hinton Oswald (St. Louis: Concordia, 1972), pp. 25-34.

36. "Thou hast despised all who depart from Thy judgments." "But to them it appears that . . . their own opinion is not unjust, in fact is not their thought, but a certain divine revelation. All this their pride and love of their own ideas brings about. Here the word 'thought' is taken for council and prudence or wisdom as in Ps. 1:1, 'in the council of the ungodly.'" Martin Luther, "Psalm One Hundred Nineteen," in *Luther's Works, Vol. 11,* pp. 493-94.

another metaphor, from Proverbs 30:20: "This is the way of an adulteress: she eats, and wipes her mouth, and says, 'I have done no wrong.'"[37]

Luther's comment on the "seat of scoffers" also applauds the Vulgate's translation for emphasizing the social implications of such sin: *in cathedra pestilentiae non sedit* ("does not sit in the seat of the community of pestilence"). Luther says: "Although 'pestilence' is not a literal translation, it is a very adequate expression; for the Hebrew refers to mockers or to the scornful" ("Psalms 1 and 2," p. 290). The Latin is faithful, though not accurate, says Luther, because it grasps the genesis of idolatry in the inward-facing human heart, which puts on an outer face of self-justification that creates social momentum. Idolatry is a gangrene that destroys by projecting itself outward through teaching into the social matrix. This yields a polarity between a self-worshiping church that has only a semblance of truth, God, and liturgy (thus becoming a servant of the devil, who appears as an angel of light [2 Cor. 11:14]), and the church that "desires a beneficial way, in a sense a more secure way, a holier foundation, or to be called God's church."[38] As ungodliness is social, so too is godliness. It can be attached by God to a people and passed down from parents to children, yet no individual is thereby exempted from delighting in God's law and exercising the faith in God that constitutes blessedness, for "there is no respect of persons with God (Gal. 2:6)" ("Psalms 1 and 2," p. 290).

This delight is Luther's reference point in interpreting the often-discussed hatred statements of the Psalms. In his comment on the prayer of Psalm 26:5, "I hate the company of the evildoers, and I do not sit with the wicked," he describes how delight generates an increase in the discriminatory capabilities. Delight includes a discerning hatred of the semblance of truth that is actually the self-worship of the kingdom of Satan. Delight in God's law thus serves a heuristic function in resisting some words and desires in love: "Where the Word of God is involved, there hate comes in, and love is out. But where my person, my property, my reputation, or my body is involved, there I should render [my neighbor] complete honor and service. These are God's property, given by God to help the neighbor."[39] In this way the prayer to hate

---

37. Luther, "Psalm One," in *Luther's Works, Vol. 10,* p. 12.

38. Martin Luther, "Auslegung vieler schoener Sprüche göttlicher Schrift, daraus Lehre und Trost zu nehmen, welche der ehrwürdige Herr Doktor Martius Luther vielen in ihre Bibeln geschrieben," in *Luther deutsch: die Werke Martin Luthers in neuer Auswahl für die Gegenwart, vol. 5: Die Schriftauslegung,* ed. Kurt Aland (Göttingen: Vandenhoek und Ruprecht, 1990), pp. 341-42.

39. Luther clarifies his point by indicating one biblical example of this wise hating (David and Ahithophel, 2 Sam. 15:31). Martin Luther, "Psalm 101," in *Luther's Works, Vol. 13, Selected Psalms II,* ed. Jaroslav Pelikan, trans. Alfred von Rohr Sauer (St. Louis: Concordia, 1956), pp. 177-84.

the semblance of truth is actually a request that we may be sharpened in our understanding of what is ours and what is God's. This "hatred prayer" is, in fact, a prayer that "keeps faith in motion" because it commits us to the continual critical displacement of our recurrent pagan impulses of self-defense, pride, and covetousness by delight in God's law alone. "Once and for all I say: see that you always separate most widely and distantly the law of the Lord from the laws of any men, and watch with all your diligence that the two, confused into one chaos . . . do not miserably destroy you" ("Psalms 1 and 2," p. 294).

Luther summarizes these two verses by sharply formulating his claim that Christians cannot and must not talk about ethics without first and always making it an inquiry into faith.

> For it is impossible to teach the works of any kind of laws without peril unless one first teaches faith in Christ as the better part of doctrine and with greater zeal. Paul uses eleven chapters of the Epistle to the Romans to make faith the foundation, and then five to build life on this foundation. Again, in the Epistle to the Galatians he spends five chapters on faith and only one, the sixth, on life. He does likewise in other epistles. In the Gospel Christ demands only faith. ("Psalms 1 and 2," p. 294)

Luther sees the conclusion of verse 2 as extending the point. In beginning with faith, we can see that the ensuing task of understanding right human action lies somehow within the task of "delighting" and "meditating" on God's law. His German translation renders the Hebrew word חֵפֶץ *(hepes),* "delight," as *Lust,* which draws out the Hebrew's focus on desire.[40] This translation counters the Vulgate's *voluntas,* which had come to accrue Aristotelian associations with the will and its direction to proper ends. We have seen why Luther felt the verse could not be urging "desire" as a general concept of will directed to general goods. This is a verse about "delight in the law of the Lord," insisting that "law" be defined in relationship to Scripture rather than a general metaphysics. Making a cross-reference to Psalm 119:47 ("And I meditated in Thy commandments which I love"), he concludes: "[L]ove, will or good pleasure, delight (all of these are understood by the Hebrew word used here) bring it about that he should be a zealous meditator on the law of Christ, which the scornful person forgets."[41] Delight in God's law is not the rational direction of the will to appropriate ends; it is

---

40. A change which he does not, in fact, press in his first lectures, though he is clearly struggling there to free the text from scholastic interpretations.

41. Luther, "Psalm One Hundred Nineteen," p. 452.

the affective impulse that drives the whole being, including the rationality, deeper into the law of God.

This delight is not a natural attribute, "for human nature is intent and inclined to evil, as the divine authority says (Gen. 8:21)" ("Psalms 1 and 2," p. 295), but can only be a gift from heaven. Humans are capable of delight in the law as a means of gaining stature before God or other onlookers, but we cannot love it simply as holy, just and good. "From all this it becomes clear that if this psalm is not understood of Christ alone, it becomes a mirror and a goal toward which the blessed man must strive" ("Psalms 1 and 2," p. 295). This is because Christ was the first human whose attachment to the law of the Lord was spontaneous and willing, cheerful and totally voluntary, and devoid of the fear of punishment. Through the Spirit, Christ himself brings such delight into the world, not through violence or force, which would not produce true conversion, but gratuitously. This sets up a first methodological boundary to theological exegesis and ethics. Their primary task is not to ask, "Why is this command given to me?" thus beginning to catalog the irritations at God that justify disobedience. Instead, inquiry into the moral meaning of Scripture is to "consider, not why, but how and how quickly a thing is to be done" ("Psalm One," p. 16).

This first methodological ground rule leads to a second: the Christian life is not discovered in the pursuance and contemplation of the "great" deed, but in the patient obedience to the lowly and mundane commands that shape everyday decisions. Translated into modern terms, Christian life is not discovered first in deliberation about the injustice of embryo experimentation, but in the exploration of parenthood in all its rich connections with our activities as neighbors, coworkers, and citizens. The blessed meditate *into* the law, and because Scripture is the medium of that law, we must not try to fit it into our ethical frameworks, but we "must take the utmost care that we do not quickly believe our own idea and that we must expound scripture in all humility and reverence, because scripture is the stone of offense and rock of scandal for those who are in a hurry. But scripture turns that rock into pools of water [cf. Ps. 114:8] for those who meditate on the law of the Lord" ("Psalm One," p. 19). The task is not to take the "big questions" to Scripture, but to meditate into the law in daily life, to go to it, and to let Scripture create the questions.

To "meditate," הָגָה *(hagah)*, Luther continues, is to "examine, to investigate, in general, to treat verbally" ("Psalms 1 and 2," p. 296). This emphasis on the preaching of Scripture is a well-known and critical feature of Luther's theology, because through it he overcomes the idea of language as a sign system that only points to reality but is not the reality itself. On first glance it is evident that "the church is not a pen-house but a mouth-house," because Christ did not devote himself to writing but to preaching.[42] But this historical observation rests on a deeper point about the structure of God's work in the world. Oswald Bayer points out that we can understand Luther's "Reformation discovery" as the hermeneutical realization that words spoken in worship, such as "I absolve you," do not signify another reality but establish a new state of affairs: here speech is not a sign pointing to something else, but is reality itself. "Therefore, in distinction to the Western philosophical tradition, which sees the person distinguished through its intellect from other living creatures, Luther by contrast sees 'nothing more powerful, or nobler work of a person . . . than speaking,' since 'through speaking the person is most distinguished from other animals, more than through character or other works.'" Bayer concludes: "'God' is grasped as the one who in the oral word promises himself to a person in such a way that this one can rely on him."[43]

Luther grounds the role of speech in this account on the emphasis in the Psalms, expressed in Psalm 1, that meditation on the law is verbal. He applauds Augustine's Latin translation of "utters" in Psalm 37:30 ("The mouth of the righteous utters wisdom") as *garrire*, because meditation is an "exercise of the birds," whose singing beautifully pictures the expression and re-expression of God's law.[44] To so discourse is to be "first [giving] close attention to the law and then drawing together various parts of scripture. . . . For out of this will proceed a sermon to the people which is well informed in the Law of the Lord" ("Psalms 1 and 2," p. 296). Scripture is essential to Christian proclamation because it sustains and corrects it.[45] This leads Luther to explain the procedure used to discover the positive content of verse 1's prohibitions. Using the example of the command "thou shalt not kill," he observes that these are cold and forbidding words unless we meditate on them, talk about them, and link them with other biblical discussions until God's grace emerges from them. In modern terms, Luther is using a theological locus approach in which other Scripture passages are arrayed around a passage to elucidate its depth, rather than a scholastic catalog approach, which combs all of Scripture to develop a comprehensive encyclopedia of its meaning. His theological "system" is to perpetually re-enter the whole through single verses, a

---

42. Pelikan, *Luther the Expositor*, pp. 63-64.

43. Bayer, "Luther as an Interpreter," pp. 77, 81.

44. Augustine is elaborating a metaphor inherited from Ambrose, who once wrote, "Anyone possessed of his five wits should blush with shame if he did not begin the day with a psalm, since even the tiniest birds open and close the day with sweet songs of holy devotion." Quoted in Prothero, *Psalms in Human Life*, p. 14.

45. Pelikan, *Luther the Expositor*, pp. 68-69.

process that he believes leads to the continual reversal of our perceptions. Instead of commands appearing as simple prohibitions, they direct our attention to God's work of, for example, turning speakers of anger and slander into speakers who talk of God's words and love of neighbor.

"Day and night," Luther continues, is a figure of speech urging both that meditation consume our waking hours, and that it continue through the dark and light periods of life. Only true delight in God's law is not shattered by adversity or desiccated by loss of interest.[46] Here the import of Luther's rejection of an Aristotelian definition of delight becomes clear: "Delight in God's law" displaces and resituates all other delights, because God's law is not one delight among many but is the only delight. Delight in a flower is an aspect of delight in God's law that reveals the flower as it truly is, God's work. When, for example, Noah is awed and grateful for the good deeds of his son Shem, he blesses God, as in Genesis 9:26: "And he said: 'Blessed be *the* Lord, God of Shem.'"[47] Fundamentally, for Luther, good deeds are enactments of delight in God.

Thus the desire for the law, says Luther, "is the whole life of man" ("Psalms 1 and 2," p. 297). The godly begin with

> this holy desire, and then follow meditation and external works, and after this the teaching of others as we shall see. . . . Note this well: it is the mode and nature of all who love, to chatter, sing, think, compose and frolic freely about what they love and to enjoy hearing about it, therefore this lover, this blessed man, has his love, the Law of God, always in his mouth, always in his heart and, if possible, always in his ear. 'He who is of God hears the words of God' (John 8:47); and 'Thy statutes have been my songs in the house of my pilgrimage' (Ps. 119:54); and again, 'I will delight in Thy statues, I will not forget Thy Word' (Ps. 119:6). ("Psalms 1 and 2," pp. 297-98)

The ungodly chatter about natural things, but in so doing they fall under the sway of false lords, as false visions of blessedness emanate from their own alienation from God's law. The social realm, the realm of words (in contrast to an emphasis on thought; cf. ch 4), is the realm in which human transformation

---

46. "Is it surprising if he is blessed who is gifted with this heavenly desire and has no interest in things which shatter those who have a fool's sense of blessedness?" Luther, *Luther's Works, Vol. 14,* p. 297.

47. This blessing the Lord in all things is discussed by Luther's comment on this passage in his mature lectures on Genesis in *Luther's Works, Vol. 2, Lectures on Genesis, Chapters 6–14,* ed. Jaroslav Pelikan (St. Louis: Concordia, 1960), pp. 174-78. Paradoxically, alone among modern translations, the NRSV obscures this point in its reversal of the verse's object, to "Blessed by the Lord my God be Shem." I have quoted NKJV.

takes place. Luther understands that God's remaking of humanity is visible in the way delight steers and co-opts discourse, as if the wind of the Spirit can be traced by watching the waves in the grain of verbalized social interaction.

1:3   וְהָיָה כְּעֵץ שָׁתוּל עַל־פַּלְגֵי מָיִם אֲשֶׁר פִּרְיוֹ יִתֵּן בְּעִתּוֹ וְעָלֵהוּ לֹא־יִבּוֹל

וְכֹל אֲשֶׁר־יַעֲשֶׂה יַצְלִיחַ

1:3   Der ist wie ein Baum, gepflanzet an den Wasserbächen, der seine Frucht bringet zu seiner Zeit, und seine Blätter verwelken nicht, und was er macht, das gerät wohl.

1:3   He is like a tree planted by streams of water, that yields its fruit in its season, and its leaf does not wither. In all that he does, he prospers.

Following the psalm, Luther moves on to explicate how delighting in God's words transforms the faithful. An opening connection with Psalm 92:12 ("The righteous flourish like the palm tree and grow like a cedar in Lebanon") allows Luther to suggest that the tree that the psalmist has in view is the palm tree, which (1) grows in deserts and (2) is perpetually blooming to yield (3) sweet fruit. Continuing his attempt to disentangle the psalm from its high-medieval interpretive context, he offers the rare explicit disagreement with Augustine's interpretation of the tree as representing, not the whole human being, but only the will. The tree, Luther contends, again basing his argument on an intertextual connection, is the whole man: "A good tree a good man, and a bad tree an evil man; as Christ also teaches (Matt. 7:17ff)." The tree metaphor makes an organic, developing connection between the roots of human faith described in verses 1 and 2 and the action that grows out of it. That the blessed are "planted" indicates a distinction between the cultivated tree and the wild tree, continues Luther. A planted tree is cut off from its association with and source in the community of wild trees and is artificially planted elsewhere. The desire for God's law is not in any man, "[b]ut as the Heavenly Father plants and cultivates, and transplants us out of Adam into Christ, it is conferred on us from heaven" ("Psalms 1 and 2," p. 300).

Such trees are planted beside streams of divine grace. Already in his first lectures, Luther had drawn together a rich complex of water and grace images, which are especially clearly stated in his comment on Psalm 84:6: "As they go through the valley of Baca they make it a place of springs; the early rain also covers it with pools."

> [F]aith, which is given by God's grace to the ungodly and by which they are justified, is the substance, foundation, fountain, source, chief, and the first-

born of all spiritual graces, gifts, virtues, merits, and works. 'No other foundation can anyone lay' (1 Cor. 3:11). Of this fountain the Lord says, John 4:13-14: 'If anyone will drink of the water that I shall give him, it will become in him a spring of living water welling up to eternal life.'... If one has faith, all other things gush forth from it, like water from the rock and stone.[48]

What sustains faith proves to be the dominant force determining the shape of our action. As verse 1 contrasted those who take their sustenance from the law and those who take it from human wisdom, so this verse contrasts those who are nourished by God's presence and those who are nourished by the things of this life.

> Therefore this desire, the root of this tree, located in this arid, unfruitful life, thirsts after the brooks of heavenly waters all the more, the less it finds in the world to quicken it. Thus another psalm (63:1): '... as in a dry and weary land'; and Is. 53:2: 'For He grew up before Him like a root out of dry ground.' Is it not wonderful to grow trees in sterile ground, nourished only by flowing waters? And blessed is he who, as the world grows more sterile for him, thirsts all the more for the heavenly streams. This tree does not grow in a fat land, nor the blessed man in the splendor of the world. ("Psalms 1 and 2," p. 300)

Luther can now explain that to truly meditate on God's law is to be caught up in a movement of divine grace in which Scripture necessarily gushes forth meaning. "Whoever desires to be beautifully educated ... let him surrender himself to meditation on the law of the Lord day and night and he will learn by experience that what the prophet says in this verse is true." Yet its truth is an eschatological truth. "[H]e says *beside*, that is, next to, or near, since in the future we shall walk into and be swallowed up by these waters" ("Psalm One," p. 21).

Moving his attention from the source of the Christian ethos to its outer embodiment, Luther's interpretation of the "fruit" of love of neighbor reshapes the traditional Christian claim that to be in existence is already to be a recipient of divine grace. All creatures, says Luther, participate in a great cosmic web of reciprocal relations. The sun does not shine for itself, water does not flow for itself, plants do not give fruits for themselves; every creature lives by the law of love, sharing freely of itself with its neighbors. Or rather, God

---

48. Luther, "Psalm Eighty Four," in *Luther's Works, Vol. 11*, p. 146. Notice that in these first lectures Luther is still incompletely free of the *volentas* language: it is his central focus on faith and understanding its meaning that leads him to question the focus on will and broaden its scope to include a more central component for desire in his later expositions.

intends creation to be reciprocal in this way, an intention that only the devil and humanity resist. The refusal to give of themselves transforms them from fruit-bearing plants into thornbushes and choking vines.

Using imagery derived from the deepest strata of the Old Testament (cf. Job 29:23), Luther describes the blessed as mobile conduits of the divine springs in a world dried out by sin's refusal of reciprocity.[49] To be planted beside the overflowing streams of divine grace is to become a refreshing rain in this desert.[50] This image of portable springs suggests ways around the contemporary alienation of the discourses of hermeneutics and ethics. Here reading and acting are not conceived of as needing to be brought together, but as reciprocally defining. In his commentary on Galatians (1535), Luther links the image of Christians as God's portable springs directly to his concept of "good works," elucidating its ethical implications.

> When I have this righteousness within me [earthly or active righteousness], I descend from heaven like the rain that makes the earth fertile. That is, I come forth into another kingdom, and I perform good works whenever the opportunity arises. If I am a minister of the Word, I preach, I comfort the saddened, I administer the sacraments. If I am a father, I rule my household and family, I train my children in piety and honesty. If I am a magistrate I perform the office which I have received by divine command. If I am a servant, I faithfully tend to my master's affairs. In short, whoever knows for sure that Christ is his righteousness not only cheerfully and gladly works in his calling but also submits himself for the sake of love to the magistrates, also to their wicked ways, and to everything else in this present life — even, if need be, to burden and danger.[51]

Faith lives in meditation on the divine word of Scripture, and God's grace both founds the desire to attend to Scripture and turns it into the fruit of works of love.[52]

---

49. A variant image appears in the Old Testament, of God's servants as pipes or tubes delivering divine olive oil (Zech. 4:1-14). For a discussion of the ethical implications of making human agents transmitters of divine love, see Bernd Wannenwetsch, "Caritas fide formata. 'Herz und Affekte' als Schlüssel zu 'Glaube und Liebe,'" *Kerygma und Dogma* 45 (2000): 205-24.

50. Freely translating a medley of verses, Luther explains that this new life happens when "'The law of his God is in his heart' (Ps. 37:31) and not 'his hand,' but 'his will is in the law of the Lord' (Ps. 1:2) and 'he greatly delights in His commandments' (Ps. 112:1), and again, 'I have laid up Thy Words in my heart' (Ps. 119:11)." Luther "Psalm Eighty Four," p. 145.

51. Martin Luther, *Luther's Works, Vol. 26, Lectures on Galatians, 1535, Chapters 1-4,* ed. Jaroslav Pelikan (St. Louis: Concordia, 1963), pp. 11-12.

52. Luther's basic observations are mirrored in the work of contemporary form- and historical-critic Marvin Tate (*Word Biblical Commentary: Vol. 20, Psalms 51–100* [Waco: Word

Because fruitfulness is defined as the restoration of connectivity to a creation suffering from its lack, we can see how Luther would have understood the modern gap between hermeneutics and ethics as a symptom of humanity severed from the organic relationship the Spirit creates between meditation on Scripture and fruitful human action. Such estrangements are the inevitable by-product of wrong faith: the ungodly become "captive in their distress" (Ps. 18:45), torturing themselves by losing sight of God's desire to make Scripture bear fruit, preferring instead to meditate on concepts, rules, and schedules, budgets and accounting — the whole panoply of techniques of scarcity — and in so doing they manage themselves into unfruitfulness. Imagining that these methods bring true fruit and that nothing good can be "produced" otherwise, they judge and condemn others' fruit.

But the blessed are those who do not know the gap between hermeneutics and ethics because they know they have nothing of love to offer and can neither love nor read Scripture unless they be sustained by God's grace. "Fruit in its season" is, then, Luther continues, "a golden and lovable word through which the freedom of the righteous Christian is affirmed" ("Psalms 1 and 2," p. 301). This is the heart of Luther's "Treatise on Good Works," in which this verse plays a central role.

> St. Paul also says, 'Where the Spirit of Christ is, there all is free' (Rom. 8:2). For faith does not permit itself to be bound to any work or to refuse any work, but, as the first Psalm says, 'it yields its fruit in its season', that is, in the normal course of events. We may see this in an everyday example. When a husband and wife really love one another, have pleasure in each other, and thoroughly believe in their love, who teaches them how they are to behave

Books, 1990], p. 225), who recapitulates Luther's portable springs concept in the idiom of modern biblical studies when commenting on Ps. 72:6 ("May he be like rain that falls on the mown grass, like showers that water the earth"): "[T]he first prayer is for the king to bring justice and deliverance to the poor. . . . Second to that is the plea that the king may live and give life to the land, and third is the hope that his power may go to the ends of the earth. . . . When the king gives the life of God's justice to the people, then the blessings of fertile land and far-reaching power follow. All of these themes add up to the biblical concept of *shalom* ('peace/well-being'). Though the word *shalom* appears only twice in this psalm (vv. 3 and 7), it brings together into a wholeness the political, economic, social and spiritual dimensions of life. . . . *Shalom* is the salvation which embraces all creation. . . . While the king stands in special relationship to God as the anointed son of David, the people are privileged to be able to intercede for him because they are in relationship to God as well. They pray for the life of the king in order that the king may give them life which enables them, in turn, to pray. It is a complex relationship, but when it is established, the world itself is established through it." The main difference between the interpretations of Tate and Luther is where each locates himself as exegete within the thought complex he finds in the psalm.

to one another, what they are to do or not to do, say or not to say, what they are to think? Confidence alone teaches them all this, and even more than is necessary. For such a man there is no distinction in works. He does the great and the important as gladly as the small and the unimportant, and vice versa. Moreover, he does them all in a glad, peaceful, and a confident heart, and is an absolutely willing companion to the woman. But where there is any doubt, he searches within himself for the best thing to do; then a distinction of works arises by which he imagines he may win favor. And yet he goes about it with a heavy heart and great disinclination. He is like a prisoner, more than half in despair, and often makes a fool of himself.[53]

"Fruit in season" is the divine gift of right judgment about how and when to undertake acts of love. Luther takes seriously the fact that essential parts of the Christian life lie outside the grasp of systematic affirmations, such as the knowledge of the times, the ability to sense the right moment to act, and the judgment about which act is appropriate to this particular context. When we possess this knowledge, wisdom is the "leader and director of the virtues, the judge of the times. Many produce fruit at an improper time, according to their own head and thought, and not fruit in its season, so that a person studies when he ought to be at work on behalf of others, or, on the contrary, he wants to rule and run when he ought to be praying or studying" ("Psalm One," p. 21). Such a practical skill parallels the skill of the world in practical matters, says Luther; Christians, like journeymen, must learn to be masters in matters such as knowing when to reap a harvest or when to sell a commodity. As love learns wisdom in marriage, and the apprentice learns judgment through training with the master, this wisdom is a skill of attentiveness to God's word learned and practiced within a community.

This is ethics as attentive and spontaneous action, activated by divine prompting and human need, and distinguishable from the project of developing formal moral norms within which all proper behavior is described. Though his understanding of good works matured in his later thought, Luther's first preserved sermon (on Matthew 7:12) makes clear the derivation of this interest in an ethic of good works. In the Sermon on the Mount, Luther suggests, Jesus teaches not that blessedness is refraining from harming the neighbor, but that salvation is characterized by the life of active good works — outgoing love that seeks out human need and meets it.[54] In framing ethics

---

53. Martin Luther, "Treatise on Good Works, 1520," in *Luther's Works, Vol. 44, The Christian in Society I*, ed. James Atkinson, trans. W. A. Lambert (Philadelphia: Fortress Press, 1966), pp. 26-27.

54. Luther, "Luther's First (?) Sermon, Matt. 7:12, 1510 (?) or 1512 (?)," in *Luther's Works,*

thus, Luther demotes it from its role in cataloging the goods toward which human will is properly directed, replacing it with a notion of ethics as faith's exploration of love. Ethics thus becomes a mode of reflecting on God and our social context so as to remain open conduits of the divine love.[55]

Only when such fruit is present can faith produce "leaves." Stretching the botanical metaphor, Luther understands the leaves of the blessed as their teaching, and for their doctrine and teaching to remain alive, their works of love must be alive. "'Jesus began to do and teach' (Acts 1:1), and 'He was a man mighty in deed and word' (Luke 24:19). Thus he who would be a teacher of the Word of doctrine must first show the fruits of his life if he does not want his leaves to wither" ("Psalms 1 and 2," p. 302). Faith in God alone meditates on Scriptures for its sustenance, makes spontaneous and attentive love possible, the continuity of which keeps the teaching of the faithful vibrant.

The unity of the body of Christ is a unity of purpose in meditation on Scripture. Precisely because Jesus is the one blessed man of verse 1, the whole church is included. This church delights in Scripture, making it a church of chatterers of the law — of preachers. This means that every righteous person is characterized by right faith, love of others, and words that teach this faith, for, "if he does not teach others, he certainly teaches himself, meditating in his heart on the law of God" ("Psalms 1 and 2," p. 303). It is in this way that God's word remains eternally in him. So the "leaf" of official church teaching and doctrine belongs to the whole body of Christ. The official preacher is, in effect, the designated "representative listener" of the congregation, the hearer who chatters about what he or she hears in God's law. The office of preacher can thus only be "the ear and not the tongue" — not inventing anything but only representing to the body what they are already taken into.[56]

Moving on to the "he does" of "in all he does he prospers," Luther reiterates his point that good human action is, properly speaking, divine work in humans. Based on the difference in Hebrew between עָשָׂה ("doing") and פָּעַל

---

vol. 51. This point is made via a connection with Matthew 25:42: "He does not say: I had food and you stole it from me, I had drink and you took it away from me, but rather, 'you gave me no food and no drink'" (p. 9).

55. Cf. Dietrich Bonhoeffer, *Ethics*, Dietrich Bonhoeffer Works, vol. 6, ed. Ilse Tödt, Heinz Eduard Tödt, Ernst Feil, and Clifford Green, trans. Reinhard Krauss, Charles West, and Douglas Scott (Minneapolis: Fortress, 2005), p. 271.

56. For a more in-depth analysis of this concept, see Bernd Wannenwetsch, "'Members of One Another': *Charis,* Ministry and Representation: A Politico-Ecclesial Reading of Romans 12," in *A Royal Priesthood? The Use of the Bible Ethically and Politically: A Dialogue with Oliver O'Donovan,* ed. Craig Bartholomew, Jonathan Chaplin, Robert Song, and Al Wolters (Carlisle: Paternoster Press, 2002), pp. 196-215.

("acting"), he argues that the doing of this verse is not a reference to the work of the blessed but to the divine work on and through the blessed to make them *his* works. "(Is. 19:25): 'And Israel is the work of My hands.' . . . [T]he works of God are those that He performs through creatures, especially the Word and grace, through which He works and causes us to work. Therefore let 'doing' mean to establish, arrange, and place into various church offices, and as the apostles Peter and Paul have taught, to make servants of the manifold grace of God, found churches and multiply them. Thus the believers are themselves their creation, work and product" ("Psalms 1 and 2," pp. 303-4). It is only in this sense, Luther continues, that Paul can "'bear' the Galatians (Gal. 4:19) and 'father' the Corinthians (1 Cor. 4:15). 'Are you not my workmanship in the Lord?' (1 Cor. 9:1) he says. You understand, therefore, that this 'work' of the blessed man is a spiritual one, not palaces, empires, and parades" ("Psalms 1 and 2," p. 304).

Luther interprets the "prosperity" of this verse as the flourishing of the renewed social realm called a kingdom of Spirit, which "cannot be known except through faith or experience. That this is true you will clearly see if you evaluate [the] desire [of the blessed], where blessedness alone is found, not in riches, not in honor, not in his own righteousness or virtue. Nor is it found in any good that can be named within or without man, except in this desire for the Law" ("Psalms 1 and 2," p. 298).

1:4 לֹא־כֵן הָרְשָׁעִים כִּי אִם־כַּמֹּץ אֲשֶׁר־תִּדְּפֶנּוּ רוּחַ

1:4 Aber so sind die Gottlosen nicht, sondern wie Spreu, die der Wind verstreut.

1:4 The wicked are not so, but are like chaff that the wind drives away.

The godless will not exhibit this continuity of love and teaching, promises verse 4, but will be "dispersed like chaff." This will happen in three ways, says Luther. First, they will be driven bodily by the will and indignation of other people. At every moment the ungodly are exposed to the thorns and choking vines of others' greed in having nothing other than their own, ultimately relative, ideas to hold on to. This can be restated in a second form: the wicked are driven like chaff in being carried in all directions by the wind of various doctrines, but in Christ the Christian can resist what the wicked cannot, the exposure of the intellect, heart, and conscience to the winds of the world's self-referential methodologies (Eph. 4:14). Finally, the wicked will be scattered like chaff in the last day by the "eternal stormwinds of the unbearable wrath of God" ("Psalms 1 and 2," p. 298).

This point provides Luther with another opportunity to criticize ethics as the definition of right acts shorn of concern for the context of their enactment. Some of the wicked, he says, "also produce fruit, but not in their season; yes, rather at an unsuitable time" ("Psalms 1 and 2," p. 23). This is tantamount to saying that their attempts at social reciprocity bear some external features of true reciprocity, but they do not succeed in being so. Rain is still rain even if it does not fall on the plants that need it. But the blessed do not judge their actions by their formal qualities without referring to a local context in the knowledge that good works are marked by a proper "judgment of the times" participating in the divine drama, as well as fitting within the range of what might generally be defended as loving acts. But the wicked, not being rooted in the streams of divine grace, can never get this wisdom right in being unable to discern the buffeting of their being by false doctrines.

עַל־כֵּן לֹא־יָקֻמוּ רְשָׁעִים בַּמִּשְׁפָּט וְחַטָּאִים בַּעֲדַת צַדִּיקִים   1:5

1:5   Darum bleiben die Gottlosen nicht im Gericht noch die Sünder in der Gemeinde der Gerechten.

1:5   Therefore the wicked will not stand in the judgment, nor sinners in the congregation of the righteous.

This verse Luther understands as a consolation to God's servants in seeing God puncturing the deceit of those who peddle visions of blessedness and power other than the law of God. Though the wicked tout their definitions of blessedness (which, of course, exalt themselves as prime exemplars and so augment their own power), "in truth they are never in power, and the ungodly are never among the faithful, even though they have such a brilliant appearance of life that one might think no one has a greater right to rule or to be among the believers, this is the pretense and the hypocrisy denounced in this psalm; with it they inflate themselves, become presumptuous, and deceive themselves and others" ("Psalms 1 and 2," p. 308).

The sinner refuses to judge himself, divinizing his own thoughts, and becomes God's rival. In contrast, the Christians' "great and happy pride" ("Psalm One," p. 31) is their delight in God's law, which leads them to constantly condemn their own pride. "'[E]ven if he falls seven times a day, he as often rises again' (Prov. 24:16) in that he does not excuse himself for his sins, but quickly confesses them and accuses himself." Paul provides an example of this attitude: he "chooses to be found in Christ, not having his own righteousness (Phil. 3:9). Thus he himself says that he is the foremost of all sinners (1 Tim. 1:15), which is a great and happy kind of pride" ("Psalm One," p. 34).

As in Augustine, the standard of self-judgment in Luther is the divine judgment, but, in distinction from Augustine, this judgment is not in the first instance moral but a judgment of where one's roots are planted. Luther links this verse to the judgment that the Psalms often ask of God for the Solomonic king, as in Psalm 71:1-2: "Give the king your justice, O God, and your righteousness to a king's son. May he judge your people with righteousness, and your poor with justice." Luther understands this to mean that Christ is the king who consummates these strands of the Old Testament, and so his every word is God's judgment. This word of Christ has three effects: (1) it reveals reality as it really is; (2) it divides the world, ordering and remaking it; and (3) it creates the righteous and the judged, that is, those who humbly submit to it.[57] This is the judgment to which the wicked will not subject themselves, and thus they will be subjected against their will.

Conversely, the way of the righteous is present in a special form: hidden before humans but visible to the eyes of God.

1:6   כִּי־יוֹדֵעַ יְהוָה דֶּרֶךְ צַדִּיקִים וְדֶרֶךְ רְשָׁעִים תֹּאבֵד

1:6   Denn der HEER kennt den Weg der Gerechten, aber der Gottlosen Weg vergeht.

1:6   for the LORD watches over the way of the righteous, but the way of the wicked will perish.

The godless last for a time, but because they resist the reciprocity that God wills for creation, they are offensive, like smoke in God's eyes, to be dissipated also like smoke. But faith is strengthened by being under God's eyes, having staked itself on God's intervention (Ps. 37:5).[58] In hope the blessed are thus hidden in God's Spirit, Luther concludes. Their flowering is invisible in a world defining blessedness in other terms; their greatest moments and their most beautiful discoveries are hidden to a world frantically trying to establish personal power by looking down its nose at other definitions of blessedness. Yet God watches the blessed in spirit. "Because this is the wisdom of the cross, God alone knows the way of the righteous. It is hidden even to the righteous; for His right hand leads them on such a wonderful way that it is not the way of the senses or of reason but of faith alone, which is able to see even in darkness and behold the invisible" ("Psalms 1 and 2," p. 309). The power of this

---

57. Luther, "Psalm Seventy Two," in *Luther's Works, Vol. 10*, p. 406. Luther cites as evidence for this connection Is. 9:7; Ps. 89:14; 97:2; 99:4; 33:5; and 37:28.

58. Luther, "Auslegung vieler schoener Sprüche," p. 342.

hidden community grows in its being "led from wickedness to piety; and this does not happen outwardly through violence, but through love, which prays internally and admonishes externally, with the co-operation of God" ("Psalms 1 and 2," p. 309).

Luther concludes his exegesis of Psalm 1 with one of his most important themes: the righteous must not forget that the Psalms are *prayers*. This has four implications. First, we must adjust ourselves to them in mind and feeling in order to approach God. The Psalter positions us not before men but before God, serving as "a kind of school and exercise for the disposition of the heart" ("Psalms 1 and 2," p. 310). Thus faith sings the psalms in vain if it is not affectively engaged in its singing of the Psalter, an engagement that creates a visceral repudiation of the council of the ungodly — which resides in us. Second, "when you say: 'But their delight is in the Law of the Lord,' you should not rest assured and pat yourself on the back, as if you were the one who loves the law of God. Rather, you should sigh with the greatest possible ardor to Him who alone has come to send fire upon the earth (Luke 12:49). And as long as you live, think of yourself in no other way than as one who does not yet love God's Law and who desperately needs this desire for the law" ("Psalms 1 and 2," p. 310). Prayer that loves God's law thus moves toward God and away from one's own ideas in contrast to the hypocrite's prayer, which looks outward to condemn others' sin while delighting in his own merit in the name of delight in God.[59]

Third, such a prayer cannot but be a prayer for the church as a whole also to despise the council of the ungodly, and to prosper with the fruit of good deeds and the leaves of right teaching. Finally, because the Psalter is a school for faith, there is no substitute for exercise with them. Do not believe that you cannot pray them: "First practice on one psalm, even one little verse of the psalm. You will progress enough if you learn to make only one verse a day, or even one a week, live and breathe in your heart. After this beginning is made, everything else will follow, and you will have a rich treasury of understanding and affection" ("Psalms 1 and 2," p. 310). Such exercise allows the words to serve as a path to the waters of God's grace, and they provide the opportunity for our affective being to begin to resonate with them. This is an essential way to approach any psalm: "This I want to impress on you once more in this first psalm, so that it may not be necessary to repeat it for each individual psalm. I know that whoever becomes practiced in this will find more by himself in the Psalter than all the interpretations of other men can give him" ("Psalms 1 and 2," p. 311).

59. Luther, "Psalm Seventy Two," p. 408.

Psalm 8: Doxology as Emplacement in Christ's Reign

Thus far Luther has suggested that the Psalms place prayer and praise formed by Scripture at the center of the Christian life. In his 1537 sermon on Psalm 8, he develops this claim by naming it as the work of the prophetic Christ, making Scripture the paradigmatic opportunity to "speak Christ." "Chattering" about Scripture he thus reveals as the exterior feature of the Spirit's internal generation of a Christian ethos, yielding Luther's prefatory remark as he begins his exegesis of Psalm 8: "We want to talk a little about our dear Lord and Savior Jesus Christ. For He has commanded us to remember Him till He comes, and He has also deserved never to be forgotten. To give us an occasion to talk about Him, we shall take up the Eighth Psalm of David, which was written about our Lord Jesus Christ, and follow the example of this prophet as he prophesies to us."[60]

When Luther appears to decide beforehand that this psalm is about Christ, it sets off all kinds of alarm bells for the modern reader. Luther thinks this move can be legitimated because the subject of the psalm is a king who rules in heaven and earth, and whose dominion is of Spirit and word, established through the weak and humble. This is not an allegorical reading, but one that suggests that questions raised by this text cannot be satisfactorily answered by Christians without reference to Christ. The main interpretative question the psalm raises is: how should we interpret the psalm's claim that its performance takes place within this king's dominion? To be truly sung, concludes Luther, this psalm asks us to speak about the king within whose kingdom the psalm places us.

8:2 יְהוָה אֲדֹנֵינוּ מָה־אַדִּיר שִׁמְךָ בְּכָל־הָאָרֶץ אֲשֶׁר תְּנָה הוֹדְךָ עַל־הַשָּׁמָיִם

8:2 HERR, unser Herrscher, wie herrlich ist dein Name in allen Landen, du den man lobet im Himmel!

8:1 O LORD, our Ruler, how glorious is Thy name in all the lands! Thou to whom thanks are given in heaven.[61]

---

60. Luther, "Psalm 8," in *Luther's Works, Vol. 12, Selected Psalms I*, ed. and trans. Jaroslav Pelikan (St. Louis: Concordia, 1955), p. 97 (page references to this work hereafter cited parenthetically in text).

61. For Psalms 8 and 111, Luther included his German translation within the text of his exegesis. I will follow the translations of *Luther's Works* which catch the resonances of his German. While Luther places the entire text of Psalm 8 at the head of his treatise (in *Luther's Works, Vol. 12*, p. 97), in Psalm 111 the blocks of commentary follow the citation of each verse.

Luther begins to ground his claim that this psalm is about the rule of Christ with one of several philological examinations. The subject of the psalm is יְהוָה אֲדֹנֵינוּ (*yhwh 'Adonenu*). The first word, "Jehovah," is never ascribed to anyone in the Bible but God himself. But the second ascription, *adoni,* is a common, human lordship, applied to princes and heads of houses. For example, Sarah calls Abraham her lord (Gen. 18:12), as Joseph calls Potiphar his lord (Gen. 39:8). Joseph is called *adonai,* in turn, when he is made ruler in Egypt (Gen. 45:8). Therefore, here *adonai* means "the human nature and external rule of this king over us men." And if this king is called "Jehovah our *adonai,*" "it follows that He must be true God and true man at the same time" ("Psalm 8," p. 99). Luther suggests that the combination of these words reveals "three sublime doctrines": "First, this King has two natures, that is, He is true God and man. Second, He is an undivided person; not two persons, two Kings, two Lords and Rulers; but one person, one King, one Lord and Ruler. . . . The third doctrine is that this Lord, that is, God, was to become man and receive dominion, power, and glory from the Father over all" ("Psalm 8," p. 101).

Luther then interprets the psalmist to be opening with an expression of joy and amazement that, out of this little corner of the world, "men will preach, sing, and speak about this King throughout the world" ("Psalm 8," p. 102). Not only throughout the world, says the psalm, but in earth and heaven. Who can sing such praise? Luther replies:

> This is spoken according to the nature of Christ's kingdom which is a strange and wonderful kingdom — not an earthly, perishable, mortal kingdom, but an eternal, heavenly, imperishable kingdom. The citizens of Christ's kingdom are earthly, perishable, mortal men, living in lands scattered hither and yon on earth; and at the same time they are citizens of heaven. Thy kingdom will extend as far as the world, and yet this kingdom will be an eternal, heavenly kingdom. ("Psalm 8," pp. 103-4)

Christ's subjects are in him already in heaven, though "according to the body we are scattered hither and yon among the lands" ("Psalm 8," p. 105). What Luther intends to draw out is that the heart that desires God's law and meditates on it lives in heaven in heart and soul by faith and hope. "This is what it really means to live in heaven, not with the body but with the heart and the soul in faith and hope. By faith in the Word, our heart has taken hold of life in heaven through the power of the Holy Spirit. But we must still wait till the Last Day, when our old 'bag of worms' will finally be purified and come along, too" ("Psalm 8," p. 105).

Through meditation on the psalm's words, taking them up through faith and singing them with lips and hearts, those words, via the Holy Spirit, become the means whereby the blessed may live in Christ, our eternal life. In faith and hope heaven is present to humans whose inhabitation of Christ gives them eyes to see heaven and God's graceful provision in the world around us, for now only "through a mirror darkly." Only in the end, when our sinful bodies are finally purified, will we see "face to face" (1 Cor. 13:12). Yet eschatological hope has become faith's heuristic for perceiving all things, and it is the development of this eschatological perception that is the "purpose of this ruler's dominion and kingdom" ("Psalm 8," p. 105). Luther's whole epistemological framework is thus revealed to rest on an ecclesiology with a sharply defined Christological eschatology. The sure hope of life in Christ exposes reality for what it is, allowing us to experience the life of service for which God has inaugurated his kingdom.

This Christological exegesis reveals Luther's innovativeness as a biblical exegete. He reads the verse literally, meaning that he does not see it as a mask or sign of Christ but understands it as a historical record of Israel's actual and proper hope for Christ.[62] However, because he understands Christians as grafted into this hope, it is his ecclesiology that allows us participation in this past hope, fusing the "literal" and "historical" senses.[63] Because Israel has sung this song of hope in Christ's lordship, and as an artifact of it, we also can sing it to enter its hope and be remade by its Lord.

8:3   מִפִּי עוֹלְלִים וְיֹנְקִים יִסַּדְתָּ עֹז לְמַעַן צוֹרְרֶיךָ לְהַשְׁבִּית אוֹיֵב וּמִתְנַקֵּם

8:3   Aus dem Munde der jungen Kinder und Säuglinge hast du eine Macht zugerichtet um deiner Feinde willen, da du vertilgest den Feind und den Rachgierigen.

8:2   Out of the mouths of babes and sucklings hast Thou ordained strength because of Thine enemies, that Thou mightest destroy the enemy and the avenger.

This verse, Luther continues, describes the difference in kind between Christ's power and worldly power. It sets up a polarity between the powers of force and strength — war at root — and the "kingdom of the word," the two ways of securing the unity in human society. It is not true that under all moral language lies the struggle of power against power. This is only true of

---

62. Cf. Preuss, *Shadow to Promise,* pp. 189-90, 211.
63. Cf. Pelikan, *Luther the Expositor,* ch. 5, esp. p. 107.

the world alienated from God. In this psalm, says Luther, we discover a power different in kind from worldly power. Christ's power is with the word of the gospel, the good news about Christ the King that is spoken by "infants and sucklings."

Nietzsche and Luther agree that the word is powerful, but they disagree about what its power is. Its true power, according to this verse, is in founding a heavenly kingdom of praise. This is God's way of stilling the "avenger," the biblical characterization of the rebellion of earthly strength and power against Christ. Christ's work is to make a fool of this anti-power, thereby showing the power of the spoken word, hope, and the Spirit, says Luther. Quoting Colossians 2:15, he continues: Christ "degrades himself below all men, as it is written in Psalm 22:6: 'I am a worm and no man; scorned by men, and despised by the people.' . . . In such physical weakness and poverty He attacks the enemy, lets Himself be put on the cross and killed, and by His cross and death He destroys the enemy and the avenger" ("Psalm 8," p. 110).

As Christ once triumphed, so he continues. Jesus sent his disciples out armed only "with comfort and joy. . . . So He begins His strength and His kingdom; He could not do it more foolishly before the world" ("Psalm 8," p. 111). This foolishness triumphs in the cross, but triumph it is: "Emperors, kings, and the potentates of the earth must hang their heads and confess that they cannot defend themselves against it" ("Psalm 8," p. 111). The human war to assert itself against God is revealed through innocent words — as wantonly destructive tragicomedy. In Christ, says Luther, God humiliates this pride.

> I want to begin foolishly so that in their great cleverness they might become fools and dunces, so that they see and know that all their riches, power, reason, wisdom and cleverness are mere nothings before Me. Therefore, just as they go with force, reason, wisdom and cleverness to spite and boast, so I turn right around and under the noses of the rich, powerful, wise and clever I put nothing but poor, weak and simple people, who have neither house nor home, but are strangers and exiles on the earth (Heb. 11:13). In this I take joy and pleasure: because they brag of their power and wisdom, I meet them with nothing but weakness and foolishness. ("Psalm 8," pp. 113-14)

Luther understands this dynamic of the cross to be the secret inner history of the world, operative in all times and places. Therefore, to open one's mouth to praise it is to participate in the triumph of Christ's rule. Given the antagonism between the power of strength and the power of the word spoken in humility, we can see why Luther defines the "infants" of this verse as "plain, simple, unsophisticated people, who are like infant children in that they set aside all reason, grasp and accept the Word with simple faith, and let themselves be led and directed by God like children" ("Psalm 8," p. 108). "Sucklings" extols a satisfaction in God's words that does not desire to "supplement" Scripture with the addition of human dreams and embellishment. A prerequisite of participating in the work of God's kingdom is to take God's Word, Scripture, as sufficient and clear in itself, even when it does not yet seem to have revealed its meaning.

The words that Christ uses to defeat the enemy must be learned, a learning that is not memorization but a remaking, a schooling. "As a child goes to school to learn the Our Father and the Creed, so we must also go to church to hear and learn the Gospel. . . . Those who hold God's Word and desire His wisdom, let themselves be taught and learn" ("Psalm 8," pp. 114-15). The meaning of this odd emphasis on childlike faith in Scripture by the highly educated Luther makes sense if we ask what Luther does not do. He refuses to inquire about any supposed ontological mechanism whereby uttered words defeat evil. Nor does he ask how the gospel is established in hearts through words. He refuses to enter into a metaphysical attempt to explain these relationships, taking it on faith that the kingdom is present; not only present, but because the word "mouth" here is singular, it is present in unity. The use of the singular "mouth" suggests "the unanimity of the faithful in praising Christ. So also the apostle says 'that with one mind and with one mouth they may glorify, etc.' (Rom. 15:6). For they believe, teach and proclaim the same thing."[64]

The question about the relationship of praise and human action is thus revealed to be one about how we might participate in the unity and order of this kingdom, rather than a question about the mechanics of *how* God through Scripture and his Spirit creates this Kingdom. Luther constantly emphasized that the aim of theology is not to know God in himself, but as he is for us and, consequently, how we are to follow him.[65] The psalmist describes the blessed as infants and sucklings, Luther insists, in order to emphasize that only by relying on God's word in Scripture do we discover in them clear and sufficient provisions sustaining us as participants in Christ's conflict with disorder. This is a great comfort from the very mouth of God, who says, according to Luther: "'Let it be sufficient for you that I am your great Lord, be satisfied. It is My way to begin in weakness. I am founding and establishing My kingdom through your mouth. . . . I shall not cast you into hell but abide with you and strengthen you'" ("Psalm 8," p. 117).

---

64. Luther, *Luther's Works, Vol. 10*, p. 89.
65. Cf. Paul Althaus, *The Theology of Martin Luther,* trans. Robert Schultz (Philadelphia: Fortress, 1966), ch. 20, "The Freedom of the Gracious God."

8:4   כִּי־אֶרְאֶה שָׁמֶיךָ מַעֲשֵׂי אֶצְבְּעֹתֶיךָ יָרֵחַ וְכוֹכָבִים אֲשֶׁר כּוֹנָנְתָּה

8:4   Wenn ich sehe die Himmel, deiner Finger Werk, den Mond und die Sterne,
        die du bereitet hast:

8:3   For I shall look at the heavens, the work of Thy fingers, the moon and the
        stars which Thou art establishing.

The establishment of Christ's sphere of dominion is not an occasional
affair: the up-building of a peaceful rule follows its assault, says Luther. "David believed in such a future glory of the children of God and the renewal of
the creatures. He rejoiced at it from the bottom of his heart and stood in the
certain hope that he would see the heaven, moon, and stars prepared and renewed by the finger of God. God postponed this glory so that all the saints
have to wait for it" ("Psalm 8," p. 120). Note that Luther understands the historical David's hope to be normative. David sings of a promised new creation
with such certain hope that he glimpses the sight that will only be exposed to
full view in heaven. In this fierce holding to the promise of God, he really does
possess a knowledge of that new creation on which "the angels long to look"
(1 Pet. 1:12).

David's joy in the promise of the new heaven and earth binds him to
God because he has been given new perception of the truth of creation. His
joy is the presence of that future, that new kingdom of Christ's power. Thus
Luther's eschatological and ecclesiological reading meets the earlier Christian interpretation of this verse as speaking of the church. "Therefore, 'I will
see thy heavens' means that men will see 'Your apostles and disciples.'"[66]
Here an important difference between Augustine and Luther emerges. Augustine's understanding of the *totus Christus* rests on a theory of an ontological relationship between Christ and the church, what was later dubbed a
mystical union. The unity of Christ and the church is conceived with the
help of a metaphysical conceptual relationship. Luther, however, takes the
unity of the Christ and his church to rest on the unity of word and deed that
springs from a unity of faith and hope. The church is that community unified in faith and hope because it is gathered around Scripture as God's word
guiding them in the present. It is a community that lives only in verbalized
praise.

8:5   מָה־אֱנוֹשׁ כִּי־תִזְכְּרֶנּוּ וּבֶן־אָדָם כִּי תִפְקְדֶנּוּ
6   וַתְּחַסְּרֵהוּ מְּעַט מֵאֱלֹהִים וְכָבוֹד וְהָדָר תְּעַטְּרֵהוּ

66. Luther, "Psalm 45," in *Luther's Works, Vol. 12*, trans. E. B. Koenker, p. 272.

8:5   was ist der Mensch, da du seiner gedenkst; und des Menschen Kind, da du dich sein annimmst?

6   Du hast ihn lassen eine kleine Zeit von Gott verlassen sein. Aber mit Ehren und Schmuck wirst du ihn krönen.

8:4   What is Man that Thou art mindful of Him, and the Son of Man that Thou dost care for Him?

5   Thou wilt let Him be forsaken of God for a little while, but Thou wilt crown Him with honor and adornment.

Verses 4 and 5, says Luther, further elucidate the shape of Christ's rule by clarifying how the work of Christ is both the decisive moment in the conflict with evil and reveals the meaning and experience of the kingdom that is enlisted in his conflict with sin. Again, Luther bases his Christological interpretation on a close reading of the Hebrew text.

Luther considers the subject of verse 4 to be the king of verse 1, based on the complex conceptual field that these two verses set up. We must keep in mind that he has already noted that his reason for reading the psalm at all is to talk about Christ. But in so doing he also aims to understand how to meditate on God's law. He understands the Hebrew word אֱנוֹשׁ (*enosh*), "man," of verse 4 to emphasize the afflicted frailty of humans, as in, for example, "Let the nations know that they are but *enosh*" (Ps. 9:20), or "As for *enosh*, his days are like grass" (Ps. 103:15). The verse's second word for man is *adam*, which means all humanity. Luther concludes that the psalmist "calls Christ אֱנוֹשׁ 'man,' because of the trouble and sorrow He had on earth. He calls Him 'son of adam' or 'son of man' because of His nature, that He was born of a human being rather than immediately created by God as Adam was created from a clod of earth or Eve was made from Adam's rib. Christ was born in an ordinary yet supernatural way, God's work being mediated through flesh 'by the Holy Ghost of the Virgin Mary,' as the Christian creed teaches" ("Psalm 8," pp. 122-23). Not only did God subject himself to the normal travails of humanity, but he suffered himself to be spit on and mocked as a human — and this as his chosen *modus operandi!* How could this be God? What an offense to natural understandings of blessing! Yet, says Luther, quoting Psalm 118:22-23, "The stone which the builders rejected has become the chief cornerstone. This is the Lord's doing, it is marvelous in our eyes."

If verse 4 is about the physical humiliation and suffering of Christ as part of God's work, then verse 5 is about his spiritual suffering. In his exegesis of this verse, Luther is well aware that the Hebrew says וַתְּחַסְּרֵהוּ מְּעַט מֵאֱלֹהִים, "you made him a little lower than Elohim," but he is led by his

Christological focus to ask, "What does it mean for Christ to be 'a little less than God'?" His mind turns to Job, the upright man forsaken by God. It is God-forsakenness that is death, he argues, in being indistinguishable from the turning away of God's face, which is a harbinger of the destruction of the wicked. Only certain faith and hope live through such death. Satan attacks Job, and God allows the attack only as a means to further his work and Job's faith. This experience of the spiritual suffering of Job illuminates the work of Christ, which finds full expression in the cry of the cross, "My God, my God, why have you forsaken me?" (Matt. 27:46).

Luther asks himself, "If I, as a part of Christ's kingdom, am to correctly convey the meaning of Christ's experience of being 'a little less than God', how might I say it?" His response is to retain the figurative LXX translation in his: "Eine kleine zeit von Gott verlassen sein," that is, "You will forsake him for a little while." The translation links the believer's experience of the invisibility of God and the work of Christ on the cross in order to elucidate what Christians should expect to experience in Christ's kingdom on earth. The beginning and completion of Christ's kingdom "happened in this way," concludes Luther, with this rationality,

> that the Lord, our Ruler, true Man and Son of Man, travailed with body and soul in His tender humanity. . . . On the cross He was utterly forsaken, and they gave Him vinegar to drink in His great thirst. All creation behaves as though it were against Him. He hangs in the air and is suspended on high and has nowhere on earth to place His foot. There is no one to sympathize with Him or comfort Him. That is His suffering.[67]

Christ's suffering, because it is ours by participation, brings ours to light. In it we learn how God both teaches and protects the certain hope and sure faith that grounds Christian love. The faith displayed during Christ's wrestling with a God who has become invisible is the template of Christian hope. "A Christian must know definitely that his suffering will have an end and will not endure forever, lest he become like a rejected Judas and despair and blaspheme God. Therefore St. Peter says [1 Pet. 1:6]: 'A little suffering'; and Psalm 8:5: 'To lack God a little while,' so that a Christian may look beyond his trouble and behold its end."[68]

As Christ's suffering illumines the Christian life, so does his resurrection, which is his "crowning with glory and honor." Luther finishes his philological work on verse 5 by looking at the כָּבוֹד (kabod), "honor," and הָדָר (hadar),

---

67. Luther, "Psalm 45," pp. 127-28.
68. Luther, *Luther's Works, Vol. 13*, p. 382.

"adornment," which crown Christ. *Kabod*, he says, means overflowing with goods: "Him who was forsaken by God and by all creation will be elevated to such glory and honor that all the angels of God will adore him" ("Psalm 8," p. 129). Those glorifying him are thus Christ's "glory"[69] and "adornment." The Hebrew word *hadar* (adornment) means splendorous clothing, says Luther, and this fulfills Christ's promise to array the nations around himself (Matt. 25:31-32). As Christ's natural body is adorned by the resurrection, his eternal adornment is his "spiritual body, which is his congregation" ("Psalm 8," p. 130). This resurrection is Christ's coronation with earthly and heavenly power, his securing of his adornment with spiritual followers.[70] The power of this redemption to reorder all creation is the subject of verses 6-8.

8:7   תַּמְשִׁילֵהוּ בְּמַעֲשֵׂי יָדֶיךָ כֹּל שַׁתָּה תַחַת־רַגְלָיו

8   צֹנֶה וַאֲלָפִים כֻּלָּם וְגַם בַּהֲמוֹת שָׂדָי

9   צִפּוֹר שָׁמַיִם וּדְגֵי הַיָּם עֹבֵר אָרְחוֹת יַמִּים

8:7   Du hast ihn zum Herrn machen über deiner Hände Werk; alles hast du unter seine Füsse getan:

8   Schafe und Ochsen allzumal, dazu auch die wilden Tiere,

9   die Vögel unter dem Himmel und die Fische im Meer und was im Meer gehet.

8:6   Thou wilt make Him Lord over the works of Thy hands; Thou hast put all things under His feet,

7   All sheep and oxen, and also the beasts of the field,

8   The birds of the air, and the fish of the sea, whatever passes along the paths of the sea.

These verses, says Luther, expound Christ's earthly rule. As previously mentioned, the Hebrew here, מָשַׁל *(mashal)*, means to have dominion, ruling as humans rule.[71] But only God can rule "all things"; therefore, this is an inductive proof that Christ is God, born in eternity, but lord in time.[72] Such

---

69. Luther, "Psalm Fifty," in *Luther's Works, Vol. 10*, pp. 230-31.

70. Here Luther is consciously reformulating Augustine's notion of the *totus Christus*, the influence of which is plain in Luther's earliest Psalms lectures; cf. Luther, "Psalm Eighty Four," p. 139, n. 11.

71. "In Judges 8:22 some men of Israel say to Gideon, 'be lord over us, you and your son and your grandson also; for you have delivered us out of the hand of Midian.' But Gideon answers, 'I will not be lord over you, and my son will not be lord over you; but the Lord will be lord over you. . . . Thus also Christ is to be made Lord, so that all might obey Him, men and angels.'" Luther, "Psalm 8," p. 131.

72. Luther, "Psalm 45," pp. 285, 132.

power cannot be attributed to Adam (Gen. 1:8), whose dominion was only of human reason over the fish, birds, and animals. "Here the text reads much differently: 'Thou hast put all things under His feet,' excluding nothing but the Father, who has subjected everything to the Son (1 Cor. 15:27). And this dominion extends to angels, men, and everything that is in heaven and on earth" ("Psalm 8," p. 133).[73]

This leads to a sharp rebuke of what, ironically, has come to be a familiar debasement of Lutheranism. "[W]e should not get some such idea as this: 'If Christ has a special, peculiar dominion and kingdom, He has nothing in common with Adam's dominion and kingdom.' The Christians must still live in the world. Where are they to stay and find something to eat and drink, if Christ has nothing to do with Adam's kingdom and the world is their enemy and will not grant them even a crust of bread?" ("Psalm 8," p. 135). In his comment on Psalm 45:12 ("Since he is your lord, bow to him; the people of Tyre will seek your favor with gifts, the richest of the people with all kinds of wealth"), Luther develops what we might call a political and economic "penumbra effect" of the gospel. The life-form of the gospel, by existing in the world, suggests some basic outlines of the secular rule that is necessary for this kingdom of the Word to survive. Because Christ is over them all, kings can only be humanity's foster fathers and are therefore responsible to God to keep open the social space within which the church carries on its work of proclamation.

> If there were no prince anywhere who embraced the Gospel there would be no place, no peace, no food, no clothing. The church would expire in short order. Therefore God has raised up certain princes who foster, support, and sustain the godly. . . . Necessarily, then, he comforts the church here, that there will not be lacking holy men and daughters of the church, also among the powerful and rich of the world, to maintain and defend the church, so that the statement of the psalm may be fulfilled (Ps. 110:2): 'Rule in the midst of Thine enemies.' ("Psalm 45," pp. 290, 292)

In his first lecture series, Luther took a more eschatological line on these verses, reminiscent of the "bomb crater" image of God's intervention in time that played such a central role in Barth's *Epistle to the Romans.* "[T]his is what Christ did. In lowliness, weakness, and shame He stripped the whole world of its strength, honor, and glory, and altogether annihilated it and transferred it

---

73. Interestingly, Luther thought that the statement of Christ's dominion in Ps. 8:6 made it an appropriate text for exorcism. In his table talk Luther tells of having confronted a poltergeist with these words. Luther, *Luther's Works, Vol. 54,* p. 280.

to Himself . . ." ("Psalm 8," p. 89). But unlike Barth's *Romans*, Luther's wrestling with the imagery of this psalm yields a more constructive ecclesiological and soteriological result. This eschatological impact is not just a negation of the world but a reorganization of its political and economic structures. Yet we must call this a penumbra effect of God's work, because it is only an exterior effect, an important though secondary result of his creating a kingdom of hope, faith, and love. In this sense, Barth's crater image was (as he came to realize) only an inversion of the critical force of God's work, and thus it necessarily overlooked the positive nature of the gospel's reordering of human social life.[74]

The contrast between the emphasis of the early Barth on critical negation and the criticism by superabundance of Luther's image of Christ's universal dominion gives a clearer view of how God works to bring about a new creation. By developing his focus on the moral power of human desire, Luther sets up a typology of human faith. "Sheep and oxen," says Luther, are those who accept that the glory in their works has been stripped away and who become tame, gentle, submissive to one another. "Sheep" are the quieter "moons" in the ordered constellation of Christ's church, and the "oxen" those of greater faith ("Psalm 8," pp. 89-90). The in-breaking of God's grace has the earthly effect of arranging a church whose internal order brings humanity into its true flourishing.

The wild animals are those sinners who have been corralled into the walls of the church but remain wild, not amenable to obedience to men. The fish are those outside the church. Christ's work accomplishes its purpose in oxen and sheep, bringing human wandering desires into a social network where they find a settled place and become productive. Yet this must not

---

74. This penumbra effect suggests powerful resources for Christian ethics. The gospel of Christ lives in the freedom of gathering and preaching the word, and the freedom from worry about the provision for the morrow that is embodied in Christ's life. Faith lives this political and economic freedom even in the absence of the proper conditions for its realization, i.e., political tyranny and economic want. Yet the implication of this gospel is that good government, even if not living in faith, should nevertheless be one that allows the life of faith to be carried out. We can thus claim by theological analogy not that the state *is* the church but that responsible secular government should minimally provide freedom of speech and gathering, and provide a minimum of economic security for all. Barth's *Community, State and Church* systematically develops the implications of this penumbra effect for an ethic of secular government. Oliver O'Donovan's *Desire of the Nations* develops a sharply observed historical account of the reality of this penumbra effect on the shape of Western political structures. What is surprising in this connection is that the implications of this penumbra effect for secular economic life have so rarely been theologically explicated in the last decades, as attempted, for instance, by Oliver O'Donovan in *The Ways of Judgment* (Grand Rapids: Eerdmans, 2005), ch. 14.

make us smug, warns Luther, for Christ has been given dominion over all creation; therefore, "even those who are most vagrant and slippery in the deep are under Christ" ("Psalm 8," p. 90). Some fish, he notes, are kept in fish ponds, though not tamed, while domestic animals can become unproductive if the growth of their rampant appetites is unchecked. What Christ does in his dominion, Luther concludes, is create a kingdom of those stripped of their earthly glory but ordered in their unified desire to crown Christ in praise.

8:10   יְהֹוָה אֲדֹנֵינוּ מָה־אַדִּיר שִׁמְךָ בְּכָל־הָאָרֶץ

8:10   HERR, unser Herrscher, wie herrlich ist dein Name in allen Landen!

8:9   O LORD, our Lord, how majestic is Thy name in all the lands!

"David concludes this psalm just the way he began it. He thanks the Lord, our Ruler, for His great and inestimable blessing, for establishing such a kingdom and calling and gathering His church, which gloriously praises His name throughout the world and thanks Him in heaven" ("Psalm 8," pp. 135-36). Luther understands himself to be following David's example in urging his readers to join the author in praise of God's work. With the psalmist, we are to live in hope of the victory of Christ's rule, a hope that finds expression in praises and thanks to God. We have noted that Luther considers his whole exegesis to be such praise, following "the example of this prophet as he prophesies to us" ("Psalm 8," p. 97).

Several conclusions can be drawn about what Luther has been doing in his "singing" of this psalm. His basic assumption is that the psalm participates in Christ's incarnation, serving his prophetic work. This leads Luther to emphasize that rightly understanding it depends on including the whole Christ story, from its beginning in heaven to its conclusion with Christ adorned with the lives of the saints. His emphasis is not on knowing all of God's "metaphysical workings," or on the constant awareness Christ's Word creates of those aspects of the soteriological drama that can be spoken by babes. The passion narrative recounted in Psalm 8 begins in heaven. Christ is pictured as coming down to suffer under the world's power to inaugurate his continuing of this struggle through the mouths of babes. Thus the psalm itself, by facilitating the doxological recounting of God's own story, facilitates what it describes: the victory of Christ's lordship recapitulated in a fresh outworking of his victory through weakness.

Luther does not set God on one side and humans on another, trying to define each and their relationship to each other; he simply looks for an opportunity to verbalize the story of God, the retelling of which involves him deeper in it. The story he tells is not outside his own search, pertaining to another independent actor, but is his story only because Christ's. Luther is not thinking about how to get in touch with a God somehow beyond and over him; he is verbally and methodologically thinking through the contours and categories of his inclusion in Christ's own victory.

By understanding the gospel in this way, Luther concludes that moral deliberation and human action are properly oriented only when humans immerse themselves in the drama of Christ's work. We can say, then, that Luther does not think of humans as "story-telling animals," an image that emphasizes human creativity, but as "drama-suffering animals" or "story-permeated things."[75] Human creativity comes to life in perceiving what it means that Christ's one triumph clarifies or rewrites all other narrations of world events. The subject of theology is this new creature with God, who has been taught her place in the one drama and no longer must generate her own drama, or wander around story-less and lost.[76]

In a phrase, Luther is telling us to understand this singing, chattering, and verbal meditation as orienting us within Christ's victory. Our abstraction from our Creator and our alienation from Scripture is self-imposed. To begin to know where we are in God's working, and thus to know who we are, does not demand hermeneutical or ethical method; rather, it demands trust and hope and a willingness to observe and experience faith firsthand. Preaching tells the story of Christ in as high topographical relief as possible, as an invitation to embrace the place we find ourselves in Christ's rule. Praise makes it possible for us to collaborate with God's attempt to explain our role in the divine drama. Luther's quest is thus for deeper awareness of the reality that is happening to us, rather than a program for changing our lives. Awareness, he believes, is found in exploring the microcosm and heart of reality that is the Christ story. Luther explores Scripture in order to become familiar with Christ's kingdom, going backward and forward through Scripture's account of it in microcosm. This, he concludes, is the Christian "way" (Psalm 1) of being human. Christians are those journeying on this way, exploring this law, and meeting together in the united recognition of the dominion of this Lord.

Again, this implies that every psalm can be read as part of such an exploration. Every psalm includes within it a hermeneutics of itself because

---

75. He is not claiming this on the basis of a general human anthropology, but is making a theological observation about the form of redeemed humanity. Cf. Stanley Hauerwas, *Performing the Faith: Bonhoeffer and the Practice of Nonviolence* (Grand Rapids: Baker Books, 2004), ch. 5, "The Narrative Turn: Thirty Years Later."

76. Cf. Hans G. Ulrich, *Wie Geschöpfe leben: Konturen evangelischer Ethik* (Münster: Lit Verlag, 2005), ch. A4, "In der Tradition der ethischen Exploration," pp. 198-225.

Christ is to be heard in every psalm: the presence of Christ is the rescue that the Psalms ask for, receive, and praise.

Psalm 111: The Lord's Supper as Inflaming Praise

Having found Psalm 8 to draw attention to Christ's work of "adorning" himself with the church, Luther interprets Psalm 111 as elucidating the role played by the church in the redemption of all creation. He focuses this account on how God grants humans new desire for him in the celebration of the Lord's Supper. Luther interprets David to be offering Psalm 111 to inflame the gratitude of the faithful for God's provision of the Eucharist.[77] Because the transformation of the affections plays such a central role in Luther's ethics, such "gratitude inflammation" is essential for the renewal of the Christian mind, perception, and behavior. This further clarifies how praise is located by Scripture, within the church, both of which frame his ethic of doxology.

Luther's 1530 treatise on Psalm 111 is an occasional piece, dedicated and addressed to the Christian nobleman Kaspar von Kröckritz, exhorting him and all Christian nobles to take their political responsibilities with proper Christian seriousness. The treatise is of great interest because it displays Luther's consistent belief that moral exhortation is only properly undertaken as "chattering" about Scripture, through which Luther intends to inflame a deeper appreciation of God's grace, especially as embodied in the Eucharist. Moralizing in Christian ethics is counterproductive; only an inflamed appreciation of God's grace transforms Christian living. An ethos of doxology aims to serve the renewal of the heart as the center of Christian ethics, displacing a focus on human willing and its ends. Therefore, the bulk of Luther's treatment of Psalm 111 is devoted to seeking a renewed heart and affections. The renewed heart is one that explores the breadth and depth of God's grace in the particular places given for each individual to love others. This is the basic presupposition of what we have called the penumbra effect of the gospel, in that the renewal of humanity through the Spirit generates ripples of moral renewal throughout the social fabric. And via the witness shed by this renewal, God tempts the world to journey to seek his face at the place he has given himself to be known: Christian worship.

Luther's exegesis of Psalm 111, which relates the Christian Eucharist to Israel's Passover celebration, also gives us an especially close view of his under-

---

77. Martin Luther, "Psalm 111," in *Luther's Works, Vol. 13*, p. 353 (page references to this work hereafter cited parenthetically in text).

standing of the unity of the two testaments. Easter, he says, is another name for the divinely commanded annual celebration of God's freeing Israel from the living death of slavery in Egypt (Exod. 12:42). "Therefore it seems to me that this psalm was composed for the Easter festival. Here David wanted to provide a model for the people and to put words into their mouths, showing them how they should express such praise and thanks" ("Psalm 111," p. 355). But, Luther continues, this Easter festival has been abolished by Jesus Christ, who has himself become the Easter lamb (1 Cor. 5:7), thus instituting a "far greater festival."

The Christian eucharistic celebration is the continuation of Israel's Passover as a remembrance of Christ's claiming of his church. "He defeated our enemy, the devil, death, and sin, and led us out of the real Egypt into the real Promised Land, that is, eternal life" ("Psalm 111," p. 355). So, although the original Passover setting for which this psalm was written is abolished, its inner truth continues unbroken in the Eucharist. Luther defends this transposition of Israelite into Christian ritual by referring to Paul's interpretation, in which the latter calls Christians the true Isaac and Christendom the real Sarah and Jerusalem (Gal. 4:22-28). "Thus we may also well apply, interpret, and sing this psalm for the holy Sacrament with no harm done" ("Psalm 111," p. 355). One of the effects of this transposition is to make it a daily remembrance: the annual celebration of Easter is continued for "ancient memory's sake," but, in fact, every day is Easter for Christians. Each day is shaped by a constant awareness, remembrance, and praise of Christ's suffering and alienation during his crucifixion — and the new thing of his resurrection.

This is not a simple translation of Israel's worship without remainder, but it rests on the assumption that Christian worship is only legitimate if it continues the genuine relationship of Israel with the God depicted in the Old Testament. Luther is firmly committed to the proposition that the Christian Eucharist is not properly understood without explicitly taking account of its roots in the Passover festival; nor is Psalm 111 properly sung as praise of God's grace in Christ unless it is understood simultaneously as David's praise of God's work of salvation in Egypt. This leads Luther to undertake an experiment unique in his writings. He interprets the psalm twice, the first time reading it as Israel's praise in the context of the Old Testament, and the second time, building on the first, as the church's praise of God's grace in Eucharist.

Rather than giving a full account of how Luther relates Passover and Eucharist in his exegesis of Psalm 111, my aim will be to complete the description of Luther's ethic of doxology. Clearly, Luther has advanced the subtlety and nuance of Christian biblical interpretation by arguing for a close study of the local Old Testament setting of a biblical text that will ultimately be interpreted in a Christian way. It is an approach that came deeply to shape modern exegesis in establishing the viability of the claim that the accuracy and nuance of New Testament interpretation rest on a fine-grained appreciation of the wide range of distinctions and traditions of which the Old Testament is made up. At the same time, this approach raises questions that Christian interpreters cannot avoid, especially interpreters of Luther, that is, the problem of supersessionism. After outlining how Luther understands the celebration of the Eucharist to orient the Christian community within God's remaking of the orders of human social existence, we will return briefly to discuss whether Luther's exegesis has the resources to avoid a supersessionist theology. I will suggest that it does, but only if we take seriously that worship in faith, hope, and love is at the same time an ethos.

Luther's insistence on attending to the Hebrew context of the Psalms leads him to treat each line of Psalm 111 separately, as its acrostic structure suggests. I will follow Luther in this ordering.

111.1a הַלְלוּ יָהּ אוֹדֶה יְהוָה בְּכָל־לֵבָב

Aleph. Ich danke dem HEERN von Ganzem herzen.

Aleph, I will give thanks to the LORD with my whole heart.

Luther begins with a terse summary of the theological position we have seen him developing in Psalms 1, 8, and 118. Genuine singing of this verse (1) comes from the affective level of human being, the desiring being, and (2) genuinely thanks and praises God and not human strength. Here Luther emphasizes that this performative congruence has a pneumatological basis and an ethical result.

> [T]he emphasis here is on thanking with the 'whole heart' so that it may be a heartfelt, profound, and genuine thanks and not one which says with the mouth: 'Thank God!' and with the heart: 'There is no God' (Ps. 1:1). It is an art, an art of the Holy Spirit, to give thanks or to say 'Thank God!' from the heart. And if someone can say this from the heart, you need not worry that he is proud, stubborn, dissolute, and savage, or that he will turn against God with all his goods. ("Psalm 111," p. 365)

Praise is thus simultaneously a confession of human sin and divine might,[78] which has the effect of loosing the praiser from the selfish grasping for earthly power that denudes human society and all creation.

---

78. See his extended discussion of the relationship of confession and praise in the first lectures: Luther, "Psalm One Hundred Eleven," in *Luther's Works*, Vol. 11, p. 371.

111.1b   בְּסוֹד יְשָׁרִים וְעֵדָה

Beth. Im Rat der aussrichtigen und ynn der gemeine.

Beth, In the council of the upright, in the congregation.

This "council of the upright" is the counterpoint to the "counsel of the wicked" of Psalm 1:1. If wickedness forms a council that exploits and denudes sociality, then the essence of the council of the upright is its nature as a conduit bringing divine new life into the world's broken social dynamic. The claim that the purpose of this council is the renewal of the world is based, first, on the observation that it is a gathering, and thus a public body, structurally open to the unbelieving world. Such a community is embedded in all parts of society, and is separated from it only by its explicit praise of Christ's lordship ("Psalm 111," pp. 356-57). Luther uses this social understanding of worship to rule out, on the one hand, private masses in which no human hears Christ proclaimed (1 Cor. 11:12, 26) ("Psalm 111," p. 366), and, on the other hand, the movements that set up screens in a futile attempt to separate the wheat from the chaff by constructing a barrier between the praising congregation and the nonpraising world ("Psalm 111," p. 373). If the church is the congregation of the upright, it is essential to its public nature that it is always attracting those whose doxology is misdirected: "[S]ince the assembly of the righteous cannot exist except in the congregation, where the evil are mixed in, therefore both should be taken together" ("Psalm 111," p. 373).

The unity of this congregation is of both the "leaf" of doctrine and the "fruit" of good works (Ps. 1:3) as created by the Spirit. "There must be living saints wherever the Sacrament and worship of God are sincerely administered; for this cannot happen without the Holy Spirit, as St. Paul declares (1 Cor. 12:3)" ("Psalm 111," p. 365). The unity of these saints is in their "faith, hope, and charity, though they are apart in place and time, they are nevertheless one in charity and faith" ("Psalm 111," p. 373).

111.2a   גְּדֹלִים מַעֲשֵׂי יְהוָה

Gimel. Gros sind die werk des HEERN.

Gimel, Great are the works of the LORD.

The origin of this unity of faith, hope, and love is the community's shared praise of the works of God (v. 1a). Because the coming verses focus on more specific aspects of God's work, Luther understands these first verses of praise as general praise of all God's works, the whole cosmos, which is worthy of praise because it was created to sustain and preserve human existence. Creation is a proximate form of God's care for us, a discovery that the "new creature created in Christ through his Holy Spirit" (Ps. 8:3) makes in praising it ("Psalm 111," p. 374). "[O]ne must meditate on the works of God and consider them well, then one will discover how wonderful and great they are, and then the heart will find in them nothing but admiration, pleasure and joy" ("Psalm 111," p. 358). Therefore, the divine work this verse praises is — and participates in — the generation of a righteous community that is discovering creation as it really is, leading Luther to regularly link this verse with Mary's *Magnificat* (Luke 1:49): "He has done great things for me."[79]

דְּרוּשִׁים לְכָל־חֶפְצֵיהֶם   2b

Daleth. Ersucht zu all yhrer lust.

Daleth, Studied by all who have pleasure in them.

Here Luther again meditates on a biblical statement to discern what it rules out, in this case ingratitude for God's grace in creation. Most people never consider the biological and meteorological wonders that sustain them, being

> used to them and saturated with them like an old house with smoke. They use them and root around in them like a hog in a bag of feed. They say: 'Oh, is that such a great thing that the sun shines, or fire warms, or water gives fish, or the earth yields grain, or a cow calves, or a woman bears children, or a hen lays eggs? That happens every day!' ("Psalm 111," pp. 366-67)

Luther makes his point and practices it at the same time: doxology does not overlook or disdain any of God's blessings, nor does it express a generalized thanks that is unspecific. It is a practice of naming each "fire that warms and water that gives fish" as finely textured and proximate divine care. Doxology makes these gifts visible as forms of God's love in all their glorious particularity. "This is what it means to study the works of the Lord: to search them out, to meditate on them, to examine them, and to consider how it would be if they had not been created. Then one finds in them pure admiration and pleasure. But only the upright do this, as Psalm 92:4 says: 'Lord, Thou makest me glad with Thy works.'" Scoffers, conversely, sing only an anti-doxology here:

---

79. Luther, "Psalm One Hundred Four," in *Luther's Works, Vol. 11*, p. 316.

"Poor and unimportant is what God creates, and it is to be despised to the point of weariness and disgust" ("Psalm 111," pp. 367-68). Praise dethrones the illusion that our life depends on the processes of "biological life" or other physical processes, revealing in them the lordship of the divine life-giver.

Evolutionary cosmologies provide an obvious counter-example in taking the intricacy of material order as nothing more than the necessary conditions for our existence. The upshot, as Luther predicted, is that when these conditions are threatened, I fear for my very existence.[80] The good news is that creation is a gift for humanity to love and enjoy as one cannot a "necessary premise," an insight orienting Christian thinking about the environment. An ethic of doxology makes it possible for Christians to engage in care for the environment as a form of trust in God's promise that he will uphold his work of creation.[81] As Karl Barth famously paraphrases the point, creation is for the purpose of the covenant, and creation is upheld as part of God's overflowing fulfillment of his promises not to forget his community of praise and thus all humanity.[82] The world does not know that the universe is created *ex nihilo*, and so its very existence is an argument against its impulse to rely on its own skills for its continuing existence. Those who praise are learning how little they contribute to their own creation and thus how they are surrounded by divine love as intimately present as the air they breathe. That God created *ex nihilo* is the primal humbling of humanity, our confirmation as reliant beings. The meaning of this statement is one we are continually learning within a universe already in motion and maintained by the divine working.

It is important to clarify the methodological implications of Luther's ethic of doxology. Naming the doxologies and anti-doxologies of our age is an essential critical task of Christian ethics. However, the theological stability of this approach depends on the orientation of our descriptions of anti-doxology by a clear view of the doxology we understand contemporary practice to be rejecting. In this respect, to take one example, Amy Laura Hall's excellent genealogical cultural history of the contemporary anti-doxologies of American family life, *Conceiving Parenthood*,[83] gains its rhetorical force by as-

---

80. Hans Jonas's *The Imperative of Responsibility: In Search of an Ethics for the Technological Age*, trans. Hans Jonas and David Herr (Chicago: University of Chicago Press, 1984), provides a perfect example of an ethic based on a "heuristic of fear" that we will, through our technological exploits, lose the "heritage of evolution"; see ch. 2.I-II.

81. This point is further discussed in ch. 9, p. 334.

82. Barth, *Church Dogmatics*, III.1, trans. J. W. Edwards, O. Bussey, and H. Knight (Edinburgh: T&T Clark, 1958), para. 40.

83. Amy Laura Hall, *Conceiving Parenthood* (Grand Rapids: Eerdmans, forthcoming).

suming that there are subcurrents in her audience with some sympathy for "the least of these" who are rendered nonpersons by modern ideology. But what if this is not the case? Or what if we speak to a church and world that truly believe some children are not "us"? Hall quite rightly parallels Luther in suggesting that Christians cannot properly interrogate modern reproductive practice without asking, "Who is my neighbor? When was it that we saw you hungry or thirsty or a stranger . . . and did not take care of you?"[84]

Yet we can and must ask how Christians are properly to know this stranger, how we are to derive the categories that make the true stranger visible, and doxology teaches us this: "Children are indeed a heritage from the LORD, the fruit of the womb a reward" (Ps. 127:3). Christian theology must not assume that anti-doxology can only partially obscure what only God's word can make plain. It may indeed discover that the fertility of creation has come to appear as rottenness in the eyes of our contemporaries. When this occurs, Christian theology can only undertake cultural criticism as lament. William Stringfellow provides one example of such a lament when he explicitly orients his (rather impressionistic) critique of anti-doxology and its ethical practices by way of the doxologies of Psalm 137 and Revelation 18:1-8.[85] Luther has suggested why and how Hall's fine-grained cultural studies and Stringfellow's criticism as lament might be combined.

הוֹד־וְהָדָר פָּעֳלוֹ 3a

He. Sein thun ist lob und schmuck.

He, Full of honor and adornment is His work.

We are again reminded of the theological importance of translation in noting the difference between Luther's German and the English translation (taken from *Luther's Works,* cf. note 61). What the English puts in the third person, "Full of honor and adornment is His work," Luther puts in the second person: "Your work *is* honor and adornment." That is, God's works are not "full of" but "are" honor and adornment. Because creation already praises him, it stands as a divine address through creation to creation. It is not the task of human praise to look around creation to find good things to praise, which would put us in the role of having to make value judgments and be-

---

84. Hall, "Better Homes and Children: The Brave New World of Meticulously Planned Parenthood," *Books and Culture* (Nov./Dec. 2005): 18.

85. William Stringfellow, *An Ethic for Christians in a Strange Land* (Eugene, OR: Wipf and Stock, 2004).

stow validity on creation in the way a parent praises a child to encourage good behavior, for example. Praise is the human way of *participating* in the great doxology that creation already is. The implication is that human praise is not something we produce but is something we must learn: doxology begins not in the decision to pull up our bootstraps but in abandoning our refusal to join the chorus already under way.

Here Luther's close attention to the Old Testament context also yields a surprising set of connections of particular relevance for Christian ethics.

> This is the second reason for praise. Here the psalmist approaches the festival of Easter and the Easter lamb. But once again he refers to all God's works in general, not especially to creation or other wonderful acts, but to all his ordinances and institutions, which he established by his Word and Command — such as the station of father and mother, of priests and Levites according to Moses' Law, of servant and maid, marriage, the station of lords and subjects, Sabbath and feast days, worship and church order, and the like. ("Psalm 111," p. 358)

What do these orders mean in the light of Christ? "[T]hat a servant, maid, son, daughter, man, woman, lord, subject, or whoever else may belong to a station ordained by God, as long as he fills his station, is as beautiful and glorious in the sight of God as a bride adorned for her marriage" ("Psalm 111," p. 368). The mechanics of this transposition of Israel's relationship to God's ordering of social life become clear in Luther's exposition of the next verse.

3b   וְצִדְקָתוֹ עֹמֶדֶת לָעַד

Vau. Und seine gerechtigkeit bleibt ewiglich.

Vau, And His righteousness endures forever.

God is not content simply to create praisers with no relationship to historical reality. His intention is for his creation to be full of honor and majesty and that it combat the dissolution and disorder of creation by disciplining and ordering it. Working backwards by following the *ordo cogniscendi* through Luther's exposition, we can uncover the logic of God's working to order all creation. Though the discussion does not take up much of the essay, it is here that Luther cashes out what all this means for Christian political ethics, for von Kröckritz, and for his fellow Christian noblemen.

Luther has already suggested in his exegesis of Psalm 8 that, because Christ is Lord over creation in the manner of a human lord, he is establishing a righteousness that will last eternally within the realm of mundane, earthly affairs. This explains why Luther speaks first of the church as he outlines how God's eternal righteousness is established in history. Commenting on the "righteousness that endures forever," he says: "[T]he real application of this verse to us is that here we thank God for the office and work of Christ and His apostles. He is the real Caesar; and they are the real princes in the spiritual estate, conducting the office of the ministry. Here in these spiritual offices there is real honor and adornment in saving souls from sin, death, and the devil" ("Psalm 111," p. 370).

In verse 3b, God's "righteousness," צְדָקָה (sedaqah), can also be translated "his justice." The righteousness that Christ is establishing forever is his justice, a justice most apparent in his holding together his people by ordering them, setting up princes and correct teaching among them, as well as festivals of remembrance and practices of proclamation. This realm of living justice and peace is his eternal heritage and the eternal heritage of humanity. By "living justice" Luther means the justice of Christ embodied in the church through the Spirit. With this move he intends to cut off attempts by Christians to claim that it is morality that is eternal rather than Christ. Morals, for the church, are time-bound attempts by the church to state what the rule of Christ over human action means, statements that, because subject to the one eternal truth of Christ, are always subject to revision and restatement under the discipline of theological wisdom.[86]

In remembering the work of Christ, the praising community embraces its being given the fruitful internal divisions of a body that replace the destructive divisions of self-exaltation. Paralleling God's ordering of the formless waters of Genesis 1, which are divided into land and sea to be richly populated by fish and animals, the tumultuous political chaos of the world raging against God and itself is carefully reordered to form stations within which humans can flourish: the wandering "fish" are made productive and generous "oxen and sheep." "And God has appointed in the church first apostles, second prophets, third teachers; then deeds of power, then gifts of healing, forms of assistance, forms of leadership, various kinds of tongues" (1 Cor. 12:28).

The experience of this churchly ordering prepares believers to see that God is also working in a similar way to order all society for peace. "[N]owhere among men on earth is there a people like the Christians, who understand so well and can teach so well what worldly stations are. They alone know and teach that these are divine ordinances and institutions.

---

86. Luther came to this insight early and linked it with Ps. 111:3 as early as his "Explanations of the 95 Theses," p. 108.

Therefore they alone can truly thank and pray for them in their churches" ("Psalm 111," p. 370). This verse is God's promise to create the political order and peace, which is the condition of continuing human life. Doxology thus forms a community that can see and defend the beauty of social order as God's grace in a world that rarely recognizes the divine nature of all political peace, a momentous claim for Christian political ethics. Moral theology is, in this view, understood not as the attempt to generate political insights through the development of detailed ethical prescriptions for society, but a vocation to redirect attention to the proper source of political will for solutions. Christians alone can express the inner meaning of the divine gift of political order and fecundity, which some people see but incorrectly describe.

Those who live within political orders without constantly recognizing them as a divine gift, Luther continues, wittingly or unwittingly rebel against them as "dangerous stations which arose by chance, contrary to the will and command of God" ("Psalm 111," p. 370). Luther's point is that, if we think of political order as a human construct, we cannot escape the politics of suspicion, rooted in the worry that government is merely an imposition of political force serving the self-interest of those who rule. Here Luther touches on the heart of the debate between those who see all politics and social ordering as manifestations of the will to power and those who try to meet this challenge in modern liberal fashion by saying that political order is mandated not by actors but by "reason." Luther agrees with the former that, without God, humans do use politics for selfish and thus destructive purposes, while he is also in agreement with the neo-Kantians that the political work of social ordering can be defended only by referring beyond human authority. Yet Luther is able to tie these together — as neither side can — by praising the ongoing divine work of sustaining the political peace that exists, an ordering that is more dynamic than the inherent stasis of "eternal reason" and more capable of building trust than the politics of suspicion.

Clearly, Luther is further suggesting that the sacred political order (often referred to as part of civil society) generates a positive undercurrent on which secular political order depends. But Luther is not equating the church with one of many groups that make up civil society, because the sacred and secular are not symmetrical concepts. The opposite of the praise and the ordered social space it creates is not the secular, but the blindness and rebellion against a whole range of God's gifts in the form of stable social order. In such a world, a Hobbesian war-management political strategy is the most generous account of political order that secular thought can give, which always appears as an arbitrary power struggle.

Luther's suggestion is that praising God reveals political order as a gift, which makes possible a much more positive account of political order that embraces Christian service within it. Here Charles Taylor rightly grasps the essentially theological nature of Luther's view of social order and how, historically, it led to a hallowing of daily life. This hallowing of daily life was secularized, in turn, to produce some of the essential facets of our modern secular world.[87] Viewing through our modern secular lenses, we easily overlook Luther's insistence on the theological importance of not understanding the secular political realm as *without* God. The secular political order is a particular kind of order, provided by God, which formally recognizes that even those who rage against him are given space to live. But this political space is received by Christians as a gift of grace that makes possible service of others. Luther is not simply glorifying political order-making ("all social order in principle a good thing") but is offering a theological account that makes it possible for Christians to appreciate the moments of justice within secular political life, an appreciation that makes living within it ethically productive. Luther's suggestion is that, in one's job, marriage, and political and economic life, one serves the Lord who establishes justice in these orders for a human society that does not fall into chaos because God sustains it even for those who reject him.

Luther now makes explicit how one might discover what parts of social order are established by God and what parts are accidental features of sociality. His logic follows the argument he has used in relation to the church: because we are included in Christ, we know that God cares for the whole world by ordering it for peace. And because Christ cared for Israel's whole social existence, we can see that he took time to set out for them precepts about household economy, political life, and the order of their worship. Luther makes clear that God preserves "the station of father and mother, of priests and Levites according to Moses' Law, of servant and maid, marriage, the station of lords and subjects, Sabbath and feast days, worship and church order, and the like" ("Psalm 111," p. 358)[88] even for those who despise them, in order to restrain avarice and destructive greed. God spoke this order into existence at creation and maintained it through the decrees he gave to Israel, to which the church is attentive. In emphasizing the centrality of God's speaking for revealing the order of creation, Luther explicitly refers his formulation to the concerns of the natural law tradition ("Psalm 111," p. 369). Yet he insists that, while the divine stations and orders have been es-

---

87. Charles Taylor, *Sources of the Self: The Making of the Modern Identity* (Cambridge, MA: Harvard University Press, 1989), pp. 218, 256.

88. These are the *Stände* discussed by Bonhoeffer in ch. 5, pp. 91-93.

tablished by God so that "there may be a stable, orderly, and peaceful life, and that justice may be preserved" ("Psalm 111," p. 369), he refuses to allow that we may at any time have unmediated access to them. The primary function of the doctrine of Christ as Word or Logos is preventing either the separation or equation of God's creative word and redeeming act.[89] The only access to both is in praise.

The stations can be inhabited by those who do not praise their Creator, but they can only be truly known within the acknowledgment of praise, which is characterized by joy and thankfulness. Any attempt to defend them on other than doxological grounds will appear arbitrary and confusing. Access to the orders that ground social flourishing is through meditation on God's words, and meditation becomes wisdom and understanding only in those who discover God's grace in the order of social life by exploring it in action. Here praise is again established as performative congruence that reaches far beyond the speech act, that is, it is "a really good understanding if you acted accordingly in your life" ("Psalm 111," p. 386).

זֵכֶר עָשָׂה לְנִפְלְאֹתָיו   4a

Zain. Er hat ein gedechtnis gemacht seiner wunder.

Zayin, He has made a remembrance of His wonderful works.

We come now, says Luther, to the chief subject of the psalm, the Lord's Supper. "Christ calls it His remembrance when He says (1 Cor 11:24): 'This do in remembrance of Me'" ("Psalm 111," p. 371). The Lord's Supper is a liturgical form sustaining the perpetual remembrance of God's works, a claim defended by reference to the logic of Passover: the celebrants did not offer sacrifice, but they consecrated a lamb[90] as a collective recollection of God's mighty deeds of liberation. As Israel was commanded to recall its divine liberation from temporal death, so in the Lord's Supper, Christians "should contemplate, diligently regard, and consider what a glorious and beautiful work it is that Christ has delivered us from sin, death, and the devil. Here one should consider what our condition would be if these wonderful works had not been performed for us" ("Psalm 111," p. 373). In this turning of disor-

---

89. Pelikan, *Luther the Expositor*, pp. 53-54.

90. Jacob Milgrom has ratified the correctness of Luther's insight through a close examination of the difference between consecration *(terumah)* and sacrifice *(tenupah)*, as differentiated, for instance, in Lev. 10:14: ". . . but the breast of the תְּנוּפָה *(tenupah)* and the thigh of the תְּרוּמָה *(terumah)*." See Milgrom, *Leviticus 1–16: A New Translation with Introduction and Commentary*, vol. 1 (New York: Doubleday, 1999), pp. 473-81.

der into order, we see what a grace it is that God orders the church, society, and all creation.

Again, the accessibility of this grace tempts us to complacency. Just as we tend to become jaded about God's grace in creation and political preservation, we also become blasé about the Lord's Supper: "In short, we cannot sufficiently marvel at it and contemplate it in eternity. And yet, when we hear about it, we clods . . . yawn about it and say: 'Oh, is this the first time you have ever seen a rotten apple drop from a tree?'" ("Psalm 111," p. 373). It is not accidental that Luther again illustrates his point with the metaphor of fruitfulness. Doxology sees and praises God's provision and care for fertility and new life in all its forms, especially in the worship service. Anti-doxology cannot comprehend how worship is formed, like creation and political order, to express God's fecundity, seeing in the pinnacle of that fecundity only self-delusion and blemishes. The heart renewed for wonder is the heart that is redirected to perceive all of God's acts and thus to find ever-new ways to be a conduit of divine love within the space God has created for us to live.

4b   חַנּוּן וְרַחוּם יְהוָה

Heth. Der gnedige und barmherziger HERR.

Cheth, The LORD is gracious and merciful.

If we refrain from partaking in the Lord's Supper because we believe we are not good enough and God will reject us, we do not yet grasp the work of the cross and the grammar of grace and mercy it affirms. If we insist that Christ's work is not pure grace and mercy, we refuse God's self-designation in Christ and prefer — for our own reasons and in our own strength — that God be the angry judge. In this respect God is as we presume him to be. "As they believe, so it is done to them. If He is to be gracious and give blessings, it must be toward those who need the blessings; if He is to be merciful and patient, it must be toward those who need it" ("Psalm 111," p. 376). This is a terse statement of a regularly recurring idea. "It is certain, then, that for bold and satisfied spirits, whose sin does not prick them, mass is of no value, for they have as yet no hunger for this food, since they are still too full. The mass demands and must have a hungry soul, which longs for the forgiveness of sins and divine favor."[91] The proper source of this hunger is the subject of the next verse.

---

91. Luther, "Treatise on the New Testament, That Is, the Holy Mass," in *Luther's Works, Vol. 35, Word and Sacrament I*, ed. Theodore Bachmann, trans. Jeremiah Schindel (Philadelphia: Muhlenberg Press, 1960), p. 110.

טֶרֶף נָתַן לִירֵאָיו 5a

Teth. Er gibt speise denen, der ihn furchten.

Teth, He provides food for those who fear Him.

This is a praise of the *form* of sustenance being received in the Lord's Supper. Though physical food is present, what is nourished in this eating is the soul. This is why those who do not hunger but are devoid of fear, who are smug and untroubled, feed on their own opinions rather than the Eucharist. Grace is received only by trees thirsting for heavenly water. For those who know they are "planted" — transplanted from the community of sin — their awareness of misery and sin sustains the thirst for God's vivification that makes them a conduit for God's rain in a dry land. The Lord is "pitying the wretched and making the miserable one able to have mercy on others, so that He is not only rich toward His own, but also abounding, causing them to make others rich" ("Psalm 111," p. 379).

יִזְכֹּר לְעוֹלָם בְּרִיתוֹ 5b

Jod. Er gedenckt an seinen bund ewiglich.

Yodh, He is eternally mindful of His covenant.

This means nothing less for Luther than that, in the Lord's Supper, Jesus unites himself with humanity, making us part of *his* work. "It is not our institution or work but his alone; and he performs it through us and in us" ("Psalm 111," p. 377). Luther clarifies this rather counterintuitive assertion by saying, "The psalmist is not speaking of an inward remembrance in the heart but of a public and expressed remembrance, of which Christ says (1 Cor. 11:24): 'Do this in remembrance of Me.' This takes place through preaching and the Word of God. This remembrance, which He instituted . . . endures 'eternally,' to the end of the world" ("Psalm 111," p. 377). Luther's point is that in the worship service, with its foundations in praise, the preaching of Christ, and his remembrance in the Lord's Supper, Jesus Christ is entering the public sphere of human space and time, the renewal of all creation radiating out from this point. Stated in negative terms, worship creates a vacuum that attracts sin and wretchedness, revealing it not abstractly, but by transforming it into the order of peace. Open traffic at this point sustains God's remaking of human social life and all creation, and blockage here — due to human self-reliance — allows all creation to lapse again into lifeless waste. As the Lord's

Supper is God's work of renewing creation, in partaking of it we become part of God's work of reclaiming the whole creation for himself.

6a   כֹּחַ מַעֲשָׂיו הִגִּיד לְעַמּוֹ

Caph. Er verkundigt seinem volck die krafft seiner werck.

Caph, He has shown his people the power of his works.

This verse allows Luther to further develop the claim that Christ performs the Lord's Supper in its participants. The works through which Christ has shown his people his power are for us to have

> drowned our sin in His blood, killed our death in His body, and by his death and resurrection conquered and cast down the power of the devil. . . . These are different works, more wonderful than when He drowned King Pharaoh in the Red Sea (Ex. 14:28), slew King Sihon, and killed King Og (Num. 21:33-34). About these wonderful works Christians are to preach forever — although, as he says, they really do not do the preaching but the Lord does it. He does not want it to be our work and it really is not; but He instituted it and gives us Spirit and grace for it, while He Himself does it through us. ("Psalm 111," p. 378)

As David sang of the exodus of Israel from Egypt, the church sings its harmony, the praise of being rescued from sin into peace.

6b   לָתֵת לָהֶם נַחֲלַת גּוֹיִם

Lamed. Das er yhn gebe das erbe der Heiden.

Lamedh, In giving them the heritage of the Gentiles.

Again, we get a closer view of the penumbra effect of the renewal of all creation that Christ works through the church. Israel was given the spoils of Egypt, a physical heritage. But under the rule of Christ, the whole existence of the gentiles is co-opted by grace and added to the church, which returns it in renewed form. "[W]here once there existed Gentiles, living and continuing, there are now Christians, as Psalm 2:8 also says: 'I will make the Gentiles Thy heritage.' All this is done through the preaching of His mighty acts. By this the Gentiles are spiritually displaced and their idols destroyed. For His Word is effective and does not return void (Is. 55:11)" ("Psalm 111," p. 378). Christian worship continues the ongoing process of making visible the spiritual power of the cross as it frees the world by continually questioning its gods of power, success, and comfort ("Psalm 111," p. 380).

מַעֲשֵׂי יָדָיו אֱמֶת וּמִשְׁפָּט

7a

Mem. Die werck seiner hende sind warheit und Recht.

Mem, The works of His hands are truth and justice.

The service of the church to the world is to bear within itself the painful grinding away of the idolatrous self. This is a paradoxical pain, as we undergo what appears to us as a loss of power and a being forsaken by the gods of fortune. Only the church can show the world what it looks like when freed from its enslavement to idols, and only true faith can praise Christ in the midst of this suffering of the cross:

> Therefore it is correctly called the work of His hands; and this is to be proclaimed continually among Christians so that they follow Christ in His suffering and become like Him. He too was shaped and prepared in this manner, not merely that He might redeem us from the devil, but also as an example which we should follow, as St. Peter says [1 Pet. 2:21], and to which we should be conformed [Rom. 8:29] . . . not everyone has the skill to sing this verse to God and to thank and praise Him in troubles and sufferings. Only the Christian can do that. ("Psalm 111," pp. 379-80)

The world can only be disillusioned and broken by the loss of its idols, but the Christian sees in it redemption, and even comfort.

נֶאֱמָנִים כָּל־פִּקּוּדָיו

7b

Nun. Alle Seine gebot sind rechschaffen.

Nun. All His precepts are trustworthy.

Here a line from Psalm 1, "meditates on God's law day and night," echoes strongly. Idolatrous wandering is replaced by the desire to walk in his justice. This means that his law, his precepts, can actually be walked in: they will open up the world as known by God's righteousness and justice in becoming the path that human life explores to discover the "righteous works which are honorable before God and profitable to the neighbor, works like giving help and advice, like being patient and considerate, like teaching, praying, and the like" ("Psalm 111," p. 380).

8a   סְמוּכִים לָעַד לְעוֹלָם

Samech. Immer und ewiglich werden sie erhalten.

Samekh. They are established forever and ever.

Without access to these trustworthy precepts, the way of righteousness would be lost to us; in other words, we would not find our way back to the meeting with God that is the source of the Psalter. These precepts are handed on by a community that retains knowledge of God's righteousness and justice in the forms of right worship. "The axiom is (Is. 40:8): 'God's Word endures forever.' And if God did not persist so firmly and vigorously, or if it had been up to us, not a single word of the entire Holy Scriptures or of the Gospel would have remained, and there would be neither Baptism nor Sacrament. . . . The devil would long since have eliminated them from this world" ("Psalm 111," p. 381).

This community for which Christ has preserved his word is also — and essentially — becoming the place where real individuals are born, whose behavior is conformed to Christ.

8b   עֲשׂוּיִם בֶּאֱמֶת וְיָשָׁר

Ain. Geschehen ynn warheit und aussrichtig.

Ayin, To be performed with faithfulness and uprightness.

It is important to emphasize that Luther, unlike the caricature that has arisen in strands of the Lutheran tradition, is not espousing quietism or easy grace; rather, he makes the opposite claim — that Christians really are made new. He has already made this claim as strong as possible by saying that God maintains a real church of living saints. However, he contends that these saints only continue as saints in their refusal to abrogate to themselves the good works God may have done through them.

> We should thank and praise God that He preserves His teaching not only in a book or in the pulpit or by the spoken word. He also gives grace that men keep it and live according to it. It is not merely preached; it is performed in deeds. Pious Christians and living saints on earth, who have pure faith and do genuine good works, must continue on earth, as this article of our Creed demands: 'I believe in the Holy Christian Church.' ("Psalm 111," p. 381)

Again, Luther's understanding of hiddenness and visibility is the foundation for his framing of the issue: the conduits of God's grace are kept open when believers have a clear view of their sinful divergence from Christ and thus are conscientious in confessing these divergences; yet when they observe their merits, they see only Christ. God's way into the world is blocked by the human tendency to focus on the "formation of the self" and the idea that one can somehow accrue good deeds: Christian deeds are good only as they transmit Christ's work as participants in Christ's love for the world. "Consequently, even the saints do not boast about their own strengths, although they might delight and rejoice in them by referring them to Him who gave them. Either one is extremely absurd: both to be proud in poverty and to be proud in someone else's clothes."[92]

פְּדוּת שָׁלַח לְעַמּוֹ 9a

Phe. Er sendet seinem volck erlösung.

Pe, He sent redemption to His people.

Now, Luther continues, the psalmist praises God that he gives succor and respite to Christians as they participate in his struggle against the world's dissolution. Their cross, like Christ's, lasts only for a time. Here Luther recapitulates two points that we have seen in detail above. First, God protects the church by checking political tyranny. "[A]s Luke writes (Acts 9:31) that after the persecution directed against St. Stephen the church 'had peace everywhere and built itself up in the fear of God'" ("Psalm 111," p. 382). Second, God comforts Christians because, like Christ on the cross, in faith they may look beyond their suffering and see its end because they "lack God only for a little while" (Ps. 8:5).

צִוָּה־לְעוֹלָם בְּרִיתוֹ 9b

Zakec. Er gebeut seinem bund ewiglich.

Sadhe, He has commanded His covenant forever.

Luther now turns to speak of the place of the individual in God's reclamation of the world. The center of this reclamation is the creature that listens to God's Word. Thus, the dynamic visible in the reclamation of the whole world is happening within each believer. The world, suggests Luther, is not transformed by *coming* to church, but *within* the church God conforms the world to Christ. The church is not yet spotless, but it becomes spotless as it

---

92. Luther, *Luther's Works, Vol. 10*, p. 240.

partakes of Christ's life by praising the cup (the Lord's Supper) and the words of Christ's commands (Scripture, preaching, doctrine) as the path (Ps. 1:1) on which "the church itself does not follow its own work and word, but the Word of God. It knows that it can err and blunder and that it must amend and change those blunders and errors according to God's Word, which alone cannot err" ("Psalm 111," p. 383). The church is the crystallized deposit formed as God comes close to humans through his multilayered grace. Only as they are receptive to these graces do they become such a deposit, retaining a solidity not of material but of enduring deeds. "Thus the forgetfulness of the ungodly is eternal, and their remembrance is temporal. Psalm 9:6 reads: 'Their memory has perished like a sound,' that is, it is only of brief duration like a sound, however clear and loud it was" ("Psalm 111," p. 389).

9c   קָדוֹשׁ וְנוֹרָא שְׁמוֹ

Kuff. Sein name ist helig und hehr.

Koph, Holy and venerable is His name!

"[A]lthough His name has resounded in all the world, it is nowhere regarded as holy and sublime except in the council of the upright, or among Christians, among whom alone His wonderful works are also recognized and praised" ("Psalm 111," p. 384). Having been shown the error of praising human works and placed under the tutelage of God's decrees, this council of the upright has "the great and indescribable honor that we have been named by God's name, having been baptized in it and called by it. Thus His name and our name become one, because we have the kind of God that does such great things for us" ("Psalm 111," p. 384). Paralleling a central Augustinian insight, Luther continues: "If you want honor, then give God all honor; keep nothing for yourself before Him except shame. . . . And behold, as soon as you do this, you are already full of an honor that is greater than the honor of all the kings, one that abides forever" ("Psalm 111," p. 385). Thus Christians themselves become the "power that you [God] display among the people" (Ps. 77:14).[93]

10a   רֵאשִׁית חָכְמָה יִרְאַת יְהוָה

Res. Den HERR furchten ist der weisheit anfang.

Resh, The fear of the LORD is the beginning of wisdom.

93. Luther parallels Ps. 111:9 and 77:14 in Luther, "Psalm Seventy Seven," in *Luther's Works*, Vol. 11, p. 28.

The psalmist concludes with an exhortation and instruction. Having already discussed the importance of the fear of God in interpreting the phrase "He provides food for those who fear him," Luther, as early as his first lecture on this psalm, uses the repetition of the injunction to emphasize that the wisdom of God is not a static possession but a path opening into an eternal exploration of faith: "This life does not have the end of wisdom, but always the beginning, since it is infinite" ("Psalm 111," p. 383). By the time of his mature Psalms commentaries, Luther had developed this insight into a tight conceptual complex, which was clearly displayed in a 1526 exposition of Psalm 112:1. What does it mean to fear God? "It is really nothing else than to keep God in sight." But this understanding of eyes fixed on God "is nothing else than the worship of God." Such worship, in turn, rests on the life of repentance that "wants to have all his life directed according to God's will." Such desire does not issue in a moral code but in an ethos of attentiveness that "needs no code of conduct" ("Psalm 111," pp. 396-97).

Here Luther makes one final equation to further clarify the logic of this complex with reference to the church's worship, eucharistic celebration, and its attitude toward Scripture. The result is a rich description of what it means that faith is a path of exploration: "Whoever earnestly regards God's Word as God's Word knows very well that he will forever remain its pupil and disciple. The others become masters of God's Word at first flight and brashly render opinions and personal judgments on it. . . . To fear God is the same as to fear and honor his Word, for without God's Word we can have no God" ("Psalm 111," p. 386).

שֵׂכֶל טוֹב לְכָל־עֹשֵׂיהֶם 10b

Schin. Das ist eine seine flugheit aller, die darnach thun.

Shin, A good understanding have all those who practice it.

Here Luther reiterates his claim that a tree should be judged by its fruits (behavior) and not its leaves (teaching). The effect is to extend and clarify what he means by his belief in true singing. As he discussed in Psalm 118, true singing — true understanding — is conformity of action to doxology. "(Titus 1:16): 'They profess to know God, but they deny Him by their deeds'; and again (1 Cor. 4:20): 'The kingdom of God does not consist in talk but in power.' . . . It is to these Master Smart Alecks and know-it-alls that David speaks and says: 'Yes, you are smart, and you know it all, but it would be a really good understanding if you acted accordingly in your life'" ("Psalm 111," p. 386).

229

Chau. Des Rhum bleibt ynn ewigkeit.

Tav, His praise endures forever.

Luther concludes by stating the reverse side of his insistence that the blessed are those who praise God and not themselves. If this is true, then Christ himself is embodied in the person of faith who, being adorned by God's own Word, "has eternal glory and honor, and his praise will have no end; for he is adorned with the name of God, which is eternal, and he is decorated with divine glory, which has no end"("Psalm 111," p. 387). By beginning with a definition of blessedness, which disavows all human contribution to God's eternal justice and righteousness, Luther ends by saying that this very human being is "decorated with divine glory."

It is important to draw out exactly how Luther can begin by saying that faith is utter renunciation of our own ideas and yet conclude with the assertion that humans are God's glory. Luther believes that, by analyzing the praises of God recorded in Scripture, we can discover how to enter the conversation that alone makes human action possible, unified, and enduring. He asks about the relationship of God and humanity not in order to describe it, but he assumes that the meaning and relationship of all things can be discovered only in praising the one we do not yet understand. In this way our talking about God finds its proper place in talking to God. With this move Luther transforms all talk into talk about God; or, to put it another way, Luther understands all human discourse to find its proper orientation and place in its linkage with God-talk. Feuerbach inverts Luther's insight by saying that all God-talk is projected talk about humans; yet in doing so he grasps something critical about Luther's project: talk about all things is either talk about God or talk about man, but cannot be a mixture of both.[94]

That theology is theanthropic for Luther is a claim about the form of God's interventions in human affairs. Feuerbach thinks that he increases the utility of theological talk by translating God-talk into talk about human qualities; but Luther argues that only through reflection on and, more importantly, participation in the God-man Christ do the categories of anthropol-

94. Unlike much later modern theology, in his two main works, *The Essence of Christianity* (1841) and *The Essence of Religion* (1851), Ludwig Feuerbach does not reject doxology but reorients it toward humanity. About Feuerbach, Barth reminds us: "He, too, is singing his *Magnificat.*" Karl Barth, *Protestant Theology in the Nineteenth Century: Its Background and History,* new edition with intro. by Colin Gunton (Grand Rapids: Eerdmans, 2002), p. 521.

ogy, ethics, and hermeneutics emerge. Feuerbach, of course, denies this participatory aspect of Luther's insight. For Feuerbach, the idea of human goodness, the saint, is in fact the foundational axiom that modern theology uses to resolve philosophical questions.[95] In defining sainthood as a participatory relationship to Christ as ruler of all creation, Luther effectively counters this tendency. It is by praising, praying, and preaching the working of the one God that God's people debunk the other gods, and they recognize their supposed powers as gifts of the one God. Thus Luther blunts the force of Feuerbach's accusation, while agreeing that it exposes fatal flaws in many of the forms of Christian theology. In confessing that we do not, in fact, know what it means to be good Christians are committed to continually investigating what it might mean by meditating on God's words.

Barth's appreciation of Feuerbach's point is illuminating. He argues that there has been a cleavage in modern theology between the rational ideal of God, as the highest instantiation of any good, and the acting, personal God of Scripture. Feuerbach deconstructs theology as the study of the "highest good" by suggesting it is simply human projection. Feuerbach's attack leads Barth back to Luther's reversal of subjectivity:

> [T]o know, to will, and to act like God as the One who loves in Himself and in His relationship to His creation means (in confirmation of his I-ness) to be a person. God is a person in this way and He alone is a person in this way. He is the real person and not merely the ideal. He is not the personified but the personifying person — the person on the basis of whose prior existence alone we can speak (hypothetically) of other persons different from Him.[96]

Barth has modified Luther solely in suggesting that we can speak about ourselves only "hypothetically": Luther has suggested that we do not *think* ourselves into knowing this personifying person, but we *practice* the repetitions of praise and celebration to which we can point as confessions of our real personhood. Barth would not deny this in principle, though in practice his theologizing regularly asks, not how we preach and praise ourselves into personhood, but about the conditions for so achieving personhood.[97] In doxology, suggests Luther, we know we are in the presence of Christ.

---

95. A problem discussed in ch. 2.

96. Karl Barth, *Church Dogmatics* II.2, ed. G. W. Bromiley and T. F. Torrance, trans. G. W. Bromiley, J. C. Campbell, Iain Wilson, J. Strathearn McNab, Harold Knight and R. A. Stewart (Edinburgh: T&T Clark, 1997), p. 285; cf. pp. 284-93.

97. A point discussed in ch. 4.

Feuerbach, insofar as he has a constructive idea, claims that talk about idealized humanity is productive for situating ourselves in the world, but we could make it more productive by simply admitting that we are only talking about our ideal of humanity. Luther's deeper response to this objection is to suggest that it overstates our human ability to transcend the ways of thinking and acting handed down to us. We must have a richer account of the genesis of novelty in thought and action. By giving a central place to the praise of the one God, Luther suggests that this is possible only as we open ourselves to a powerful and continual transformation out of our old thought schemas and idolatries. No conceptual schema can generate this novelty, which is by definition always beyond the thought schemas through which we perceive ourselves and which sustains our blindness and ethical confusions.

Luther sees the fact that God enters our world to relativize even our thought schemas as a divine assertion of the fecundity of the first command: (1) we worship our own alienated powers, claiming that we are bound to obey them against God's word, and thus we are under the lordship of multiple gods; (2) God reveals himself to us through his works, giving us a thirst we cannot ourselves muster up for his justice and righteousness; (3) the revelation of the magnitude of God's grace comes through the exploration of faith in praise and incites praise through inflaming our gratitude for that grace; (4) in praising the scope of God's power over all, and thus embracing our place as one of God's working projects, we come to see how his Lordship over all things functions; (5) an insight that brings to light the ways we remain loyal to powers other than the one God. Psalm 111 is paradigmatic in focusing our attention on God's work of bringing all creation back into its place within the economy of his working.

The essential point that Luther presses on us with increasing insistence is that we must understand how praise makes loving others possible. When captive to ourselves and other false lords, we are torn apart, conflicted, subject to the wrath of God, and to be diffused like chaff. "That is why," says Luther in his introduction to Psalm 111, "I have labored diligently in teaching and in exhorting people to be grateful. That is also why I bring this psalm to the attention of Christians, that they may not merely become willing and inclined to gratitude, but may also have definite, fixed, and fitting words and ways to praise and thank God" ("Psalm 111," p. 353). Gratitude is the essential condition of being reclaimed by God from our dissolution, and the emphasis on "definite, fixed, and fitting words and ways" indicates the means of our reclamation. Our salvation into Christ is to be included in his words and his body through singing, preaching, and eating.

Luther, the Jews, and the Problem of Supersessionism

A concluding note is in order regarding Luther's (and the Christian tradition's) supersessionism. Though it is anachronistic to call the premodern Christian tradition anti-Semitic (a term coined in 1879),[98] moderns are rightly attuned to the resonances between modern anti-Semitic beliefs and behavior and the belief that Israel has been superseded by the church. This sensitivity may help us articulate the relationship between the church and synagogue with more theological clarity than Luther did. To do so, we must be able to look beyond the historical fact that some of the later Luther's truly horrific statements against Jews[99] were exploited by a generation of National Socialist ideologues (though perhaps not as directly forming them as was once assumed)[100] in order to reassess his theology. His reading of Psalm 111 has raised worries along these lines in his comparisons of Passover and the Eucharist when he uses terms such as "our Easter" and "their Easter" ("Psalm 111," pp. 362-63), saying that Christ has delivered Christians in a "different" way than God did Israel out of Egypt, and appearing to denigrate the latter with comments such as "those ancient wonders cannot be compared with these. They are hardly even a type or symbol of these wonderful works" ("Psalm 111," p. 372). Luther contrasts his certainty that David truly understood the meaning of the psalms he wrote with the situation of contemporary Jews, for whom "'the veil of Moses covers their heart,' says St. Paul (2 Cor. 3:15)" ("Psalm 111," p. 363). His conclusion is that Christians alone can truly sing the Psalter.

Here Luther proves to be both a man of his age and deserving of censure. He — along with all Christianity — had not yet learned that most terrible lesson of modernity: that the subjugation of Israel and the razing of the temple in CE 70 by the Romans was not a proof that God had finally rejected Israel; nor were the centuries of European anti-Semitism, with the climax in the holocaust.[101] On Scripture's own terms, such survival can only be due to

98. Cf. Steven Ozment, *A Mighty Fortress: A New History of the German People* (New York: HarperCollinsPublishers, 2004), ch. 10, p. 205.

99. The high point of Luther's comments on the topic was his 1523 treatise, "That Jesus Christ Was Born a Jew," in *Luther's Works: vol 45, The Christian in Society II*, ed. Walther Brand (Philadelphia: Fortress, 1962), pp. 195-230; the low point was in 1543: "On the Jews and Their Lies," in *Luther's Works: vol 47, The Christian in Society IV*, ed. Franklin Sherman (Philadelphia: Fortress, 1971), pp. 121-306. The issue is sensitively discussed by Heiko Oberman in *Luther: Man between God and the Devil*, trans. Eileen Walliser-Schwarzbart (New York: Image Books, 1992), pp. 292-97.

100. Ozment, *A Mighty Fortress*, pp. 98-99.

101. Robert Jenson, *Systematic Theology, vol 2: The Works of God* (Oxford: Oxford University Press, 1999), p. 193.

God's faithfulness to his covenant, preserving a holy remnant from Israel. From this vantage point, it is possible to develop a clearer view of what Luther might and should have said on the subject.

First, however, we should take Luther's exegetical practice seriously. Luther was in constant dialogue with Jewish and other biblical interpreters, engagements that undeniably increased his exegetical sensitivity. This gives us a first glimpse of the importance of the Jewish (and academic) textual traditions for a contemporary theological reading of Scripture. Though Luther did not himself explicitly discuss the methodological implications of such a three-way dialogue, in practice his constant grappling with Jewish, humanist, and scholastic interpretations allowed him a productive critical distance from received Christian allegorical interpretations, often suggesting new ways forward for his own exegesis. Luther's practice suggests that Christians need dialogue with divergent exegetical traditions because such conversations teach different forms of sensitivity to the text not otherwise available. Such engagement assumes that Christians should not pretend that Jews and Christians are alike; rather, we must admit that, interpretatively, we are "outsiders" to each other. But we are "outsiders bearing a family resemblance," and that proximity makes attentiveness especially important to the prospect that Jewish exegesis will make Christian exegesis more faithful.[102] Such a claim rests on the Christian confession that the church is an eschatological community, whose members may at times lie outside of its visible institutions. The same hope holds for those who uphold the traditions of biblical exegesis sustained in the academy. That contemporary Christian exegesis has access to well-developed nonconfessional or non-Christian exegetical traditions is a great opportunity, as long as Christian exegesis owns its confessional and ecclesial grounds for entering this dialogue.

In Luther's defense, we should also say that his theological and exegetical interest is in clarifying how Christians gain access to Scripture, not primarily in explaining the relationship between Jews and Christians. In giving pride of place to the Old Testament Psalms, he is clearly asking how Christians can be included in Israel's praise. David, says Luther, undeniably expressed the genuine divine word, and thus Christian theology exists under constant questioning: Can we participate in this praise? This amounts to an assertion that David's praise is paradigmatically complete and axiomatically the condition for Christian praise. Christian praise accesses these words not by modifying them but by preserving their living heart. This allows us to say that Luther's use of

---

102. Stephen Fowl and L. Gregory Jones, *Reading in Communion: Scripture and Ethics in the Christian Life* (Grand Rapids: Eerdmans, 1991), pp. 116-17.

the phrases "our Easter" and "their Easter" should not be interpreted as a radical separation of the Passover and Eucharist, because if "our" Christian Easter is in genuine continuity with David's Easter, its main difference is occupying a different place in the one drama of Christ's kingdom.

This also implies that God's deliverance of his people in the Old Testament cannot be understood as less than or inferior to the work of Christ, as Luther sometimes appears to be saying: all God's works must be understood as the extensions of this one act (John 5:46; Luke 24:44-45).[103] Christians can participate in God's works in Israel's history recorded in the Old Testament only because they are encompassed in Christ's one work.[104] This can be defended in one way by saying that the hope that all people would join Israel's praise is part of *Israel's* praise. Psalm 117 ("Praise the LORD, all you nations! Extol him, all you peoples!") is not atypical in placing all people in God's sphere of power and inviting all into Israel's praise.[105] The New Testament's claim is that Christ is the definitive form of this divine invitation. Thus, if the prophetic Christ is not at work in David, then Christians cannot sing these songs.[106] At just this point Luther relies on a Jewish exegetical technique that was also present in the New Testament. David was considered in early rabbinic interpretation to have "done everything Moses did,"[107] an exegetical move paralleled by the writers of the New Testament, who considered Jesus to have done everything both David and Moses did. Clearly, this model does not force a Christian supersessionist reading of Judaism any more than Judaism implies that David superseded Moses. Similarly, Christians can say that the Psalms are David's five books to the five books of Moses' Torah and Jesus' five-part Sermon on the Mount. The three are not radi-

---

103. The thought is visible in Luther, "Treatise on the Last Words of David," p. 268, and, as we have seen, in Augustine; cf. ch. 6, "Doctrine as Hermeneutics in Augustine."

104. Cf. Francis Watson, *Text and Truth: Redefining Biblical Theology* (Edinburgh: T&T Clark, 1997), pp. 179-84.

105. See also Ps. 22:27; 33:8; 45:17; 47:2, 8-9; 66:1-2, 16; 72:11, 17; 82:8; 86:9; 96:7-10; 99:1-3; 102:15; 117; 138:4; 148:11.

106. See Luther's discussion of Psalm 8 in this chapter.

107. William Braude, trans., *The Midrash on the Psalms*, vol. 1 (New Haven: Yale University Press, 1959), p. 5. This collection of rabbinic interpretations of the Psalms has grown in a process of editorial accretion during the period from the third to the thirteenth centuries, but began as an arrangement of older materials, the oldest of which are probably from the first century. Though William Holladay may be correct in concluding that this midrash "played only a minor part in Jewish literature" (*The Psalms through Three Thousand Years*, p. 148), his suggestion that this is due to the late date of its assumed final redaction is perhaps overly hasty (and too reliant on Jacob Neusner's chronology). See the detailed discussion of dating in Braude, pp. xi-xiv, xxv-xxxii.

cally different in the way historical criticism would have it, but they are moments in a temporally extended "musical" relationship whose movements climax in Christ. This climax is not something apart from Moses and David, nor from God's grace to us. Christians can find this contemporaneity in the Old Testament, such as in Joshua 24:6: "I brought your fathers out of Egypt, and *you* came to the sea."

To understand the situation of Christian praise in this way does not yet resolve all of our questions, but it implies that Luther was mistaken to suggest that the Jews have been wholly excluded from the covenant with God; and he should have confined himself to expounding to the best of his ability how Christ opens that covenant to gentiles. Luther correctly understood that the New Testament is making room on the margins of this account for Israel's rejection and God's "choosing instead the filth and refuse of the world."[108] Yet this does not commit Christian theologians and exegetes to the belief that the New Testament, and especially Paul, sets out a picture of what the "rejected Jews" always and essentially are. "*If* Paul found negative exemplary significance in the way of life he had once practiced as a Pharisaic Jew, the historical specificity of the exemplar must still be maintained. In this way, theological exegesis of Paul's texts can avoid the danger of negative stereotyping that is theologically irrelevant and ethically problematic."[109]

Luther inadequately appreciated the New Testament's affirmations that God has not rejected his people (Rom. 11:1). Furthermore, in most cases in the New Testament, the "people of God" remains Israel, into which the church must be grafted (Matt. 2:6; Luke 2:32, with the exception of 1 Pet. 2:9). The "people of God" remains an eschatological concept (Eph. 1:14; Rev. 21:1-3). As a result, Christians should not expect to find the boundaries of faithful Judaism any more visible than that of the church (Matt. 13:30).[110] Christians must allow that in God's purposes the Jews have a vocation, if nothing else than to witness to the almost entirely gentile church that "life with God is not their due reward, not their natural possession, not theirs to demand or extort, and they can learn that perhaps best by learning that *others* have a prior claim, *others* are God's first love, *others* have become (also by grace) God's quasi-natural family."[111] Christians must confess that these separate vocations will

---

108. Quoted in Pelikan, *Luther the Expositor,* p. 94.

109. Francis Watson in Karl Barth, *The Epistle to the Philippians: 40th Anniversary Edition,* introductory essays by Bruce McCormack and Francis Watson (Louisville: Westminster John Knox, 2002), p. xlii.

110. Jenson, *Systematic Theology,* pp. 191-93.

111. Eugene Rogers, *Sexuality and the Christian Body: Their Way into the Triune God* (Oxford: Blackwell, 1999), p. 178.

be united in Christ's coming (Rev. 7). Until then, unless it is to undermine its own foundations, "the church must indeed call Jews to be baptized into the church of Jews and gentiles and think that when this happens it obeys God's will; but she dare not conclude that the continuing separate synagogue is *against* God's will."[112]

This position will continue to raise important questions to be discussed with due sensitivity in Christian-Jewish relations. In these discussions Christians should hope to hear from God's people deeper meanings of the content of God's word. Our differences must not be minimized in these discussions, or Christians, through their own disingenuousness, can again risk closing down such conversation with Jews. Yet Christians can only begin that conversation by explaining that we understand ourselves to be part of the community that can sing the Psalter through the work of Christ, who reveals that there is no real monotheistic religion without the Spirit's creating a community of praise. We have seen that Luther glimpses the work of the Spirit in all lives oriented by such praise. "It is an art, an art of the Holy Spirit, to give thanks or to say 'Thank God!' from the heart. And if someone can say this from the heart, you need not worry that he is proud, stubborn, dissolute, and savage, or that he will turn against God with his goods" ("Psalm 111," p. 365).

With this statement Luther opens the door to a twofold assertion about the relationship of Scripture and ethics in a Jewish-Christian context: Christians must allow for Jews' participation in the praises of David in a genuine way, and in so doing may glimpse God's providing for the upholding and sustaining of creation and society. Jews, too, may know God's ordering of the community of the righteous and praise its Orderer. In singing the Psalms they have often witnessed to the church that the order of creation is known and loved only through the divine command and blessing of God's Torah. Christians and Jews can meet in their recognition of God's grace in protecting humanity in these ways from its own sinful self-assertion against God. If this is true, then Jews and Christians can further agree that Psalm 111, first and most sharply, questions the "blind and senseless world" ("Psalm 111," p. 368), which resists praising God's works and precepts because it refuses to call on his name. In so doing, the psalm's *positive* force is to hold open the discussion of the proper name of God, which Christians must insist is known only through Jesus Christ. At the same time, the psalm's primary *critical* force is against the rejection of the God of Abraham, Isaac, and Jacob by a rebellious world and the wisdom it tries to construct on its defiant assertion that talk of God is talk of man in a loud voice.

112. Jenson, *Systematic Theology,* p. 193.

PART III

Singing the Ethos of God

CHAPTER 8

Ethical Exegesis: What Have We Encountered

The next two chapters constitute Part III, the book's concluding section, where I undertake the constructive task for which the survey of Part I and the immersion in historical exegesis of Part II have prepared us. We have come to the point of directly facing the conflicts and problems generated by bringing together this disparate collection of exegetical and ethical methodologies. Not only do the contemporary treatments of Part I show evidence of deep methodological differences, but their approaches to both biblical hermeneutics and Christian ethics diverge from that of Augustine and Luther at numerous points. And, as we have also seen, neither do Augustine and Luther share a common exegetical method. It is tempting simply to assert that we face methodological heterogeneity deep enough that any attempt to harmonize them will do violence to the legitimate considerations of the respective approaches. In this chapter I will suggest that the proliferation of methodological presuppositions clears the way to reconceive biblical interpretation as a continually developing craft through which we are drawn into the divine drama and ethos. In the terms of the psalmists, like all the acts of faith, the reading of Scripture is not a destination but a path.

One of the main observations of Part I about the shape of the contemporary discussion has been reinforced by our immersion in Part II in the exegetical tradition: contemporary approaches too often define their exegetical and ethical methodologies with insufficiently integrated reference to both the form and content of Scripture. The Psalms exert a pressure for precisely this integration, says Patrick Miller: "The full hearing of the Psalms will be greatly enhanced when the familiar tendency to abstract content from form or to empty form of its content is overcome."[1] The Psalms press us to

---

1. Patrick D. Miller, *Interpreting the Psalms* (Philadelphia: Fortress, 1986), p. 17.

look behind the questions "What does the Bible say about Christian ethics?" and "What does it mean that Christian ethics must appeal to Scripture?" to discover a more complex question: "How do we allow the scriptural form and content to shape both our exegetical and ethical methodologies? How do we perceive their inner unity?" I propose to put this question to the Psalms. The task will be to ask Scripture the question of its role in Christian ethics. As such it will be an exploration of Luther's *sola scriptura* principle. But this principle includes within it the claim that we begin learning to live with God by practicing talking to God, not by means of a theoretical reflection on such practices. Having said that, in this chapter I undertake hermeneutical reflection as a defense of — and elucidation of — the undertaking of the task in chapter 9.

This chapter begins by reconceiving Christian ethics as the task of making the grammar of our lives explicit by bringing it into contact with Scripture. It then develops an account of this process as God's way of drawing humans into the divine drama. Within this drama, Scripture is part of God's giving himself to us and thus transforming us. The result is the suggestion that Christian ethical and exegetical judgments are indispensable forms of the church's confession of the work of the triune God. In such a confession, faith steps out in hope of meeting God on the path of obedience. A final section discusses some of the interpretive tools used in chapter 9. The main proposal of this chapter is that perceiving the fundamental unity of biblical form and content demands a reaffirmation of the primacy of the craft of biblical interpretation, limiting and circumscribing the centrality of hermeneutical theory in contemporary discussions.

Chapter 9 follows this discussion of method with an exegetical exploration of the relationship between Scripture and ethics. Here the task is to attempt to think Christian ethics within the scriptural world of the Psalms. The chapter rests on the interpretation of two psalms: I take Psalm 130 to portray the birth of Christian faith, a faith that from its first moment has a relationship to Scripture and an ethical posture; with Psalm 104, I develop this analysis by showing how this doxological faith is enriched and taught to face creation, both in singing *about it* to God, in *singing*, and in singing *to God.*

Our Way of Living with God:
Ethics as Active Incorporation into the Divine Grammar

A close reading of Augustine and Luther revealed a broad agreement that Christian faith, properly understood, is a perpetual engagement with Scripture. Faith reads Scripture in and with the congregation, thus facilitating the moral renewal of that community. We also saw that their understandings of this renewal diverged in many ways, but within one broad agreement: that Christians exegete Scripture as a form of praise, and they do so as those who sing because they are already within the realm of Christ's lordship. From this perspective, our contemporary sense of the foreignness of the Bible and the Christian tradition appears as an expression of insecurity about whether we are participants in God's ongoing drama with humanity. If we are not one with the community that wrote and interpreted these texts, we have ceased to participate in the unity of the "one holy, catholic and apostolic church" we confess to be God's work. That God's working has indeed preceded us is marked by our having, in fact, these tangible ancient texts in our hands and in fact being engaged in the struggle to understand this witness of our forebears in the faith.[2]

Reading the Bible in Christian ethics turns out to be a question about how we can live within Christ's rule, becoming actors in his drama. How do we become aware of where we are in this rule rather than rejecting it or stumbling along without seeing it? This is a quite different beginning point than the inquiries of hermeneutics (How do I read well?) or ethics (What should we do?), taken on their own; yet it comprehends both questions. In their own ways, Augustine and Luther have emphasized that gratitude to God is the condition for knowing where we are, and thus knowing how to act. It remains to unpack the hermeneutical implications of the claim that Scripture informs us of God's works, making collaborating with them possible and thus rendering our works good.

We return to the example of foreigners finding their way into a new language and culture. Trying to find our feet in a foreign culture, as Taylor and Augustine have noted, is similar to trying to discover where we lie in a culture's conception of moral space. In noting the performative nature of language, Luther and Wittgenstein have emphasized that we enter cultures by learning their languages. These observations suggest that it will be fruitful to explore Christian ethics not as "creating" a better world but as the discovery of the world of God's working through exploring his words. Because we do so as sinners whose alienation from God is still being overcome, examining the divine ethos through the metaphor of foreignness is especially helpful in clarifying the mechanics of this discovery, and the role of Scripture within it.

The experience of foreignness has many hues. It always begins mono-

---

2. Cf. Robert Jenson, *Systematic Theology: Vol. 2, The Works of God* (Oxford: Oxford University Press, 1999), p. 280.

chromatically, as interest, lack of interest, or indifference. We tend to explore those cultures we find inviting and full of promise. Yet this inviting aspect can easily turn threatening, and we may even experience this attraction and repulsion simultaneously, or in wildly fluctuating combinations. The psalmist hints at these dynamics by picturing the entry of the world into the church with the image of a wild ass coming in from a life in the desert to an oasis full of life (Ps. 104:11, discussed in ch. 9). Discovering our way into life with God is an experience in which we can see that many competing crosscurrents of our inner and outer lives are claimed and rearranged. The forces of attraction to God are fanned to life by the Spirit, so that life with God may become a familiar and inviting path, enabling the prayer "Lead me in the path of your commandments, for I delight in it" (Ps. 119:35). But as Augustine and Luther have both pointed out, this sense of fulfillment in traveling with God does not eradicate the cross- and counter-currents of temptations and sinful impulses. Scripture both gives us access to this sphere and arms us against losing it again by exposing the trackless wastes of self-absorption for what they actually are. By implication, Christian ethics is the second-order discipline of reflecting on this process with the aim of facilitating God's claiming of human thoughts, passions, and actions through Scripture.

The most helpful theories for negotiating new cultures are those that reveal patterns and enable educated guesses about how to participate in the ongoing stream of social interaction. Consider again our foreigner, freshly arrived in an unfamiliar country. Let us assume that she wants to stay for a long time and desires to know the culture, to fit in as best she can, to become a participant in the flow of life and thus to learn from the inside what the culture has to teach. The first hurdle she faces is learning the language, and in the process she slowly discovers that she is learning not merely a language but a new way of life. Even if she has prepared for her arrival by studying the language in books, there will be much to learn about how that language is used, and therefore what it actually means. If she has not been prepared by study, she must begin by pointing to things that she and her hosts can identify as distinct objects, though not yet with shared words, with all parties tacitly assuming that in time words can be found for objects.[3] This process continues in her asking questions about the necessities of life: what people eat, what these eating utensils are, and so forth. She explores the way her hosts meet the necessities of life, and is often surprised that, though all people eat, her hosts eat unfamiliar things that are given names not corresponding to once-

3. A claim that is, of course, arguable; the opposite position is articulated by the analytical philosopher W. V. O. Quine in *Word and Object* (1960).

familiar dishes. Then come practical phrases such as "I want . . ." or "Where is . . . ?" or "How do I . . . ?" It is important to note that she does not really know a language until she is immersed in the cultural praxis that grounds and sustains it.[4]

Anthropologists sometimes call these intertwined praxological and linguistic rules defining a group's character a "grammar." Visible surface differences often appear to radically divide cultural groups sharing basic presuppositions.[5] For instance, police officers and criminals often share a single set of rules about what is allowable or not in criminality and policing, though these vary from culture to culture. In our culture, physical violence against children or the elderly is considered to be despicable under any circumstances, by both camps, a distaste that unites the two groups as a single moral community. Social groups may display radical surface differences and a complex variety of ordered sets of middle differences that nevertheless rest on a deep unity of practice and presupposition that renders them identifiable as a group.

The "grammar" of such group behavior is sometimes explicitly grasped, but it is most often implicitly understood. It is, however, capable of being described in terms of the maxims, standards, and beliefs that guide the group's discrimination, decision-making, and automatic reactions to social stimuli. These standards and beliefs are held in place by exemplary or guiding examples that anchor what is thought of as "normal" behavior. Thus the ethos shared by groups is attached in a wide range of ways to its use of language. Admitting that a society is made up of many communities and sub-roles (factories, bowling clubs, and so on) allows us to talk about multiple levels of social grammar, and thus to affirm the communitarians' recognition of the importance of social roles in shaping our character and decisions. Allowing that our behavior is shaped by many overlapping and interlinked communities gives us more fine-grained critical access to these patterns of behavior. My in-

---

4. "Someone coming into a strange country will sometimes learn the language of the inhabitants from ostensive definitions that they give him; and he will often have to guess the meaning of these definitions; and will guess sometimes right, sometimes wrong." Ludwig Wittgenstein, *Philosophical Investigations*, trans. G. E. M. Anscombe (Oxford: Basil Blackwell, 1968), #32. See also Fergus Kerr, *Theology after Wittgenstein* (Oxford: Basil Blackwell, 1986), p. 71; James McClendon and James Smith, *Convictions: Diffusing Religious Relativism*, rev. ed. (Valley Forge, PA: Trinity Press International, 1994), esp. ch. 6. This point is not only intracultural but intercultural. For instance, though it is important that we not think of the mentally handicapped as inhabiting a culture separate from ours, their biochemical processes often cause their thinking and behavior to *appear* to be a threatening foreign culture. Thus, just as when we enter a foreign culture, affection makes us different people.

5. Cf. Kate Fox, *Watching the English: The Hidden Rules of English Behaviour* (London: Hodder and Stoughton, 2004), pp. 1-2.

terest here is not in establishing or refuting the philosophical claim that we can have no experiences without language; I aim merely to gain an analytical purchase on human behavior. Though we learn many behaviors without having them ever brought to verbal description, my suggestion is that behavior *transformation* is best approached by way of attention to our language.

To learn a culture, then, is to learn a complex but somehow coherent web of grammar. Just as a native speaker must as a child, our foreigner learns words in their *Sitz im Leben*, and so, also like a native speaker, she cannot always give a definition for a word or the reasons for acting in a certain way, despite knowing perfectly well how to use words or "fit in" socially. Here we are reminded that dictionaries are one sort of description of a language, and not the language itself. Language is a web of living interconnections. Words "mean" connections to other words, a web of interrelationships that constantly fluctuates. Words are defined primarily by their use, which is not a denial that they refer to things, but a comment on how we must learn what they refer to: this is not first a matter of getting to the "essence" of the meaning of words, but understanding how they are used and with what other words, ideas, and practices they are connected. Learning and translating languages is grounded in the act of assuming that "I think I know what this person is saying." At this level, all reading (cultural and textual) is a guess about implied authorial intention as communicated through the social clues and language that define it.

This makes it obvious that translation is a creative, active, and laborious process of synchronizing one web of language and culture with another. There may be words for one object in two languages, but what these words imply and what other connections they make may give a completely different resonance to the object named. To inhabit the new culture, we must seek to understand its grammar, and we must attempt to go into the culture it assumes, as artificial as this inevitably seems at first. Robert Jenson pinpoints the theological insight this suggests: "Those who interpret Scripture in and for the church are compelled to keep trying to say what it says, and by the mere claim that Scripture does say *something* to us; the struggle itself is the hermeneutical principle."[6] This emphasis on the church's struggle must be paired with the confession that the struggle is productive, not because of the church's efforts, but because it is God's Scripture. Learning a language is possible, as is learning a new grammar of living. We can now say with proper theological, linguistic, ethical, and sociological complexity that the church partakes of a complex, many-layered divine grammar that is nevertheless uni-

6. Cf. Jenson, *Systematic Theology*, p. 280.

fied in a describable way. Through Scripture God claims our action for the divine order, not out of but wholly within the many orders of human sociality. This transformation can be described via an analogy with the processes of being absorbed into any culture, with the caveat that the divine grammar is primarily accessible in Scripture. As Yoder has emphasized (ch. 3), the grammar of God's work in Jesus Christ is the bringing of a divine ethos into all social roles in a way the world cannot anticipate or understand on its own terms.

By now it is apparent that what anthropologists call social grammars, Christian ethicists often call "ethos" or "character." Like the anthropologist, the ethicist engages in a descriptive task of exposing contemporary social grammars to view. But unlike anthropology, Christian ethics does so to facilitate their assessment, critique, and possible reformulation in the light of the work of Christ. In short, Christian ethics describes and evaluates the grammar of human behavior as a joyous participation in the transformation of the Christian mind and action. It is the discipline of continually attempting to comprehend the grammars of Scripture and our present in all their rich interconnection. The simultaneity of this process is essential because Scripture provokes us to ask questions about aspects of the grammar of our daily lives. At the same time, we continually turn to Scripture with moral questions that lead us to study it with a focus and clarity that is existentially grounded, thus facilitating the discovery of aspects of the biblical grammar never before perceived.[7]

In order for such an approach to function, we must be clear that there is no such thing as a "scriptural discourse." Scripture is the meeting place of all discourses. Discourses can be objectified, described, and their limits mapped — none of which are true of Scripture. To take a text as Scripture is to deny that it is susceptible to this objectification: we are infinitely "suspicious" that it runs far beyond us. Attempts to dismiss the Bible's moral relevance with the claim that its authors "couldn't have known" about our moral dilemmas or conceptual distinctions are sure signs that the Bible has ceased to be Scripture for that interpreter, for whom some other text or group of texts has become Scripture, against which the Bible must now be justified.

These observations have obvious implications for how we conceive language critique to relate to Christian ethics. Language shapes perception, and moral decisions are bounded by our perceptions of reality. One metaphor reveals (creates) one reality, and another draws out a different set of features of experience. We can exist within multiple language worlds, but only one world of action. Action is a conclusive interpretation. To act is to be oriented by the perceptions and hunches about the true or real framed in some language. It

---

7. Cf. Francis Watson, ch. 4, pp. 58-59.

has been the fundamental assumption of this study that language situates our action, giving us ways of conceiving what is and what is not possible in the world. If this is true, then we can see how the active participation in the process of our grammar being synchronized with the grammar of Scripture is the essence of Christian ethics.

In this view, renewed human action will not proceed from the formulation of new moral rules within old frameworks of perception, something that only creates irresolvable existential contradictions. To take one example: If I believe that my life will have no meaning unless I act to create it, then the biblical Sabbath command confronts me as a barrier to my fulfillment. If I attempt to observe it, I do so as a Stoic, gritting my teeth and "lying idle" for a day, or as a utilitarian, obeying only because it makes possible my doing more on other days. I conform to the letter of a moral rule within the reigning rationality with which it clashes, and I do so without interest in discerning its inner truth.

Becoming aware of the inexhaustibility of Scripture (like becoming aware of the vast diversity of foreign cultures) begins with appreciating it. The example of the acclimatization of the foreigner has been intended to illustrate the phenomenon of being reshaped as we are drawn into Christ's lordship. Scripture teaches Christians that the form of language is a divine gift that provides access to our redemption. This sets up a new understanding of "biblical criticism" because it means that all our language is susceptible to being questioned and reformulated. To speak of "singing" Scripture is to say that, theologically conceived, criticism is not properly the work of a detached observer but a clarification from within belief of the scope and import of that belief.[8] Criticism is repentant collaboration with a Creator who is always present in his creation, who has not ceased to speak. We are still learning his grammar from him. Language and its meaning are thus not simply "there," but must be taken up in order to learn what it means through inhabiting it. In singing "The right hand of the LORD does valiantly," we are judged to not yet know what these words mean precisely in being taught their meaning. Thus gratitude to God for the form of language is indelibly tied up with the content he has given this form in Scripture. The language patterns given in Scripture have a singular uniqueness that lead us back into the ways of life out of which they were born. In the course of engaging with the community being drawn

---

8. The theological anthropology of this account needs more conceptual development than I can provide here, but would look something like what Günter Bader has developed in *Psalterium affectum palestra: Prolegomena zu einer Theologie des Psalters* (Tübingen: J. C. B. Mohr [Paul Siebeck], 1996).

into this grammar, we come to learn its words as we are synchronized with its way of life. The two happen simultaneously. The life-form of the church points us to its grammar in Scripture, even as that grammar reforms and re-shapes the grammar of that community.

The interpenetration of form and content in Scripture entails a further claim developed by Luther. Skill in hermeneutical theory is not the key to Scripture, because familiarity with its content is irreducible. We must con-stantly grapple with Scripture *(lectio continua)* and we cannot avoid the occa-sional second-order reflection on this process. However, this depends, Luther reminds us, on our first learning "to make only one verse a day, or even one a week, live and breathe in your heart."[9] Luther is surely right that, once we learn something of this skill, "whoever becomes practiced in this will find more by himself in the Psalter than all the interpretations of other men can give him."[10]

In reading Scripture we are exposed to the grammar of the Christian life in Christ. The Bible is not a grammar "handbook" in which we can see and study the naked structural form of life with God, grasped and described at a meta-level. Rather, it is the place where God's way of life can be felt and grasped, where we can "taste and see that the Lord is good" (Ps. 34:8). In New Testament terms, it opens life within the "law of the Spirit" to us; in Old Tes-tament language, this grammar is the Torah, which encompasses all of God's works, the study of which brings life. These different formulations are not identical, but because they are separated in the development of the Bible, we can explore their difference and unity in a structured way. It is this force of Scripture to shape our inquiry into God's ways that validates Scripture ever again as God's chosen form of self-mediation, thus forming the basis and foundation of the life-form that is Christian faith.

Luther and Augustine ask that the Psalms lead them more deeply into the divine form of life. This is not a question about how to enter the commu-nity of faith, because it assumes we have already been co-opted by the Spirit. Thus the question is, how are we more deeply immersed into the grammar of life with God? This is to ask how we are generated as people whose form of life is consistent with the grammar of God's own life. How do we become or-dered and stable by the imparting of the divine presence? Properly speaking, this is the only question of Christian ethics. According to the Psalms, we enter the grammar of Scripture by learning how to live as a conversation with God.

---

9. Martin Luther, "Psalms 1 and 2 from Works on the First Twenty-two Psalms, 1519 to 1521: A Composite Translation," in *Luther's Works, Vol. 14, Selected Psalms III*, ed. Jaroslav Pelikan (St. Louis: Concordia Publishing House, 1958), p. 310.

10. Luther, "Psalms 1 and 2," p. 311.

This use of the concept of grammar can be clarified by comparison with three related projects. The concept of doctrine or the Christian story as a regulative grammar plays a central role in George Lindbeck's postliberal theology. He understands ontological statements such as "Jesus is Lord" to be first-order beliefs sincerely held by the practicing faithful, and doctrines and narratives to be the intrasystemic rules that help us to know whether we correctly understand and enact them. Doctrine is a grammar that tells us that the crusader's cry of "Jesus is Lord" as he slays an infidel may be true as an ontological affirmation, but it runs against the whole pattern of God's will as Christianity has understood it through the ages. Religious practice and utterance are thus understood to be true only as uttered performatively, as a way of life, and so the good performance is judged by its correspondence to the grammar of its ontological and intrasystemic references.[11]

Lindbeck's proposal and mine agree in emphasizing that the primary way to claim the truth of Christianity is to proclaim it in speech and act. This means we also agree that the forms of living and believing of Christians are constantly in flux. "It is only in dead or imperfectly known languages and religions that no new words are used, truths uttered, or feelings expressed" (Lindbeck, p. 84). The primary difference is where we locate the continuity of the community that lives and proclaims Christ. Lindbeck's use of "grammar" is an inversion of Calvin's claim that the Bible is the lens through which Christians view all reality (p. 90, n. 23). This yields the claim that "languages and religions" or "the Christian story" are the lenses through which the Bible and the world are interpreted (p. 83). Because Lindbeck is concerned to talk about all religions and not just Christianity, in my view he wrongly dismisses Calvin's espousal of Scripture as itself the "framework or medium within which Christians experience" (p. 84). I have contended that Calvin is right to conceive doctrines as topographical and pedagogical arrangements of Scripture, crystallized traditions of biblical interpretations that guide, but do not bind Christian interpretation.[12]

Telford Work allows Scripture the more central grammatical role Lindbeck denies it in referring to his project as an exploration of the claim that "Scripture is God's rhetoric."[13] He bases this claim on the affirmation that there is an "intrinsic connection between *ethos* and *logos* in the Bible."[14]

---

11. George Lindbeck, *The Nature of Doctrine: Religion and Theology in a Postliberal Age* (Philadelphia: Westminster, 1984), pp. 64-66.

12. Calvin, *The Institutes of the Christian Religion*, I.vi.1.

13. Telford Work, *Living and Active: Scripture in the Economy of Salvation* (Grand Rapids: Eerdmans, 2002), p. 59.

14. Work, *Living and Active*, p. 63.

Scripture serves God's reorientation of Christian existence to cohere with his being. Because God has risked committing himself to us by making himself accountable to his word, humans are shown the divine ethos and are drawn into their proper rhetorical shape. When gaps are assumed to exist between the words of Scripture and God's ethos and logos, Christians lose the ability to know what they must be conformed to for their redemption. So far, this is almost precisely the position developed in this study.

By calling the Bible God's rhetoric, however, Work emphasizes the Bible's ability to shape our speech and action so that through us God can persuade others to change. This tack has an ineradicably apologetic slant. My suggestion is that, in calling the Bible the divine grammar, our attention is focused not on apologetics, how God uses his faithful to persuade others, but on ethics — how God through Scripture shapes our action. Work's emphasis on rhetoric has the advantage of emphasizing how Christian action speaks louder than words. However, the grammar metaphor directly focuses us on primary questions of how we remain in God's story, which fund any meaningful definition of Christian witness.

In chapter 3 we saw that this focus on the divine claiming of our action through Scripture is the primary emphasis of Richard Hays's concept of "focal images."[15] Yet we also saw that, as in Lindbeck's grammar, it is these "focal images" and *not* the biblical text, that become methodologically essential in his project of "mapping" our lives onto "the pattern of the New Testament's story of Jesus" (Hays, p. 302). The concept of focal images helps Hays unify the disparate biblical materials and spur analogical reasoning across the temporal gap between our lives and that of the Bible, but it does so by picturing Scripture (or the synthetic "biblical narrative") as a static template on which our narratives are measured and cut or squeezed to fit. My proposal is similar to Hays's in that I seek the Bible's unity and encourage analogical reasoning from Scripture to our contemporary contexts, but dissimilar in where I locate this unity. The metaphor of grammar has the advantage of emphasizing the dynamic and interpretative nature of reading and living. We "apply" images but "enact" or "sing" within a grammar; and "singing" draws out much more forcefully the recurring return to the text of Scripture and life that the "application" of "images" does not so naturally emphasize.

In addition, Hays develops focal images as a method of ensuring balanced and coherent biblical interpretation. But once making that move, Hays

15. Richard Hays, *The Moral Vision of the New Testament: Community, Cross, New Creation: A Contemporary Introduction to New Testament Ethics* (San Francisco: HarperSanFrancisco, 1996), ch. 10.

is forced by the richness of the biblical witness to use several focal images, putting him in the position of needing a third-order methodology about how they might be weighted in relationship to one another in particular ethical discussions. This has the effect of overemphasizing hermeneutical theorizing in asking us to develop a facility in a complex metadiscourse so that we can grasp the ethical relevance of a given biblical passage. The metaphor of grammar allows us more effectively to accomplish what Hays tries to do with the appeal to narrative as an ordering device: different biblical genres and narratives must be related in a process that is inevitably interpretive and ongoing.

Grammar is irreducibly complex and yet unified in a multipolar way. It has no "center," and it is only properly or improperly practiced; that is, when its various complex relationships, rules, and exceptions are grasped, it becomes a serviceable mode of existing and communicating within a given community. To try to pin this movement down in "images," whether one or many, is equivalent to saying that the performance of living with God can no longer develop in a way fundamental to the idea of "learning a grammar." Grammar always remains open to debate. There is no external judge to adjudicate disputes about proper performance. The whole community "owns" the language, and as a whole seeks and relies on the Spirit for its maintenance. This amounts to an eschatological caveat about our claims to knowledge: we are to learn and perform Scripture, but without claiming we possess an external point of reference from which we are capable of freezing interpretation in life and exegesis.

The practical gain in this change is twofold. While Hays struggles to explain how human reason and experience and the church's tradition inform our reading of Scripture, thinking of the Bible as a grammar *assumes* that it is interacting in various ways with a vast range of grammars that may or may not be consonant with it. In asking how the various grammars of our lives fit with the biblical grammar, we seek to "translate" ourselves by actively facilitating the synchronization of our meaning frameworks with Scripture. In this interaction we are co-opted into God's work of drawing what we "know" into scripture as the *norma normans*. This is the sense of Luther's *sola scriptura*, which Hays rejects (p. 209) but unknowingly restates when he says, "[E]xtrabiblical sources stand in a hermeneutical relation to the New Testament; they are not independent counterbalancing sources of authority" (p. 296). My claim that Hays has shifted the locus of moral authority away from the text and toward its synthesis is confirmed in his unwitting — and dissonant — reformulation of the *sola scriptura* principle that follows: "In other words, the *Bible's* perspective is privileged, not ours." One immediately wonders whether "focal images" are the Bible's perspective or ours. *Sola scrip-*

tura does not mean that we know nothing but the Bible: it means that the key to Scripture *is* Scripture, and that this key comprehends and criticizes all that is, including our interpretive schemas.

In using the metaphor of the Bible as a grammar, we are able more clearly to expose the Bible's function in the divine reclamation of the diverse rationalities partitioning and fragmenting our lives. Scripture's unity is, therefore, not of itself, but in the unified grammar of the divine life that faith seeks in the diverse moments and strands of the biblical witness and in our lives. Hays suggests that, because Jesus' death and resurrection are God's decisive act, the New Testament is to be hermeneutically privileged over the Old Testament (p. 309). Surely Augustine has taken this insight to its proper conclusion by assuming that the unity of the whole Bible is premised on Christ's person and work, which reveals God's eternal way of being. The Logos, actually and logically if not temporally, precedes the writing of Scripture. Christ's own working (not the texts that discuss it nor the concept of Christ's being) thus has equal interpretive priority over all biblical texts. But at the same time, because we hear that Word within his body, the reception of that Word by the community, as collected and elucidated in doctrine, cannot but make a claim on our interpretations.[16] Jesus' arrival in human history added nothing new to the divine grammar in which Abraham hoped and participated. What is new in the Christ event is Jesus Christ's speaking to his church without the mediation that comes before and after through his Word and Spirit, which constitute the unity of his body.

God's Way of Living with Us: Scripture's Place in the Divine Self-Communication

This definition of Scripture as the grammar of the Christian life is intended to be understood in realist terms. I am suggesting that the unity of Scripture's grammar is in God's action alone. Without this presupposition, the Bible naturally fragments into a million irreconcilable pieces. Having said this, we can further say that to be taken into God's action is to have creation revealed as a divine work. That Scripture reveals where we are in creation thus rests on a confession about the relationship of God's work to the world. To affirm in faith that all discourses meet in the economy of God's own action, and that this economy is disclosed in its relevant features in Scripture, depends for its coherence on God's actually having imparted himself to creation. That creation has structure only as an artifact of the divine work is another way of

---

16. Cf. Jenson, *Systematic Theology,* pp. 270-71.

saying that he has communicated himself to it. According to Scripture, this *communicatio idiomatum* is the foundation of all creation (Gen. 1–2) and each human being (Job 10:8ff.; Ps. 139:11ff.).[17] Scripture's grammar corresponds to the rationality of the Logos, the truth of Christ, serving God's reorientation of the rationality of human speech and action. It follows that we can orient ourselves within creation only by confessing it to be the enduring artifact of God's creative work; rejecting this claim renders us formless and void (Gal. 5). Creation is not God — its order is imparted to it for us, but it is God's order and thus truly understood only by knowing him.

This is not to imply that rebellion against God can destroy God's gift of existence in a single stroke. Creation has its own proper solidity patiently suffering human sin. This observation allies Christian theology with all forms of empirical research. Because creation is ordered by God's hand, the clarity of detail achieved by empirical research about creation's many levels of order can be understood as an agnostic or unwitting theology: that is, talk about God and his gifts that does not know itself as such. When scientific knowledge is seen with eyes that wonder at God's work, it yields new appreciation of the multiplicity and comprehensiveness of divine provision for and care of life. The discovery of the richness of the "text" of order left in materiality by God's working facilitates our rediscovery of creation's multifaceted relationship to the text of Scripture. A dialogue about, and exploration of, the world's social and material order in wonder at its Creator is thus an indispensable component of the discovery of the complexity of God's self-description in Scripture.

"Grammar," then, as I am using the term, does not primarily point to utterances or specific sentences, but it is about the rationality of *Mitteilung*, "communication." It is a way of exposing to view the content of our conversational life with God. Kierkegaard asks how we can have any "part" of God, and he finds that we do so *Mit-teilung* — literally, "with a part of" conversation. Even if we must take seriously the fact that we converse with a God who is invisible, we nevertheless receive the whole of God in a hidden manner as we converse with him.[18] He communicates his own idiom to us in Christ. In the "happy exchange" of justification, Christ not only takes our place, as is so often emphasized, but we take Christ's place before the Father. This is why Jesus teaches us his prayer: these are Jesus' own words to the Father. Therefore,

17. On the parallel with God's *creatio ex nihilo,* see Hans Walter Wolff, *Anthropologie des Alten Testaments* (München: Christian Kaiser Verlag, 1973), ch. 11.

18. Soren Kierkegaard, *Concluding Unscientific Postscript to Philosophical Fragments,* vol. 1, ed. and trans. Howard Hong and Edna Hong (Princeton, NJ: Princeton University Press, 1992), ch. 2.1, pp. 72-80; Kierkegaard, *Philosophical Fragments,* ed., trans., and intro. Howard Hong and Edna Hong (Princeton, NJ: Princeton University Press, 1985), pp. 66-71.

to pray as Jesus prays is to come to know the Father as Jesus knows the Father and to thus embody the life of Christ. The theologically central point is that we threaten the reality and sophistication of the practice of this communication *(communicatio idiomatum)* if we displace the primacy of actual communion with second-order reflections on how this might be possible or how it ought to proceed if we were to begin.

The practice of Eucharist emphasizes the importance of not critically distancing ourselves from communal worship and the materiality of God's self-communication through concrete forms of worship. In the Eucharist we move within his active and concrete handing-over of himself to us — thus making us real. He breaks himself up into digestible installments and gives himself to us in order to keep us in being.[19] Eucharist is our active submission to Christ's struggle with our order, his taking it up in order to draw us into a new order. He takes up *logos* to change and reshape our *logos* into conformity with the *Logos*. His relationship to us as handworker is thus shown to have its *ratio* in the divine *communicatio* with humanity.

The Lord's Supper is "for the forgiveness of sins" (Matt. 26:28) because in moving into its realm we confess that our performance of worship does not save, but that God must ever again give himself in it. At the same time, these are not merely occasional self-bestowals, because it is through his self-gift that we have bread and wine to offer that (his) earth has given and (his) human hands have made. He is not separable from or identifiable with his creation, yet is bound to it in such a way that we are not left wondering about the God who is radically other than these forms Scripture calls his love.[20] Sin, conversely, imposes a different grammar, altering practices and metaphors in the attempt self-referentially to exploit the many levels of creation's order that sustain our relationships with God and one another with the purpose of accruing a supposed benefit to the self.

The emphasis of such an explorative theology has momentous implications for the Christian understanding of engagement with non-Christians. Bonhoeffer puts the point unequivocally. "The more exclusively we recognize and confess Christ as our Lord, the more will be disclosed to us the breadth of Christ's Lordship."[21] Christians can only engage in fruitful dialogue with the

---

19. Douglas Knight, "Speaking Humanity," in Murray Rae and Steven Holmes, eds., *The Person of Christ* (London: Continuum, 2005).

20. Jaroslav Pelikan, *Luther's Works: Companion Volume: Luther the Expositor: Introduction to the Reformer's Exegetical Writings* (St. Louis: Concordia, 1959), p. 173.

21. Bonhoeffer, *Ethics*, Dietrich Bonhoeffer Works, Vol. 6, ed. Ilse Tödt, Heinz Eduard Tödt, Ernst Feil, and Clifford Green; trans. Reinhard Krauss, Charles West, and Douglas Scott (Minneapolis: Fortress, 2005), p. 344.

world if they know that all they have is faith in the illuminating power of the Spirit of the Christ offered to us in Scripture. Therefore, *sola scriptura* must be understood as a restatement of *sola fides* and *solus Christus*, with the result that the one truth of all reality is exposed as Christ.

One implication of this intertwined set of claims is expressed by the concept of the "clarity of Scripture," which explicates the certainty of faith that the Spirit of the self-revealing God will meet faith in Scripture, and that Scripture is sufficient for this task. "[A] well-rounded theological account of *claritas*, far from undermining the validity of hermeneutical work, recovers the proper vocation of hermeneutics, precisely by reinserting the activity of interpretation into the overall structure of God's communicative fellowship with humankind."[22] The Christians' confession that God also meets them in their commitment to the neighbor sets up a powerful incentive and framework for engaging with contemporary cultural currents. It is this faith in the promise of the Spirit's appearing and the unity of all God's works and Word that propels Christians into dialogue with all seekers of truth, sustaining it by making bearable the repeated disorientation and embarrassment of entering new discourses and exposing familiar ones as idolatrous. This faith is a guide that keeps us from becoming lost in proliferating views of reality or cut off from Scripture by taking familiar discourses as "true" without querying whether their grammar coheres with the Logos, whose grammar we encounter in Scripture.

The reverse is also true. The church does not know Christ and thus does not know itself when it has not yet found the connection between its usual modes of speaking and the Bible. It has not yet plumbed the depth of Luther's insight that all talk is in some way talk about God. It still believes that some of its talk retains a place separate from God. It is at this point that those people who confess that they are outside the church and yet wrestle with the Bible, connecting their own discourses with its words and images, can challenge the church more sharply to question its own discourses that have floated free of Scripture.[23] The promise of grace is that Scripture exposes us to the whole of God's actions in creation, and thus all human discourses meet there, whether for affirmation or judgment. Therefore, the task of faith is to discover these connections in wrestling with Scripture, and so seek the re-integration of the discourses that order our lives. Christians, because they have this promise of

---

22. See John Webster, "Biblical Theology and the Clarity of Scripture," in Craig Bartholomew, Mary Healy, and Karl Moller, eds., *Out of Egypt: Biblical Theology and Biblical Interpretation* (Carlisle: Paternoster Press, 2004), p. 355.

23. John Steinbeck's *East of Eden* is one example of the exploration of the inner meaning of a biblical text by a "secular" writer, in this case the Cain and Abel story.

the unity of all discourses, need not fear that engaging in any discourse will falsify Scripture. Engagement with others in such hope sustains the patience necessary to grow into new discourses and re-examine familiar ones, knowing in faith that the connections of this discourse with praise will in time also begin to appear.

If Christian ethics is the connection and critique of the discourses that determine our moral lives with Scripture, then its first aspiration is not necessarily to develop a comprehensive ethical schema. Instead, it may aim at much more limited but penetrating projects of the analyzing and reformulating of a single or limited complex of specific grammars in which our society is currently captured. With this in mind, my aim in the next chapter's exegesis of Psalms 130 and 104 will be to indicate where these psalms meet and claim various contemporary discourses within which the world conceives its moral options.

Good Works as the Craftwork
of Exegetical and Ethical Judgment

This strong emphasis on the concreteness of the procedure whereby God communicates himself to us leads to a revitalization of hermeneutical method. Again, Robert Jenson encapsulates well what we have discussed in Part II of this book: "Churchly interpretation of Scripture is interpretation done in the course of activities specific to the church: missionary preaching, liturgy, homiletics, catechetics, endurance of suffering, governance, care of souls, or works of charity. . . . [T]here is no way to list in advance what roles Scripture may play in these different enterprises and their changing historical situations."[24] The result is a new appreciation for the importance of knowing the content of Scripture and the exegetical tradition, so often marginalized in contemporary hermeneutical discussion.

The heavy emphasis we saw in Part I on general and formal features of reading, and the deep influence of self-reflexivity on the formation of the questions we take to Scripture, has made it particularly difficult for contemporary exegetes to recognize the sheer particularity of the church's Bible reading. Richard Longenecker's *New Testament Social Ethics for Today* provides an interesting example of how those engaged in constructive Christian interpretation often feel compelled to describe what they are doing within the rubric of hermeneutical method. In substance, Longenecker's biblical ethic is an in-

---

24. Jenson, *Systematic Theology*, p. 277.

terpretation of one New Testament passage, Galatians 3:28: "There is no longer Jew or Greek, there is no longer slave or free, there is no longer male and female; for all of you are one in Christ Jesus."[25] His intent is to show how the Christian tradition has come to rule out some ways of interpreting the verse, while validating others. He shows that the tradition has had reasons to view the passage as more important than some other passages (such as those where slavery is unreflectively embraced, for example); and it has in turn set this passage alongside other passages by which it is interpreted (such as Christological passages). Longenecker traces the history of the development of this interpretation to show how the Christian tradition arrived, via a particular historical route, at a particular biblical topography (as we did in Part II). What he claims to be doing, however, is laying out a "developmental hermeneutic." This leaves us with the impression that what he has displayed is a method of interpretation rather than a way of giving a lesson in the content of the tradition relative to one passage. Despite this, the force of his account is generated by his fine-grained attention to the one particular tradition he is investigating rather than the attractiveness of any general set of rules (methodology) he might have developed (but did not) about how people in religious traditions should interpret their scriptures.

The study of Scripture is the devotion of a unique community to a singular text. Therefore, what comes to be overlooked in contemporary biblical hermeneutics is a point essential to Luther: Christian biblical exegesis as meditation on Scripture is grounded in learning the unique connections between passages of Scripture, thereby discovering the biblical topography. This process of discovering the biblical topography is both essential to Christian exegesis and ethics — and inescapably particular. Each generation must undertake the task anew, because it can never be fully described in general terms. General theological reasons may at times be given for or against a specific connection between biblical texts, and suggestions may be made of proper ways of getting to know Scripture.[26]

---

25. Richard Longenecker, *New Testament Social Ethics for Today* (Grand Rapids: Eerdmans, 1984).

26. Longenecker gives one such (relatively praiseworthy) set of rules: "To be a Christian theologian today, therefore, requires (1) extensive familiarity with the Scriptures, (2) extensive familiarity with church history, (3) discernment in appreciating the essence and direction of biblical statements, (4) discernment in distinguishing between advances and pitfalls in the history of Christian thought, being able to identify the lines of continuity which exist between every true advance and the New Testament, the touchstone for Christian faith, and (5) creative ability to say what all this means for Christian faith and life today amid the complexities of varying ideologies and competing lifestyles." *Social Ethics for Today*, p. 22.

But such second-order and preparatory comments must not displace this basic insight: until the intervention of modern concepts of reading, biblical interpretation was defined as a very particular facility of enriching the understanding of a given passage by making connections, and quite often novel connections, with other passages in a way that brings added theological density and explanatory power to both. Thus, general reasoning and guidelines cannot be used to rule out the surprising connections that keep a tradition alive. The process of showing how certain passages may be interpreted takes place within our activities of cultural and theological interpretation, as we try to discern what a specific text has to say today. This is not to imply that biblical interpretation is radically *ad hoc*. Attentiveness and rigor remain prerequisites. But this attentiveness to the nuance of Scripture and the way it links with our experience is best understood as a craft.

The considerations that remain central in this view can be illustrated by noting how a judgment about the proper *context* in which a theological claim is taken to be morally relevant is as important as judgments about the proper *content* of any given theological claim. Indeed, it may turn out that the problem of Christian moral theology is less concerned with making correct general statements about Christian behavior, and more with the process of developing sensitivity to perceive when and how intervention is appropriate at all.[27] Here the discourse of ethics is crucial because it asks the question beyond how right and wrong theological arguments are established: When and how should we begin to think about right and wrong behavior at all? When we do, how should we use moral arguments — and, more than that, inhabit them? The use and inhabitation of Christian descriptions of reality happens in irreducibly particular circumstances and thus depends not only on a grasp of the systematic connections of theology but also on having been shaped into people who know how to ask for and discern the Spirit's appearance. This suggests a concept of the "clarity of obedience," which conceptually parallels the idea of the "clarity of Scripture" in that both conceive human action as sustained by dependence in faith on the reliability of God's speaking. Faith in the clarity of Scripture is revealed as ethical in scope.

The ethical aspect of the clarity of Scripture is that willingness and increasing facility in venturing concrete exegetical judgments is a precise correlative of willingness and facility in making individual ethical judgments in real time. As various writers have helpfully indicated, interpretation is not finished until we enact it in a self-involving way. Such judgments are not free-floating exercises of the will but are made with reference to prior exemplars,

---

27. Bonhoeffer, *Ethics*, pp. 365-66.

from whom we have learned specific concepts and doctrines, but also an ethos and aesthetic of action. We must learn to sense opportunities for the good judgment that is "evaluated primarily by its ability to improvise, to balance individual inventiveness with adherence to a tradition of prescribed conventions — which means that elements of risk and unpredictable achievement are inescapable features."[28] We must also continually grow in this ability, because "the Spirit reserves much . . . so that we may always remain his pupils." This admission does not make ethical and exegetical judgments more tentative, but it emphasizes their aspect as active confessions made in faith, hope, and love. Such an account seeks not to judge the Spirit but to elucidate as clearly as possible how Scripture conceives of calling on God and following God by holding together the active and passive moments of prayer and good works. In so doing, exegetical and ethical judgments are confessed to be fully human, but human as judgments seeking to follow God's one eternal action in the present.

Right Christian action continues in God's story because it hears him (Job 12:4), speaks to him (Job 13:1), and knows that without this conversation its most powerful wisdom is vanity, which will lead us into a pathless waste (Job 12:24). Only God can claim his church for a course of action, but God does so claim it, and Christian ethical action is a living confession embodying that truth. The willingness to confess in the form of such judgments can proceed only out of the preparatory work of observation and hearing of the saints, deep thought about their lives and teaching, and the development of general (doctrinal) descriptions of God's action. But this preparatory work itself rests on a faith that God will speak and bring clarity precisely through activities of faithful study that hasten toward particular instances of the divine advent.

I have suggested that such a position is a confession that Christian ethical judgments dare to claim that God has made specific claims on our existence through Scripture and the Spirit. If we believe that Scripture is clear, and that the Spirit, through various media, gives clear direction in life, then action that has prayerfully consulted Scripture to judge and synchronize the relevant discourse with Scripture should be considered faith's informed con-

---

28. Quote from p. 80 of James Fodor and Stanley Hauerwas, "Performing Faith: The Peaceable Rhetoric of God's Church," in Stanley Hauerwas, *Performing the Faith: Bonhoeffer and the Practice of Nonviolence* (Grand Rapids: Baker Books, 2004), pp. 79-109. I avoid calling these improvisational judgments "performances," as do Fodor and Hauerwas, because I find it difficult to disentangle the appropriate reference of "performance" to formed activity from the inappropriate self-consciousness entailed in the "show" or "stage play" resonance, a problem that is exacerbated by the authors' contrasting performance as activity with prayer as receptivity.

fession *as* action.[29] A true Christian ethical statement ventures in faith to propose a specific action in specific circumstances, and it does not take the form of a general claim about the good. The saying and the doing are both equally acts of witness. Such ethical ventures, to be Christian, must refer to Scripture, either directly or indirectly, through the community or doctrines that Scripture has shaped.

To take this approach is to conceive of ethics as training in discerning how to follow God. A "good work" is one that embodies this following in real time, and is judged not solely on its coherence to general ethical guidelines but regarding its character as embodied faith. We discover our being in Christ when we give up our moral detachment and say, "Biblical text *X* and ethical consideration *Y* meet here in this situation, and demand a response." It is in such judgments that God meets us (Eph. 2:10). This does not make truth subjective, but the action aspect of the complex confession of faith is made visible. Nor do good works so conceived aim at the building up of merit, but they aim at a progressive entering into a rationality to more actively and deeply understand it. The desire to do good works is both critical and a desire we must pray for, not having the will on our own. This was a prominent theme in Part II, and we will return to it in the final chapter.

Learning the proper modesty and perspicuity of the craft of theology in communities of faith is especially important when properly doctrinal statements are by definition considered immodest in the social context in which they are being uttered (external to the community of faith). I illustrated this point in Part I by tracing the various responses to the biblical texts on roles within marriage. Admitting this reshapes the way we ask theological questions. For instance, William Cavanaugh, in *Torture and Eucharist*, asks how we are to understand and practice the church's beliefs about excommunication in a way resistant to false images of society forced on a nation by political corruption or totalitarianism.[30] Of course, such inquiries demand clear doctrinal reflection, but of a kind that is shaped by a much wider range of demands than simple systematic coherence.

Luther's discussion of translation helps to clarify these connections. At a practical level, biblical translation depends, as a craft, on connecting two worlds of meaning. One is the language use of the average person. At the same time, the translator must be attentive to two levels of meaning within

29. "Hearing is the miracle of God. . . . This miracle is the office of the Holy Spirit." Karl Barth, *The Holy Spirit and the Christian Life: The Theological Basis of Ethics,* trans. R. Birch Hoyle, foreword by Robin Lovin (Louisville: Westminster John Knox, 1993), p. 11.

30. William Cavanaugh, *Torture and Eucharist: Theology, Politics and the Body of Christ* (Oxford: Blackwell Publishers, 1998).

the text — its linguistic grammar (Hebrew, Greek, or Latin) and the intertextual logic of its relationships to other biblical narratives and statements.[31] Once the translator is fully immersed in the grammar of the language of his contemporaries does it begin to be possible to make the judgments necessary to see the relevance of Scripture for the contemporary world. Semantics is the discipline of making judgments about how one grammar is interacting with another and is basic to grasping cross-influences. Luther says that he seeks in that semantic task to test his theological decisions and linkages by reference to the church fathers (his masters), with the aim of drawing people (his apprentices) into faith in Christ (Christ's grammar) ("On Translating," pp. 197-98). This process of linkage is both a craft in a practical sense and a discipline in a spiritual sense, and it demands a God-fearing, experienced, and trained heart (pp. 193-94).

Exegesis is theology taking place in close attentiveness to God's Word, and it is accomplished in myriad small theological decisions distinguishing and linking the Bible with the unique configurations of our common language. The translation of a single word can thus have momentous ethical implications, to which we can make appeal in moral theology without recourse to a cumbersome synthetic account of the supposed ethical content of Scripture. This kind of biblical interpretation cannot be learned from an instruction manual; it must be learned as a craft. This entails a continuous sensitivity to our social and cultural context, the logic of our lives, and Scripture simultaneously and in equal measure. The task is complex: it demands apprenticeship to those who can teach us the forms of judging how it is to be done. Apprenticeship is always practical, and Christian interpretation is always ecclesial.

The essential point is that the interpretative strategy I have outlined is the one demanded by the material, the diversity of Scripture itself, and the diversity of interpretation that forms the Christian tradition. This strategy rests on faith's confession of God's facility in using diverse influences to enrich his body. The Bible, as part of Christ's body, draws in the whole diversity of human discourse, as Christ draws all meaning into his lordship. The physical layout of traditional Jewish biblical commentary reflects the nature of Christ as Torah: the biblical text is ringed with various commentators, with differing interpretations, who stand side by side, thus demanding the development of the skill of reading for today. I have followed a similar procedure. Placing the exegesis of Augustine and Luther side by side does not reveal uniformity;

31. Luther, "On Translating: An Open Letter," in *Luther's Works, Vol. 35, Word and Sacrament,* ed. E. Theodore Bachmann (Philadelphia: Muhlenberg Press, 1960), pp. 189, 195-96.

rather, it suggests shared priorities that are not reducible to the methodological congruence sought by modern hermeneutical sensitivities. This approach highlights the necessity of developing the ability to make judgments about Scripture and society in real time, and doing so within the community of faith. The interpretive rule I am suggesting begins in faith within the living *ecclesia,* and trusts its ability to pass on its thick rationality rather than simply a hermeneutical theory. "Ethical" reading is another name for ecclesial reading: it seeks to learn from the saints the reality that praise opens up.

Rather than trying to answer certain preformed questions with the help of Scripture and tradition, this means that we must attempt to position ourselves within the acoustic realm of Scripture. Within this space, our attempts to listen to God will constantly engender the need to listen to the voices of those who have read before us. Of course, what it is that needs to be heard and which particular insight of which thread of the Christian exegetical tradition (or of other discourses) will appear to fit within the acoustic realm of Scripture cannot be predetermined. What factors and arguments will shape our final judgments must be left to the very dynamic of the procedure. This is not *ad hoc* in the sense of requiring no preparation, but in the sense that it is methodologically unpredictable. What tools we take up as interpreters of Scripture and culture must constantly surprise us. Its fertility requires continuous and close study of the Bible and the tradition and an ongoing willingness to venture biblical and cultural exegesis.

Engagement in this interpretation may not leave us time to give a full account of our hermeneutical presuppositions (as this study attempts) before proceeding to our own exegesis. Such background explanations are suggested, of course, by the nature of "meditation" as coherent and textually attentive thought. Yet the hermeneutical discourse must be distinguished from the sort of venture of interpretation undertaken in chapter 9. The work of this final chapter must be allowed its own voice as exegesis of Scripture, facilitated — but not justified — by the previous chapters with their hermeneutical focus. I am not claiming that the book of Psalms contains the whole of the biblical witness without remainder, but it can help advance an interpretive proposal that I believe is especially promising for a contemporary church struggling with having distanced itself from Scripture.

Relocating Hermeneutics

In the course of Part II of this study, we saw how Luther and Augustine are united in going to Scripture to know God, but divided by their interpretive practices and hermeneutical frameworks. For example, Luther is simply not interested in establishing an explicit critical relationship with Augustine's hermeneutical presuppositions in the way the contemporary discussion would lead us to expect. We are left asking about the proper place of hermeneutical theorizing in Christian exegesis. This amounts to a question about the role of criticism in exegetical/ethical interpretation.

Some definitions are in order here. It is essential that we distinguish the practices of biblical and cultural interpretation from hermeneutics and explain their relationship. *Interpretation* is the use of practical tools and approaches in the attempt to come to grips with a text or context. These include textual and cultural criticism, as well as conceptual approaches, such as the fourfold method, Christological or sociological presuppositions, and so forth. We cannot make sense of texts without a "toolbox." But what this toolbox contains will vary from interpreter to interpreter. All interpreters use their tools with the regularity to which those tools commit them; but if our interpretation is to grow in sophistication and sensitivity, we should expect that the tools at our disposal, and the ways we use tools, will continually develop.

In the apprenticeship in reading that we receive from the community of faith (and other reading communities) we learn to interpret in ordered, methodological steps, even if we cannot describe those steps in abstract terms. We often simply know what "works" to produce readings that seem reasonable. However, it will always be the case that the tools we inherit when we learn to interpret come with a vision of why we interpret, what counts as a coherent reading — and these shape our interpretive judgments.[32] In general terms, method is a structured *habitus,* or practice, by which aspects of experience are made visible and thus accessible to criticism. To discard it would imply the embrace of arbitrariness or anarchy and the loss of orientation that would entail. What needs to be clarified is the method of faith. Here again I will develop Luther's suggestion that the method of faith is a kind of prayer and practice from which understanding grows.[33]

Hermeneutics is second-order reflection on the way we use the tools of interpretation, that is, which tools we use and how. A theological practice of hermeneutics would not claim to be exposing the "true" interpretation, but it assumes that it is through interpretation that the church partakes of the grammar of the divine life. Its role is to make interpretation more self-conscious and thus

---

32. David Kelsey, *Proving Doctrine: The Uses of Scripture in Modern Theology* (Harrisburg, PA: Trinity Press International, 1999), pp. 167-70.

33. Gerhard Sauter, "Das Gebet als Wurzel des Redens von Gott," in *Glaube und Lernen* 1, May 1986 (Göttingen: Vandenhoek & Ruprecht): 21-37.

attentive to God. Hermeneutical reflection can take various forms, but it functions like a university lecture in bricklaying: it may spur the bricklayer already conversant in the basic skills of the trade to experiment with familiar methods to produce novel results or to give up counterproductive habits. Discussions of theory thus have great critical value for those with some basic skills. But such lectures are an extremely poor substitute for apprenticeship in the practices of mixing mortar, aligning bricks, and so on. The port of entry into the Christian tradition is a reading of Scripture, not a theory of reading.[34]

It is thus incorrect to claim (as Paul Ricoeur does, for instance) that conceptually understood, general hermeneutics must come before special or particular (read biblical) hermeneutics.[35] The historical reality is that the writing of and being drawn into a scriptural tradition were highly developed long before the suggestion that this can only follow a discussion of general hermeneutical theory. Thus the discourse of general hermeneutics, insofar as it advances biblical exegesis, does so by making that exegesis more self-aware as a participant in the faith that arises through and with the production of, and continual engagement with, its Scripture.

This is not to oppose hermeneutics per se, but to question the central place it has been given in modernity. Interpretation is the irreducible foundation on which hermeneutics must rest, which can only question, clarify, and suggest different interpretive possibilities in a piecemeal fashion. But it cannot become a master discourse (1) displacing the learning of basic skills of interpretation, or (2) generating a claim that we must engage in it before engaging in interpretation.

The structure of this study emphasizes our continual reliance on the experience of interpretation by placing the attempt to explain its exegetical insights after an extended immersion in particular readings, rather than prefacing them. The gain of this approach is that it takes seriously the communal location of learning the skills of interpretation, while it takes the text of Scripture more seriously than do the communitarians of chapter 2. It follows the approaches of chapter 3 in taking the text of Scripture seriously, while it denies the claim that we must first build up a synthetic superstructure (a hermeneutical claim) before having access to Scripture for ethics. It also reckons with the possibility that our general observations and theological claims may be flawed (ch. 5), thus maintaining that interpretive practice is more basic

---

34. We have seen that, for Augustine, this came through the person and teaching of Ambrose. St. Augustine, *Confessions,* trans. and intro. by Henry Chadwick (Oxford: Oxford University Press, 1991), V.xiii-xiv.

35 Paul Ricoeur, *From Text to Action: Essays in Hermeneutics 2* (London: Athlon Press, 1991), p. 89.

than theoretical reflections. Such practice takes place in the immediacy before Scripture that maintains the proper theological primacy of ethos over ethics, of interpretation over hermeneutics. This position draws on the theological conceptions presented in chapters 4 and 5, but attempts to explicate these claims within an interpretive rather than a hermeneutical framework.

No academic discipline can be posited as privileged or primary in its relationship to Scripture, including biblical studies. The only solidity to which Christian faith can cling in its exploration of the Bible is Christ as body, head, and Word. Any concept or academic discipline that makes itself the arbiter between rival interpretations would have to be established as another axiomatic truth. My point is, rather, that only Christ (as person and as body) and his Word (as bound to Scripture) can be objects of Christian faith. As Douglas Knight says, Scripture and tradition are thus distinguishable but utterly interwoven. Theology's role is not to police the borders between the two; instead, its role is "continually to cross it and transport its goods back and forth between doctrine and liturgy and Scripture. It must understand that words are in the service of works, and the works are in the service of the community, that is to say, of loosing the captives and binding them into the community of God, securing their place in plurality, and the works are themselves adopted by the Spirit and reintegrated into the words of God."[36] Again we encounter the basic question of faith: the choice between faith in human activity (in this case in the form of hermeneutical sophistication) or the appearing of God to renew our interpretation and thus continue our story with him. But to argue for the latter requires something like Luther's ethos of doxology, in which Scripture plays an irreducible role in shaping a community whose whole existence is understood as an artifact of God's working.

From this viewpoint we can see that, at its best, the church's engagement in the discourse of biblical hermeneutics is an inquiry into how people become aware of themselves by becoming aware of God through his Word. At its worst, it becomes a way of letting second-order discussion displace first-order engagement with Scripture and society, thus marginalizing the importance of dialogue with God. Augustine and Luther can be understood as reflecting on Scripture as a way more clearly to articulate the processes of God's claiming his people. For them the Psalms are a context of discovery through which faith receives its identity by engaging in an incredibly rich drama (with a grammar) in which we are made characters (those who are being taught to participate in and practice this grammar).

36. Douglas Knight, "Liturgy as Exorcism," http://www.douglasknight.org/mambo/content/view/51/38/.

Thus a unique feature of the Psalms to which Luther has drawn our attention is emphasized: the Psalms never leave the place from which theology must always begin afresh — the soteriological, or redemptive, moment. Again, the weight of my analysis rests on the claim that form and content are so intertwined in Scripture that we misunderstand it when we pull them apart.[37] For the most part, modern hermeneutics deny the possibility that the interaction with Scripture is a living, generative process, an exploration. The Psalms press us to take seriously the claim that, as we read Scripture, we are in a conversation with God on which we can critically reflect. The basic assumption is that the subject *(Sache)* of theology cannot be separated from this praxis of exploratory prayer and the biblical forms given to sustain it.

This beginning emphasizes the need for Christian ethics to discuss the specific genesis of the Christian ethos in me. How do I come to talk about God at all? Praying as direct attentiveness to God is exposed here for the first time as the point from which the whole Christian tradition develops. Christian faith is grounded on the particularity of the divine address. The tradition is composed of those who participate in this "place" where the tradition is created. Philosophical hermeneutics has no choice but to find revelation elsewhere. Heidegger's sophisticated and influential hermeneutics, for instance, finds its revelatory moment in the negation of death, Arendt's in birth.[38] In contrast, Christian faith, hope, and love spring from something counterintuitive yet experienced as wholly positive, a new creation.[39] Prayer and praise are human activities of faith and are simultaneously an effect of God's action on us and our action of preparing the way for God to speak to us. This re-emphasis of talking to God as the heart of theology also returns revelation to its proper place as speech, as opposed to the understanding some have of revelation as a mere creature that is actually capable of being handled and therefore manipulated to our ends. The point of theology is lost when revelation becomes generalized in this way, when "scripture" is turned into "text."[40]

37. For a vigorous defense of this claim, see Jan Fokkelman, *Reading Biblical Narrative: A Practical Guide,* trans. Ineke Smit (Leiden: Deo Publishing, 1999), esp. ch. 2 and p. 97.

38. Martin Heidegger, *Being and Time* (a translation of *Sein und Zeit,* trans. Joan Stambaugh (Albany, NY: State University of New York Press, 1996), Division II.I: "The Possible Being-a-Whole of Da-sein and Being-toward-death," pp. 219-46. Hannah Arendt, *The Human Condition* (Chicago: University of Chicago Press, 1958): "The Disclosure of the Agent in Speech and Action," pp. 175-81.

39. Bonhoeffer, *Ethics,* pp. 309-11.

40. Gerhard Sauter asks how to locate God-talk within talking with God. Sauter, "Das Gebet als Wurzel," pp. 21-37.

Umberto Eco perhaps puts this better, and certainly more provocatively, by stating the inverse. The "texts" that are interpreted by secular hermeneutical rationality cannot, by definition, be said to refer to all that exists and might possibly exist. Therefore, as soon as a "text" becomes "scripture," it cannot but appear to hermeneutical rationality to be generating what he calls "overinterpretation."[41] We do not believe that "normal texts" point to all that exists, and Eco suggests that we can spot people treating texts as Scripture precisely in the way they produce interpretations that betray their continual suspicion that there is always something more and deeper to be learned from them. From this perspective, Christian doctrine is both the systematic affirmation of Eco's "overinterpretation" and the attempt of the faith community to channel it to keep it faithful to the God who speaks through it. Suspicion that a text means more than we have yet grasped — and thus at least in principle touches on all possible knowledge — is the basic relationship of Christian faith to Scripture. This was another feature of Christianity's relationship to Scripture that Luther attempted to draw out with his doctrine of *sola scriptura.*

The most significant feature of this emphasis on the primacy of interpretive practice is the refusal to take up an observer's point of view from which this whole process might be judged. As Luther has emphasized, "The Spirit reserves much for Himself, so that we may always remain His pupils."[42] This confession that Scripture is clear but our understanding is not yet complete must shape our hermeneutical, ethical, and critical theorizing. To begin in that way corrodes the insistence on beginning with the discourse of "method" that characterizes post-Enlightenment philosophy.

Chapter 9 will undertake an exercise resembling a biblical commentary, but not of the kind with which we are familiar today, precisely because what I will say is not methodologically predictable. It is not the "yield" of a previously developed set of exegetical steps. Nor does it "build" on the results of biblical scholars, systematicians, or ethicists, or even the exegesis of Augustine and Luther. Rather, it is a response to the challenge implicit in this tradition to begin reading Scripture before and with them, and from one's particular vantage point, with its particular moral, methodological, and spiritual questions and political context. It is a strategy that seeks to develop skills, not by deciding beforehand how the task should be approached, but

---

41. Umberto Eco, with Richard Rorty, Jonathan Culler, and Christine Brooke-Rose, *Interpretation and Overinterpretation,* ed. Stefan Collini (Cambridge, UK: Cambridge University Press, 1992), pp. 52-53.

42. Luther, "Psalms 1 and 2," pp. 284-85.

by beginning the task of bringing these particularities to Scripture in the openness that these questions may themselves be overturned in the interaction. We have denied that one can first summarize the ethical content of Scripture (as Childs and others have attempted) before asking it ethical questions. With the re-emphasis of the primacy of interpretation, I am suggesting that the proper alternative is to begin, continue, and finish by continually taking the risk of interpretation.

In joining Bonhoeffer and others in the questioning of the primacy of method, this project is not unprecedented in the field of biblical ethics. Yet in Part I, I have indicated the ways in which the theological implications of such a position, and the range of new conceptual problems that follow, have not been sufficiently appreciated. This "downsizing" of theory leaves the biblical interpreter in a maze of relationships between things and beings, whose meaning and claim on our action cannot be adjudicated by reference to a narrative-eye view. We are thrown back from the formal considerations of modern philosophy and hermeneutics onto the material activities both of reading and of Scripture within the community of faith. From this vantage point, I have suggested that, surprisingly, the post-Barthian framework of biblical theology (ch. 4) remains insufficiently radical in describing reading from the angle of an observer who stands seeing the full sweep of salvation history rather than "general" history. It is thus most comfortable describing the "divine person" at work on the community of faith. The Psalms suggest a different route in depicting a path, necessarily out of sight ahead, that the subject must continually traverse in the course of being transformed. The Psalms press us to understand ourselves as undergoing a redemption guided by texts, in which direct conversation with God is the only constant — and thus the generative condition.

The only thing we need add to this emphasis is its corollary: the more tools to which we have access for interpretation, the better. As we have seen, interpretive traditions supply these tools that give us access to aspects and levels of Scripture we may never have noticed otherwise. But appreciation for interpretive tools and the communities that developed them (most often non-Christian) must not be used to disparage the biblical interpretation of the Christian tradition as insufficiently sophisticated. We interpret from communities, not from hermeneutical affirmations or interpretive tools, even when we use them (as we must). Christian interpreters must remain aware that tools and theories bind us to worldly rationalities and thus may alienate us from the community of faith if we do not take care to retain the primacy of God's speaking.

Theological Exegesis: Its Presuppositions and Tools

The foregoing suggests an attempt to display at least a few of the presuppositions and tools I use in the exegesis of the next chapter. Chapter 9 is an experiment that asks the question "What is the role of the Bible in Christian ethics?" as an exegetical theologian rather than as a hermeneutical theoretician. It is important to keep in mind that chapter 9's interpretation of Psalms 130 and 104 is exemplary and unfinished, but not tentative or halfhearted. It is the fully invested and fully human exegetical and ethical effort that sustains the Christian tradition. The presuppositions and tools discussed below do not determine that interpretation, but retroactively they clarify and facilitate that interpretation. The remainder of this chapter is devoted to explicating what seem, on reflection, to be some of the more important tools in my own interpretive toolbox. This means that what follows cannot possibly be an exhaustive description of my hermeneutic; but I offer it in the hope of becoming more aware of the most central and articulable presuppositions of my approach (cf. ch. 1). This is an engagement in hermeneutics that attempts to give reasons for my interpretative moves and refutes various objections to it. But on my own grounds, this hermeneutical discussion does not legitimate my exegesis but critically sharpens aspects of an interpretive practice learned from many teachers in the community of faith.

Metaphor as the Fundament of Scripture and Language

An essential presupposition of the approach presented here is its appreciation of the fundamental breadth and flexibility of metaphor, and its centrality in human perception. Metaphor is not primarily a syntactical form, because it takes many linguistic shapes to form the fundament of all linguistic meaning.[43] The point is most sharply put by Friedrich Nietzsche: "What, then, is truth? A mobile army of metaphors, metonymies, anthropomorphisms, in short a sum of human relations which have been subjected to poetic and rhetorical intensification, translation, and decoration, and which, after they have been in use for a long time, strike a people as firmly established, canonical, and binding."[44] Nietzsche is suggesting that we are mistaken when we assume

43. Janet Martin Soskice, *Metaphor and Religious Language* (Oxford: Clarendon Press, 1985), p. 18.

44. Friedrich Nietzsche, "On Truth and Lying in a Non-Moral Sense," in *The Birth of Tragedy and Other Writings,* ed. Raymond Geuss and Ronald Speirs, trans. Ronald Speirs (Cambridge, UK: Cambridge University Press, 1999), I:146.

that we can escape from metaphorical language into a more basic conceptual mode, a mistake the concept of ontology makes particularly tempting (for theologians at least). Concepts are valid but second-order forms of thought, Stephen Webb suggests. "Concepts imitate the capacity of metaphor to create meaning by new constellations of groups of words, but what metaphors do spontaneously, concepts accomplish consciously, using the metaphorical genius for synthesis to reach new understandings of the structures of reality."[45] The creative potential of metaphorical speech funds the generation of the novel connections that rejuvenate a language, thus feeding all other forms of speech. Therefore, it is the core form of speech to investigate if we want to discover the genesis of an ethos through language.[46]

Analytic philosopher Janet Martin Soskice has elucidated in more conceptual detail how all language is metaphorical and how metaphorical language can be realistic. Even the most "objective" knowledge is oriented by root metaphors whose vagueness and insightfulness are indispensable in allowing flexibility of investigation that establishes insights about things and relationships that fact-language describes. Researchers in cognitive psychology, for instance, are guided by computer metaphors (programming, storing, indexing, etc.) at the same time that researchers in computing science perceive through psychological metaphors (artificial intelligence, memory, and so on). Each metaphor provides terms and places them in the field of experience in ways that direct attention and guide exploration without over-specifying the entity or relationship being investigated.[47] Despite constantly relying on metaphor's realism to guide thinking and perception, Soskice correctly points out that "few contemporary English writers on religious language are free from a residual empiricism, which, whatever the intentions of its proponents, is fundamentally incompatible with traditional transcendental Christianity" (Soskice, p. 142). Thus, when modern Christians lose a living sense of Scripture, it is not because they have no practical experience of vineyards, kingship, and so forth, leaving them unable to grasp biblical metaphors; rather, it is because the Bible's metaphorical heart has been smothered by a positivist literalism (pp. 159-60).

Metaphors do not have two distinct subjects, but they link and integrate

45. Stephen H. Webb, *Re-Figuring Theology: The Rhetoric of Karl Barth* (Albany, NY: State University of New York Press, 1991), p. 35.

46. The most serious contemporary challenge to this privileging of metaphor comes from philosophers who combine Wittgensteinian language-game theory with Idealist categories to reinvigorate concepts as the basic form of human linguistic agreement. For such a "semantic rationalism," see Robert Brandon, *Making It Explicit*.

47. Soskice, *Metaphor*, ch. VII.

previously unrelated associations, shaping perceptions of both (p. 135). Therefore, though modern philosophers have most forcefully made the hermeneutical observation about the centrality of metaphor, my suggestion is that, in so doing, they express the centrality of biblical interpretation within Western intellectual development. This is marked in English by the overwhelming predominance of references to biblical interpretation in the early use, and therefore the definition, of the word "metaphorical."[48] The embedding of scriptural interpretation in the foundations of Western culture makes possible the realization in Western philosophy that all language is fundamentally metaphorical.

Metaphors are the form words take, and words reveal the world. "The sacred literature thus both records the experiences of the past and provides the descriptive language by which any new experience may be interpreted" (Soskice, p. 160). This is not a general claim about the way all languages are supposed to function, but a theological observation about biblical interpretation. Scripture is highly metaphorical on its very surface: "In the beginning was the Word . . . and the Word was God . . . in him was life, and the life was the light of all people" (John 1:1, 4). Exploring this metaphorical surface reveals that it is not a substitute for realistic language but is the only realistic language adequate to the reality it describes.

This biblical emphasis on metaphorical language carried into early Christian theology in the priority of liturgy and hymnody in the generation and regeneration of doctrine.[49] The centrality of song and prayer in Israel's experience of God is based on a deep connection between the source of praise and the reality of God's presence.[50] Song is a basic form of Israel's theologizing, because it is concomitant to a theology of advent. Song precedes but is properly accompanied by the more analytical and critical work of doctrinal and canonical formation.

This claim would need further development than I can offer here, but it is bolstered when we observe the regular recurrence of inset poetry at critical points in the Old Testament. It is a pattern we also see in the New Testament, in passages such as Luke's canticles (Luke 1:46-55, 68-79; 2:29-32) and the

---

48. "Metaphor," *Oxford English Dictionary*, 2nd ed. (Oxford: Oxford University Press, 1989).

49. Bernd Wannenwetsch, "Singen und Sagen: Zur musisch-musicalischen Dimension der Theologie," *Neue Zeitschrift für Systematische Theolgie und Religionsphilosophie* 46 (Berlin: Walter De Gruyter, 2004): 334-36. I am not claiming that this relationship of poetry and divine advent is unique to Christian faith. The view was also present in Greek thought, and was associated with the god Dionysius, as in Plato's *Phaedrus* (238d).

50. The more general thrust of Wannenwetsch's "Singen und Sagen."

Christ hymn of Philippians 2:6-11. This suggests a theological account of the unity of Scripture oriented by the poetic or hymnic interjections we find in Scripture, beginning in Genesis (2:23; 3:14-19; 4:23-24; chs. 8–9), explicitly breaking into song with Moses' Song in Exodus (ch. 15) and culminating in the depiction of redeemed humanity as "praising creatures" in Revelation (chs. 1, 4, 5, 11, 15). Biblical scholars often note that these songs play important interpretive roles in the narratives they punctuate, and that the most signifi-cant pronouncements in narratives are often put in poetic form.[51] I am sug-gesting that this compositional habit is not accidental, but is an expression of the essential structure of life with the trinitarian God.

The implication is that, for each generation that takes up Scripture, song should be understood as a prime way of entering this tradition of faith, tracing back to the experience-insight and thus the hermeneutic of Scripture to join the community who wrote the initial song. This is a hermeneutically focused interpretation of the early church's exegetical practice as summarized in the fifth-century formulation *lex orandi, lex credendi* ("the law of praying [sets] the law of believing"). The fact that high points in the biblical narratives are so regularly linked to the singing of songs can lead us, as Augustine noted, to look on these songs as playing a unique role in the intratextual reading of the Bible, as well as revealing the deep structure of the generation of faith.

Scripture is, in its essence, something to be sung, which means to be read in the mode of praise by the church. Robert Jenson concurs:

> The first and foremost doctrine *de scriptura* is therefore not a proposition *about* Scripture at all. It is rather the liturgical and devotional instruction: Let the Scripture be sung, at every opportunity and with care for its actual address to hearers, even if these are only the singer. The churches most faithful to Scripture are not those that legislate the most honorific proposi-tions about Scripture but those that most often and thoughtfully sing and listen to it.[52]

Such singing cannot be confined to the collective worship of the church; but if it is truly sung, it is embodied in the continuing praise of the church as it

---

51. Cf. James Watts, "'This Song' Conspicuous Poetry in Hebrew Prose," in Johannes C. de Moor and Wilfred Watson, eds., *Verse in Ancient Near Eastern Prose* (Neukirchen-Vluyn: Neukirchener Verlag, 1993), pp. 345-58; see also Jan Fokkelman, *Narrative Art and Poetry in the Books of Samuel: A Full Interpretation Based on Stylistic and Structural Analyses* (Assen, the Netherlands: van Gorcum, 1981-1993).

52. Jenson, *Systematic Theology II*, p. 273. With apologies, I have taken the liberty of re-placing Jenson's metaphor of reading and hearing with singing and listening to emphasize that *every* churchly reading is properly a song of praise, as Augustine and Luther taught us.

scatters to its daily pursuits throughout the week. To say that Scripture is to be sung is both a statement of scriptural topography and a description of how this topography reshapes perception.

Wittgenstein illustrates the point with a story in which an observer looks through a window on a cold winter night and sees someone sitting in a chair inside a house.[53] What is the person doing? Watching TV? Thinking? Mourning? The list of reasons we might come up with to construe the case one way or the other is limited only by the background stories we can concoct to explain the perception we have of that person. And each story causes us to emphasize — and, more importantly, to perceive — different details of the experience. Another example: A bird makes noise, but does it sing? We call the bird's activity "singing" because we apply to its behavior a metaphorical linkage with humans as we characterize our own behavior. In so doing, we anthropomorphize the bird. We create a topography of perception simply by being forced to interpret raw experience through some metaphor, image, or story in order to capture it as perception.

This view of language is fully exploited in the Bible, where the literal is constituted by the proper use of the metaphor. Metaphor indicates, exaggerates, and explains the relationships of specific features of reality to orient us to the reality the utterance illuminates.[54] A paradigmatic example is Jesus' statement to Peter after a great haul of fish: "From now on you will be a fisher of men" (Luke 5:10).[55] What Peter will now see — and, more importantly, live — as a follower of Christ is created by this use of metaphor. This is not analogical imagination as a special rational operation of connecting the past with the present; but it is analogical thinking as the basic structure of reason. Here thinking about the world is continually rethinking to what biblical metaphors appear to commit us. A bird does not sing, for instance, if we define (human) singing as part of a cultural complex expressing the whole depth of the human experience of the universe. For humans, singing is almost always a singing of words, an insight obscured by the original metaphor. Yet the Psalms press us yet again in a new direction by saying that all creation sings praise (Ps. 148). How and when we apply the metaphors that orient us in ethical decisions is a skill of judgment learned in the school of scriptural exegesis.

We may be more used to the metaphors that frame our "common sense" (such as the ubiquitous yet pernicious "making history"), but this does not

53. The theoretical explication of this discussion is contained in Wittgenstein, *Philosophical Investigations,* IIxi, 216e.

54. See Colin Gunton, *Yesterday and Today: A Study of Continuities in Christology,* 2nd ed. (London: SPCK, 1997), pp. 150-53.

55. Cf. Fokkelman, *Reading Biblical Narrative,* pp. 203-5.

make them any more true than the biblical metaphors with which we have lost touch. When we are faced with unfamiliar (even unpalatable) biblical metaphors, such as, "I have calmed and quieted my soul, like a child quieted at its mother's breast" (Ps. 131:2a), we face words that induce a "metaphorical shock"[56] that asks us to consider realities we assumed were unreasonable to juxtapose. It is worth pointing out that most of the modern discussions surveyed in Part I, including the thought of Wittgenstein on which I have drawn here, are focused on epistemological questions. "Shock," however, is an affective experience. Metaphors cannot themselves generate affective experience, but they can facilitate divine intervention into our affective life more readily than factual language can. Such shocks do not automatically become occasions for growth, however, unless they reorient our affections by being embraced in faith through a process of prayer and meditation.

It is no accident that Jesus' teaching is characterized by the call for repentance couched in the shocking juxtapositions of his parables. It is not fanciful to suggest that this was a transformative rhetorical practice learned in the school of Scripture (Luke 2:46). We should not be surprised, then, that it is through such words that the Spirit continues to work, inflaming believers to meditate on and respond to unsettling juxtapositions and so have their affections reoriented. The Psalms serve such affection inflammation in offering a universe of images by which God can grab human affections. We cannot put ourselves into the song of praise, but as we find ourselves in it through our singing of it, we discover the reality it contains, because doxology inflames us to look and to live. It inflames us, as Luther and Augustine have emphasized, because it is part of God's work reorienting our passions, remaking our hearts (Ps. 51:12).

This re-emphasis of metaphor separates my approach from more philosophical or analytical theologies (most notably that of Thomas Aquinas), which strive to establish the basic univocal nature of biblical words.[57] There are variants of this approach, such as that of Thomas's fourteenth-century interpreter Nicholas of Lyra, that try to broaden such a definition by proposing a double literal sense.[58] While Lyra's two references turned out to be historical

---

56. This term is taken from Hays, *The Moral Vision*, p. 301.

57. Thomas Aquinas, *Summa Theologiae*, I q. 10 repl. 1; discussed in James Preuss, *From Shadow to Promise: Old Testament Interpretation from Augustine to the Young Luther* (Eugene, OR: Wipf and Stock Publishers, 1999), p. 51.

58. So Lyra: "For example, in 1 Chron. 17, the Lord says of Solomon: 'I will be a father to him, and he will be like a son to me.' And this is understood as speaking of Solomon literally.... Now this same authority ... is used by the Apostle, writing to the Hebrews, *as having been said literally of Christ*. This is evident for the following reason: the Apostle uses it to prove that Christ

and Christological, my suggestion is that the multiple levels of textual reference opened up by the Psalms are comprehensible only as referring to multiple aspects of the one, authoritative divine economy centered in God's work in Christ.

Doctrinal frameworks constitute an essential "strategy of containment" that prevents the web of allusions, quotations, and the inhabitation of unfamiliar metaphors from becoming completely indeterminate and thus interpretively useless. Yet doctrines do not in themselves generate the new readings that sustain the community's growth and continuation. The "logic of external constitution" developed by Augustine and Luther serves us well here. Christians are formed in their dialogue with Christ through the Spirit, as they are drawn out of their self-identification and into life with and named by the triune God. Their unifying interpretive focus is always beyond themselves, something that is being discovered. Doctrine points ever again to Christ, the fundamental source and boundary of Christian interpretation, the one who has the bounty to reveal new insights and to judge and cut them off.

Interrogating the Cross Traffic between Grammars

The centrality of metaphor places demands on our interpretive tools. One approach that attempts to meet these demands has come to be called "intertextuality." Beth LaNeel Tanner finds that it has been used throughout the Christian exegetical tradition, though calling it a new "methodology" began with French literary critics of the 1960s and '70s.[59] This literary approach emphasizes that writing continually reuses older materials, either through direct quotation or allusion. Current academic practice makes this explicit through the use of footnotes, but older texts did it through the use of identical words (i.e., quotation, which was almost always devoid of the modern convention of quotation marks) and the reuse of distinctive ideas (allusion).

To think of texts in this way allows us to understand how language is alive only when it is being used, and how metaphors draw on this living use to

---

was greater than the angels. But such proof cannot be made through the mystical sense, as Augustine says. . . . The aforesaid authority, then, was fulfilled literally in Solomon, yet less perfectly because he was a son of God by grace only; but in Christ [it is fulfilled] more perfectly, because he is a son of God by nature. Now, although *each exposition is literal,* simply speaking, still the second one, which concerns Christ, is [also] spiritual and mystical in a derived sense, in that Solomon was a figure of Christ." Quoted in Preuss, *From Shadow to Promise,* p. 68.

59. Beth LaNeel Tanner, *The Book of Psalms through the Lens of Intertextuality* (New York: Peter Lang, 2001). This discussion is drawn from chapter 1.

try to communicate novel insights. Tanner gives two examples of how language can be used to interlink normally separate grammars of life. The first is uttered by the proud owner of a new boat: "This is the Cadillac of boats!" Though Cadillac makes cars, not boats, "[t]he word 'Cadillac,'" says Tanner, "serves as a norm for a particular culture and as a metaphor for a successful life. The purpose of the sentence by the author was primarily the communication of information concerning the boat, but the metaphor introduces a process of cultural intertextuality that brings the current text into conversation with the contemporary culture" (Tanner, p. 8).

Such interlinkings of meaning can also be diachronic, linking the writer's age with a past age or ages. Here the author may make connections never "intended" by the original author. Tanner cites the example of the way the term "Camelot" has taken on a range of new meanings for contemporary Americans.

> Before 1960, Camelot was a mythical place from a novel about King Arthur and his court at Camelot. But after 1960, Camelot became the metaphor for a historical presidency. The mythical Camelot was transformed into a metaphor for the life and work of President John Kennedy and his family. Then after Kennedy's death, the representative term 'Camelot' was again transformed, this time into an American myth about this particular period of history. The name Camelot survived, but was redefined twice by the readers of this era. (p. 8)

For our purposes, it is important to note that each "redefinition" did not in fact change the grammar of the initial use of the term, but emphasized parts of it and in a way that served to interpret the present reality to which it was being applied, emphasizing some of its "royal" aspects. In this layering of diachronic moments, the interpreter finds a metaphor to yield useful purchase on experience and thus orient responses to it.

Tanner observes that such an approach meshes well with the work of modern biblical critics who are also engaged in showing the synchronic intertextual connections between the Bible and its culture and between biblical books. Thus the various modern critical methods sensitize us to the details of how the cultural and linguistic forms of Israel's scriptures and neighbors are "reused" by biblical authors. As Tanner traced the novel and meaning-creating reuse of the words "Camelot" and "Cadillac," biblical scholars have explicated the linkages generated within the "canonical consciousness" of biblical writing and editing. They thus display the processes of challenge and meaning negotiation occurring in the development of Scripture.

Once biblical texts are approached in this way, it is apparent that modern biblical interpreters, however objective they conceive their interpretations to be, are also reading and rereading Scripture to augment or critique trends in their own society. Regina Schwartz reminds us of the bias of biblical scholars that, as we saw in chapter 1, was such a concern to Schüssler Fiorenza: ". . . the German historicism that gave birth to biblical scholarship is no mere positivism (as if there were such a thing); rather, every archeologist's spade and every philologist's verb ending is deeply inscribed with politics" (quoted in Tanner, p. 31). Exegesis in an intertextual mode serves to expose the political and ethical force of exegetical frameworks. Francis Watson rightly encourages us to become aware of the synchronic and diachronic referents of our interpretation. Tanner presses for an increased self-reflexivity about this awareness in order to expose the ways that communities of moral formation are not the place where we must bridge synchronic and diachronic influences, but are the standing nodes in the continual cross-traffic between them.

The important question at this point is whether the proliferation of hermeneutical connections is a theologically irrelevant by-product of human creativity at work, or can be conceived of as a process that enriches Christian interpretation. By tracing the intertextual linkages proposed by a given writer, we can begin to see how his or her interpretative schemas generate different biblical topographies. As the practice of hermeneutics changes, new unities are found in the biblical witness, and new biblical topographies are constructed by referring to one's starting metaphor, of which "the author's theology" and "what really happened" are two. Interpretations turn out to be versions of reality defended by reference to the biblical texts. What historical critics call a historical "context" is understood by faith as the location of God's presence in reality, making Scripture the record of God's work of drawing humanity to himself by revealing himself and co-opting and transforming Israel's form of life.[60] Exegesis as the exploration of the divine grammar forces us to make explicit our account of Scripture and to do so in a way that makes sense of the Bible within the contemporary church's exegesis and ethic, and the processes of cultural gathering, writing, and editing that are basic to the formation of Scripture (the question addressed in ch. 4).

Outlining the relationship of this approach to historical-critical methods will illustrate some of its implications. If we think of exegetical traditions

---

60. On the theological meaning of the historical critical method as part of Christ claiming his own history, see D. Gerhard Ebeling, "Die Bedeutung der historisch-critischen Methode für de protestantische Theologie und Kirche," in *Wort und Glaube*, 3rd ed. (Tübingen: J. C. B. Mohr, 1967), ch. 1.

as discourses, it immediately becomes obvious that discourses are formed in, and shaped by, their interaction with different discourses. The current hegemony of discipline language emphasizes the appropriate discreteness of discourses, while underplaying the fact that traditions are necessarily in motion, changing and being changed by their interactions with other traditions. We might more accurately say that discourses change because individuals are themselves involved in different traditions of truth or different truth discourses. Because in each discourse different truths appear, immersion in a new tradition brings new insights. The conclusion of chapter 7 emphasized that Christians need dialogue with other exegetical traditions in order to reveal the text anew to them. Dissent about scriptural interpretations focuses us on Scripture (and not hermeneutical theory) as the court of appeal, and, more importantly, reveals which interpreters place themselves under God's rule.[61]

The lesson that Christians should learn in dialogue with historical critics is not the one they so often learn, that we are a different community from Abraham and Paul. The church is a single community, but there are different times and places within it. Christian interpretation properly wrestles with the historical distance between Moses and Jesus, and Jesus and Paul. The church only thinks about these people as part of a single drama, and as such it is essential that the church's way of conceiving its biblical topography take proper theological account of these historical distances.[62] Bad exegesis of the Psalms, for instance, is not the kind that sees unities between the world of the psalmists and the work of Christ, but the kind that moves too quickly between the two, taking no account of the intervening narrative of God's self-revelation.

As with the church's interaction with modern historical criticism, we cannot predict how the meeting of different interpretive traditions will affect the structure of the respective traditions involved. Nevertheless, because Christ's reign is the source of all truth, we can say with some certainty that in such meetings new and usually profitable insights are offered to each tradition. Good readings are ones in which multiple traditions meet to reveal new complexities of God's truth. This is to affirm and even strengthen Watson's exhortation to take the world seriously by saying that those who truly listen to the world hear God's Word better. From the beginning, Christian interpreters freely immersed themselves in secular or pagan discourses, understood

61. Gerhard Sauter, *Gateways to Dogmatics: Reasoning Theologically for the Life of the Church* (Grand Rapids: Eerdmans, 2003), p. 217.

62. Jenson, *Systematic Theology*, p. 281.

through the metaphor of "plundering the Egyptians" (Exod. 12:35-36).[63] To learn what a strange discourse can bring to the interpretation of Scripture demands entering it sympathetically, yet seeking to clarify the points at which its grammar denies the God of Scripture. The text of Scripture does the work of holding these different interpretive communities in dialogue, a dialogue that cannot but yield new sensitivities to its contours.

63. Stephen Fowl, *Engaging Scripture: A Model for Theological Interpretation* (Oxford: Blackwell, 1998), pp. 179-82.

CHAPTER 9

Exploring the Place of
Christian Ethics in Scripture

As the previous chapters have indicated, this chapter is best understood as a conversation with Augustine, Luther, and the thinkers surveyed in Part I, as well as more diverse discourses. My primary interest in entering this conversation has not been the comparison or judgment of the various contributions, but the discovery of how each helps to illuminate the place of Christian ethics in Scripture. In this chapter I will indicate where these conversation partners have enriched and sensitized engagement with the text. The resulting exegesis is the constructive heart of this book and cannot really be called theirs — or mine — but must be understood as the tradition "live," an event in the intergenerational dialogue of a community of faith as it learns anew what it means to walk with God.

Psalm 130: Thematizing the Ethos of Prayer:
Prayer as the Context of Christian Ethics

Christian ethics must continually combat its tendency to collapse into either a simplistic validation of cultural presuppositions or a blanket reaction against them. Yet when the methodological place of divine action in Christian ethics is muddied (as we saw it to be in much of the contemporary discussion), this collapse is inevitable. To avoid this problem, Christian theology must constantly seek to clarify how God generates a community that has its own ethos, distinct and distinctly Christian. How does the church begin to see itself as "other" than the world? This chapter turns to the Psalms to ask this question by way of phenomenological and textual inquiry. How do we begin to think of ourselves as part of God's story? How does speaking to God relate to Christian ethics? How does prayer become present and even an integral part of our awareness of the world?

Praying is a practice in which a new world of faith appears, as Psalm 104 will show. But before moving on to ask how the Christian ethos becomes more complex and differentiated in its relationship to self and the world, we must clarify how it is that praying comes to seem "reasonable" at all. Christian theology is not in the first place interested in the substance of humankind, but its generation, because its vantage point is eschatological hope.[1] Christians thus endorse the psalmists' confession that creation cannot endure without its redemption. "The Lord watches over the way of the righteous, but the way of the wicked will perish" (Ps. 1:6). Psalm 130 is a prayer of one who faces the prospect of perishing.

שִׁיר הַמַּעֲלוֹת מִמַּעֲמַקִּים קְרָאתִיךָ יְהֹוָה: 130:1

אֲדֹנָי שִׁמְעָה בְקוֹלִי תִּהְיֶינָה אָזְנֶיךָ קַשֻּׁבוֹת לְקוֹל תַּחֲנוּנָי: 2

130:1 Out of the depths I cry to you, O Lord.
2   Lord, hear my voice!
      Let your ears be attentive to the voice of my supplications!

For the ancients, "depths" named the horror and helplessness of humanity before the external and internal chaos that threatens to swallow it. Israel's scriptures portray it as lying somewhere beneath the fury and random destructiveness of the ocean's thunderous and crushing waves (Ps. 42:7). The metaphor is elaborated in other Old Testament passages that at times emphasize the experience of being under a volume of chaos and destruction, which descends with a thunderclap to crush humanity. In other places the depths are reached via a slower devouring, or rather entombment, of the flood (Ps. 69:2). These sketches of impending disasters are the closest the Old Testament comes to a description of the experience of hell, with the fearful violence of the surface waves being only the precursor to the final horror of being irrevocably discarded from God's life.[2]

This experience is portrayed in narrative at several points in the Old Testament. Jonah repents under the sea's waves, inside the belly of that avatar

---

1. See Dietrich Bonhoeffer, *Sanctorum Communio: A Theological Study of the Sociology of the Church,* Dietrich Bonhoeffer Works, vol. 1, ed. Clifford Green, trans. Reinhard Krauss and Nancy Lukens (Minneapolis: Fortress, 1998), pp. 56-58.

2. Cf. Lamentations 3:54-55. Jeremiah's (and Joseph's) incarceration in a well by people who rejected their divine messages are also prototypical images of the swallowing by waves of the suffering servant, whose existence is preserved only by remaining in God's sight.

of destruction, the "great fish."[3] Through such scenes the biblical authors indicate that the gateway to life with God is the discovery of the limits of our ability to help ourselves. Walther Zimmerli thus concludes his survey of hope in the Old Testament:

> It was precisely where man was led to the edge of human hopelessness that every look turned away from man and his immanent possibilities. There was at no place a "principle of hope" that was generally held or believed by man, no existential hope to be discovered in the existential understanding of man or his world. Rather, it became clear that it was precisely where the sharpest criticisms of hope were loudest, that man in a frightening recklessness threw himself upon the one he was conscious of as coming to his people, or in the broadest meaning, to his creation.[4]

For Israel there is only one hope: calling on God and waiting for his arrival, a calling with all the practical and affective urgency of the drowning swimmer. In the Psalms we see an impressive certainty about this hope, but one that is gained through the undermining of all hopes for human plans, thought systems, and strength to save. The Psalms transmit that certainty of hope to those for whom it is an impossibility, who know no action of theirs can save, and nothing can distract them from the horrors before them. In so doing, they offer God's hope and shear away false hopes.

The secular or pagan worlds can also reach this despair at human powers; indeed, if a distinctive feature of modernity is the loss of the belief in the immanence of Jesus Christ, postmodernity might be defined as modernity's loss of confidence in its own ability to realize its dreams. Theodor Adorno has plumbed this crisis of hope, crying out with some eloquence against the false hopes of his age, and expressing his shame at participating in them.[5] His rich appreciation of the moral falseness of his age shares with the psalmist a sense of hopelessness at human power. But unlike the psalmist, Adorno has given up hope in God, and claims to have given up on principle any hopeful narrative that might point a way out of his dilemma. Thus the paradox: What generates Adorno's protest? Can he protest, really cry out, unless he has hope for something more? Or, more pointedly, what exactly makes his moral criticism

---

3. It is in this sense that the whale represents the radical evil of the cosmos that Herman Melville's *Moby Dick* so profoundly grasps, though without the hope of biblical faith.

4. Walther Zimmerli, *Man and His Hope in the Old Testament* (Naperville, IL: Alec R. Allenson Inc., 1968), p. 161.

5. Theodor Adorno, "Fish in Water," in *Minima Moralia: Reflections from a Damaged Life,* trans. E. F. N. Jephcott (London: Verso Editions, 1978), pp. 23-24.

of his age possible? If we are as deeply caught up in the moral falseness of our age as Adorno (and most postmodern thought) assumes, where does the perspective of the lament come from? Luther sets this question in a theological context: "We are all in deep and great misery, but we do not all feel our condition."[6] Utter hopelessness and self-satisfaction share the trait of not crying out. Still we must ask: Why do some feel the evil of an age, while others are apparently immune to any notice of it?

The crying out of these verses stands on a razor's edge between expressing our needs as we understand them, making demands of God, and a crying for God not of human origin. That God wears away human hopes (Job 14:19) and sparks the latter cry of faith has been the unanimous conviction of the Western theological tradition. Humans may hear of God and believe, but God gives faith, which, though not yet perfect, is nevertheless real.[7] This Spirit-taught cry expresses the deepest longings and sufferings of humanity toward God (Rom. 8:26), but shorn of the reliance on the ideologies we once believed would satisfy them.[8] Before God, in prayer, we articulate for the first time a true appreciation of our location. This verbalization of our situation is the first moment of a true inhabitation of it. No longer able to lie to ourselves about who we are, our lies before God about ourselves and others appear for the first time to be what they are — lies. In this prayer we discover ourselves in sin without an exit point in sight.

Such cries are the first step out of the oblivion to which humanity against God consigns itself. Crying marks the borderlands of human existence. This cry may be the cry of demand, of anger, or the helpless gasp of fear and confusion of human birth. But this is not all humanity was meant to be, and the cry of the psalmist is more than this simple cry of bewilderment and loneliness. It is a cry to Yahweh.

"I cry to you, O LORD." The invocation of the proper name of God, Yahweh, shapes the whole framework of the Old Testament.[9] This psalm is

---

6. Martin Luther, "Psalm 130, the Sixth Penitential Psalm," in *Luther's Works, vol. 14: Selected Psalms III,* Am. Ed., ed. Jaroslav Pelikan (St. Louis: Concordia, 1958), p. 189. Augustine makes the same point: "When the wicked have reached the depths of evil, them [God] despises. . . . They are very deep in the deep who do not even cry out from the deep." Augustine, *Nicene and Post-Nicene Fathers, Vol. VIII: St. Augustine: Expositions on the Book of Psalms,* ed. Philip Schaff (Edinburgh: T&T Clark, 1996), p. 613.

7. See Thomas Aquinas, *Summa Theologica,* II.II q. 6, a. 1 and 2.

8. Dietrich Bonhoeffer, "On Psalm 119," in *Meditating on the Word,* trans. and ed. David McI. Gracie (Cambridge: Cowley Publications, 1986), p. 117.

9. Gerhard von Rad, *Old Testament Theology: Vol. I, The Theology of Israel's Historical Traditions,* trans. D. M. G. Stalker (New York: Harper and Row, 1962), pp. 179-87; Hans-Jochim Kraus, *Theology of the Psalms,* trans. Keith Crim (Minneapolis: Augsburg, 1986), pp. 20-23, 31-33.

unique in invoking the name in every couplet: we might say that it is nothing more than an elaboration of the act of calling out to God by name. Throughout the Old Testament such an invocation of Yahweh's name is linked to an evocation of the divine presence that is the ground of the worshiping community. Israel came to recount its corporate journey as an enactment of Yahweh's command to "seek the place that the LORD your God will choose out of all your tribes as his habitation to put his name there. You shall go there . . . then there will be the place where the LORD your God chooses to make His name abide" (Deut. 12:5, 11; cf. Num. 6:27).[10] Thus the name simultaneously invokes God's gift of himself to Israel, his dominion over its sphere, and his freedom to remain inaccessible.[11] This relationship of proximity and transcendence is expressed in the worshipers' addressing God with a proper name, יְהֹוָה (Yahweh), and a title expressing obedience or subservience, Lord, אֲדֹנָי (adonai).

The combination of a name and title by the psalmist expresses the character of faith as life that seeks God despite this presence and absence, admitting that, like all persons, God is free to address us as he sees fit. We do not see God's being, but for his silence he has given us his name, to which we may hold fast. "Holding fast" evokes the strong affective component of calling on the name: true calling is an affective and volitional embrace of Yahweh that makes the transition from relation to relationship possible.[12] The fact that faith must continually traverse the distance between hope and sight, holding only to this name, has methodological implications for Christian ethics, says Hans Ulrich: "The name of God, which will be present with faith, continually opens up discoveries. Straight away this name lets these openings be distinguishable as discoveries. Anyone who follows in the dramatic of *aliquid quo nihil maius cogitari posit* [that than which nothing greater can be thought] will discover the novel. Those who follow other names instead of God's name will make other discoveries: possibly the (dubious) name of God, which does not call God 'Creator' but 'Author of all things' or something else."[13] Many gods will promise to satisfy human distress cries, but the psalmists hope in one God, this named God, whose pres-

---

10. Cf. Exod. 20:24; 33:19; 1 Kings 8:28-29.

11. Sandra Richter, *The Deuteronomistic History and the Name Theology:* leʾakkēn ʿmô šām *in the Bible and the Ancient Near East*, Beihefte zur Zeitschrift für die alttestamentliche Wissenschaft 318 (Berlin/New York: Walter de Gruyter, 2002).

12. Cf. Francis Martin, "The Psalms as a Particular Mode of Revelation," *Nova et Vetera* 3, no. 2 (Spring 2005): 279-94.

13. Hans G. Ulrich, "Fides Quarens Intellectum: Reflections toward an Explorative Theology," trans. Brian Brock, *International Journal of Systematic Theology* 8, no. 1 (2006): 52.

ence has made their crying possible, but whose freedom demands remembering and hope from humans. Yet only the experience of something beyond our own powers sustains the hope of renewal and transformation. That the name is known marks God's presence, but that it must be called upon marks God's invisibility. It is through inciting people to such worship that God opens the way into himself (Job 28:23, 27-28).

The name is the anchoring center of the textual space created by Scripture's many literary forms: psalms, narratives, laws, prophecy, and so forth. "The referent 'God' is at once the coordinator of these diverse discourses, and the vanishing point, the index of incompletion of these partial discourses."[14] While Ricoeur does not clarify whether the God so described actually exists or is only a hermeneutical presupposition demanded by the Bible's heterogeneity, Psalm 130 suggests that we do not know God until he has caused us to call on his name. It is meaningful to say that the name of God unifies the diversity of Scripture and explains the open-ended nature of interpretation only if this God continues to meet us in our interpretative efforts.

Theology that begins here is not best described as the explication or updating of a deposit of historical faith claims. It is more properly understood as joining a collective probing of God's unseen purposes for his people. Because this probing clings to this peculiar name, it seeks to know the ways of this God. Early Christians found that those ways converged in Jesus Christ, whom New Testament writers explicitly linked to the divine name.[15] These followers could simply refer to themselves as name-followers, as John Howard Yoder points out:

> An *epikaloumenous* is literally "a confessor," "one-who-calls-himself-by-the-name-of," or "one-who-invokes-the-name." Before the Christians were called Christians they were perhaps called *epikaloumenoi*, "callers upon the name." In Acts 9:14 and 21, Ananias says in his vision of Christ sending him to Paul, that Paul is feared by "all those who call upon thy name." Paul's conversion was called "calling on his name" (Acts 22:16b).[16]

God's revelation of his name is thus the entry point into a new being characterized by praise of God's work in Christ.

14. Paul Ricoeur, "Philosophical Hermeneutics and Biblical Hermeneutics," in *From Text to Action: Essays in Hermeneutics 2* (London: Athlon Press, 1991), p. 97.

15. Cf. Luke 2:21; John 12:13; Acts 2:21; 4:12; 15:17; 1 Cor. 1:2; Rom. 10:13; James 2:7; Rev. 3:12; also discussed in Richard Bauckham, *The Theology of the Book of Revelation* (Cambridge, UK: Cambridge University Press, 2005), pp. 26-30.

16. John Howard Yoder, *Preface to Theology, Christology and Theological Method,* intro. by Stanley Hauerwas and Alex Sider (Grand Rapids: Brazos Press, 2002), p. 159.

Though the cry of these verses looks like an individual cry, its formulation in traditional words tells us that it is also an act of clinging to God by clinging to the words of a community that is itself characterized by its clinging to God's name.[17] The psalmist, in life-threatening distress, trusts the words of the faithful, those whom God has protected and preserved, and who have thus left words that point the way back to the font of their own salvation. That place is invisible to the singer; but by taking up these words, the psalmist also takes up their hope and attitude of repentance, without self-justifying or claiming innocence of participation in the destructive chaos raging within and without.[18]

The cry of these verses, then, is not the cry of despair. It is the cry of the one awakened to the name of God. Being so awakened repositions the petitioner under the heaven of eternity (2 Cor. 5:16): the remaking into a new being has not yet properly begun, but her distance from it has been glimpsed. Yet the realization already differentiates the psalmist from others in the depths. As Moses called upon Yahweh at the Red Sea, so the Christian ethos begins ever anew in our cry to God to show himself and open a way for us through the wall of chaos before and behind. "Was it not you who dried up the sea, the waters of the great deep; who made the depths of the sea a way for the redeemed to cross over?" (Is. 51:10). In Christ the depths of human life are discovered in their essential relationship to the eternal one whose name is Yahweh. In this depth, Jesus' Sermon on the Mount is irrelevant, nonsense, or offense — certainly otherworldly. Yet the preacher of these words is both the way to God's face in a broken world, God's laborious searching out this way for us (Job 28:27), and the face of God himself.

The relationship set up between "Yahweh" and "Lord" has sharply countercultural implications in redefining modern conceptions of power. The Psalms do not put us in the position of the abject subservience owed to earthly kings simply because they are powerful. Instead, they are songs to God because he saves. "Lordship" is commandeered from a power discourse for a setting within God's salvific working. God is praised not because he had the skill to fabricate the universe, but because his involvement with us is actively working to save us. If we define power as the potential for action, we overlook the psalmists' constant reminders that God's power is always bound to and recognized in specific acts that only he can do.[19] The psalmist sings: "You are the one who forgives"(v. 4), not "You are powerful."

17. These verses echo many passages, such as Jonah 2:2: "I called to the LORD out of my distress, and he answered me; out of the belly of Sheol I cried, and you heard my voice."

18. Neh. 1:6; cf. also v. 71; 2 Chron. 6:40.

19. Cf. Bernd Wannenwetsch, *Political Worship: Ethics for Christian Citizens* (Oxford: Oxford University Press, 2004), pp. 321-23, 356-57.

It is only on the basis of being taught to see this character of God's action, and not the potential reach of his hidden power, that we can praise him. If he is hidden, sometimes exercising his power as vengeance or capriciousness, then our praise is in vain. It is only because he tells us what he is doing that we can praise in all circumstances. The God named in the Psalms is always addressed on the basis of his works, continually forcing us back to them, releasing us for praise from our human awe at the potential exercise of power, and the subservience to demonic lords that it entails. The lordship of earthly powers relies on the persuasive force of potential to act and of pageantry, but the lordship of Yahweh is one of proximity and the enabling of communal life. The Exodus story is God's story because he has involved himself in human affairs; he actually did lead Israel out of Egypt, they were enabled to hear and respond, and they were transformed.

This transvaluation of our definitions of political power by God's governance teaches us that good human governance is focused on and judged solely by its acts of mercy and justice. The Psalms sharply locate human governance within divine governance. "Even in the songs of praise, the Psalms are not the hymns and prayers of a church triumphant that exists in liturgical security; they are a language of the עניים, the 'poor,' the 'people that was chosen and bidden to travel a new and better way among the nations.'"[20] The Psalms, therefore, question tools and strategies of political mastery. The power of governments is not potential firepower, for instance, but actual acts of peacemaking and community-building. The power of any technology is not its ability to remake all things, but its ability actually to facilitate human flourishing. Stated the other way around, if the power of medicine is not to heal, it is simply its ability to do anything with the human body. If the power of a government is not to sustain peace, it is to control and manipulate. The psalmist's understanding of God's lordship retrains us to see that good works are what are truly powerful, not the potential to have broad impact if we were to act. This is an important insight for Christian ethics, because we easily equate our definitions of powerful humans with God's power. In so doing we project our fallen relationships onto God with the question, "Who has the most power?" By exploring God's working, we expose the human attraction to "power potential" as self-alienation, through which we cede our ability to criticize the demonic exercise of power.

Therefore, these verses are the distressed prayer of sin-sickness and separation, which readily admits that it is consumed by hostile powers. It expresses awareness of moral brokenness and the mortal threat to existence that

20. Kraus, *Theology of the Psalms*, p. 16.

is wandering off into the dead ends of sin. The appearance of God's name, like lightning illuminating a dark street, allows us to see that we, too, have lost our way and are mired in insoluble tangles. I see that I am sunk, with many others, in the depths, aware but powerless, enlightened but blind. Yet, as it is supremely encapsulated in 1 John 1:9-10: "If we confess our sins, he who is faithful and just will forgive us our sins and cleanse us from all unrighteousness. If we say that we have not sinned, we make him a liar, and his word is not in us." The psalmist puts it this way:

אִם־עֲוֹנוֹת תִּשְׁמָר־יָהּ אֲדֹנָי מִי יַעֲמֹד׃ 130:3

כִּי־עִמְּךָ הַסְּלִיחָה לְמַעַן תִּוָּרֵא׃ 4

130:3 If you, O LORD, should mark iniquities,
   Lord, who could stand?
4   But there is forgiveness with you,
   so that you may be feared.[21]

The Old Testament knows much of God's hatred of sin, and the fear of judgment that it rightly produces in humans (Gen. 3:10; Exod. 3:6; Deut. 5:5; 17:13, Ps. 119:120). But the fear of God can also refer to reverential awe and adoration (Exod. 15:11; Deut. 7:21; 10:17; 28:58, Ps. 47:2; 111:9). At Sinai these two senses of fear are in interplay. The Israelites see that God is present with them, as indicated by the smoking of the mountain, and they fear judgment, to which Moses responds: "Do not be afraid; for God has come only to test you and to put the fear of him upon you so that you do not sin" (Exod. 20:20). The terror of judgment is to give way to reverence and obedience. The "fear of the Lord" is thus a concept that holds faith and ethics in the closest relationship: "The fear of the LORD is hatred of evil. Pride and arrogance and the way of evil and perverted speech I hate" (Prov. 8:13; cf. Lev. 19:14; 25:17: Prov. 16:6; Ps. 36:1).[22]

The concept carries into the New Testament, even intensifying the Old Testament's understanding of faith as the "fear of God." In the *Magnificat*, Mary praises God that "His mercy is for those who fear him from generation to generation" (Luke 1:50), including herself as one who fears and is raised up. The first Christians are depicted as having the fear of the Lord (Acts 9:31), and subsequent Christians are enjoined at many points also to have it (2 Cor. 7:1; Col. 3:22). Those Christians who walk in the law of Christ's Spirit are those

---

21. Here the NRSV overly sanitizes the Hebrew with "revered."

22. My treatment is indebted to John Murray's excellent summary of the ethical meaning of the fear of the Lord in Scripture; see Murray, *Principles of Conduct: Aspects of Biblical Ethics* (London: Tyndale Press, 1957), ch. X.

who have been taught to fear by Christ's fulfillment of the prophet Isaiah's words: "The spirit of the LORD shall rest on him, the spirit of wisdom and understanding, the spirit of counsel and might, the spirit of knowledge and the fear of the LORD. His delight shall be in the fear of the LORD" (Is. 11:2, 3a). The Christian life in all its mundane moments (Col. 3:22) and highest sanctification (2 Cor. 7:1) is realized only by God-fearers. The upshot is that, rather than conceiving of the Psalms as written in an age before the "innovations" of Jesus Christ were apparent, Christ's life should be understood as introducing gentiles to the full depth of Israel's fear of God.

"Who can stand" is a phrase that expresses the fear of judgment: the beginning of holy fear is the realization of our complicity in sin (Ps. 36:1; Rom. 3:18). "Whoever, therefore, does not consider the judgment of God, does not fear; and whoever does not fear, does not cry out," says Luther, "and whoever does not cry out, finds no grace."[23] The word translated as iniquities, עֲוֹנוֹת (avonoth), refers to deviation in the sense of being bent, or in the sense of having taken the wrong path — in which the will has been an active participant.[24] If God is to "act as an overseer or watchman, a preserver or protector," שָׁמַר (shamar), of these wrong turns, who will stand his wrath? Jesus again validates this Old Testament reiteration of the centrality of the fear of God in emphasizing its ability to overwhelm the fear of men (Matt. 10:28; Luke 12:4-5; cf. Ps. 3:6; 27:1; Rom. 13:1-7). Such fear, says the writer of Hebrews, becomes an incentive to diligence and perseverance in faith (Heb. 4:1).

The important point is that the specter of judgment evokes fear, but the fear of judgment is not in itself regenerative. Recognizing the severity of God's wrath against evil, the psalmist clings to the words of Yahweh Adonai, which echo through the Old Testament: "Those who love me, I will deliver; I will protect those who know my name. When they call to me, I will answer them; I will be with them in trouble, I will rescue them and honor them. With long life I will satisfy them, and show them my salvation" (Ps. 91:14-16). God's presence changes things, regenerating and overturning.[25] No innate spiritual-

23. Luther, "Psalm 130," p. 190.

24. Marvin E. Tate, *Word Biblical Commentary, Vol. 20, Psalms 51–100* (Dallas: Word Books, 1990), pp. 15-16; see also Francis Brown, *The Brown-Driver-Briggs Hebrew and English Lexicon* (Peabody, MA: Hendrickson; reprint, 1999), p. 5771.

25. Commenting on Psalm 13, James Luther Mays rightly points out: "The petition is twofold: a plea to be heard (v. 3a) and a plea for help (v. 3b). This twofold petition is also typical of such psalms, but the distinction between God's healing and helping is more formal than real. Any word that faith can take as an answer from God is help that breaks the loneliness of isolation and brings vitality to a waning hold on life." James L. Mays, *The Lord Reigns: A Theological Handbook to the Psalms* (Louisville: Westminster John Knox, 1994), p. 56.

ity, nor anything within created reality, can speak such an answer and such deliverance.

Isaiah 6:1-5 depicts how God's appearing evokes this awe and reverence, simultaneously generating and orienting the fear of judgment.

> I saw the Lord sitting on a throne, high and lofty; and the hem of his robe filled the temple. Seraphs were in attendance above him . . . and one called to another and said: "Holy, holy, holy is the LORD of hosts; the whole earth is full of his glory." And I said: "Woe is me! I am lost, for I am a man of unclean lips, and I live among a people of unclean lips; yet my eyes have seen the King, the LORD of hosts!"

Because God has made himself present, our uncleanness is revealed in the same moment that we are drawn into a relationship of awe, obedience, and dependence (Ps. 139:1-6, 13-16, 23-24; Acts 17:26-28; Rom. 11:33-36; 1 Cor. 8:6; Rev. 4:11). "It is a fearful thing to fall into the hands of the living God" (Heb. 10:31).

The fear of judgment does not exist in abstraction from the great "nevertheless" of verse 4: "But there is forgiveness with you, so that you may be revered." The word used here for forgiveness, סְלִיחָה (selichah), carries a specific meaning, and it comes to prominence in relatively later prophetic texts.[26] In these passages we hear God's chosen crying for God to return his care to a people lost in the byways of unfaithfulness. In such a state, the fear of God is, to use Luther's image, the chisel knocking away the old man's reliance on other powers. As fear removes reliance on powerless forces, the new man being built up by the Spirit can emerge, a sculpture of hope in Yahweh alone made from the rough stone of fear and idolatry. "God deals strangely with His children. He blesses them with contradictory and disharmonious things, for hope and despair are opposites. Yet his children must hope in despair; for fear is nothing else than the beginning of despair, and hope is the beginning of recovery."[27] Whoever fears God — and desires his grace in hope — no longer fears other powers. The New Living Translation of verse 4 gets the sense almost perfectly: "You offer forgiveness so that we might learn to fear you." This judgment is the freeing of all creation.[28]

Hope has a powerful heuristic value, a feature that makes it liberating.

---

26. Dan. 9:9; Neh. 9:17; see Hans-Joachim Kraus, *Psalms 60–150: A Continental Commentary,* trans. Hinton Oswald (Minneapolis: Fortress, 1993), p. 466.

27. Luther, "Psalm 130," p. 191.

28. Martin Buber, *Right and Wrong: An Interpretation of Some Psalms,* trans. Ronald Smith (London: SCM, 1952), p. 15.

Divine forgiveness is a truly creative thing, opening paths not illuminated when we did not know the name of God.[29] Hope in this name in a world trusting in its own powers means that we go from being nameless to having a name because named by the Lord. While still in the depths of his disaster, Job articulates this insight with stunning assurance: "My eye has seen all this, my ear has heard and understood it" (Job 13:1). In these verses the psalmist indicates that it is God's action of forgiveness that opens human perception and creates human identity, a reversal of the common-sense order of causality made explicit in Psalm 119:49: "Remember your word to your servant, in which you have made me hope."

What emerges from these considerations is a quite unfamiliar dramatic of sin. By talking about "wrong paths," the psalm implies that what is important about sin language is not that it can be applied to others' actions, but that God can use it to convince us that we are participants in the rebellion against him. It is forgiveness that reveals our culpability. This is a momentous statement in its exposure of our enormous propensity to use moral language for no other purpose than self-justification and the condemnation of others (Luke 18:4-14).[30] The power of God's appearing is its ability to break our habits through forgiveness, undermining our certainties and orientations in order to bring us back, not simply paying for our guilt. Forgiveness is not a cleansing of something we have accrued as a consequence of our behavior, but a dramatic divine intervention in which those wandering off into their destruction see their trajectory, are forcibly headed away from it, willingly repent, and are shown a new way. A general doctrine of forgiveness cannot provide this comfort, only the actual experience of God's particular forgiveness.[31]

This interpretation emphasizes the connection between right action and salvation history. The Christian ethos is not simply about "right acts" but is related in essence to being within the present trajectory of God's story. Not being part of that story is what defines being mired in the dead ends of sin. It is this history of God with his people that makes the concept of deviance

---

29. See Hannah Arendt's discussion of the constructive power of forgiveness: "Irreversibility and the Power to Forgive," in *The Human Condition* (Chicago: University of Chicago Press, 1958), pp. 236-43.

30. Bonhoeffer famously made this point (drawing on Luther) with the phrase "ethics is sin." See "Ethics as Formation" in Dietrich Bonhoeffer, *Ethics*, Dietrich Bonhoeffer Works, vol. 6, ed. Ilse Tödt, Heinz Eduard Tödt, Ernst Feil, and Clifford Green; trans. Reinhard Krauss, Charles West, and Douglas Scott (Minneapolis: Fortress, 2005).

31. John Owen, "A Practical Exposition upon Psalm CXXX," in *The Works of John Owen*, Vol. VI, ed. William Goold (Edinburgh: Banner of Truth Trust, 2000), pp. 397, 409. Thanks to Rob Price for drawing my attention to this fascinating work.

thinkable, that we have lost this particular path and story. By dwelling on the renewing power of forgiveness rather than sin, the psalmist indicates that Christian vocation is always toward a specific ministry of reconciliation (2 Cor. 5:18), and not just away from sin.[32] Living within this divine story, continuing the narrative of Scripture, depends not on "staying clean" but on developing prayerful sensitivities to God's ongoing work through waiting, hearing, and following. Without God's constant forgiveness, we do not see our sin; and without the exposure of our sins and our repenting of them, we remain in the deadening byways down which other gods have enticed us.

John Owen's massive study of Psalm 130 yields this summary of its content: "The psalm expresses the *experience* of the psalmist and the working of his faith, the state and condition of a *soul greatly perplexed,* relieved on account of grace, and acting itself toward God and his saints suitably to the discovery of that grace unto him."[33] The laudable analytical precision of this summary raises two points that are illuminating in the context of our discussion. The first is that, though Owen emphasizes the importance of the experience of divine presence, he does not set this experience within a definition of faith as an activity. His reading understands experience with the Puritans' introspective focus on the descent of the soul into sin, marked not in reference to the activities of faith that were misdirected, or actions that were done without faith, but in reference to the constant uncovering of the depths of guilt and disquiet in the soul. This inward focus determines how we are to search for the assurance of forgiveness. The result is a heavy emphasis on clinging to the promise of forgiveness in verse 4, but without any reference to assurance as an artifact of undertaking the practices of hoping of verses 5 and 6.[34] Owen's interiorizing of experience, however, allows us to see that the vulnerability of walking in hope must be equally emphasized: assurance is both the result of past experiences of God's presence and faith's active reliance on future appearances.

Second, while Owen imports an introspective concern into the psalm, he does properly emphasize the continuing role of the experience of lack or need in faith. To feel need is, ultimately, to have an awareness of the lack of God's face shining on us. Thus, at its deepest root, all prayer is petitionary

---

32. Karl Barth, *Church Dogmatics,* II.2, ed. G. W. Bromiley and T. F. Torrance; trans. G. W. Bromiley, J. C. Campbell, Iain Wilson, J. Strathearn McNab, Harold Knight, and R. A. Stewart (Edinburgh: T&T Clark, 1997), pp. 419-49.

33. Owen, "A Practical Exposition," p. 329 (italics added).

34. Many Puritans besides Owen found these verses particularly rich, John Bunyan being a notable example; cf. Rowland Prothero, *The Psalms in Human Life* (London: John Murray, 1909), p. 248.

prayer. Christian prayer includes thanksgiving, repentance, and worship, but these are expressions of the essential fact that humans need God, that they must in all their words and actions come ever again to him with empty hands. Thanksgiving, repentance, and worship are thus essential to prayer; they cannot be abstracted from it, but are the form of human explicit and verbal calling in need upon God.[35]

This petitionary prayer, to be prayer at all, must also be wholly concrete. Jacob's wrestling with God at Jabbok (Gen. 32:24-32) and Jesus' wrestling with the Father in prayer at Gethsemane (Matt. 26:36-44) were not expressions of a general feeling of need; rather, they were life-and-death struggles with God in which particular needs were verbally exteriorized. As Luther discovered in Psalm 111:2b, we do not recognize God's works by thanking him in generalities, nor do we ask for his presence if we ask in general.[36] Felt needs are reminders of the lack of God's presence or favor, and petitionary prayer exposes them to God. At precisely these points, therefore, we discover either our false hopes or the divinely given path into an order we do not yet know or experience. By continually following the fear of God into our own dark places, we actively participate in their being made new by Christ's light. Fear of our own need meets the fear of God, a meeting the psalmist does not seek to limit, but something he exhorts Israel to actively live into. The sheer volume of lament, or petitionary, psalms (such as Psalms 6, 77, 79, 80) indicates that prayer addressing a felt need to God is a central component of the path of faith. To describe the faithful as "God fearers" expresses the negative side of hope, the abrasive and transformative quality of walking in hope in a sinful world, of hoping amidst — and as part of — a sinning world under judgment.

130:5 קִוִּיתִי יְהוָה קִוְּתָה נַפְשִׁי וְלִדְבָרוֹ הוֹחָלְתִּי:
6 נַפְשִׁי לַאדֹנָי מִשֹּׁמְרִים לַבֹּקֶר שֹׁמְרִים לַבֹּקֶר:

130:5 I wait for the LORD,
   my soul waits,
   and in his word I hope;
6 my soul waits for the Lord
   more than those who watch for the morning,
   more than those who watch for the morning.

---

35. Barth, *Church Dogmatics*, III.4, ed. G. W. Bromiley and T. F. Torrance; trans. A. T. Makay, T. H. L. Parker, H. Knight, H. A. Kennedy, J. Marks (Edinburgh: T&T Clark, 1996), pp. 97-102.

36. See chapter 7, p. 214.

The chiastic arrangement of these two verses emphasizes "waiting" and "hoping," and thus the practical and affective action of supplication.[37] The word for waiting, קָוָה *(kavah)*, indicates eager expectation; it is expressed in modern English by metaphors such as "a neck craned in expectation, waiting for a glimpse of a loved one." This urgency is captured in the translation of the 1662 Book of Common Prayer: "My soul fleeth unto the LORD." Such hope theologically transforms the association of morning with divine help and deliverance common among ancient sun worshipers.[38]

It is easy at this point to become overly focused on Israel's cultural borrowings rather than the transformation of these ideas within Scripture. Whereas the rising of the sun was awaited as the coming of a god among ancient peoples such as the Egyptians, the Old Testament reinscribes the image by embedding it in the divine command that every Passover begin with a commemoration of the vigil of the Israelites on the day they found their freedom from Egypt (Exod. 12:42). Because references to Israel's cry of distress and salvation from the byways of oblivion are followed by thanks for a divine rescue, it is easy to see how this psalm came to be associated with the Exodus. Both the annual Passover celebration and the text of this verse celebrate the momentous dawn arrival of Yahweh to rescue a people doomed to dispersal and oblivion.

Thus the psalmist indicates the object of his hope, God's salvific appearance in human events, and in doing so invites us into the doxology that marks the outer boundaries of true faith. In these verses we see crying turn to singing, the darkness of hopelessness and formless hope enlightened by true hope.[39] Because this portrayal comes to us through Scripture, we begin to see how Scripture is inextricably intertwined with Christian hope. Scripture shapes Israel's waiting by teaching how and for whom to wait and hope. Here the word is not conceived as a barrier that separates us from knowledge of God but as a life raft that allows us entry into the way of his salvation.

"I wait for the LORD, my soul waits, and in his word I hope." Yahweh alone is awaited by name, a waiting that takes the form of hope in his word. The Hebrew דָּבָר *(dabar)*, usually translated as "word," has a range of meanings, including message-communication-promise, action-response, or even

---

37. These verses have been the object of much text-critical debate. For a defense of the Masoretic text, see Leslie Allen, *Word Biblical Commentary, vol. 21, Psalms 101–50*, rev. ed. (Nashville: Thomas Nelson, 2002), p. 526, n. 5a.

38. Cf. Ps. 5:4; 30:6; 46:6; 49:15; 90:14; 92:3; 143:8; and Is. 33:2.

39. Barth, *Church Dogmatics, Vol. IV.I, The Doctrine of Reconciliation*, trans. G. W. Bromiley (Edinburgh: T&T Clark, 1956), p. 605.

matter-thing.[40] For this reason Israel comes to understand all words as intelligible by reference to Yahweh's most enduring action toward Israel, the message-communication-promise that is Torah. This word comprehends God's salvific acts and all the acts he demands of humans, and thus all other words. It is an insight that frames that massive meditation on the Torah as the path of faith, Psalm 119. Verses 146-147 put it this way: "I cry to you; save me, that I may observe your decrees. I rise before dawn and cry for help; I put my hope in your words."[41] The locus of Israel's hope is Scripture, God's word. Jesus Christ learned righteousness from Scripture and the faithful community shaped by it (Luke 2:46), and as their ground, is bound to them, says Luther. "[T]his same Word and promise of God is the whole content of the new man, who lives not by bread but by that same Word of God (Matt. 4:4)."[42] It is in sharing the hope of Israel in this word that the church is grafted onto Israel. "Faith comes from what is heard, and what is heard comes through the word of Christ" (Rom. 10:17).

But more must be said about the specifically textual mediation of this hope to avoid falling into the problem of thinking only of Scripture as a barrier to, or inferior medium of, God's self-revelation. Luther follows the Vulgate's emphasis on the continuous quality of waiting by making the verb continuous: "My soul waits for the Lord, from one morning watch to the next."[43] Waiting is not a onetime event, but is, he argues, the continuous attentiveness implied in the very word "Lord." Christians are to continue to scrutinize the Old Testament because it was not set aside by the fulfillment of the patriarch's hope. Israel's hope was not a "sign" of Christ, because they truly hoped for what they did not see, just as Christians must. This formulation recovered for the Christian tradition the idea that Scripture is not the "way to" God's words, but is literally "God with us" in teaching us how to hope in God.[44] The Christian life of faith, hope, and love is an earnest, diligent, and persevering waiting for and wrestling with their Lord, a tenacious clinging to his words, while waiting continually, as did the patriarchs, for his advent.

130:7 יַחֵל יִשְׂרָאֵל אֶל־יְהוָה כִּי־עִם־יְהוָה הַחֶסֶד וְהַרְבֵּה עִמּוֹ פְדוּת׃
8 וְהוּא יִפְדֶּה אֶת־יִשְׂרָאֵל מִכֹּל עֲוֹנֹתָיו׃

40. Tate, *Psalms 51–100*, p. 71; *Brown-Driver-Briggs*, p. 1697.

41. See also Ps. 119:74, 81.

42. Luther, "Psalm 130," p. 192.

43. "Meine Seele wartet auf den Herrn von einer Morgenwache bis zur andern." Martin Luther (1534 translation).

44. James Preuss, *From Shadow to Promise: Old Testament Interpretation from Augustine to the Young Luther* (Eugene, OR: Wipf and Stock Publishers, 1999), pp. 189-90, 211.

130:7 O Israel, hope in the LORD!
    For with the LORD there is steadfast love,
    and with him is great power to redeem.
8   It is he who will redeem Israel
    from all its iniquities.

"O Israel, hope in the LORD!" It now becomes evident with striking clarity that Israel is this kingdom of "waiters," desiring that their hope be fully determined by the name in which they hope. Such waiting is an active participation in being transformed. Drawing on one etymology of "Israel," Luther observes: "The name, too, is suitable; for Israel means a 'wrestler with God' (Gen. 32:28). Now all who wait for the Lord so firmly that they wrestle, as it were, with God are the true Israelites."[45] This prayer and wrestling transcends human laments in the recognition that, though earthly events have precipitated the cry of protest, it is God's self-bestowal that is the true need. God's power over all things, and the inadequacy of human requests, replaces the supplicant's distress at the horror of human life with the deeper horror faith glimpses, that God will leave us to negotiate such tribulations without his divine appearance.[46] The psalmist seeks a concrete act of redemption — not an abstract, inner feeling — but a presence that changes hearts, minds, and events.

Rabbi Jonathan Sacks fills out what is meant by saying that we are given our identity through the embodied communal enactment of Scripture. He recounts the way the truth of his life crystallized during childhood as he repeated with his grandfather at Passover, "This is the bread of affliction which our ancestors ate in the land of Egypt." This, Sacks says, was moral education: "To have moral commitments, even an identity, we must first belong."[47] Moral education is here understood not as being generated in the first instance by being told how to make choices, but, as Charles Taylor has described in more detail,[48] in learning where we are, who is near us, identifying with a community that "knows" where we came from and where we are going. Sacks could, of course, criticize or embrace the story that claimed him; but this

---

45. Luther, "Psalm 130," p. 193. Nigel Biggar rightly notes that this is one of the central rubrics within which Barth defines Christian ethics (the phrase "the hastening that waits" comes from the eschatological ethic of 2 Pet. 3:12), but does not draw out the roots of the approach in Luther's appropriation of the Old Testament. See Nigel Biggar, *The Hastening That Waits: Karl Barth's Ethics* (Oxford: Clarendon Press, 1993).

46. Zimmerli, *Man and His Hope*, pp. 32-33.

47. Jonathan Sacks, *The Politics of Hope* (London: Jonathan Cape, 1997), p. 175.

48. Discussed in ch. 5: "Metaphysics, Epistemology, and the Primacy of the Moral."

foundational experience of identity circumscribed what would count as a reason for or against accepting the story. In a real sense, any thinking he did could only be internal to this story, until he came to identify himself with another community of practice. He concludes: "A tradition is not a system but a way of life. It contains many divergent, even conflicting strands. It can be taken forward in different ways. A tradition never, in and of itself, resolves disagreements. Instead, it is the arena within which [disagreements] take place."[49]

So the "I" who cries out both draws on the community's words and comes to enjoin the community to hope: "Oh Israel, hope in the Lord." In doing so, the church confesses that its hope is defined by God's Word precisely in its confession that the Spirit creates that community who wrestles with Scripture as its form of hope in God. The community says, "This text articulates my hope," and thus it affirms that "this text speaks [of] us." This is an active understanding of the relationship of text, community, and meaning. To wait for God is to join with the community of faith, whose Scripture records and thus gives access to the hope for life, reality, and the present that defines the Christian ethos. The church is not primarily a physical location or an institutional organization: it is a unity of hope about its source that produces an acting and speaking together, and thus it is a world of social meaning in all contexts (see ch. 6). This *polis* exists and speaks not to remember the great deeds of its founders, or to provide space for great human deeds to be recounted,[50] but to recall the saving deeds of God and ask for his presence, a recounting and supplication that constitutes the true unity of the church.

The church is placed by God's love in the position of enacting in love its faith and hope in the faithful and recurrent appearance of the One it calls to by name. It bases its knowledge of reality on the name of God, which "is no self-reassurance that this name can reveal expert knowledge, through which we can connect ourselves with God," but "is a testing and exploration of the novel that came into the world: what happens and what has happened where people are seized by this name, by the God of this name."[51] Christians are those catching hold of themselves by testing the world in hope, ferreting out their allegiance to hopeless gods in light of this name. They are, in short, actively offering themselves to conformity with God and his Word, and so "by the mercies of God, presenting [their] bodies as a living sacrifice, holy and ac-

49. Sacks, *The Politics of Hope*, p. 156.

50. Concerning this political understanding of Heidegger's concept of "world," see Arendt, *The Human Condition*, pp. 192-99.

51. Ulrich, "Fides Quarens Intellectum," p. 53.

ceptable to God, which is [their] spiritual worship which follows the *Logos* and the *ratio Dei*. And let your life-forms be changed, in order to find out what is the will of God, the good and acceptable and perfect."[52]

The prayer of the psalmist exhorts Christians continually to remember that the source of the renewal of human life rests on the intervention of Yahweh. This means that the new thing that is awaited at the appearance of God is not a new thing if we already have a name for it. To pray for specific solutions rather than deliverance returns God to the status of a pagan god, from whom people expect ratification of their old, unrepentant being. True hope waits and prays for mercy; if we have hope in anything other than God's name, we do not wait, Luther concludes: "They have no doubt about His aid, but they do not give it a name."[53] The only name in whose power the Christian can hope is Christ, and that hope excludes any hope for the outcome of history other than the triumph of that name.

The essential point for Christian ethics is that it must serve this church, the community waiting in hope for God's action. The church must thus remain clear about its true threat, says Augustine: the turning away of God's face. This one fear drives out the teeming fears of all other societies striving to secure their own existence without God's help. Christian faith is grounded in God's decision not to let us wander away from him, and it issues in action exploring what the arrival of this God means in a world waiting on other powers. Such "waiters" are the artifacts of the creative action of a God whose being is steadfast love. In Luther's hymnic interpretation of Psalm 130, he develops his image of God carving a people, this time not focusing on the means (fear) but on the source of the humanity shaped by a new hope: "So does Israel take a fitting form, to be created by the Spirit, and as thy God dwells with thee."[54]

There is a fatalistic fear of the future that may shape our action and an activism that takes history by the throat: both embody the sin against the Holy Spirit by deigning to live as if the future were not God's. To wait for God's dawn is to persevere in acts of love sustained by faith and hope when the world and our reason see no path forward. The witness of such perseverance is to make visible the power of God's appearance. It is to live in reliance that the Spirit will give us resources that we did not know we had: to raise and not abort a disabled child, to live and not give up life when facing terminal illness,

52. Ulrich's paraphrase of Rom. 1:2, in "Fides Quarens Intellectum," p. 54.

53. Luther, "Psalm 130," p. 192.

54. "So tu Israel rechter Art, der aus dem Geist erzeuget ward, und seines Gotts erharre." *Evangelisches Gesangbuch*, p. 557.

to persevere in marriage, to live with the "untouchables," or to pastor a difficult church. The faith that is shown paths unknown to the spirit of the age is only possible when the fear of death has truly died. "Princes persecute me without cause, but my heart stands in awe of your words. . . . Great peace have those who love your law; nothing can make them stumble" (Ps. 119:161, 165).

The source of the countercultural force of these new creatures, the psalmist continues, is God's חֶסֶד *(hesed)*, often translated as "steadfast love." He is causing this love to רָבָה *(rabah)*, grow, increase, overflow and thus פְּדוּת *(peduth)*, "ransoming the lost," which carries the sense of purchasing from slavery to begin a joint story. It is this ransom that makes possible the exodus from waywardness. God's *hesed* love has the bounty to make Israel its own by ransoming them out of all — meaning the totality of — their iniquities. Every byway is cut off and exposed as sinful. God's loyal love is the source of human holiness, creating חֲסִידִים *(hasidim)*, those loyal to or devoted to God, responding to God's love with devotion and faithfulness.[55] Because God loves loyally, he creates those who love loyally: "I love the LORD because he has heard my voice and my supplications. Because he inclined his ear to me, therefore I will call on him as long as I live" (Ps. 116:1-2). *Hesed* refers to the obligation assumed by one person to act on behalf of someone who is helpless without it.[56] Jesus emphasizes the centrality of this idea in the parable of the Good Samaritan. Because God helped us in our needy state, we are enabled to be steadfast, empowering lovers — as he has been to us. Or rather, we become carriers of his empowering, steadfast love, which remains with us as long as his face shines on us.

Scholars have argued that it has been the ransom reference of these verses that inspired the early church to include Psalm 130 with the Penitential Psalms.[57] They understood the redemptive power of Yahweh's *hesed* as culminating in the redemption accomplished in Christ: "In him we have redemption through his blood, the forgiveness of our trespasses, according to the riches of his grace that he lavished on us" (Eph. 1:7; cf. Rom. 3:23-24). This connection's deep structure emphasizes the external constitution of the Christian ethos: to be ransomed is to be co-opted from without for a new way of life. Christian hope, with its creative power, comes from outside us and, through the advent of God's loyal love, creates us; it is comforting because it is based on a trusting relationship that we have not created.

This is to understand the life of the people of God as the procession of

---

55. *Hasidim* occurs twenty-four times in the Psalter. Tate, *Psalms 51–100*, pp. 34-35.

56. Tate, *Psalms 51–100*, p. 13.

57. Allen, *Psalms 101–50*, p. 255.

Israel toward Christ. Israel is drawn from the depths, separated, dried out from its idolatries, and set on a new path. The basis of this movement is not self-assurance but faith, which clings to the word that comes to us about who we are meant to be. Faith lives on the way of the prodigal son: from confusion and rebellion, through repentance, into the presence of God. This makes the title of Psalm 130 particularly appropriate, "a song of מַעֲלוֹת," of ascents. The term is used in the Bible to refer to the ascending of stairs; but it takes on a religious meaning in metaphorically referring to Israel's journeying "up" to Jerusalem for the three great pilgrimage feasts, or to the priests' ascending stairs to the altar in the temple. For this reason it is applied to the songs that are thought to have accompanied such ritual processions: Psalms 120-134. Luther catches this resonance by translating it as *Wallfahrtslied,* "a pilgrimage song." The people of Israel, as the "waiters," sing this song in the midst of a journey, an exploration of the world in the new light that Yahweh's loyal love in Christ throws on the world. This community finds its form in relationship to the texts that record life in the light of that love, through which a community of hope has been, and is being, formed.

To summarize thus far: Psalm 130 has emphasized that Christian ethics must go into and through calling on the name of God. Jesus puts this in the words of the *Shema:* "'Hear, O Israel: the Lord our God, the Lord is one; you shall love the Lord your God with all your heart, and with all your soul, and with all your mind, and with all your strength.' The second is this, 'You shall love your neighbor as yourself.' There is no other commandment greater than these" (Mark 12:30-31, par.; Matt. 12:28-34; cf. Deut. 6:4). To love God completely is the irreducible first word of the great commandment; but its second word is "love your neighbor as yourself." This second command is not second in temporal and practical sequence, as though we must get loving God right before we get on to loving the neighbor. But it is second in structural relationship: love of neighbor is defined by the God who loves us. Psalm 130 has illustrated the reasons for this priority and the love that calling on the name of Yahweh entails. From this perspective, loving the neighbor now appears as loving the neighbor *in the way* God loves the neighbor, and *at the same time* that God appears to the neighbor, that is, as his creaturely means.

Psalm 130 has led us into deeper reflection on the role of prayer in the Christian life. This has yielded the discovery that prayer is an ethos. To live as one "waiting for the Lord" is fundamentally and sweepingly different from all other forms of life. Praying contextualizes the whole of the Christian life in each of its moments, thus framing all choices about action. In this sense prayer is not a "practice" but a *Lebensraum,* a space within which we can live. As Luther puts it, the life of faith is nothing other than prayer, which makes prayer, as John Webster notes, "not simply an extension of antecedent subjectivity but rather that in which I first become subject."[58] The active faith of prayer sustains human action, whose shape is defined by its origin and *telos* as response to divine activity. This prayer also places us in the community of the church, marking our fate as that of the church and reminding us of the setting of our struggles within the vocation of the church. Prayer is a form of life together with God, his community, and the world.

We might call this space "faith," but this does not catch the sense that it requires the constant verbalized meditation in which we give ourselves into God's lordship that is prayer. Faith is the essence of the Christian ethos, and to call prayer the proper form of faith's embodiment is to contrast it with unfaith as the frantic search for security in other sources. That the Christian ethos is basically prayer becomes visible in noting how we can interrupt, judge, and refine all that we do with prayer (Neh. 2:4-5). This reshapes the method of Christian ethics by de-emphasizing the attempts exhaustively to classify proper acts in favor of understanding the dynamics and dramatics of continuing in God's story. Judgments about our present become as important as judgments about right actions in general, thus recovering a role for the theological context of ethical deliberation lost to modern Christian ethics.

Psalm 130's emphasis on waiting makes eschatological expectation the frame around all further inquiry into God's redemptive and creative works. From a soteriological — and therefore ethical — perspective, this priority of eschatology is extremely important. That Christian ethics begins in hope relativizes and re-creates our common-sense notion that the creaturely or material realm is the most obvious reality, and the redemptive and eschatological successively more obscure. Faith is taught the turn from abject terror at the forces of inner and outer violence to hopeful certainty in the face of those same forces: "God is our refuge and strength, a very present help in trouble. Therefore we will not fear, though the earth should change, though the mountains shake in the heart of the sea; though its waters roar and foam, though the mountains tremble with its tumult" (Ps. 46:1-3). Psalm 104 shows us how the reversal of this perception is accomplished, as God creates a kingdom that is becoming increasingly differentiated and able to distinguish what God is doing in the world. The waiting of Christian faith does not remain an interminable waiting for God's saving arrival, having no other prayer than Psalm 130; but it is taught a more finely attuned waiting for God's many inter-

---

58. John Webster, *Word and Church: Essays in Christian Dogmatics* (Edinburgh: T&T Clark, 2001), p. 260. See the discussion of faith in ch. 7, pp. 183-84, 187-89.

ventions in the life of earth and its creatures. In singing Psalm 104 we willingly participate in the discovery of the universe of God's working.

In the eschatological prayer of faith, humanity receives God's steadfast love and thus begins a transformation from undifferentiated, wayward, lost beings into a community on a path into a new richness of order and fulfillment. The prophet Isaiah (43:19-21; cf. 35:7-10) encapsulates the hope of this newness in a way that ties together many themes of Part II:

> I am about to do a new thing;
> now it springs forth,
> do you not perceive it?
> I will make a way in the wilderness
> and rivers in the desert.
> The wild animals will honor me,
> the jackals and the ostriches;
> for I give water in the wilderness,
> rivers in the desert,
> to give drink to my chosen people,
> the people whom I formed for myself
> so that they might declare my praise.

The focus of Psalm 130 on expectancy and forgiveness is a concise summary of the entryway into the proper response of faith to God's whole world of creating. To confess our powerlessness to God, to wait and to be forgiven, is the form of this divine working. The earthy concreteness of this order into which God subsequently introduces us is the subject of Psalm 104: God does not just live and work in himself, but works to bring a new order of praise to all creation.

Psalm 104: Praise as Learning to Live within God's Works

If Christian ethics aims to facilitate attentiveness to God's activity, then the investigation of the origin of the Christian ethos must lead into the question of how it is shaped and how it grows. How does God turn the rebellious into children and saints? How does God claim the diversity of created things and knit them into a whole that remains diverse, but undergoes a fundamental re-ordering? How are we taught to recognize where God is working in the world, taught the art of seeing his work and hearing his voice? How are we to understand the world as created by the work of the Spirit in a way that can orient our action, giving concreteness to the heuristic of hope? The methodological question we must now address is this: How does the origin of the Christian ethos described in Psalm 130 unfold to comprehend the whole range of contemporary ethical questions?

I will suggest that Psalm 104 reveals the following relationships. Verses 1-4 show how God's name is expressed in his works. We know creation rightly only if we know it as God's work and seek to harmonize it with the divine working. Singing the praises of God's works teaches us how to discern and thus collaborate with the work, method, will, and nature of God. But we must be taught to know God through the works in which he is most himself. The main body of the psalm, verses 5-26, elaborates the metaphor of each thing finding, or enjoying, its place in the whole varied landscape of God's creation. The basic metaphor is God's provision of all creation with its places, which are varied, interrelating, and mutually supporting. We can also see that what is said of creation is also meant of the church, meaning that Jewish and Christian exegetical traditions have legitimately found this psalm to shed light on many ethical questions. The practical import of the metaphor is to emphasize that (1) created, social, and textual diversity are divine gifts within which (2) God's saving action creates and sustains true social unity.

We will see that this praise of the diversity of creation is the psalmist's way of introducing believers to the interrelationships of the diverse but ordered unities of God's works in the biblical canon, in the various offices and strands of the church, in the varied nature of the exegetical tradition, and in the social roles of human life. The central concerns of Psalm 104 help us to see in each of these spheres the form of God's working to bring all creation to find its place in the unity of worship. Diversity is truly expressed as held together and oriented in worship. The diversity of the Bible is thus a good thing, leading into God's diverse works, as it simultaneously leads us into the correlative political unity of the church, and back out to know the proper unity of human political life. This approach, when growing out of the insights gleaned in Psalm 130, clarifies how we are to "love our neighbor as ourselves" in work, politics, and family life, in which "worry not" becomes the orienting moral hermeneutic.

In conclusion, the final verses of Psalm 104 show how meditation and singing call the church to a worship within which its ethos is continually renewed. The psalm's cumulative effect is to undermine attempts to read it as describing our daily experience of created cause and effect, in which the course of history progresses according to natural causality, and evil and decay appear as independent powers. We will see that such a reading obscures the aspects of both creation and *ecclesia*, which are essential in Christian ethics. Rather, the psalm is addressed to a *community of hope* that is unified in *song* about *God's action*. To this praising community the Spirit is an active force, guiding the faithful into their places in the body of Christ, through the activity of the congregation and God's Word. The biblical text wraps up the whole cosmos, interprets it, transforming human perceptions of the material and social worlds. The theological judgment that this psalm appropriately addresses the concerns raised in this book is a statement both about the essential contours of the biblical topography and about where its contours push those who ask what it says about Christian moral renewal.[59]

A Creation Psalm?

Within modern biblical studies, Psalm 104 is often defined as a creation hymn.[60] The main reasons for this are the proximity of its content to the Egyptian Hymn to the Sun[61] and a wide range of links with the first chapter of Genesis.[62] It is thus unsurprising that Gerhard von Rad would cite Psalm 104 as a rare example illustrating that "Israel was in fact sometimes able to speak of the world as creation without making any particular mention of Yahweh's saving activity."[63] Despite von Rad's unique theological and textual sensitivity, he still sides with many modern interpreters who see this as essen-

---

59. As ch. 8 emphasized (pp. 258-59, 278-79), Christian theology and worship cannot avoid making such judgments about which passages throw the most light on given questions. These theological judgments parallel those that go into the construction of lectionaries. It is thus particularly interesting that a plausible reconstruction of the daily psalms of the second temple (Psalms 24, 48, 82, 94, 81, 93, 92) emphasizes the themes central to my exegesis of Psalm 104. Peter Trudinger, *The Psalms of the Tamid Service: A Liturgical Text from the Second Temple* (Leiden: Brill, 2004).

60. This designation leads to its being grouped with Psalms 8, 19, 29, and 148.

61. See below, p. 312.

62. "The correspondences are striking," notes Leslie Allen. "The sequence of material is largely the same: light, the concept of the heavenly waters, the draining of the waters from the earth, vegetation, the sun and moon as timekeepers, sea creatures, and the provision of food. Moreover, the overlap of vocabulary is remarkable, especially לְמוֹעֲדִים, 'for seasons' (v. 19 = Gen. 1:14); חַיְתוֹ, 'animals' (vv. 11, 20 = Gen. 1:24); עוֹף־הַשָּׁמַיִם, 'birds of the sky' (v. 12 = Gen. 1:26, 28, 30); עֵשֶׂב, 'grass' (v. 14 = Gen. 1:11-12, 29-30); and מָקוֹם, 'place' (v. 8 = Gen. 1:9)." Allen, *Psalms 101-50*, pp. 41-42. However, Kraus argues that these are only "loose allusions" and not "literary dependence." Kraus, *Psalms 60-150*, pp. 298-99.

63. Gerhard von Rad, *Old Testament Theology: Vol II, The Theology of Israel's Prophetic Traditions,* trans. D. M. G. Stalker (New York: Harper & Row, 1965), p. 357. It is a position that has been influential in Psalms interpretation; for instance, Walter Brueggemann follows this line with "no reference to covenant or torah" in *Old Testament Theology: Testimony, Dispute, Advocacy* (Minneapolis: Fortress, 1997), p. 455; so does Konrad Schaefer: "It makes no reference to Israel or her history," in *Psalms: Berit Olam Studies in Hebrew Narrative and Poetry,* ed. David Cotter (Collegeville, MN: Liturgical Press, 2001), p. 257.

tially and solely a creation psalm, which may be a reaction to the unanimous opinion of premodern interpreters that this could not possibly be the case. I will defend the legitimacy of many of the modern concerns, while also seriously considering those of precritical interpreters. Both draw our attention to important textual features.

It is often too hastily assumed that premodern readings of Psalm 104 are vastly different from the conclusions of modern scholarship. Klaus Seybold observes that the psalm is "poetry at the highest level," by which he means that the conceptual and linguistic structure is manifest, and it is manifestly multivalent in the complex way that we expect from good poetry.[64] There are a range of words that anchor the psalm's central themes and entail well-documented double references. In each case, the theologically more "primitive" references have acquired a more conceptualized meaning. I will discuss these in detail in the course of the psalm, and it is only necessary to indicate them now: *nephesh* (throat/life), *'or* (daylight/light of revelation), *shamayim* (heavens/sky), *mayim* (waters/chaos), *mal'ach* (messengers/angels), *ruach* (wind/spirit),[65] and phrases such as "comes on the clouds."[66]

Eight of the psalm's thirty-five verses are *tricola*, indicating its basic skeletal structure.[67]

104:1 Bless the LORD, O my soul.
> O LORD my God, you are very great.
>> You are clothed with honor and majesty,

3 you set the beams of your chambers on the waters,
> you make the clouds your chariot,
>> you ride on the wings of the wind,

14 You cause the grass to grow for the cattle,
> and plants for people to use,
>> to bring forth food from the earth,

15 and wine to gladden the human heart,
> oil to make the face shine,
>> and bread to strengthen the human heart.

24 O LORD, how manifold are your works!
> In wisdom you have made them all;

---

64. Klaus Seybold, *Introducing the Psalms,* trans. R. Graeme Dunphy (Edinburgh: T&T Clark, 1990), p. 70.

65. Ps. 104:3, 4, 29, 30 (103:16). For further references, see Tate, *Psalms 51–100,* p. 22.

66. Cf. Ps. 68:5-7; 18:10; Deut. 33:26; Is. 19:1; Tate, *Psalms 51–100,* p. 176.

67. See Jan P. Fokkelman, *The Psalms in Form: The Hebrew Psalter in Its Poetic Shape* (Leiden: Deo Publishing, 2002), pp. 110-11.

the earth is full of your creatures.
25 Yonder is the sea, great and wide,
    creeping things innumerable are there,
      living things both small and great.
26 There go the ships,
    and Leviathan that you formed
      to sport in it.
29 When you hide your face, they are dismayed;
    when you take away their breath,
      they die and return to their dust.

These verses express wonder at God's ordering activity, a "plain meaning" that directs our attention to the *inclusio* of both Psalms 103 and 104: "O bless the LORD." Even at first glance we find an orientation to praise, and thus we can understand the psalm as exemplifying the proper content and order of praise and the community of praise. Our task, then, is to clarify what, precisely, the psalm urges us to praise.

In this task, the approaches of both the modern and premodern interpretive communities can shed new light on Psalm 104. The modern emphasis on creation may renew our appreciation for creation as creation, and so, unlike some premodern interpreters, we can explore what this might mean for ethics. But we have shown the importance of the premodern emphasis on the unity of all things in the one God's working. Properly understood, God's creative work is of a piece with the form of action known in his redemptive works.

Psalm 104 raises a question that forces us to clarify how we are to understand the connection of God's creative and redemptive works. Even if we insist that the psalm is purely about created life, the wealth of zoological detail begs for explanation. Why include the wild ass, beasts of the field and forest, birds of the air and nesting birds, cattle and wild goats, storks, rabbits, and the leviathan? This question about the quantity of detail is heightened when we note that the psalmist begins his praise of the earth's animal life with a patently unattractive animal, the desert ass. In introducing this particular animal first, the author asks us to make a decision: Was the wild ass chosen for a reason? And what was it? Because this is the first animal of a series that the reader meets, any answer we give must account for the whole series. Luther asks, "Why does [the psalmist] mention this one species [the ass] among so many animals, if he does not aim at being understood spiritually?"[68] Other

---

68. Luther, "Psalm One Hundred Four," in *Luther's Works*, vol. 11, *First Lectures on the Psalms, Psalms 76–126*, ed. Hinton Oswald (St. Louis: Concordia, 1976), pp. 329, 338-39.

Old Testament references to the desert ass corroborate Luther's suggestion that at this point we must unpack its metaphorical implications. A reference in Hosea 8:9 shows the ass as an example of willfulness, while Jeremiah 2:24 emphasizes the animal's lust, and Job 24:5 its desert-dwelling nature. My exegesis draws on this latter resonance in a way that makes the negative character features of the other passages intelligible. In Psalm 104 these character features become a theological resource. As I explained in the last chapter, my procedure will be to flesh out the theological meaning of the metaphors the biblical author has used.

Some contemporary critical exegetes have recognized that the psalmist's animal metaphors are only accessible to some form of theological or intertextual interpretation. It seems evident that all animal references in the Psalms should be interpreted as theologically multivalent.

> Rarely is an animal *just* an animal in the Psalter. In some cases, the delineation between zoological classification and metaphorical significance is not clearly marked. Those psalms that refer to animals *without* explicit metaphorical significance — i.e., those that reflect on the goodness of God's creation — become indirectly fraught with metaphorical significance by virtue of their association with the vast majority of psalms that do deploy animal imagery figuratively. To read the Psalter as it was codified by the second century B.C.E., that is, to view the Psalms as a *book,* is to imbue *all* references to animals in the Psalter with some degree of connotative force, even in their purely creational contexts, that they would not otherwise have in isolation.[69]

Even if Brown is overstating his case for effect, there remains good reason to believe that the animals of Psalm 104 would not have been read in a purely literal manner. The New Testament writers certainly did not, Augustine notes. Paul, for instance, assumes in at least one passage that the Old Testament instruction about animals also, or possibly even primarily, refers to church order (1 Cor. 9:9-10).[70]

A postcritical perspective allows us to emphasize more sharply than either modern or premodern interpreters that, when this psalm talks about the order of the animal kingdom, it means to shape our perceptions of both the animal and human social order. The obvious obscurity of the psalm's zoolog-

---

69. William Brown, *Seeing the Psalms: A Theology of Metaphor* (Louisville: Westminster John Knox, 2002), p. 152.

70. St. Augustine, *Expositions of the Psalms 99–120: Volume 5*, ed. Boniface Ramsey, trans. and notes, Maria Boulding (New York: New City Press, 2003), p. 148.

ical parade sets us off on a deeper investigation of the manifold nature of divine truth. According to Augustine, "the obscurity of the divine word is beneficial in this respect: that it causes many views of the truth to appear and to be brought into the light of knowledge."[71] This exploration is the opposite of unconstrained interpretive play, a playful embrace of the given text of Scripture and creation (104:24).

But how do the multiple levels of reference fit together? The text of Psalm 104 also provides another set of hints. The references this psalm makes to the surrounding psalms are important in this respect. Norbert Lohfink and Erich Zenger point out that Psalms 103 and 104 are so interwoven "that the two psalms can simply be read as 'twin psalms.' The Midrash Tehillim also regards Psalms 103 and 104 as an overlapping composition when it explicitly compares the summons that occurs five times in the two psalms combined 'bless the Lord, O my soul' (103:1, 2, 22; 104:1, 35) with the five books of the Torah."[72] There are other obvious links as well. Psalm 103 (vv. 19-22) closes with the image of Yahweh erecting a royal throne in heaven, with which Psalm 104 (vv. 2-4) begins. The only two appearances of the "ministers of Yahweh" in the Psalter occur here (103:20-21; 104:4). Both give prominent place to the idea of humans returning to dust (103:14; 104:29) and focus on God's establishment of his rule. Finally, the "just order" of 103:6 is explicitly understood as the deliverance of the oppressed and despised. It is this focus on just order that we will see links God's creative and redemptive works, Genesis and Sinai, wonder at creation, and Torah obedience. Psalm 103 relies on Exodus 33–34, as 104 is in dialogue with Genesis 1.[73] In both cases, covenant establishment is the central theme.

These connections ground a strong case for the claim that Psalm 103 sets 104 in a redemptive framework, asking us to read 104 as a further explication of the conspicuously placed "his kingdom rules over all" (103:19). The implication is that, rather than thinking of Psalms 103 and 104 as related psalms that nonetheless address separate topics, Psalm 104 asks us to think about the topic of 103, God's one rule, in a more complex way — that is, as the dynamic of his rule of all things. This allows the psalmist to (1) praise the goodness of God's work of creation and (2) use this order to explicate the form of God's redemptive activity, as creating an ecosystem of peace and praise. This amounts to (3) giving a more general description of Israel's his-

---

71. Augustine, *The City of God against the Pagans,* ed. and trans. R. W. Dyson (Cambridge, UK: Cambridge University Press, 1998), XI.19.

72. Norbert Lohfink and Erich Zenger, *The God of Israel and the Nations: Studies in Isaiah and the Psalms,* trans. Everett Kalin (Collegeville, MN: Liturgical Press, 2000), p. 185.

73. Lohfink and Zenger, *The God of Israel,* p. 188.

tory, which is the theme of Psalm 105. So we may also read Psalm 104 as an account of the inner dynamic of the rising and falling of Israel's history. This rising and falling is an expression of God's work to separate the peoples and make them his messengers by purifying and ordering them in a new and unfamiliar way. To put the case this way is to allow that the canonical complex of Psalms 103–105 has been arranged to suggest to Israel the integration of God's creative and redemptive works.

It is an integration not defined by the horizontal, by its movement from creation to exodus, but by the vertical. From verse 2, the participles of alternating verses (2, 3, 4, 5, 10, 13, 14, 19) emphasize that the psalm's primary referent is God's creative activity and thus not primarily its result. This point is theologically critical: for Israel, creation is never just of the world, but is also of Israel. "In innumerable hymns and historical psalms in the Psalter the deeds of Yahweh in history and creation are recited and praised in close connection with each other."[74] Talk of God's creative work is thus always open to this simultaneous focus on creation and redemption, whether the foregrounding theme is God's works of redemption (Ps. 103, 105–106) or creation (104). The redactors of the Psalms have arranged them to make the message unmistakable: God's redemptive work locates and situates the proper human response in creation.[75] This renders any attempt to read Psalm 104 as "purely" about humans and the world a dubious undertaking.[76]

Here again, that the psalms are song and prayer proves exegetically and ethically determinative. We must account for the fact that the psalm is sung by the redeemed community, and calls it to praise. As a psalm rather than a narrative description, it guides a community into the practice of singing, "O LORD, how manifold are your works! In wisdom you have made them all; the earth is full of your creatures" (v. 24). Such a song inspires an appreciation of God's ways of creating and sustaining a universe diverse in its harmony. Thus the psalm transmits to us the psalmist's reflection on the proper content of praise, inviting us into it, anchoring a community that asks, "What is God's work?"

This community does not sing about God's being (metaphysically defined), nor the effects of God's works, but about the works to which faith must be attuned. Its singing of creation is thus a means of talking about the different modalities of God's presence: not his potential presence, or possible

74. Kraus, *Theology of the Psalms*, p. 62.

75. James Luther Mays, *The Lord Reigns*, ch. 2, esp. pp. 15-16; see also Lohfink and Zenger, *The God of Israel*, ch. 6.

76. See Karl Barth, *Church Dogmatics*, III.1, trans. J. W. Edwards, O. Bussey, and H. Knight (Edinburgh: T&T Clark, 1958), p. 240, and II.1, pp. 106ff.

omnipresence, but his actual omnipresence as omni-caring. God is not the "one who can do everything" but the great lover and caring one, a handworker creating the whole cosmos and his people, providentially upholding and ordering both. In the divine working the two are one. To sing of God's creative activity is to sing of our own creation as material and justified beings.

Singing, therefore, emerges as a powerful locus of communal reorientation. Islamic scholars, for reasons that worried the writers surveyed in chapter 1, have become newly attentive to the ways ritual repetition resists critical analysis.[77] This is an important insight, and it has grounded critical biblical studies. But a postcritical and post-Constantinian Christian church must learn to appreciate again the importance of an immersion in Scripture in which criticism continues to function, but not in a way that makes it impossible to take Scripture up in praise. In communal praise we discover the sharp distinction between observing God's many works and a willing participation in God's creation. Such an "inside" vantage point can perceive the proper differentiation and unity of the various divine works. Here we need not conceive of the divine works as related in some sort of A+B+C sequential fashion (with its roots in Platonic symbol systems), because the one God's works must ultimately be united.[78] Thus the praise of the one God transforms and overcomes many things we commonly sharply distinguish: "O LORD, how manifold are your works! . . . The earth is full of your creatures"(104:24).

This category reorientation is most obvious in the confession that Christians cannot praise creation without new creation, a statement based on

77. Jane Dammen McAuliffe, "Reading the Qur'an with Fidelity and Freedom," 2004 American Academy of Religion Presidential Address, *Journal of the American Academy of Religion* 73, no. 3 (Sept. 2005): 626.

78. Perhaps no theologian has delved as deeply into this question as has G. W. F. Hegel. His main interest is in showing how things that appear to be separated are in fact interrelated, mediated. See "The Absolute Idea," in G. W. F. Hegel, *Science of Logic*, trans. H. D. Lewis (Atlantic Highlands: Humanities Press International, 1969), pp. 828-34. This insight grounds his whole system of thought, determining his understanding of Christianity. It is an insight tied to the life of the immanent Trinity as the mediation of the Father and the Son in the Spirit (see Hegel, *Encyclopaedia of the Philosophical Sciences in Outline and Critical Writings*, trans. E. Behler [New York: Continuum, 1990], §467, pp. 260-61), which sets up an account of the mediation of the different attributes of God (see Hegel, *Lectures on the Philosophy of Religion. Volume III: The Consummate Religion*, trans. Peter C. Hodgson [Berkeley: University of California Press, 1985], p. 271) and accounts for the activity of the economic Trinity (see Hegel, *Encyclopaedia*, §§468-470, pp. 262-63). Thanks to Martin Wendte for many stimulating discussions about the relevance of this point.

the psalmists' insistence that we worship one God.[79] This insistence also accounts for Israel's rewriting the theology of the sources on which its own psalms often draw.[80] Ancient creation prayers are offered to the creation, or simply recount the events of creation; they are not addressed to a creator above and apart from creation. Only this latter presupposition allows the natural world to be conceived as a messenger of the divine, as Psalm 104 portrays it. Israel's monotheistic hymnody explicitly refutes the dualisms of the Hymn to the Sun. In the metaphorical universe of Psalm 104, the lion is no longer the twin of the poisonous snake, nor do lions inhabit a nighttime world conceived as having a power to threaten from beyond God's reach.[81]

For our psalmist, night is also God's, and it is also good. This raises the opposite problem: Does such a reading out of the power of evil properly appreciate creation as it is? Is creation as harmonious as the psalmist seems to suggest? Are modern Western minds that are raised on evolutionary cosmology and capitalist social conceptions meant to forget the entirely less prosaic power of the struggle for existence? Or maybe Psalm 104 expresses the "satisfied and assured assertion of orderliness" of the "economically secure and politically significant."[82] We must face the possibility that here the speaking

79. "What creative work fills the earth? All trees and bushes, all animals, both wild and tame, and the whole human race itself. . . . Nonetheless we should attend even more closely to that particular creative work of which the apostle says, *If anyone is in Christ, there is a new creation. The old things have passed away, and lo, everything is made new!* (2 Cor. 5:17)." Augustine, *Expositions of the Psalms*, p. 169. For a more detailed discussion of the methodological centrality of eschatology in Christian ethics, see Hans G. Ulrich, *Eschatologie und Ethik: Die theologische Theorie der Ethik in ihrer Beziehung auf die Rede von Gott seit Friedrich Schleiermacher* (München: Christian Kaiser Verlag, 1988).

80. This despite insufficiently theological Christian assertions to the contrary, as in Walter Brueggemann, *The Message of the Psalms: A Theological Commentary* (Minneapolis: Augsburg, 1984), p. 31.

81. C. S. Lewis, *Reflections on the Psalms* (London: Geoffrey Bless, 1958), pp. 86-89. Contemporary biblical scholarship concurs. Samuel Terrien, after a detailed discussion of divergences between the two hymns, suggests that the Israelite poet probably did not know the Hymn to the Sun directly, receiving it through a mediating culture. Terrien, *The Psalms: Strophic Structure and Theological Commentary* (Grand Rapids: Eerdmans, 2003), pp. 715-16. For a textual comparison, see John Eaton, *The Psalms: A Historical and Spiritual Commentary with an Introduction and New Translation* (London: T&T Clark International, 2003), p. 516.

82. Brueggemann, *The Message of the Psalms*, p. 26. He continues on p. 27: "This does not make these poems suspect, but it permits us to read them knowingly, for not everyone experiences life this way and can speak so boldly about it. Life is well-oriented only for some, and that characteristically at the expense of others." This chapter will argue that this suspicious historicizing completely misses that the order into which the psalm introduces us is *not* the order of human oppression sustained by the "economically secure and politically significant," but the order of God's *subduing* of that oppression.

members of life's macabre pantomime are wishfully dreaming themselves into a blind optimism about the world.

Amidst a universe characterized by destructive forces of awesome scope, the human experience of creation cannot but be an ambiguous one: matter faces mind as a dangerous cipher, experiences of created beauty as question rather than answer. What, for instance, is actually beautiful about a sunset? Either it is nothing, since it is a random confluence of a physical phenomenon with neurological receptors whose firing, in itself, has no meaning. Or it may, conversely, confirm our romantic "sunny optimism" that the world is, after all, a pretty good place.[83] The disappointment that follows this inherently unrealistic view eventually becomes its opposite: the belief that "nature absolutely paints like the harlot, whose allurements cover nothing but the charnel house within."[84] Oswald Bayer pinpoints the theological question at stake here: "If the world is not believed as something promised, then it becomes, as Nietzsche appropriately said, 'a thousand wastes, silent, cold.' In such silence and such coldness Luther experiences the wrath of God."[85]

But creation may also strike us, as it does the psalmist, as a manifestation of God's faithfulness in revealing the beauty of his glory in a broken creation seen in all its fury and violence. This is a psalm expressing serene confidence in the order of world processes, and a joy in them, despite the experience of a world that is perpetually, crushingly, engulfed in violence and suffering. Of the Creator, Barth rightly asks: "Where and how far will the world picture as such testify to an order and harmony in which we can directly perceive the divinity and wisdom and power of the Creator? Can we rightly understand Psalm 104 for even a single moment without the commentary of Revelation 21:1-5?"

> Then he showed me the river of the water of life, bright as crystal, flowing from the throne of God and of the Lamb through the middle of the street of the city; also, on either side of the river, the tree of life with its twelve kinds of fruit, yielding its fruit each month; and the leaves of the tree were

---

83. Joseph Conrad has a sharp eye for the essential anti-realism of romantic optimism. "Everything in the world reminded him of her. The beauty of the loved woman exists in the beauties of Nature. The swelling outlines of the hills, the curves of a coast, the free sinuosities of a river are less suave than the harmonious lines of her body, and when she moves, gliding lightly, the grace of her progress suggests the power of occult forces which rule the fascinating aspects of the visible world." Joseph Conrad, "Freya of the Seven Isles," in *The Nigger of the Narcissus and Other Tales* (London: Oxford University Press, 1975), p. 355.

84. Melville, *Moby Dick*, ch. 42: "The Whiteness of the Whale."

85. Oswald Bayer, "Luther as an Interpreter of Holy Scripture," in Donald McKim, ed., *The Cambridge Companion to Luther* (Cambridge, UK: Cambridge University Press, 2003), p. 82.

for the healing of the nations. There shall no more be anything accursed, but the throne of God and of the Lamb shall be in it, and his servants shall worship him; they shall see his face, and his name shall be on their foreheads. And night shall be no more; they need no light of lamp or sun, for the Lord God will be their light, and they shall reign for ever and ever.

Barth's question presses for further investigation: "I ask: Can we, in a genuine, linguistic, historical explanation of Ps. 104, disregard for even a single moment the fact that it is only from this point — because in the Psalm itself this [new creation] is first read into the cosmology of natural man with prophetic and apostolic authority, and only then read out of it — that there can be and actually is the praise of God in the ordered harmony of His creation which constitutes the content of this Psalm?"[86] Psalm 104 answers that praise in no way minimizes the forces of evil in the world, but confesses that they are comprehensible only as that which God "makes sport of."

Praising God the Enlightener, Lover, and Creator

104:1 בָּרֲכִי נַפְשִׁי אֶת־יְהוָה
יְהוָה אֱלֹהַי גָּדַלְתָּ
מְּאֹד הוֹד וְהָדָר לָבָשְׁתָּ׃
2a עֹטֶה־אוֹר כַּשַּׂלְמָה

104:1 Bless the LORD, O my soul.
      O LORD my God, you are very great.
      You are clothed with honor and majesty,
2a   wrapped in light as with a garment.

"Bless the LORD, O my soul." Psalm 104 begins where Psalm 130 left off, an opening on which the rest of the psalm is an extended meditation. Only in blessing the Lord do we ally ourselves with his working, and declare our readiness to cooperate with it. From such a beginning we can appreciate that this is not a psalm about creation but a singing about creation as an exploration of calling on the name. To sing of creation, as the psalm proceeds to do, is one of the many possible ways to call on the name. As we will see, for the psalmist it is only in praise of the name that the creature discovers herself or himself as creature.

    Given that Psalm 104 is an exploration of God's name, it is appropriate

---

86. Barth, *Church Dogmatics*, II.1, ed. G. W. Bromiley and T. F. Torrance; trans. T. H. L. Parker, W. B. Johnston, Harold Knight, J. L. M. Haire (Edinburgh: T&T Clark, 1997), p. 114.

that it begins with language that evokes a royal meeting in which servants bow (1 Sam. 14:22) and superiors give their blessing (2 Sam. 13:25). Thus בָּרְכִי *(baruch)* can be translated either "bless" or "kneel"; but in the Psalter, when it is directed toward God, it also becomes a synonym for praise. Yahweh as King has blessed his servants (Gen. 1:28, for example), and here his servants acknowledge that blessing by returning it. The psalmist is exploring creation understood as a blessing by those who kneel.

Verse 1's "O my soul" is the familiar translation of נַפְשִׁי *(naphshi)*. Like the English word "heart," the noun נֶפֶשׁ *(nephesh)* carries a wide range of metaphorical meanings. One is simply "life": the ancient understanding of biological life was focused on breathing, the process by which air moves in and out of the body. The English "heart" functions in a similar way, denoting life by referring to what is understood to be the body's most important organ. This points to a range of wider significations that refer to the vital affective motions we denote in English as "soul." This reference to the "soul," the essential inner being, can be reduced to indicate lives *simpliciter,* as in "3,000 souls were lost that day." *Nephesh* is thus a poetically loaded term that functions as does the English "heart" in both referring to the biological life of the body and indicating at the same time movements in the deeper affective parts of human existence. It emphasizes energy and movement as supremely evident in speech and breathing. It is this totality of human energy that Yahweh claims for himself. "You shall love the LORD with all your heart, with all your *nephesh,* and with all your might" (Deut. 6:5).

One unfamiliar implication of the Hebrew conceptual complex is its linkage of several dynamic aspects of human existence — the breathing and sustaining activity of the mouth and throat through the intake of nourishment. Life is not only breath but food, and the right food is necessary to sustain life. Whereas the English "heart" most often links with romantic images such as "giving one's heart for love," which point to specifically romantic pairings, *nephesh* highlights the longings of the empty stomach, or compares receiving the essential blessings of human life to the satisfaction of the fulfilled stomach. Moderns believe they can die of a "broken heart," which means to die by losing one's true romantic love. But the Hebrew word complex intimates that one dies of having wrong desires, of "surviving by eating the wrong things," or of starving from privation of the things that preserve human existence. In Psalm 34:9-10, lions suffer hunger, but the *nephesh* who tastes God (v. 8) feeds on God, because praise is continually "in my mouth."[87] Here righteous desire and praise is literally a life-and-death matter.

---

87. Brown, *Seeing the Psalms,* pp. 153-54.

The polyvalent meaning of *nephesh* is often interwoven with a rich set of theological reflections on what sustains human life, on view here in the two main themes that anchor the content of Psalm 104. The first is רוּחַ *(ruach)*. It is translated as "wind" in verses 3 and 4, as well as in 103:16. In verse 29 it is translated as "breath," here meaning human breath, and in verse 30 as "spirit," meaning God's Spirit. Elsewhere it means the human spirit of jealousy or courage (e.g., Num. 5:14) or the divine Spirit that fills humans with divine wisdom or prophecy (Exod. 31:3).[88] The term refuses to draw any sharp boundary between the "natural" and the "supernatural": the core of the conceptual complex as used in the Old Testament is simply that this kind of movement, that of moving air, characterizes God's presence more than other kinds of movement or nonmovement. The notion that God is present as wind thus emphasizes the complete indebtedness of living things to his presence. For Israel, life is in breath, which is so memorably depicted in being breathed into Adam in the second creation account. The substance of humanity is not dust, says verse 29, but this breath, without which humans, like animals, pass away. The term *nephesh* holds together the notion that God gives breath with the singer's continuing existence as constituted by the possession of this breath.

This further clarifies the meaning of the *inclusio*, which might be translated in this way: "Bless Yahweh, my *nephesh*, because I live in returning this breath in praise to its maker. I live in taking words of praise upon my lips. I am a creature who lives in answering God, in God answering God." In the Hebrew cosmology, all breathing things live only in this answer, as the final psalm reminds us: "Let everything that breathes praise the LORD! Praise the LORD!" (Ps. 150:6). After beginning in Psalm 1 with the quest to understand the blessed life, the Psalter concludes by answering that blessedness is to have praise claim the whole existence of the praising animal: "All that is within me, bless his holy name" (Ps. 103:1-2, 20-22; 104:1, 35).

In writing of God's works, the psalmist feeds on humanity's proper food and invites others to this table. In writing he simultaneously exhorts his own inner being and the community of faith, reminding both to constantly recall that they only exist to praise. The psalmist writes and calls to song because, if life is to have value, I/we must be determined by praise. Praise thus generates a constant critical relationship to the currents within us that repudiate the eschatological hope that God is at work. This writing-as-praise-and-exhortation

---

88. For a survey of the 389 uses of the term in the Old Testament, see F. W. Horn, "Holy Spirit," in David Freedman, ed., *The Anchor Bible Dictionary, vol. 3, H-J,* trans. Dietlinde Elliot (New York: Doubleday, 1992), pp. 262-63.

is the pinnacle of human creative endeavor in collaborating with the divine creative work that is the subject of this psalm. Human creativity is not *ex nihilo,* but novel re-expression of God's praiseworthiness.

The second sentence of verse 1, "O Lᴏʀᴅ my God, you are very great. You are clothed with honor and majesty," opens up verse 1's dense affirmations into the themes that will take up the bulk of this psalm. It extols Yahweh as the only power, a Lord who arrays himself in beautiful and varied works. There are again royal resonances to the terms "honor" and "majesty." Having suggested that human life exists in praise, the psalmist so constructs his work as to make clear that he is not talking about it but engaged in it, showing the implications of the belief that "I live in praise" *through* praise. To live in praise is an embodied confession that praise is the only way to feed on God's works, in which one becomes certain of being the work of the God who orders all creation.

The divine outflowing that is God's works is the subject of the next phrase: "You are clothed with honor and majesty, wrapped in light as with a garment." The parallelism of this line tells us that the "majesty and splendor" of God as the Lord who clothes himself in his works is related to his being clad in light. The Bible is rife with light imagery that gives us a closer view of what "wrapped in light" might mean. Again, the linkage to Genesis 1 is obvious: light was the first of God's creations. Roaming further afield, we note that the Israelites had light during the plague of darkness on the Egyptians (Exod. 10:23). In 2 Kings 7:9, morning light is linked with the dispensing of justice, and in Job 3:16, 20, to see the light of day is to exist. The author of Job also says that light is the wisdom of God, which explains why Psalm 97:11 ("light dawns for the righteous") and Psalm 130:6 ("My soul waits for the Lᴏʀᴅ more than watchmen for the morning") understand the genesis of justice and the appearance of God as inseparably linked. This meaning coalesces in the references to a range of mediators as light: God's word (Ps. 119:105), the law (Prov. 6:23), and Israel itself, which shines because it has these words (Is. 42:6). Thus the conclusion of Psalm 36:9: "In Thy light [transmitted in these ways] we see light."

Therefore, we might summarize the meaning of this sentence as: "You cover yourself with the power to illuminate, and thus to lead and draw to yourself, thereby bringing into existence both justice and all materiality." With this wording the psalmist directs our attention to the inner logic of divine action, the works in which God is most himself. All God's works revolve around his self-revelation and overflowing. In short, God covers himself with the emanation of his wisdom, which leads people to and into the trinitarian life: "You discover a lifesaving way to yourself and for this are to be praised" (Job 28:20, 27).

It is from this perspective that glory and splendor are to be understood.

The light in which God wraps himself creates the clothing of his works. Thus his beauty cannot be abstracted from his power, and his works are an explanation of his form of power.[89] His power is not arbitrary or autonomously operating, but it ties itself to certain works, to work with certain ends. This limiting of divine power to the purpose of searching out a way to himself explains the New Testament's fondness for characterizing Jesus as light. The prologue to John makes this linkage with the light of Genesis 1 explicit, calling Jesus the light of the material creation and of the new creation that is the kingdom of God. Jesus is thus named as the meaning of the many divine works through which God mediates his goodness to humanity.

Jesus calls himself the "light of the world" (John 8:12; 9:5), and so do his disciples (Matt. 5:14). John the Baptist (John 5:35) and the gospel itself (2 Cor. 4:4) are also referred to as divine light. Conversion is to be "called out of darkness into this marvelous light" (1 Pet. 2:9) and to become children of light, following light and transmitting it (1 Thess. 5:5; Eph. 5:9; John 12:36). In all of this, God's power is conceived as enacting a work: the enlightenment of the world, an enlightenment specified in its means, method, and result. Christian doctrine has drawn these points together to yield a sharp definition of the clarity of Scripture. "The economy of God's communication of himself by scattering the darkness of sin, reconciling lost creatures, overcoming ignorance and establishing the knowledge and love of himself, is the dogmatic location of the notion of *claritas scripturae*."[90] Scripture is both a description of God's enlightening work and a point at which he has chosen to concentrate it.

The preceding chapter discussed the irreducibility of metaphor in providing access to the reality of faith. The metaphorical intertwining of physical light and holy lives, and of the breath of life with the divine animating Spirit, illustrated clear and intentional metaphorical interweavings. We can now ask what this means in concrete terms for our understanding of Christian ethics.

What we must first say, with reference to light, is that this psalm seeks to undermine the belief that there is a "real" light and a "metaphorical" light. The true light is the garment in which God has wrapped himself. God is the one who makes and names and thus orders light; it is his work and his glory. Therefore, the "truth" of light is no more to be equated with our commonsense perception of its material manifestation than it was for Israel, whose

---

89. Cf. Barth, *Church Dogmatics*, II.1, p. 653.

90. John Webster, "Biblical Theology and the Clarity of Scripture," in *Out of Egypt: Biblical Theology and Biblical Interpretation*, ed. Craig Bartholomew, Mary Healy, Karl Möller, and Robin Parry (Milton Keynes, UK: Paternoster, 2004), p. 361.

neighbors believed that the sun was God, or one of the gods. The metaphor of God's work as light constitutes a realistic claim about the interrelationships of the universe's created light and God's working. This doxology sets us in a trajectory in which we will discover what it means that light is simultaneously God's working and the effect of this working. In the same way, *nephesh* is real when it sings. It is not somehow "fulfilled" or "completed" in singing; it truly exists in singing. Thirst and desire for God's law are physical moments that occur bodily in our daily lives,[91] just as God physically enlightens, bringing about his light in the world. What we take as insubstantial "metaphorical" meaning is turned on its head; the eschatological truth is revealed to be more concrete than what we once took to be "reality."[92] By using the power of metaphor to explore light as God's invitation to himself, the psalmist cannot but deconstruct our certainty about light.

Augustine beautifully expresses this reversal by referring to angels. The angels are so certain of their knowledge of the triune God that "they know every created thing not in itself, but in this better way: that is, in the wisdom of God, as if in the design by which it was created."[93] Talk of the angels allows Augustine to contrast eschatologically determined perception and purely human perception. For humanity, the evidence of sensation is the most firm certainty, the knowledge of God and the protological and eschatological ground of all things ephemeral. Bonhoeffer's comment on Psalm 119:18, "Open my eyes, so that I may behold wondrous things out of your law," expresses how God's law creates the gratitude through which God's creative and eschatological works become visible: "The one whose eyes God has opened to see the Word beholds a wonderland. What until then appeared to me as dead is full of life, what was full of contradictions is resolved in a higher unity, the harsh demands become a gracious law. In the midst of human words, I hear God's eternal word. In ancient stories I recognize the contemporary God and his work for my salvation."[94]

What, then, is light? Here the poet refuses to limit the polyvalence of language. Light is the sun; light is wisdom; light is Israel. But light is, essentially, that in which God clothes himself. Barth hits on the inner meaning of this polyvalence: "What is constituted once and for all with the creation of

91. Bernd Wannenwetsch, "Walking the Ten Words: Exploring the Moral Universe through the Decalogue" (unpublished paper).

92. Joachim Ringleben, "Metapher und Eschatologie bei Luther," *Zeitschrift für Theologie und Kirche* 100, no. 2 (2003): 223-40.

93. Augustine, *City of God*, XI.29.

94. Bonhoeffer, *Dietrich Bonhoeffer's Meditations on the Psalms*, trans. Edwin Robertson (Grand Rapids: Zondervan, 2002), p. 88.

light is the law of the history willed by God."[95] Light is God's minister, revealing God. Thus the sun and moon serve their true purpose and reveal their true being only as representatives and witnesses of their nature as participants in the law of the history willed by God. In this way they are known for what they are, God's garment.

The books of Isaiah and Revelation emphasize this point by recounting how the sun will one day be superfluous as a light source, not replaced but eclipsed by the light of God himself in the new creation: "The sun shall no longer be your light by day, nor for brightness shall the moon give light to you by night; but the LORD will be your everlasting light, and your God will be your glory" (Is. 60:19; cf. Ps. 121:5-7). That this is not an abstract "metaphorical" statement, but one that is concrete in the present, and is thus freighted with social and political implications, is revealed in Revelation 21:23-24, where heaven is a city that "has no need of sun or moon to shine on it, for the glory of God is its light, and its lamp is the Lamb. The nations will walk by its light, and the kings of the earth will bring their glory into it."[96]

The "what is light?" line of questioning again clarifies methodological questions about the relationship between the Bible and Christian ethics. Verse 2 addresses God with the words "You are . . . wrapped in light as with a garment," understanding "light" as having a complex referent. On the one hand, it points to the true teleology and thus meaning of what we commonly understand as light in a scientific sense. Light is revealed as both a physical phenomenon and the possibility that created reality can be explored in faith to discover the law by which God arrays himself in the glory of the universe. To sing this as blessing on the God who so works is to cling to these words in such a way that all perception is reoriented around the first commandment: "Thou shalt have no other gods before me."

This not only broadens but narrows our interpretive options. If we want to see God, notes Calvin, we must take seriously that he is clothed, not naked. "That we may enjoy the sight of him, he must come forth into view with his clothing; that is to say, we must cast our eyes upon the very beautiful fabric of the world in which he wished to be seen by us, and not be too curious or rash in searching into his secret essence."[97] At the same time, because

---

95. Barth, *Church Dogmatics*, III.1, p. 120.

96. Cf. Bernd Wannenwetsch, "Representing the Absent in the City: Prolegomena to a Negative Political Theology according to Revelation 21," in L. Gregory Jones, Reinhard Hütter, and C. Rosalee Velloso Ewell, eds., *God, Truth, and Witness: Engaging Stanley Hauerwas* (Grand Rapids: Brazos Press, 2005), pp. 167-92.

97. John Calvin, "Psalm CIV," in *Commentary on the Book of Psalms*, vol. IV, trans. James Anderson (Grand Rapids: Baker, 1989), p. 145.

we are enfolded in this divine clothing, none can claim that God hides him-self, only that he is too close to be seen properly. God's works are on display, but on such a scale that they are all too easily overlooked. That God is clothed in his works is the psalmist's description of the grammar of God's working, a grammar that demands a topography of all human sensation. Its basic claim is that God is the self-revealer and lover of all. The art of understanding all his works begins in praise of this God.

All this is incipient in the opening verse of the psalm, as the remainder of the psalm shows. The psalmist does not add new themes, but he deepens and clarifies the connections laid out here. Verses 2b-4 repeat the logical com-plex of 1-2a, now recounting the divine self appearing in the majesty and splendor of creation. Creation is not left alone, but is arrayed as God's maj-esty, and the mechanism of this arraying is God's attention to the importance of an ordered and comprehensible self-revealing.

Divine Presence and the Renewal of Language as Political Space

104:2b נוֹטֶה שָׁמַיִם כַּיְרִיעָה:

3 הַמְקָרֶה בַמַּיִם עֲלִיּוֹתָיו הַשָּׂם־עָבִים
רְכוּבוֹ הַמְהַלֵּךְ עַל־כַּנְפֵי־רוּחַ:

4 עֹשֶׂה מַלְאָכָיו רוּחוֹת
מְשָׁרְתָיו אֵשׁ לֹהֵט:

104:2b You stretch out the heavens like a tent,
3 you set the beams of your chambers on the waters,
you make the clouds your chariot,
you ride on the wings of the wind,
4 you make the winds your messengers,
fire and flame your ministers.

The literal meaning of the next sentence appears obscure in a modern context: "You [Yahweh] stretch the heavens like a curtain [forming a roof] and build with beams your rooftop chamber on top of the waters." Isaiah 51:13 is one of many passages expressing the same idea. "You have forgotten the LORD, your Maker, who stretched out the heavens and laid the foundations of the earth." This is another way of saying that God has created the whole. Heaven and earth is the backbone pairing describing what we think of as the universe.[98] The psalmist thus communicates that "God created the whole by

---

98. Barth, *Church Dogmatics*, III.1, p. 19.

taking up residence with it. Outside of his act of building this place as his residence, nothing exists."

Here the reference to the "tent" or "curtain" that God stretches has caused discussion among biblical scholars about whether this is a reference to the temple.[99] My suggestion is that it is such a reference, again based on the dual reference of the words the Hebrew poet places together here. שָׁמַיִם (shamayim) means both "heavens" and "sky," at once the visible upper part of creation and the invisible abode of the divine. That this abode is built on the waters has the same dual reference. As previously discussed, "the waters" metaphorically links the terrestrial oceans and the danger, evil, violence, and fragility of existence. Thus, for the ancient Israelite, "to build your tent on the waters" is an unmistakable reference to the formation of a people who worshiped in a tent after God's work of salvation at the Red Sea: "You divided the sea before them, so that they passed through the sea on dry land, but you threw their pursuers into the depths, like a stone into mighty waters" (Neh. 9:11). Out of the ocean of social strife (Ps. 2:1-3) God draws forth his temple among the nations.

The author of Genesis makes a similar association in portraying the Garden of Eden in Genesis 1–3 as a temple or sanctuary of divine construction. Before the Fall, humanity was meant to multiply in faith and reliance on God, thus expanding this blessing to include the whole world. After the Fall, the Babelites congregated and tried to subject the sanctuary to human control. It is in this broken world that Yahweh must begin again to build his sanctuary in the world through an Exodus. That the universe is the work of God's hand means that its structures are built to serve as a meeting place: a temple in which the sea has been contained to become a piece of furniture in God's redemptive cosmos (2 Chron. 4:2-6). On these grounds we can see Augustine's point in commenting that to sing "you build your home on the waters" is to praise God's almighty power at creation, as well as his strength in weakness in building his tent among and through the human work of preserving and expositing God's Word.[100]

Jewish midrash comes to a related conclusion when it asks further about the foundations of the earth. The rabbis list the various substances on which the world was built and find Job 26:7 the perfect summary: "He hangs the earth on nothingness."[101] This nothingness is not an independent power,

99. Allen, *Psalms 101–50*, p. 39.

100. Augustine, *Expositions of the Psalms*, p. 114.

101. William Braude, trans., *The Midrash on the Psalms*, vol. 2 (New Haven: Yale University Press, 1959), pp. 170-71.

yet a surd of the world's utter nonexistence remains within it in the ocean of violence and disorder. That God's arrival is linked to this threat is indicated by saying that "Yahweh comes on the clouds as chariots." The Hebrew refers to dark, foreboding clouds. The image implies that proximity to the real threat of impending doom and dissipation *(Anfechtung)* is the context of Yahweh's arrival. This anti-Baal polemic reclaims the awe and fear associated with the storm clouds of the bull-god's arrival for Yahweh, thus asserting that sublime weather is also within Yahweh's sphere of control. It is only those who cry out to his name in the face of the raw forces of nature and human rebellion that Yahweh answers, say the rabbis. "The Holy One, blessed be He, came on two clouds for the sake of Israel. On one cloud God came unto Egypt, as is said, *Behold, the Lord rideth upon a swift cloud, and cometh unto Egypt* (Is. 19:1). And on the other cloud God came unto Sinai, as it is said *Lo, I come unto thee in a thick cloud*" (Exod. 19:9).[102]

Paralleling the Hebrews 1:7 quotation of this verse as referring to angels, the midrash concludes that the end of the verse, "fire and flame your ministers," speaks of angels made of fire. However implausible this might seem to the modern mind, it nevertheless appears to have more substance than many modern interpretations. Leslie Allen provides us with a typical example of the curious noninterpretation of modern biblical scholarship in his comment on this verse: "The descriptions of theophany are derived from Baal imagery and were doubtless used for polemical purposes originally." Despite his general sympathy with the New Testament, he takes the interpretation of the writer of Hebrews, and implicitly the midrash at this point, as "grammatically possible, but contextually improbable."[103] By "grammatically possible" he means that מַלְאָכָיו *(mal'akaw)* can be translated "his angels" or "his messengers," a concession that fatally undermines his intention to avoid interpreting this passage.

If our reading of verses 1-2a is correct, then, the whole psalm is about God's messengers in the processes of his revelation of his glory. It is a psalm about the medium of God's self-revelation, developing a breadth of appreciation of the ways that God is present with the world. It is a psalm about God *making* messengers. The verb for "making" is the same as the "and God made" of Genesis 1:31 and 2:2, both of which emphasize a fashioning activity, a constructing. Hebrews 1:7 describes the Father speaking these words of the Son's making of servants. We might thus conclude that this is a psalm about the medium, Christ, through whom Yahweh "fash-

---

102. Braude, *Midrash on the Psalms*, p. 170.
103. Allen, *Psalms 101–50*, p. 45.

ions [again the same verb] his servant according to his steadfast love" (Ps. 119:124).[104]

These connections shed new light on the meaning of "he makes winds his messengers, flaming fires his servants." Studying the Hebrew has given us more detail about what role fire serves: it becomes a servant in the sense of a royal minister. This is a designation that is applied to all who serve the king in the previous psalm (103:21): "Bless the LORD, all his hosts, his ministers that do his will." Along with fire comes the wind, also deputized by God as a messenger. The Hebrew for wind here is the multivalent רוּחַ *(ruach)*, its second appearance in this psalm. Thus we might paraphrase verse 4 this way: "Flames *are* his envoys and flames are *on* his envoys as Yahweh arrives on the wings of *ruach,* the wind that is spirit."

This intertwining of God's appearance with wind and fire was clearly an influence on Luke the evangelist. The Pentecost account of Acts 2:1-4 takes up all the aspects of Psalm 104's divine theophany, "clearly derived from Baal imagery."[105] The wind is loud and violent (resembling a storm wind) and accompanied by fire. The messengers of flame and fire are interpreted by Luke, not as angels, but as fire carried along with the divine presence like the pillar of fire in the wilderness. Similarly, the wind that is called God's messenger in Psalm 104 is here called the *pneumatos,* the Holy Spirit, but again using a Greek word that does not sharply distinguish the Spirit from rushing wind. That Luke dares to make such interpretive decisions about the meaning of the Old Testament theophany manifestations is interesting and important, but it is not our main focus here. Of greatest interest for our purposes is how this pairing is understood to cause those on whom the Spirit falls to speak in other tongues. What is the meaning of Luke's combining the Old Testament description of the divine appearance with this utterance in foreign languages? And why here in the narrative of the early church?

At Pentecost, the immediacy of the Holy Spirit causes words of praise and proclamation to spring to human lips.[106] Like the light that God created

---

104. Most English versions translate עֲשֵׂה as "deal with," but perhaps a more literal translation (such as Young's Literal Translation) better catches the aspect of God's servants always being his creations: "Do with Thy servant according to Thy kindness."

105. "When the day of Pentecost had come, they were all together in one place. And suddenly from heaven there came a sound like the rush of a violent wind, and it filled the entire house where they were sitting. Divided tongues, as of fire, appeared among them, and a tongue rested on each of them. All of them were filled with the Holy Spirit and began to speak in other languages, as the Spirit gave them ability."

106. Luther, "How Christians Should Regard Moses," in *Luther's Works, Vol. 35: Word and Sacrament I,* ed. and trans. E. Theodore Bachmann (Philadelphia: Fortress, 1960), p. 163.

and that gives the world time to be with him, language is the condition for human communication and thus communion. Given the central role played in the Old Testament by the covenant, ratified by the blessing that heads this psalm, this structural and structuring function of language is revealed as one of the most important of the divine gifts. For this reason the Old Testament's prohibitions against lying, false oaths, and the false use of God's name are prominently placed and regularly elaborated.[107] The authors of Genesis soon unpack the implications of the Fall by way of the Babel narrative in which the tragic loss of the communal fabric sustained by language is recounted. Human self-exaltation inexorably calls down the divine punishment of language confusion and thus political fragmentation.[108]

The Bible's interest in lying is not in the question of the margins, "Is it appropriate to lie?"[109] Rather, it investigates the question of what it means to value language: What does it mean to use language to praise God in and for the gift of language? Such a formulation demands the development of a sensitivity to language as a locus of social trust and receptivity through which faith aims to praise at all times, for instance, by speaking less often and with more thoughtfulness. Such a position allows that an "untruth" may in fact be a thoughtful and faithful use of language to love others in the way that — and at the time that — God loves them (cf. Exod. 1:15-21; Joshua 2:1-7).[110] This

107. The protection of language is prominent in both tables of the Decalogue (Exod. 20:7, 16): the violators of language are regularly excoriated in the Psalms (cf. Ps. 120; 10:7), and in the prophetic literature the eschatological people are pictured as having no lies in their mouths (Is. 53:9; Zeph. 3:13). The latter metaphor carries straight into the New Testament (Rev. 14:5). See Murray, *Principles of Conduct,* ch. VI: "The Sanctity of Truth."

108. Augustine comments on Ps. 137:6 ("Let my tongue cling to the roof of my mouth, if I do not remember you, if I do not set Jerusalem above my highest joy"): "May I be struck dumb, he means, if I do not keep you in mind, for what is the point of speaking, what is the point of singing, if one does not sing Zion's songs? The song of Jerusalem is our own language. The song that tells of love for this world is a foreign tongue, a barbaric language we have picked up in our captivity. Anyone who has forgotten Jerusalem will therefore be dumb before God." Augustine, "Exposition of Psalm 136," in *Expositions of the Psalms: 121–150,* ed. Boniface Ramsey, trans. Maria Boulding (New York: New City Press, 2004), p. 236.

109. The typical modern formulation of the question is evident in Immanuel Kant, "On a Supposed Right to Lie from Philanthropy," in *Practical Philosophy,* trans. and ed. Mary Gregor (Cambridge, UK: Cambridge University Press, 1999). Kant's reason for designating a lie as wrong is that it renders social contract and thus law impossible. He thus ties the concept of lying to the concept of logical truth: any evasions of the complete truth would destroy the rational principle of honesty.

110. The theological tradition has often wrestled with such passages, and has striven to mitigate the seriousness of charitable falsehood. Thomas Aquinas's discussion of lying also begins with the question of whether lying is permissible, but concludes that various sorts of lies

would not be a defense of lying on principle, but an explanation of why Christian ethics aims first to allow people to continue in God's story rather than simply to defend moral concepts or principles.[111] This means that the fundamental definition of a lie is a denial of God as he has shown himself in the world, in Jesus Christ, the man for others.[112]

Modern humanity's aversion to physical pain obscures Scripture's more direct interest in the Fall of humans as speaking and thus political animals. Given the Bible's weighty imprecations against lying and false oaths, we do well to reconsider our modern sense that the confusion of languages is less of a burden than the other punishments of the Fall. Psalm 63 sets up a basic division in humanity between those who invoke God's name and the lies of speakers who sow confusion and chaos, making the world a desert (Ps. 63:1). As previously noted, the sin of Babel is not simply building the tower, but the attempt to use God's name to legitimate human plans and co-opt the blessings God designated for sharing. The power of language, instead of serving communal life, is teamed with human technological knowledge not to continue life with God but to overcome him to possess and control his gifts. This contrasts with the building activities of Noah, in which the latter built a massive structure to follow God, and at his instruction. The Babelites' punishment is political disunity, which the always-practical Luther, referring to contemporary experience, illustrates well: "I myself do not understand an Italian nor does an Italian understand me; and so there exists a natural opportunity for enmity between us." In short, "as a result of this division of languages hearts were disunited, customs changed, and dispositions and endeavors altered. Consequently, you can truthfully call it the seedbed of all evils, since it has caused political as well as economic confusion."[113] The political and social strife that result from communication barriers are some of the concrete aspects of the waters of chaos on which God lays the foundation of his high home.

This foundation is a trinitarian one, by the Father, through the Son and

---

can proceed from love and thus are not mortal sins. Aquinas, *Summa Theologica* II.II, q. CX. But it is not until after the Reformation that arguments are made for why one *should* lie out of solidarity with God's love; cf. Bonhoeffer, *Ethics*, pp. 279-80.

111. See discussion in ch. 5, pp. 89-93.

112. Cf. Stanley Hauerwas, *Performing the Faith: Bonhoeffer and the Practice of Nonviolence* (Grand Rapids: Baker, 2004), ch. 2, "Bonhoeffer on Truth and Politics."

113. Luther, *Luther's Works, Vol. 2, Lectures on Genesis, Chapters 6–14*, ed. Jaroslav Pelikan (St. Louis: Concordia, 1960), p. 215. This point is also central for Augustine: "So true is this that a man would more readily hold a conversation with his dog than with another man who is a foreigner." Augustine, *City of God*, XIX.7.

Spirit. The Holy Spirit speaks into the heart of the punishment of Babel (Babylon), not, surprisingly, to restore the original unity of language but to create a new unity within and beyond the diversity of language.[114] Luther's comment is worth quoting at length.

> Therefore it is a great blessing and an outstanding miracle of the New Testament that by means of various languages the Holy Spirit on the day of Pentecost brought men of all nations into one body of the one Head, Christ. Christ joins and unites all into one faith through the Gospel, even though the different languages remain; and He tears down the wall (Eph 2:4), not only by reconciling us to God through His death and speaking to us in a new language but also by bringing about outward harmony, so that different flocks are brought together under one Shepherd and are gathered into one fold (John 10:16). This is Christ's blessing; and since it is common to all, differences in life give no offence. Let us, therefore, give Him the credit that through the Holy Spirit He has removed this most severe punishment, which was the beginning and seedbed of all evils and discords, and has brought us a holy harmony, even though the different languages remain. For where Christ the Mediator is not acknowledged, there is a disagreement of hearts like that of the languages, and there is a horrible blindness.[115]

Luther's claim is that, in the song of praise of Christ, different languages meet in the unity of hearts. Without this unity, diversity of languages engenders diversity in aims, and thus "renders welcome service to Satan, the instigator of wars and of discord."[116] God does not allow social unity that coalesces around self-exaltation to become the rule, but intervenes by confusing languages.[117]

But language, in the form of God's word, is also the way God has provided back into peace with himself and the neighbor. Already in our discussion of Psalm 130, we have seen the centrality of the divine word in the Psalms. In Acts 2, calling *on* the name of the Lord (2:21) is at the same time a calling of all *to* the Lord ("repent and be baptized," 2:38). This is the proper activity of the *epikaloumenoi*, the "ones-who-call-themselves-by-the-name-

---

114. "Leibniz grappled all his life with the idea of a universal script consisting, not of words, but of self-evident signs representing every possible idea. It was an expression of his wish to heal the world, which was then so torn to pieces, a philosophical reflection on the Pentecost story." Dietrich Bonhoeffer, *Letters and Papers from Prison* [enlarged ed.], ed. Eberhard Bethge (London: SCM Press, 1971), p. 53.

115. Luther, *Luther's Works*, vol. 2, p. 215.

116. Luther, *Luther's Works*, vol. 2, p. 216.

117. Luther, *Luther's Works*, vol. 2, p. 225.

of," as "ones-who-invoke-the-name." Augustine connects God's redemptive work through his Word with the verbal meditation of singing and preaching: "When you hear it said, 'Fire is God's servant,' do you think it is going to burn you? Well yes, it will, but all it will burn up is the chaff in you. God's servant burns up all your carnal desires by preaching his word."[118]

We can now again inquire into the *Leitmotiv* of this book: foreignness. Foreignness is, ultimately, the political, epistemic, and practical alienation of a world trying to save itself. The experience of political foreignness is, therefore, the artifact of the poisoning of human sociality by the power of human self-interest, which exploits geographical, linguistic, racial, and national differences. Only the Spirit truly can overcome these differences to release humans from the spiral of suspicion and the struggle for advantage. This is the political power of praise. We participate in many penultimate communities within which we share a modicum of mutual interest and advantage; yet these always contain the seeds of their own destruction. Human community is possible only when its unity is outside itself, in the confrontation of our ineradicable urge to make our own way and define our own truth.

Ultimately, this is the ground and content of Luther's and Augustine's "chattering" about Christ as commentary on the psalms. They seek to be inflamed with the divine power that is gathered at the place where God places his name. At this place a unity is created amidst the metropolitan stew of languages that represent the whole world and the centrifugal forces of social destruction embodied in the variety of their languages. But in Christ this destructive force is displaced by a movement toward a newly received center.[119] Language as barrier becomes language as the diversity of created praise. A community is born of those who seek to join with one another, not for the usual reasons of economic or political advantage, but united in mutual appreciation of their Creator and Redeemer. This is the *logic of external constitution,* which both Augustine and Luther explicated in their own ways. And both are attracted to the psalms as a place where the one diverse community of Christ's body expresses in song, and thus finds, its true unity.

The psalms are divine words given to facilitate our finding our place in the divine-human economy. The foreignness of Scripture is thus a marker of our alienation from the social existence it indicates. The divine gift is the realization that I am part of a "communion," not an "assembly": communion is

---

118. Augustine, *Expositions of the Psalms,* p. 126.

119. If I cannot speak Italian, says Luther, "if we both understand Christ, we mutually embrace and heartily kiss each other as fellow members." Luther, *Luther's Works,* vol. 2, pp. 215-16.

not just "assembled" but is an ongoing and often painful process of being ordered. In the communion of praise I am born in an action (singing) in which I seek to get into rhythm — to find my place in the harmony. Singing praise thus reveals the notes we are singing to the tune of other gods, whose liturgies create friction in the body of Christ. Such singing makes us the instruments of God.

We have agreed with the judgment of contemporary scholars that the Psalms are eviscerated when we examine either their form or their content, but not both together in their interrelationship. What we have added is the observation that this also fatally de-politicizes the Bible, in other words, represents an attempt by one political community to wrest the Bible away from a Christian community that has forgotten what it is for. In forcing the community of faith to rethink why it is possessed by Scripture, this political tussle has been of great value to the church. The church possesses the Bible only as it lives in it. By implication, in order to understand the unity of Augustine's and Luther's exegeses of the Psalms, we must join the praises they sing. The texts that inspired their praise must become ours. Finding our place in the harmony of creation's worship is a practical task, which means it must be practiced exegetically and politically.

The remainder of Psalm 104 provides a more detailed view of God's work of creating such a new community. We have come far enough to outline the relationship of what has already been said with what will be gleaned from the remainder of the psalm. The divine ordering that turns social chaos into the fruitful social harmony of the praising community is one that conforms to the subject under study: God's working, as mediated through a textual medium, in this case the Psalms. We run ourselves over, through, and into the Psalms in order to discover this rationality and to unite ourselves with the faith community that produced them. Thus, by developing a familiarity with the rationality that integrates the Psalms, we should be given a sense of the *ratio* of the journey from the order against God into the order of properly integrated differences.

Praising God's Subduing, Separating, and Feeding

104:5 יָסַד־אֶרֶץ עַל־מְכוֹנֶיהָ בַּל־תִּמּוֹט עוֹלָם וָעֶד:

6 תְּהוֹם כַּלְּבוּשׁ כִּסִּיתוֹ עַל־הָרִים יַעַמְדוּ־מָיִם:

7 מִן־גַּעֲרָתְךָ יְנוּסוּן מִן־קוֹל רַעַמְךָ יֵחָפֵזוּן:

8 יַעֲלוּ הָרִים יֵרְדוּ בְקָעוֹת אֶל־מְקוֹם זֶה יָסַדְתָּ לָהֶם:

9 גְּבוּל־שַׂמְתָּ בַּל־יַעֲבֹרוּן בַּל־יְשׁוּבוּן לְכַסּוֹת הָאָרֶץ:

329

104:5 You set the earth on its foundations,
    so that it shall never be shaken.

6   You cover it with the deep as with a garment;
    the waters stood above the mountains.

7   At your rebuke they flee;
    at the sound of your thunder they take to flight.

8   They rose up to the mountains, ran down to the valleys
    to the place that you appointed for them.

9   You set a boundary that they may not pass,
    so that they might not again cover the earth.

Contemporary exegesis has made remarkably little of what we are meant to be praising with these verses.[120] Clearly, it is wonderful that God has given the universe a lawlike nature. But this lawlike feature of creation is visible to the psalmists primarily in contrast with the threat of chaos against personal, political, and religious life. Israel knows this chaos intimately, being regularly threatened by it from within and without. What is astounding about this psalm's meditation on chaos is its refusal to cringe helplessly before it, or to speculate on its origins.[121] It is able to retain its hope through its praise not of the lawlike nature of creation but of the God who has invested and is investing himself in its order. The Psalms continually depict Yahweh overcoming the sea, Leviathan and Rahab, making them into food for his people (cf. Ps. 74:11-19). Yahweh "rules the sea" and thus "establishes righteousness and justice" (Ps. 89:9-15; 124). Ruling the roaring waves of the sea is "silencing the tumult of the peoples" (Ps. 65:5-8). God's voice is louder than this rebellious tumult (Ps. 93:3-4) and thus establishes a sphere free from it, a sphere of peace and justice, the holy hill — Zion (Ps. 24:1-3).[122] The manifest reference of these verses to the Genesis 1 separation of dry land from water also refers to God's rescue of Israel out of the nations and through the water — in short, an exodus (Ps. 77:15-20). Though the nations rage and foam (Ps. 2), God canalizes them by molding hearts (Ps. 33:6-7, 15). Creation quakes before God's voice, through which an order is created of those who hate evil (Ps. 97:3-5, 10-13).

---

120. The typical approach to the passage is to note that this is a standard Middle Eastern image of the *Chaoskampf*, the divine war against chaos. The suggestion is that Israel turned what was originally a song of praise for protection against natural forces into a hymn of praise for Yahweh's overcoming of all chaos. Such discussions of origins and the development of the concept are helpful but do not tell us how the passage functions as a prayer today. Cf. Allen, *Psalms 101–50*, pp. 45-46; also Kraus, *Psalms 60–150*, p. 300.

121. Brueggemann, *Old Testament Theology*, p. 164.

122. Cf. Tate, *Psalms 51–100*, pp. 142-43.

These metaphors of God's work of separation have the effect of re-calling Israel to its practices of worship. Commenting on Leviticus, Jacob Milgrom encapsulates the Torah's logic:

> Israel's separation from the nations is the continuation (and climax) of the cosmic creation *process*. Just as YHWH has separated the mineral, vegetable and animal species to create order in the natural world, so Israel must sepa-rate from the nations to create order in the human world. Israel is thus charged with a universal goal. . . . When [the redactor] H demands that Is-rael separate from the nations, it has in mind that Israel's *imitatio Dei* will generate a universal *imitatio Israel*.[123]

Israel's songbook shapes it to wonder at God's work and urges it to renew its attention to Scripture (Ps. 105:1-2, 45). As Israel takes this form, it calls the world to imitate God.

Given these intertwining levels of meaning, it seems unwise to claim that these verses are "about" either God's creative or redemptive works. They are about God and his working simultaneously to raise up mountains and limit the sea.[124] Such activity is at once about the blessings of God making a safe space for humans and animals to live, and about creating the real social peace that is equally necessary for human and animal life.

It will come as no surprise that the Psalms link this process of bounding the world's chaos and making it fruitful with the work of the future David. One of Israel's prehistoric, seminal, and guiding texts already directs its atten-tion in this direction, recounting how Yahweh overcame and limited chaos, but also observing that this is just the outer surface of God's ways, a whisper of his true being. "But the thunder of his power, who can understand?" Job asks (Job 26:6-14). The Psalms respond: "Then you spoke in a vision to your faithful one, and said: 'I have set the crown on one who is mighty, I have ex-alted one chosen from the people. . . . I will set his hand on the sea and his right hand on the rivers'" (Ps. 89:19-20, 25). Yahweh's defeat of the sea and its monsters (Ps. 89:8-11) is attributed to the eternal David, and it is David's chil-dren among the nations who must obey Yahweh's precepts (Ps. 89:27, 30-33). In light of these connections, it no longer seems so fanciful for Augustine to gloss the "foundations of the world" (Ps. 104:5) with 1 Corinthians 3:11: "For no one can lay any foundation other than the one that has been laid; that

---

123. Jacob Milgrom, *Leviticus 17–22: A New Translation with Introduction and Commen-tary* (New York: Doubleday, 2000), pp. 1371-72.

124. A point obscured in many common English translations, such as that of the NIV: "[T]he waters . . . flowed over the mountains" (Ps. 104:8).

foundation is Jesus Christ." This is not a tropological or extravagant reading into the text, but a sober reflection on the text and a Christian affirmation that "in the beginning was the Word, and the Word was God" (John 1:1).

The Gospel writers made the same inference. Jesus walks on the waters to save his children, responding to their cry and stilling their inner storms and the outer violence against them (Matt. 14:22-33 and par.). As Creator, Christ has his lordship take effect within the chaos of created social existence. The disciples' awe at Jesus' work and their worship of him are the calming of a raging humanity that is fearful of and angry at God, from which they occasionally lapse — individually and collectively — into the ethos of fear and rebellion. Calming them involves stilling their inner storms; the virtues of faith can only increase when the waters of temptation recede. These inner storms, says Luther, consist in "cravings and impulses of the flesh and the old man. . . . For these a limit has been set, so that they can touch and beat against, but cannot submerge."[125] The ascent of faith and descent of the flesh's unruliness happen simultaneously. Sea and hearts are both stilled at the same time, and for the same purpose, by Christ's presence, which replaces fear, doubt, and selfishness with this response: "Truly, you are the Son of God" (Matt. 14:33). Jesus Christ thus creates a sphere of justice and peace by imparting his grammar, "bounding" his children's "waters" (Job 38:8, 10, 11).

This suggests that the "virtue ethics" of the Psalms consists of a renewal through praise and the practice of meditation on the divine word. In this "virtue ethics," it is not human practices or concepts that are the source of moral transformation; rather, it is God's Spirit that generates new practices and concepts and thus new life through engaging us in praise. Such praise is not concerned with the development of a new "self," because its interest is in God. Faith is separated from its self-obsession, and the image of creation through separation recapitulates the reclamation described in Psalm 130's "I cry out." The crying out of Psalm 130 is the human side of the experience of being submerged, losing ourselves, only to be re-created by being torn in two, as Jesus' word to the demoniac re-creates him by speaking into existence a self that he cannot know on his own.[126] Again, this must be said at a corporate level: the church is submerged in persecution, and it must come out of the raging of the nations and out of its raging with the nations. God no longer floods all of creation in punishment (Gen. 8:5), but continually judges, separates, and dries up its rebellion and fear. In all this the body follows its head,

---

125. Luther, "Psalm One Hundred Four," p. 325.

126. Francis Watson, *Text, Church and World: Biblical Interpretation in Theological Perspective* (Grand Rapids: Eerdmans, 1994), pp. 247-55.

who submerged himself in humiliation and suffering before being raised up. The magnification of Yahweh in Psalm 104:1, therefore, "expounds the whole Psalm, namely, that it speaks of Christ's magnification."[127]

In a fallen world, tumult remains at the boundaries of God's reign of peace, but a real dry land has been established. This may be described, corporately, as the community of Israel (or Zion), or individually (as Augustine does), as the apostles whose lowliness is the preaching of peace.[128] God's Word rebukes the sea in two forms: as the eternal Word and through the preaching of his body, angering the nations (Ps. 2; 76:5; Hab. 3:10). The nations find odious the disparagement of the political diagnoses and the solutions to which they subscribe, and in which God's involvement plays no part. The nations are enraged when some slip from under their heavy yoke of ideology, which seeks to suppress the legitimate cultural, political, and conceptual pluriformity of the body of Christ.[129] Yet the Son has appeared and dries the moisture of the sea from the newly separated, evaporating the residue of enslavement to visions of the world in which human power is all we have.[130]

104:10 הַמְשַׁלֵּחַ מַעְיָנִים בַּנְּחָלִים בֵּין הָרִים יְהַלֵּכוּן׃

11 יַשְׁקוּ כָּל־חַיְתוֹ שָׂדָי יִשְׁבְּרוּ פְרָאִים צְמָאָם׃

12 עֲלֵיהֶם עוֹף־הַשָּׁמַיִם יִשְׁכּוֹן מִבֵּין עֳפָאיִם יִתְּנוּ־קוֹל׃

13 מַשְׁקֶה הָרִים מֵעֲלִיּוֹתָיו מִפְּרִי מַעֲשֶׂיךָ תִּשְׂבַּע הָאָרֶץ׃

104:10   You make springs gush forth in the valleys;
      they flow between the hills,

11   giving drink to every wild animal;
      the wild asses quench their thirst.

12   By the streams the birds of the air have their habitation;
      they sing among the branches.

13   From your lofty abode you water the mountains;
      the earth is satisfied with the fruit of your work.

127. Luther, "Psalm One Hundred Four," p. 326.

128. Augustine, *Expositions of the Psalms*, pp. 140-41.

129. Ideologies always reject diagnoses and solutions from outside their purview, developing strategies to silence them. Spotting these strategies is thus an important diagnostic activity in locating resistances to the gospel. See David Coyzis, *Political Visions and Illusions: A Survey and Critique of Contemporary Ideologies* (Downers Grove: InterVarsity Press, 2003), chs. 1, 7; and William Cavanaugh, *The Theopolitical Imagination: Discovering the Liturgy as a Political Act in an Age of Global Consumerism* (London: T&T Clark, 2002), ch. 1.

130. Luther, "Psalm One Hundred Four," p. 324.

Having praised God's subduing of chaos, the psalmist turns to praise the reclamation of creation as a river sustaining all creation.[131] Calvin reads this section as referring to God's creative work, emphasizing that the psalmist aims to enhance our awareness of God's caring for "brute creation."[132] More recent interpreters have noted that this way of speaking of God's creative work moves away from the "dominion model" of Genesis, to conceive of the cosmos on an "integration model." This latter model "positively assesses all of life as interdependent partners living off the earth. The planet constitutes nothing less than the hospitable household of life, the locus of God's blessing that accommodates life in all its various forms."[133] This is grounds enough to begin to think anew about the supposed anti-ecological anthropocentrism of the Bible (and the Genesis account). In this psalm the magnificent trees are literally for the birds, and the mountains are for the goats and coneys. As a meditation on God's creative work, this psalm "revels in the poetry of provision."[134]

However, there is a danger in this reading: if we do not read this psalm as about new creation, then we will almost inevitably read it as an example of some kind of "creation spirituality" in which humans bear the ultimate responsibility for maintaining creation's order.[135] This yields a reading of Psalm 104 as an ecological psalm in which the sinners of verse 35 are interpreted solely as "ruiners of the earth's order and species."[136] Creation undoubtedly groans under human mismanagement, but without framing our ecological behavior as participation in God's care of creation, we divinize creation. Or we can transform this psalm into a moralistic tract rather than a song of praise.[137] If we lose sight of the primacy of the Creator's work, it becomes impossible clearly to articulate the sin that drives the soiling of the environment and the ideologies on which it is founded — of infinite growth, promethean dreams of total control, and so forth.

If the psalmist's intent is to indicate that God cares for humans as crea-

---

131. See Sigmund Mowinckel, *The Psalms in Israel's Worship*, vol. I (Oxford: Oxford University Press, 1962), p. 87.

132. Calvin, "Psalm CIV," p. 153.

133. Brown, *Seeing the Psalms*, p. 160.

134. Brown, *Seeing the Psalms*, p. 160.

135. For one typical example, see J. David Pleins, *The Psalms: Songs of Tragedy, Hope and Justice* (Maryknoll, NY: Orbis, 1993), pp. 86-87.

136. Eaton, *The Psalms*, p. 364.

137. Brueggemann tries to split the difference by implying that this is a case of mixed genre: Psalm 104 is a song of praise that ends with a "somber ethical notice." Brueggemann, *Old Testament Theology*, p. 156.

tures in the same way as he does the rest of creation, then we should not be surprised that there is also a resonance of God's redemptive work in these "creation" verses. Verse 13 provides one such reference: "From your lofty abode you water the mountains; the earth is satisfied with the fruit of your work." In addition to the prominent reference to God's "stretching his tent" (vv. 2-3) in the heavens earlier in the psalm, God's "upper chamber" or "lofty abode" is the place from which he is said to rule the peoples in Psalm 103:19. Only because God tends it does this garden exist and bear fruit.[138] These few verses celebrate the drama of God's overcoming chaos to establish creation (cf. Ps. 74:12-15); he divides the sea and gives leviathan as food to those in the desert. The overtones of the exodus are obvious: the sea is divided, subjugation is turned into food for those in the desert, and thus the "creation" imagery rings with simultaneous political and redemptive overtones. God's enemies, human or otherwise, are being judged and pruned, converted into ordered social ecosystems by God.[139]

And so the enigmatic mention of wild asses suddenly makes more sense: the wild asses of the Middle East are famous for finding water in the desert (Job 24:5). Verse 11 presents us with the image of a beast coming in from the desert to an oasis, where birds sing in the trees, grass grows for cattle, and bread and wine cheer and sustain humans. We can imagine the wonder of discovery and the secret discomfort with the new world that is portrayed here. Again, the psalm reminds us of the progression portrayed in Psalm 130. Here an outsider is drawn in from the desert of self-feeding into an unfamiliar political order of bounty, where the last are first, and all are fed and re-created by God's Spirit (Psalm 68:6-10).

Psalm 65 presents a close parallel to these verses. It begins by saying that all flesh comes to Yahweh on account of their sins, and blesses all those Yahweh chooses to dwell in his courts. These praisers confess that it is through great deeds that Yahweh orders the natural and social worlds, and that the creation thus made survives only because Yahweh visits and waters the earth so that it brings forth appropriate fruit. The "saving food" of Psalm 103:17-18 is the covenant and the precepts. God takes up created material, writes on it with his finger, and it becomes the life source of his people. The metaphorical complex emphasizes finding water where it is given, in Scripture and from the hand of God. God gathers up creation to make a place for us, reshaping and delivering it back to us for our sustenance. It takes his speaking for us to discover this.

138. Thus Luther links this verse to 1 Cor. 3:9 and John 15:1.
139. Brown, *Seeing the Psalms*, p. 144.

Up to this point, it has not become clear how we are to understand the meaning of images such as that of the birds building nests in the trees. These are metaphors that presage a transition from direct exegesis to ethical interpretation. These verses do not *demand* specific ethical claims, but their form does *provoke* them. The passage clearly communicates that there is a proper place in God's ordering for a legitimate diversity of inhabitants. The text asks us to reflect on what it means to inhabit the ecology of social life that God creates through his word. The Christian interpretative tradition has almost unanimously concluded that "[b]easts aptly denote the nations which were wild and not tamed for God but roamed about on byways of error and idolatry."[140] The ordering of these beasts is God's co-option of them to make them conduits of his love, nourished on and dispensing heavenly water as apostles and teachers.[141]

Unsurprisingly, Augustine understands the metaphor of the birds singing in the trees as a poetic comment on the place of meditation on the testimonies of Scripture, "for they dwell in the mountains" — for example, they discuss and talk about the Spirit that flows amid the apostles.[142] If the birds are preachers, says Luther, then we can infer six implications of the imagery: (1) they "dwell," their meditation on Scripture is steady and practiced; (2) preachers are "over them," to be elevated in life and practice; (3) they are to preach "from the midst of the mountains," drawing out the inner meaning of the prophets; (4) that the birds "sing" means that preachers should not long for wealth but freely give their voice; (5) speaking boldly, flattering no one; and finally, (6) not always singing one song but saying different things in attentiveness to the audience.[143] If, as modern scholars suggest, these verses refer to the Levitical singers, we can draw similar conclusions about the work of the whole community of faith.

This oasis of peace manifests an order utterly unlike the order of the desert or the raging sea from which the people of God have been drawn. We need not fear this political order as authoritarian or denuding, though it may look like that through the demonic spectacles that make life in the desert seem just. There is an equality here, but not the mathematical equality of modernity. Because moderns have elevated the concept of equality to the supreme moral concept (as exemplified by Cosgrove's enshrining it as the only axiom of Christian ethics; cf. ch. 1), some use of the language is an inevitable

140. Luther, "Psalm One Hundred Four," p. 329.
141. Cf. Luther's discussion of Ps. 1:3 in ch. 7, pp. 187-88.
142. Augustine, *Expositions of the Psalms*, p. 146.
143. Luther, "Psalm One Hundred Four," pp. 330-31.

part of the attempt to conjure political agreement within secular liberalism.[144] If we want to engage in talk about the proper ordering of society, this will depend on a clear view of what we mean by social order, affording critical purchase on questions we commonly submit to the language of equality. The psalmist suggests that political agreement begins in praise that the earth is watered from God's high home, his temple, and that he alone provides the potable rain that refreshes his people (Ps. 68:7-9).

The whole order and beauty of the people of God is the result of its members allowing the water of the Spirit to do its work so that each may thrive in her own way. The order God creates is of a creation, both human and material, that reflects and conforms solely to the divine working in being reconciled to it. The earth is satisfied by the fruit of God's work. Any creature thus satisfied becomes a spring that rests between the forefathers and foremothers of faith.[145]

Being Subdued, Separated and Fed through Praise

מַצְמִיחַ חָצִיר לַבְּהֵמָה וְעֵשֶׂב לַעֲבֹדַת הָאָדָם לְהוֹצִיא לֶחֶם מִן־הָאָרֶץ: 104:14

וְיַיִן יְשַׂמַּח לְבַב־אֱנוֹשׁ לְהַצְהִיל פָּנִים מִשָּׁמֶן וְלֶחֶם לְבַב־אֱנוֹשׁ יִסְעָד: 15

יִשְׂבְּעוּ עֲצֵי יְהוָה אַרְזֵי לְבָנוֹן אֲשֶׁר נָטָע: 16

אֲשֶׁר־שָׁם צִפֳּרִים יְקַנֵּנוּ חֲסִידָה בְּרוֹשִׁים בֵּיתָהּ: 17

הָרִים הַגְּבֹהִים לַיְּעֵלִים סְלָעִים מַחְסֶה לַשְׁפַנִּים: 18

עָשָׂה יָרֵחַ לְמוֹעֲדִים שֶׁמֶשׁ יָדַע מְבוֹאוֹ: 19

תָּשֶׁת־חֹשֶׁךְ וִיהִי לָיְלָה בּוֹ־תִרְמֹשׂ כָּל־חַיְתוֹ־יָעַר: 20

הַכְּפִירִים שֹׁאֲגִים לַטָּרֶף וּלְבַקֵּשׁ מֵאֵל אָכְלָם: 21

תִּזְרַח הַשֶּׁמֶשׁ יֵאָסֵפוּן וְאֶל־מְעוֹנֹתָם יִרְבָּצוּן: 22

יֵצֵא אָדָם לְפָעֳלוֹ וְלַעֲבֹדָתוֹ עֲדֵי־עָרֶב: 23

104:14 You cause the grass to grow for the cattle,
    and plants for people to use,
    to bring forth food from the earth,

15   and wine to gladden the human heart,
    oil to make the face shine,
    and bread to strengthen the human heart.

---

144. Cf. Oliver O'Donovan, *The Ways of Judgment* (Grand Rapids: Eerdmans, 2005), pp. 33-34.

145. Since, even in his first lectures on the Psalms, many of Luther's reformation emphases are visible, it is remarkable and indicative of his catholicity that he can still name these giants of the faith the "many popes" that all the church must pass through. Luther, "Psalm One Hundred Four," p. 328.

16   The trees of the LORD are watered abundantly,
      the cedars of Lebanon that he planted.

17   In them the birds build their nests;
      the stork has its home in the fir trees.

18   The high mountains are for the wild goats;
      the rocks are a refuge for the coneys.

19   You have made the moon to mark the seasons;
      the sun knows its time for setting.

20   You make darkness, and it is night,
      when all the animals of the forest come creeping out.

21   The young lions roar for their prey,
      seeking their food from God.

22   When the sun rises,
      they withdraw and lie down in their dens.

23   People go out to their work
      and to their labor until the evening.

In their sweeping interest in the patterns of created life, these verses traverse a range of relationships of obvious ethical relevance. Here God's involvement in the dynamics of the creaturely world is paralleled and intertwined with his involvement in the human world. It is not until verses 24 and following that humans and animals are spoken of as a single group sustained by God; but that conclusion is foreshadowed by their close proximity throughout. It is difficult to overstate the radical nature of this unification of human and animal in its ancient context, a unification possible only within the thoroughgoing monotheism we have seen throughout the psalm.[146]

The section opens with wonder at God's provision of the plants that sustain animals and humans. The psalmist praises the divine provision of food for humans and the way that this food shapes human life by requiring labor to appropriate it (vv. 14, 23). Augustine sets this labor of cultivation in a liturgical context by saying that grass brings forth grain, grain bread, and bread the Eucharist. In so doing he notes the intertwining of the creaturely and the spiritual work, and God's Word uniting them: "Christ is the bread who descended from heaven [v. 13; John 6:33, 41] to be drawn from the earth when he is proclaimed through the flesh of his servants."[147] Ministers are to labor to bring this heavenly bread from Scripture and to feed the people, giving them strength to rejoice in God and have mercy on their neighbor as did

146. Lewis, *Reflections on the Psalms*, pp. 84-85.
147. Augustine, *Expositions of the Psalms*, p. 154.

the Good Samaritan (Luke 10:34).[148] Yet verse 14, with its "plants for people to use," reminds us that this text is not to be spiritualized. Literal, creaturely grass is created to supply food for all; the wicked are those who block its distribution, and the righteous are those who point to and protect its availability to all.

Augustine's focus on spiritual feeding prepares us for the reference in the next verse to wine. The pastoral task is to cultivate the spiritual hunger for the heavenly bread and wine (John 5:51; 14:6) in the physical hunger and thirst. But, unlike with physical food, we cannot overindulge this spiritual cup; we need not say, "Let no man be drunk" (Eph. 5:18). Instead, he says, we are invited to be drunk with the Lord's Spirit (Ps. 23:5), with faces shining with grace and good works.[149]

At the creaturely level, Augustine notes that the psalmist is clearly praising the power of wine to ease inhibitions and produce conviviality. As the psalm has already recounted God's provision of water, the additional divine provision of wine teaches us of God's "superabundant liberality."[150] This divine liberality confronts stingy illiberality and abstemiousness by warmly embracing enjoyment of what is human and bodily. The body is not simply a means to a heavenly end; it is also an end in itself. That we are bodily, and that this is a gift, makes a claim on all our living. It reminds us that we must not become killjoy workaholics, nor materialists, nor people obsessed with efficiency. Christians are not called to the functional wardrobe and the dutiful marriage bed, but to a playful[151] and heartfelt appreciation of embodiment.[152]

The seemingly abrupt shift of focus in verse 16 to the "cedars of Lebanon" will only present a problem for the interpreter who insists that this is a psalm solely about the order of creation.

There is ample evidence, however, that the psalmist is drawing on the many other references in which the "cedars of the Lord" denotes Israel (cf. Ps. 80:8-11). The Midrash Tehillim sees this as a reference to Israel's center in the temple, which had cedar paneling. This leads the rabbis to call the birds *(hasida)* that live in these trees the holy ones *(hasidim)*, the Levites, or ministers.[153] Throughout the Old Testament, great trees denote mighty and firm political structures that are upheld by the authorities God has established,

---

148. Luther, "Psalm One Hundred Four," pp. 334-35.
149. Augustine, *Expositions of the Psalms*, p. 155.
150. Calvin, "Psalm CIV," p. 155.
151. Barth, *Church Dogmatics*, III.4, pp. 553-54.
152. Bonhoeffer, *Ethics*, pp. 186-87.
153. Braude, *The Midrash on the Psalms*, pp. 172-73.

creating an ordered space for culture by attending to political stability (Dan. 4:20-22). The good king is a shelter and a refuge (Is. 32:1-2), shelter being defined by the concern for good acts of political service and not the accrual of political power.[154] Luther unpacks the idea by calling the "trees of the Lord" the "superiors, bishops, masters, men of the people, and those who are placed in office, as is clear in Judges 9:8ff."[155] In so doing, he grasps that the deep structure of this verse is an affirmation that it is God's work to create stable social structures, headed by leaders, thus making room for all people to live. This is not apart from the church, but anchored in it and its responsibility to make audible what that authority cannot know without it.[156] Faith expresses a certain wonder at political authorities, not for their own skills, but as features of the garden God tends. They are to be prayed for (1 Tim. 2:2) and constructively criticized, so that they may rule as cedars and not as thornbushes or parasites, which make no space for human flourishing.

The next two verses, 17 and 18, give us more detail about how the cedars and mountains make space for animals to flourish in them. At the creaturely level, the psalmist takes us further into God's care for all animals, both those that frequent the inaccessible and dangerous parts of creation and those to whom God has given timid dispositions and places to hide. "Wild goats" refers to the climbing goat (1 Sam. 24:3; Job 39:1), and the "coney" (similar to a marmot) hiding among the rocks tells us that this is a timid and harmless animal (Prov. 30:26).

Luther suggests that the nesting birds-storks pair parallels the coneys-goats pair.[157] If this is accurate, then we have here a description of the different roles in the one community of faith, where some are made "apostles, some prophets, some evangelists, some pastors and teachers, to equip the saints for the work of ministry, for building up the body of Christ, until all of us come to the unity of the faith and of the knowledge of the Son of God, to maturity, to the measure of the full stature of Christ" (Eph. 4:11-13). Within the singular care of God, there are different gifts and ecological niches; it is

---

154. See the comment above on Ps. 130:1-2; see also Bernd Wannenwetsch, "'Members of One Another': *Charis* Ministry and Representation: A Politico-Ecclesial Reading of Romans 12," in *A Royal Priesthood? The Use of the Bible Ethically and Politically: A Dialogue with Oliver O'Donovan,* ed. Craig Bartholomew, Jonathan Chaplin, Robert Song, and Al Wolters (Carlisle, UK: Paternoster Press, 2002), pp. 196-220.

155. Luther, "Psalm One Hundred Four," p. 335.

156. Karl Barth, "The Christian Community and the Civil Community," in *Community, State and Church: Three Essays by Karl Barth,* trans. Will Herberg (New York: Anchor Books, 1960), especially XIII-XXXV.

157. Luther, "Psalm One Hundred Four," p. 337.

the ministerial task of all, and the special task of some, to cultivate them. The kingdom has its centrifugal forces — its explorers, its stolid conservatives, and its timid youth in faith. These apparently opposing forces are held together in the praise of the one God. If animals, who cannot rationally acknowledge God's care in giving them their niches, do not attack those in other niches, how much more should God's own choir recognize the importance of its quite different but complementary ranges? In praise we each find ourselves at different points in this worship: some sing, some preach, some serve the Lord's Supper, and so on.

The proper unity of the community of praise is not homogeneity or equality but complementarity, a "sociality of harmonious difference."[158] This complementarity is so complex that it cannot be fully described. Nor, says John Milbank, need we think, "like the Nietzscheans, that difference, nontotalization and indeterminacy of meaning necessarily imply arbitrariness and violence."[159] We can no more fully describe the complementarity of Augustine's and Luther's singing than we can the praising of a tree and a frog. As the praise of the one God unites the disparate voices and modes of praise in the Psalms, so the many parts of the worship service and the many differentiated performers of that service find the proper harmony of worship's form and content as praise. They are united in exploring together the rationality of an unfamiliar political order: their common ethos is the life of ordered praise, an order modeled and discovered with Scripture. The fact that the church possesses a canon instead of a monolithic description of human life tells us something about the diversity, interrelatedness, and interpretive character of the Christian life and its irreducibly interpretive nature.[160]

Even Calvin's strictly naturalist interpretation of this psalm gives way before the phrase "you have made the moon to mark the seasons" (v. 19).[161] Here he agrees with the Midrash Tehillim, which says: "[T]he sun alone would have sufficed for the world's use. Why then did God make the moon? For fixing the time of the festal seasons."[162] In making this move, Calvin meets modern interpreters who, on textual and historical grounds, see this as a reference to the way the moon ordered sacred and festival time. Verse 19

---

158. John Milbank, *Theology and Social Theory: Beyond Secular Reason* (Oxford: Blackwell, 1990), p. 5.

159. Milbank, *Theology and Social Theory*, p. 5.

160. As discussed in ch. 4 (p. 55), it does not, however, demand a pluriformity of ethical *methodologies*, as Brevard Childs has suggested. Childs, *Biblical Theology of the Old and New Testaments: Theological Reflections on the Christian Bible* (Minneapolis: Fortress, 1993), pp. 678-79.

161. Calvin, "Psalm CIV," p. 161.

162. Braude, *The Midrash on the Psalms*, p. 173.

may thus be understood to emphasize how creation was made to support faith, the moon being an invitation to synchronize our time with the divine working. Such synchronization depends on our being taught that the moon is an address to us, as suggested by this verse. The festivals recalling God's creative and redemptive work perform the remembrance of the divine works to which the moon calls us. Singing and celebrating these works is thus an essential part of knowing what creation is. Faith is a form of attention to the miraculous nature of what is, which never would have been noticed otherwise. And as such it is the opposite of the modern, timeless, world-weariness portrayed in Sartre's *La Nausée,* where the main character, while looking at a tree, realizes to his horror the pure gratuitousness of things. Human self-construction renders matter frightening and monstrous, and its randomness mounts an all-embracing demand that we make some meaning out of it.

But for the psalmist, the moon is anything but frightening, a posture whose ethical implications we must now make explicit. We begin with a critical look at our present. What is the moon to us moderns? Does it simply reflect the sun's light? Is it a chunk of the earth randomly knocked off in the prehistoric maelstrom and now peacefully obeying the laws of gravity? Is it an essential component of a truly romantic evening? Is it part of the "destiny" of exploring nations to populate? Is it as-yet-unclaimed real estate or future raw material for low-gravity manufacture? Each of these questions points to the way the moon is incorporated into the ongoing self-definition of humanity. The moon and its light stand as a question to the speaking member of the cosmos, the same question that all creation repeats: What are you?

The moon, says Genesis 1 (vv. 3-5, 14-18), participates in the primal light that was God's first work of creation. The mention of the moon here is thus legitimately paired with its mention in verse 2: "You are wrapped in light as a garment." In praise, the moon is revealed as a representative of the day, which God separates from darkness on the first day of creation. That God calls light day is thus not an arbitrary naming, but it establishes daytime as a divine institution. Light orders space as time. All creatures participate in God's act of sharing part of his own activity, his light. This gift provides all creatures with the time within which their lives take place, whether they recognize the giver of this gift or not.

Having thus created time, God has it at his disposal. Here the meaning of light is inseparable from another strand of biblical thinking about light. Physical light, which establishes time, is given to *serve* the ministry of light, time in its essence being the space in which humans can "walk as children of light" (Eph. 5:8). Therefore, no creature really has created light or time for anything other than service to God. This does not mean that it will not be used against God; but it reveals what light and its mediators, the sun and moon, really are — invitations to divine service. Light is concrete and material; it is time and the bodies that deliver light, known in their ethical claim when they are recognized as God's work. Darkness is the absence of light, and thus of time, meaning, and *telos*. That darkness is under attack is marked by the moon being given to bring day even into the night.[163]

Therefore, the answer to the question "What is the moon?" is exposed as necessarily implicating moral and political questions. In saying what *is*, we commit ourselves to the rationality of action incipient in the description. Singing is not an "action" but a political praxis of those who are under a Lord. The Psalter is not sung to a purely transcendent God but to a worldly Lord.[164] It thus situates us to stand amid multiple layers of order held together in the one Truth, whom it teaches us to address. In doing so it creates us as beings whose *nephesh* is responsive to the one God's complex work. As multiple discourses meet in Scripture, so do multiple levels of meaning — via the work of the Spirit — coalesce around the form of God's presence in the judgment that frames action. The commitment to an interpretation ventured in praise equals a moral commitment. To sing "you wrap yourself in light" is to be committed to meeting the God of light in light, all light. This is a basic rule of reading the Psalms, which is a paradigm for all scriptural exegesis, because Scripture is only read as light from the Lord when it is read amidst a reality in which we already participate and within which we are learning to act according to God's statutes, that is, Scripture.

A more concrete example may help. Verses 20-23 marvel in the provision of separate workplaces for humans and dangerous animals. God cares for humans and animals by providing a barrier of light between them.[165] Jewish exegesis took this as a theological reason to limit the human workday to the daylight hours.[166] This is not simply because they read these verses as a moral law set into creation that established night work as evil. This would disconnect the passage from the common biblical theme of "works of darkness." Humans are made to work in the light, in consciousness and awareness, in the light of the Son, and thus to have a Sabbath rest from their own works. The shining of the earth's sun is a reminder that every morning is God's,[167]

---

163. Barth, *Church Dogmatics*, III.1, pp. 126-29.

164. Cf. discussion in ch. 7, pp. 198, 205-8.

165. Calvin, "Psalm CIV," pp. 162-63.

166. Braude, *The Midrash on the Psalms*, p. 174.

167. "The early morning belongs to the church of the risen Christ. At the break of light it remembers the morning on which death, the devil and sin were brought low in defeat, and new

and thus all time the forum for his worship. The cycling of night and day is a continuous reminder of the gulf between the human desire to take control of creation, assuming it to be a blank slate available for reshaping to satisfy our desires, and life as a praising creature for whom all time is an invitation to communal worship and service.

On these grounds we can comprehend the hope for a twenty-four-hour society as one attempt to replace a festal calendar with an economic calendar. The calendar of radical choice (the logical product of the Enlightenment) has been filled out with the rationality of capitalism, in which all cessation of work marks a loss of profitability. It is only because God's people are reminded by the moon of its different calendar, which is grounded in God's redemptive works, that it is enabled to see how the twenty-four-hour society breaks up many other social structures. The twenty-four-hour society is to human social life what the attempt to ignore the seasons is to modern agriculture and what the quest to totally control fertility is to human, animal, and plant reproductive cycles: each assumes the given orders and rhythms of night and day, but the twenty-four-hour society sees these seasons and cycles as obstructions to be overcome. Verse 19 is a prophetic word that the boundaries of creation are not all neutral. Some are placed there to promote human flourishing. This means that the moral question is not *whether* there are any such orders but *how* we should know them and attend to them.

The point that comes to the fore in this observation is that singing prepares us to make the judgments in the present that cannot be systematized beforehand. What exactly is the moon? This question had no less moral import to ancient Israel than it does in the context of a space race. To use a Lutheran concept, the moon faces us as a divine provocation to good works. Good works are the giving of honor to God for what he has done, that is, human action that confirms God's works. We discover ourselves as *nephesh* that God wholly possesses, as in Christ, in the moments when we say before God that this is what the moon is and thus means for my action; when we say that this is who the poor and the widows are, and here is creation. The psalm coaxes us to give up our moral detachment and to venture the judgment that this song meets reality here and now, where I stand in the confession that "we are God's workmanship, created in Christ to do good works, which God pre-

---

life and salvation were given to human beings. . . . The ancient hymns that call the community of faith to praise God together in the early morning are inexhaustible (Ps. 5:3; 46:5; 57:8; 88:13; 119:147)." Bonhoeffer, *Life Together and Prayerbook of the Bible*, Dietrich Bonhoeffer Works, vol. 5, ed. Gerhard Müller, Albrecht Schönherr, and Geffrey Kelley; trans. Daniel Bloesch and James Burtness (Minneapolis: Fortress, 1996), pp. 49-50.

pared in advance for us to do" (Eph. 2:10). This is the place of the holy, of meeting God in the step of faith, hope, and love.

Two things are not meant by this understanding of good works. First, this is not a dialectical moment. We can only be committed to one course of action, which can be very complex, but is singular. The moon, as we face it as an actor, can therefore not really be both potential property and an invitation to good works unless we equate the two. In this case it becomes "really" the destiny of exploring nations and only "metaphorically" a bearer of God's light. In the judgment that commits us to action, dialectics ceases. Action is the living of one interpretative possibility. Good works are not the opposite or negation of bad works but a step on a path totally unrelated to the trackless wastes of the works of darkness. Evil works are overcome not by opposing them with good acts defined against the deprivation of evil, but following the divine prompting. The good work for today is not found by directing our attention to rectifying a list of evils but by listening to discern God's engagement with human brokenness. Good works thus question a compromise logic in which actions are both bad and good: good works are simply good.

This move pushes the locus of ethical thinking back from a focus on acts to emphasize the ethical centrality of perception. The only human action that is simply good is praise; therefore, only human action that is enacted praise of God's work becomes aligned with it. This displacement of ethics from its focus on the judgment of acts to the development of a sensitivity to the ways of God's presence is indicated by Jesus' rebuke of the rich young ruler, a rebuke that proves fatal to ethics as the judgment of acts: "Why do you call me good? No one but God is good"(Mark 10:18, and par.). The main battles of Christian ethics are fought in learning and maintaining this focus. The Christian life is a life shaped by the desire for God's presence, and only as such does it have an interest in acting to remain within that presence. Its perennial enemy is the reduction of the Christian life to "Christian ethics," which loses its orientation to praise in becoming devoted to the task of ethics as the delineation of good and bad acts.

Good works and a good conscience are paired concepts. Good works are acts undertaken via hope in God and the desire for walking in his presence, his way. The good conscience rests in the constant practice of measuring all our hearts, souls, minds, and desires by the precepts of praise. The good conscience results from assurance about having directed attention to the source of good works, and good works are human actions that are grounded in the hope and desire for God that arises from this source to transform human action. This is an insight that clarifies the meaning of the "way" imagery with which Psalm 1 describes the content of the book of Psalms.

This is not to reduce the concept of truth to a subjective or existential category, but to tie it to God's works and thus provide a sharper view of the kind of activity that faith is. Because faith in the God of Scripture is explorative, good works are not "merits" that are "built up" in a linear fashion to secure participation in Christ. Rather, they are actions expressing a confession of the grammar of faith, that is, action undertaken as praise. In the judgment of the present moment, we actively close down possible readings of the many overlapping and confusing factors that face us, and thus more deeply and actively make the confession of faith, exploring God's name by walking out on the waters onto which he calls us. Action tests the Spirit, and action intending this test in praise is the good work. The desire to meet God, to be God's *nephesh,* issues in attempts at self-commitment with this shape. Jewish midrash puts this point in the form of a question: Why is the doing of God's word placed before hearing it in Psalm 103:20? "Because it is speaking of the people of Israel who stood at Sinai, willing to do the will of God even before hearkening to a word of what they were to do, for they said, 'All that the Lord hath spoken we will do, and then hearken'" (Exod. 24:7).[168] Hearing and responding in speech are the condition for traveling with God in the journey of salvation.

Thus these verses open to a messianic and eschatological interpretation. "The young lions *(kefirim)* are the nations that deny *(koferim)* the Holy One . . . the nations roaring to tear Israel to pieces. . . . When the sun of the king Messiah rises, [heathen] nations of the earth will slink away, and crouch in their dens" (104:22).[169] This Jewish interpretation is paralleled in Christian exegesis, defended not on a linguistic but on a moral reading of the image of the lions as those who live and prey on humans in the dark, but are driven inward into their unbelieving hearts when the Son appears.[170]

We can now see that these verses are an elaboration of verses 5-9. God has not wiped out those who rage in the dark; he even sustains them while they are confined to a region away from God's light. Because humans have a relationship to the light that animals do not, they can realize the relative vacuity of darkness and, like the ass, be drawn in from the desert. Yet the fact that "lions" remain reminds us of the possibility that creatures remain "devourers" for all of their days. They may be drawn by God into the church, but they enter as lions, as all the faithful do, and must be transformed amidst lambs into creatures of this nonviolent kingdom.[171] Receiving outsiders into

---

168. Braude, *The Midrash on the Psalms,* p. 166

169. Braude, *The Midrash on the Psalms,* p. 174; cf. Acts 1:16, 25.

170. Augustine, *Expositions of the Psalms,* p. 164.

171. The original and still timely basic idea of Hauerwas's *The Peaceable Kingdom: A Primer in Christian Ethics* (Notre Dame, IN: University of Notre Dame Press, 1983).

the church will always be costly, and the community that refuses this service, believing it is protecting itself from the prisoner, the addict, the abused, the immigrant, the indigent, and the handicapped, stops up its access to the divine spring of healing water.

The psalmist has now prepared us to hear the multiple resonances of this section's concluding verse. Because God's sustaining provision is twofold, material and spiritual, so human work is twofold, material but also spiritual. God draws in the unregenerate to make apostles, preachers, and teachers. These are his works, which makes his servants' work the witnessing to it through the renewal of their lives and their preaching.[172] If human work — any human work — is to be good, it must, like preaching, be service. The animals who live in the dark hunt each other, but humans are the ones who work in the divinely provided sunlight. In this divine light they seek to labor in a way that benefits all, not seeing work as a competitive sphere for scarce resources but as an arena in which we simply "gather up" God's bountiful provision.[173]

The only creatures that know this are those who sing in the way the psalmist moves on to describe.

On Finding Our Place: Wonder, Hope, and Song

מָה־רַבּוּ מַעֲשֶׂיךָ יְהוָה כֻּלָּם בְּחָכְמָה עָשִׂיתָ מָלְאָה הָאָרֶץ קִנְיָנֶךָ׃ 104:24

זֶה הַיָּם גָּדוֹל וּרְחַב יָדָיִם שָׁם־רֶמֶשׂ וְאֵין מִסְפָּר חַיּוֹת קְטַנּוֹת עִם־גְּדֹלוֹת׃ 25

שָׁם אֳנִיּוֹת יְהַלֵּכוּן לִוְיָתָן זֶה־יָצַרְתָּ לְשַׂחֶק־בּוֹ׃ 26

104:24 O LORD, how manifold are your works!
    In wisdom you have made them all;
    the earth is full of your creatures.
25   Yonder is the sea, great and wide,
    creeping things innumerable are there,
    living things both small and great.
26   There go the ships,
    and Leviathan that you formed
    to sport in it.

Having recounted the fantastic and intricate interwovenness of the world created and sustained by God's hand, the psalmist expresses in these

172. Luther, "Psalm One Hundred Four," p. 340.
173. Barth, *Church Dogmatics*, III.4, p. 527.

key verses (emphasized by a *tricola*) a crescendo of wonder: "O Lord, how manifold are your works!" Here "manifold" (or "many" in some translations) is not a numerical reference but denotes wonder at creation's many-layered, or complex, nature. This passage parallels the third day of the creation account, in which the beauty and dignity of creation are portrayed in the creation of the animals before humans. God's grace is for them in themselves, and through them for humans.[174] There is a place here for genuine glory in the order of creation, and the strict boundaries that maintain that order. The Midrash Tehillim wonders that the lives of the terrestrial and marine creatures are each so perfectly fitted for their places, one thriving where the other dies.[175] Modern science occasionally exhibits a secularized version of this wonder when it talks about the vastness of space, the complexity of the human brain, or the intricate social lives of animals.

But is this scientific wonder the same as that of the psalmist? Without a Creator, wonder at complexity is wonder at an accident. A car wreck may produce highly complex metal shapes, but, on naturalistic grounds, we have no more or less reason to wonder at these shapes than at the improbable complexity of the intact car or the mind and hands that produced it. Therefore, the best scientific rationalism can muster is an inexplicable surprise at the statistical improbability of the way things are.

Praise puts us in the opposite position. Praise perceives created order as an exhibition of the intricacy of God's work. This raises the question, addressed by the next verse, about the place of evil and suffering in creation. To see evil and yet still to praise is not fatalism but a formed appreciation that the world is ordered *for* something. God sustains the leviathan and the lion, but he aims to establish a new creation in which the "wolf shall live with the lamb, the leopard shall lie down with the kid, the calf and the lion and the fatling together, and a little child shall lead them" (Is. 11:6). In praise we see, says Barth, that creation precedes us in "self evident praise of its creator, in the natural fulfillment of the destiny given to it at creation."[176] The expression of wonder at the divine working is the beginning of this new creation.

The form of our wonder again has obvious consequences for ethics in our age. Modern science is built on an objectifying gaze.[177] Thus to be a physician is, in the first place, to be trained in the scientific disciplines that allow

174. Barth, *Church Dogmatics*, III.1, p. 152.
175. Braude, *The Midrash on the Psalms*, p. 175.
176. Barth, *Church Dogmatics*, IV.1, p. 177.
177. The point is by now almost platitudinous; see James McClellan III and Harold Dorn, *Science and Technology in World History: An Introduction* (Baltimore: Johns Hopkins University Press, 1999), ch. 12.

the body to appear as an object whose functioning needs correction. This is not in itself harmful. But only a perspective of formed wonder, wonder at the person as a created whole, can properly limit this objectification and give it a *telos* and defense in the good of the individual being examined. Otherwise, physicians can conceive of themselves as facing simply "clients" or "patients," allowing their treatment to be dictated by the discourses of scientific inquiry[178] or consumer choice.[179] Nor are patients and parents immune from these same forces. They may, for instance, face their own embryos without wonder, such as a "problem" pregnancy, or with misplaced wonder, seeing it as prehuman "stuff," wondering only at its fantastic "potential" as a source for stem cells or other medical uses. But they may also wonder at it as a child, a work of God's renewal of the earth.[180] The difference between praise and instrumentalization was already clear to Calvin: "We ought to know that the earth does not possess such fruitfulness and riches of itself, but solely by the blessing of God, who makes it the means of administering to us his bounty."[181]

Praise is thus not an "add on" in our relationship to created things: it is the criterion and marker of our proper appreciation of what it actually is. So the parent, physician, and scientist — along with most people in our age — live amidst a sea of disordered desires that breed rage against the divine order.

178. A classic example of the involuntary reduction of patient to experimental subject is the Tuskegee Syphilis Study; see Gregory Pence, *Classic Cases in Medical Ethics: Accounts of the Cases That Have Shaped Medical Ethics, with Philosophical, Legal, and Historical Backgrounds* (New York: McGraw-Hill, 1990), ch. 9.

179. The high profile of concepts such as "choice" and "the consumer" in reproductive medicine raises just these questions. The accelerating pace of medicine's ability artificially to produce conceptions remains far ahead of the medicine and financing required to care for the much more difficult and expensive pregnancies and deliveries that are produced. See Rebecca Jackson, Kimberly Gibson, Yvonne Wu, and Mary Croughan, "Perinatal Outcomes in Single-tons Following In Vitro Fertilization: A Meta-Analysis," *Obstetrics & Gynecology* 103 (2004): 551-63. This increase in medical complications has resulted in the development of a double standard regarding the care offered to "natural" and "assisted" pregnancies. See Howard Minkoff and Richard Berkowitz, "The Myth of the Precious Baby," *Obstetrics & Gynecology* 106 (2005): 607-9. Characteristically, however, the medical ethics establishment has tended to defend the commercializing forces at work in elective cesarean sections on the grounds of patient autonomy, thus undermining any wider resistance to the commercialization of reproduction. See Howard Minkoff, Kathleen Powderly, Frank Chervenak, and Lawrence McCullough, "Ethical Dimensions of Elective Primary Cesarean Delivery," *Obstetrics & Gynecology* 103 (2004): 387-92.

180. Cf. Wannenwetsch, "What Is Man? That You Are Mindful of Him! Biotechnological Aspirations in the Light of Psalm Eight," in Ralph Waller, ed., *Farmington Papers* (Oxford: Farmington Institute for Christian Studies, 2004).

181. Calvin, "Psalm CIV," pp. 164-65.

In this sea are "creeping things innumerable," but God knows and numbers the elect (Ps. 1:6).[182] Here again we cannot establish that the metaphor demands a specific interpretation, but it does provoke further reflection. Augustine cannot resist interpreting the "ships" of verse 26 as churches, the ecclesia contained in the wood of the cross, piloted by Christ, and tossed by the "tempests of temptations." There is no reason to reject this beautiful interpretation as long as we combine it with an awareness that the sea of rage, desire, and idolatry is also inside the church. Nor need we reject his linking of the leviathan with the evil one, the devil, who is the embodiment of the rage of the nations. We need not fear this rage; we need fear only God, as Psalm 130 has taught, because he is the only true power (Rom. 13:1). The devil rules the chaos where he is at home, and only those who know the dwelling place of the saints see that what seems to be glory to him is really damnation. To say God "makes sport" of leviathan is a comforting and sustaining word to those confessing their proximity to temptation and persecution.[183]

God allows the sea of chaos for only a limited time, during which he does not begrudge its creatures their own life. As such, it is at times threatening to God's children; yet from it, paradoxically, he also feeds his people. This is often extravagant, as in feeding the disciples by having them catch a fish with a coin in its mouth (Matt. 17:27), or having them catch a multitude of fish (and thus souls) large enough to sink their boats (Luke 5:1-11). Through his disciples the Lord brings a rich harvest from the rebelliousness of the Egyptians (Ps. 105:37). Scripture is not afraid to dwell on the threat of the world to God's servants that is represented by the leviathan (Job 40:15-23; Jonah 2). Yet praise trains us to see it differently, as sport or play in God's creation. If there were not some divinely laudable creativity in rebellion, there would be no spoils from which God could feed his children. This is not to validate evil, but to emphasize God's mastery over even evil for his own purposes. Rebellion does not escape God, but remains his sport, however much it strikes fear into our hearts.[184]

Creatures, even in rebellion, have real life. Despite the admixture of chaos and disorder in the world, says the psalmist, God is still wise, and "the earth is full of his riches." Nothing exists in this world in which God's goodness is not visible; the only question is *how* to rightly experience it. Humans have this work to do (v. 23): to use their real and discrete existences to think, read, and make music and art as ways of responding to and thus discerning

182. Luther, "Psalm One Hundred Four," p. 342.
183. Augustine, *Expositions of the Psalms*, p. 172.
184. Calvin, "Psalm CIV," p. 165.

the boundary God has established between chaos and redeemed order.[185] In none of this activity, however, can humanity hope to overcome the leviathan, but only to live in wonder at God's work and in trust in his care.

כֻּלָּם אֵלֶיךָ יְשַׂבֵּרוּן לָתֵת אָכְלָם בְּעִתּוֹ: 104:27

תִּתֵּן לָהֶם יִלְקֹטוּן תִּפְתַּח יָדְךָ יִשְׂבְּעוּן טוֹב: 28

תַּסְתִּיר פָּנֶיךָ יִבָּהֵלוּן תֹּסֵף רוּחָם יִגְוָעוּן וְאֶל־עֲפָרָם יְשׁוּבוּן: 29

תְּשַׁלַּח רוּחֲךָ יִבָּרֵאוּן וּתְחַדֵּשׁ פְּנֵי אֲדָמָה: 30

104:27   These all look to you
      to give them their food in due season;
28   when you give to them, they gather it up;
      when you open your hand, they are filled with good things.
29   When you hide your face, they are dismayed;
      when you take away their breath,
      they die and return to their dust.
30   When you send forth your spirit, they are created;
      and you renew the face of the ground.

These verses comprise the "hope stanza" of this song. In it the yearnings of plants, animals, and humans converge. They all hope to live and flourish, to be blessed. As we have seen, Bonhoeffer emphasizes that in the Psalms this is not simply a spiritual or inner happiness, but a real earthly prosperity: "Not blessed because you lack nothing, but because you receive everything you have from the hand of God."[186] This waiting is not for fulfillment in a future life, but for the substantial care of "daily bread," God's indispensable and multifarious material presence. The prayer of thanks at every meal is thanks that God has been present for us.

But these verses speak not only of God's material provision but also of the necessity of his presence as spirit. Thus, "give us our daily bread" is an ineradicably spiritual request for God's Spirit through which creatures flourish and are re-created, and without whom they return to dust. All creatures need food, and this implies a continuation of Genesis 1:2: without God's ongoing creative work, all life must necessarily die. God has given breath and must continue giving food, but neither one as a possession. Creatures do not take possession of a piece of divinity with their breath, for the Bible allows no blurring of the line between creature and creation. The

185. Barth, *Church Dogmatics*, III.3, ed. G. W. Bromiley and T. F. Torrance; trans. G. W. Bromiley and R. J. Ehrlich (Edinburgh: T&T Clark, 1996), p. 87; *Church Dogmatics*, IV.3.1, p. 698.
186. Bonhoeffer, "On Psalm 119," p. 111; cf. ch. 5, pp. 78-79.

divine breath creates a truly creaturely breath, which lives truly in appreciation of breath as gift.[187]

What this breath relies on is food "in due season," another temporal designation. Time in the modern sense of a flow of empty and potential occurrences is absent in Hebrew cosmology; time is an ordered space for faithful acts. "Every event has its definite place in the time-order; the event is inconceivable without its time and *vice versa*."[188] Creatures do not await some future salvation, but rather the occurrence of necessary events (Eccl. 3:1ff.). Again, there can be no such thing as "potential" provision, only the timely assurance of actual and dependable divine presence. The psalmist affirms the Lord's equitable governance by saying that a series of times will follow a definite rhythm, subject to an order (Gen. 8:22). The seasons and days, rains and new growth will continue, as will the moon to govern the seasons. And it was the moon's continuing orbit that guaranteed the continuance of festival time that sustained the community's cognizance of this provision.[189] "Yahweh has made" all these (Ps. 118:24), which serves as a promise of his continuing care.

For humans to reject this remembrance, then, is to reject God's life-giving Spirit and, like the serpent in the garden, to eat dust. With the rejection of the necessity of the Spirit's feeding us, we try to survive on our own resources.[190] We are dust that breathes, set in motion by the breath of God, fed by the breath of God, but only by his breath. So when we try to feed ourselves on creaturely loves, we eat our own damnation. Conversely, when we praise what we live on — the divine work — we live. This is the great polarity: trying to live with wonder at or disdain for creaturely things, and living from the hand of God. The former is excited by the genius or beauty of humans, or by overmastering other men and creatures,[191] the latter by being overcome, by learning what humans cannot control or create, and wondering at that. Such wonder senses moments of redemption, when the social disorder of those living by eating dirt is broken in on and a new creation inaugurated. All true order is grounded in Christ, and humans who benefit from it (alone among all creatures) refuse to praise him for that gift. Because we are all implicated in

187. Calvin, "Psalm CIV," p. 168; Childs, *Biblical Theology,* pp. 400-401.

188. Von Rad, *Old Testament Theology,* vol. II, p. 100.

189. "We must make an effort to realize how much sacral festivals must have meant to a people who completely lacked any concept of absolute and linear time to which these festivals had then to be related. The festivals, not time, were the absolute data, and were data whose holiness was absolute." Von Rad, *Old Testament Theology,* vol. II, p. 103.

190. Augustine, *Expositions of the Psalms,* p. 178.

191. Wonder at technological mastery accelerates it; wonder at political power bows before it; and wonder at earthly beauty in itself idolizes it, each with obvious ethical implications.

this anti-doxology, we still do not sing this psalm perfectly, says Augustine. Yet singing it at all allows us to see that the world is running to Christ, a spectacle that fills us with joy. The sea is still being made dry and divided, in and around us, a work that is indeed worthy of praise.

This wonder is always susceptible to the temptation of pride, and when it yields to this temptation, God turns away his face (Ps. 143:7), allowing faith to again be submerged in the waves of confusion from which it has been drawn (Matt. 14:25-32). In this process we are always taught where our wonder must lie: "What have you that you have not received?" (1 Cor. 4:7), Augustine asks. "When we *repent* of our sin we find ourselves and discover that we had no strength of our own. We *confess* to God that we are earth and ashes." Those who refuse to have a spirit of their own (Matt. 5:3) shall have the Spirit of God (Matt. 10:20). Thus is the earth renewed "for new men and women, who confess that their righteousness is nothing of their own but rather that they have been justified by God, so that his grace may be in them . . . these people for whom the whole aspect of their earth has been made new."[192]

This breath language is the Old Testament's looking forward to what is as yet hidden: the relationship between the incarnate Son and the sustaining and renewing Spirit. The interaction between the Son and the Spirit is the history of creation renewed and redeemed. We and the animals (Eccl. 3:19f.) are given the Spirit's breath for a time, and in due season, so that we may praise the Lord (Ps. 150:6). This is the textual grounds for the affirmation that God works outside the church and can use the world to teach the church how to read Scripture.[193] But at the same time, God has not bound himself to provide this sustaining Spirit to all indefinitely. The Spirit was sent out to renew the earth, to create a new earth and a new community[194] who sings this song:

104:31 יְהִי כְבוֹד יְהוָה לְעוֹלָם יִשְׂמַח יְהוָה בְּמַעֲשָׂיו:

32 הַמַּבִּיט לָאָרֶץ וַתִּרְעָד יִגַּע בֶּהָרִים וְיֶעֱשָׁנוּ:

33 אָשִׁירָה לַיהוָה בְּחַיָּי אֲזַמְּרָה לֵאלֹהַי בְּעוֹדִי:

34 יֶעֱרַב עָלָיו שִׂיחִי אָנֹכִי אֶשְׂמַח בַּיהוָה:

35 יִתַּמּוּ חַטָּאִים מִן־הָאָרֶץ וּרְשָׁעִים עוֹד אֵינָם בָּרֲכִי נַפְשִׁי אֶת־יְהוָה:
הַלְלוּ־יָהּ

104:31 May the glory of the LORD endure forever;
may the LORD rejoice in his works —

192. Augustine, *Expositions of the Psalms*, pp. 179-80 (italics added).

193. Watson, *Text, Church and World*, p. 7.

194. Barth, *Church Dogmatics*, III.2, ed. G. W. Bromiley and T. F. Torrance; trans. H. Knight, G. W. Bromiley, J. K. S. Reid, R. H. Fuller (Edinburgh: T&T Clark, 1994), pp. 361-62.

32 who looks on the earth and it trembles,
who touches the mountains and they smoke.

33 I will sing to the LORD as long as I live;
I will sing praise to my God while I have being.

34 May my meditation be pleasing to him,
for I rejoice in the LORD.

35 Let sinners be consumed from the earth,
and let the wicked be no more.
Bless the LORD, O my soul.
Praise the LORD!

As the song ends, blessing God, expressing praise for his works, crystallizes into its pure form of blessing and glorifying God *simpliciter*. We must be sure to unpack the methodological implications of this turn in order to fully respond to the question we brought to the Psalms initially: the relationship between Scripture and Christian ethics. We have seen that Scripture is portrayed as an essential part of the way into the ethos of God, and so we should see that ethos in microcosm here.

What is immediately apparent is that these are joyful words. Praise is not portrayed as something demanded, nor a law obeyed, nor a bargaining tool. What is appreciated is praised. Praise is thus a form of speech that expresses and hence fosters appreciation. It is the form of speech of those who have experienced God's presence and have been enlivened to his presence in the world. One cannot praise what one does not know, and "the decisive event for 'knowing' in biblical Hebrew is not that one looks at an object, but that one comes into touch with it."[195] "Taste and see," says the psalmist (Ps. 34:8), putting tasting before seeing because "this sweetness cannot be known unless one has experienced and felt it for himself."[196] Praise and blessing the Lord are therefore *responses*. Mary's *Magnificat*, reliant as it is on Hannah's Song, is the church's prototypical image of such an outburst of appreciation for God's working. No one can magnify God and his gifts unless he or she is raised up by God, the praising (Luke 1:46) following the raising (Luke 1:47). Out of such experience, comments Luther, "it is characteristic of the magnified and enlightened soul to magnify God in his individual works."[197]

195. Buber, *Right and Wrong*, p. 58.

196. Luther, "The Magnificat," in *Luther's Works, Vol. 21, The Sermon on the Mount (Sermons) and The Magnificat*, ed. Jaroslav Pelikan, trans. A. T. W Steinhäuser (St. Louis: Concordia Publishing House, 1956), p. 302.

197. Luther, "Psalm One Hundred Four," pp. 316-17. This thought developed throughout his life; see Luther, "The Magnificat."

We are, of course, still learning this praise. Like the grumpy senior citizen, we receive God's gifts but still find fault in them. Ultimately, this is the effect of eating dust, trying to live by focusing on ourselves. Condemned to our own ugliness, we "think that there is much ugliness in things and that God neither is nor is beautiful," says Luther; but "all things are very beautiful and rightly confessing God."[198] Only God's advent, however, can reveal this beauty to create the delight portrayed by the psalmist. The psalm praises God's presence in all things, despite creation's brokenness, and despite our own inward turnings, falterings, hesitations, and inhibitions. It is no accident that in heaven we will be freed of these wayward desires and inhibitions, freed to express delight in the one who is most worthy of it.[199] This is the eschatological promise of praise. Its ethical concomitant is that if we see the world thus, we will live and choose and act in reliance on God's sustenance, not falling into all the modes of self-protection that the fallen and self-obsessed world offers at every turn.

Praise can be sustained only in utter reliance on the divine provision and presence. The praiser asks God to glory in *his* works. We can see Augustine, in his passion to communicate this verse to his congregation, turning with his finger pointing: "Not your glory, not mine, not his, not hers, but the Lord's glory; and may it not last for a time but forever. *The Lord will rejoice in his works.* Not in your works, as though they really belonged to you. If your works are bad, they are the fruit of your sinfulness; if good, they are wrought through God's grace."[200]

It is this divine touch and the resulting human response that are indicated by the clause "he touches the mountains and they smoke." If modern interpreters venture an interpretation, they tend to suggest that this is a reference to the continuing, if marginal, presence of natural evil.[201] This may or may not be correct, given that the passage does not hint at an eruption causing loss of life. A more likely interpretation is that, like waves, volcanic eruptions evoke awe and fear. "The voice of the LORD breaks the cedars . . . shakes the wilderness . . . strips the forests bare . . . and in his temple all say, 'Glory!'" (Ps. 29:5-9). Here God's voice strips the most solid things conceivable, the rulers and the proud, of their self-assurance, causing them to utter praise (cf. Dan. 4:28-37).

The metaphorical formulation of this truth is that creation smokes in the presence of God. Sinai smokes in the giving of the Torah (Exod. 19:18), as

198. Luther, "Psalm One Hundred Four," p. 318.

199. Lewis, *Reflections on the Psalms*, p. 94.

200. Augustine, *Expositions of the Psalms, 99–120*, ed. Boniface Ramsey, trans. Maria Boulding (New York: New City Press, 2003), Exposition 4.15 of Psalm 103, p. 180.

201. See Terrien, *The Psalms*, p. 718; see also Kraus, *Psalms 60–150*, p. 304.

does all creation with God's coming (Ps. 18:12-14). Similarly, God's touch and gaze produce speech in humans (Ps. 144:5).[202] Some are inflamed with rebellious envy against truth at this touch, displaying their wrath in word and deed (Rev. 14:11; 19:3). But others emit sweet prayers of repentance, are angry about their sin, and thus their faith is renewed (Ps. 18:7-8). This sacrifice of praise and repentance is the smoking of the faithful (Song 3:6; Rev. 5:8; 8:3-4). Those that are thus renewed are "temples filled with smoke" (Is. 6:4-5) that exhibit what Luther calls "the shape of the true religion, which is confession, praise and the proclamation of God."[203] Smoke is thus a metaphor that emphasizes the interdependence of God's appearance and the generation of the human ethos of prayer.

This praying animal is the fulfilled *nephesh*, whose whole being is committed to reliance on God's working, a task that requires ongoing and continual repentance. This makes the ethos of prayer at once the cheapest and costliest sacrifice. Milgrom has shown the trajectory of development in the Levitical system toward ensuring that even the poorest Israelites could offer sacrifices.[204] Because of Christ's sacrifice, this trajectory has reached its logical fulfillment: the only sacrifice asked of humanity is the least costly and most important of human sacrifices. In Israel, praise was the work of the priests and people in the temple, with the Psalms as its songbook, which is why the Psalter is also called the "book of thanks." The offering of praise may be sung with many motives and for many reasons, but they all presume the centrality of meeting with God, and of continuing life with him.

The psalmist then requests that the *meditation* of praise be acceptable to God. The object of this "meditation" can here be translated "to him" or "on him." We have seen how meditation on Scripture is, ultimately, meditation on the work of Christ. The sacrifice of Christ opens the way from chaos to life, and praise is a meditation on this work of regeneration, and thus "on him." It is just as clearly "meditation to him": "I will sing to the Lord as long as I live; I will sing praise to my God while I have being." "While I have being" literally means "while I still am"; that is, as long as I am breathing, it will be used for praise. We see that, here again, writing and singing are center stage as the willing embrace of God's determination of human existence.

202. Martin Luther, "Psalm Eighteen," in *Luther's Works, Vol. 10, First Lectures on the Psalms I, Psalms 1–75*, ed. Hinton Oswald (St. Louis: Concordia, 1974), p. 121; also *Luther's Works, Vol. 16, Lectures on Isaiah I*, ed. Jaroslav Pelikan (St. Louis: Concordia, 1969), p. 71; and *Luther's Works, Vol. 7, Lectures on Genesis, Chapters 38–44*, ed. Jaroslav Pelikan (St. Louis: Concordia, 1965), p. 327.

203. Luther, "Psalm One Hundred Four," p. 342.

204. Milgrom, *Leviticus 1–16*, pp. 195-96.

The Epistle to the Hebrews says that Christians meditate not only *on* and *to* the glorified Christ, but they also sing *with* him: he is the church's worship leader (Heb. 2:12; Ps. 22:22). In singing the Psalms, Christians become one with Christ's body, enabling them to participate in the praise of the Father.[205] Jesus learns obedience with us and is made perfect (Heb. 5) by including us in his procession. His sinlessness is not to be understood in terms of metaphysical cleanliness but in terms of the steadfast character of his dependence on the Spirit.[206] And thus do we, with him, discern our vocation in God's will in reliance on him, within his body, and through the leading of his Spirit. For this reason the community's corporate singing also emerges as a comforting token of divine love.[207] "And that they speak these words to God and with God, this, I repeat, is the best thing of all. . . . When these words please a man and fit his case, he becomes sure that he is in the communion of saints, and that it has gone with all the saints as it goes with him, since they all sing with him one little song."[208] We learn to pray and praise in community. Our personal prayers receive their meaning only in the context of this communal work of God, as outriders to the one corporate praise. Their criterion of goodness is their aim to draw all into it.

We can now see that giving singing such a central methodological place commits us to understanding Christian ethics as serving the church's coming into tune with God's working. Different discourses, different political groupings, different aspects of created order, God's works of creation redemption, and the diversities of Scripture and its tradition of reception: all are unified as the one God's works, and their true unity is discovered only through this song of praise.

We can now make a final clarification of the methodological role of the Psalms in framing our understanding of the place of the Bible in Christian ethics. Singing the Psalter is a practice that combines the reading of Scripture and praying. Through the Psalter God has given us entry into the universe's eternal song of praise, and to take up the Psalms is to join that congregation. This means that the song the church sings is a fully earthly song of a pilgrim people and a groaning cosmos. But it is also an eternal song, being bound to the Word of revelation in Christ Jesus. Song reinvigorates the church's rela-

205. H. Orton Wiley, *The Epistle to the Hebrews,* rev. ed. (Kansas City, MO: Beacon Hill Press, 1984), p. 86.

206. Colin Gunton, *Yesterday and Today: A Study of Continuities in Christology,* 2nd ed. (London: SPCK, 1997), pp. 220-23.

207. Bonhoeffer, *Life Together,* pp. 27-35.

208. Martin Luther, "Prefaces to the Old Testament" (Preface to the Psalter, 1545), in *Luther's Works, Vol. 35: Word and Sacrament I,* ed. E. Theodore Bachmann, trans. Charles Jacobs (Philadelphia: Fortress, 1960), p. 256.

tionships with the saints of the ages, with Christ, and with Scripture. Christians collectively sing the Psalms because:

> [I]n singing together it is possible for them to speak and pray the same Word at the same time — in other words, for the sake of uniting in the Word. . . . Because it is completely bound to the Word, the singing of the congregation in its worship service, especially the singing of the house church, is essentially singing in unison. Here words and music combine in a unique way. The freely soaring tone of unison singing finds its sole and essential inner support in the words that are sung. It does not need, therefore, the musical support of other parts.[209]

The union of human voices with all creation and the saints of all ages in praise of Christ is the essence of psalm singing. Here the church experiences time as whole, not broken up and distorted. Singing brings the church into rhythm, turning it from an assembly into a communion. Therefore, it is not an incidental part of Christian worship, an "adventitious hankering to decorate," but the essence of enjoying God, doubling the Son's praise in attention to him as the Spirit glorifies the Father and the Son.[210] The singing of the community is an ethical reality in being simultaneously earthly and eschatological.

By joining the song of a community that runs itself over and through the Psalter, we discover our resistances to them. We discover that our self-image and self-reflectivity shout us down when we try to sing the Psalms. To be finding our place in worship is to be discovering for the first time the orders of self-love and false loves, which tell us that it is impossible to praise God with the Psalms. This study has suggested how conceptions of hermeneutics may constitute one such wrong love, as may concepts of theology as science, of humanity as rational beings, of social propriety, and so on. Therefore, Bonhoeffer concludes, "whether or not a community achieves proper unison singing is a question of spiritual discernment."[211] Its failures to do so reveal its idolatries. Those include using method to force social unity (such as loud music) or seeking unity through the prominent performances of strong personalities (such as worship leaders) or secular ideologies (perhaps embodied in celebrity performers).

Bonhoeffer concretizes this insight by taking issue with a range of ways Christians unfaithfully participate in the community's praise. Here "vanity

---

209. Bonhoeffer, *Life Together*, pp. 66-67.

210. The phrase and the image of the church joining in the Son's praise are those of another Lutheran, Robert Jenson, *Systematic Theology*, p. 235.

211. Bonhoeffer, *Life Together*, p. 67.

and bad taste" are not musical or aesthetic categories, but rather are theological, and thus ethical, categories. Singing reveals the ugly strategies we use to resist finding our place in the ecology of body life, displacing the central moral imperative of communal unity with lesser moral aims, as the Donatists do. The first way is through improvising on the tune, which Bonhoeffer suggests reveals an underlying belief that the harmony of the community's song is insufficient without being "filled out" with a few improvised musical flourishes. A second way to mar the community's praise tempts those with unique voices—among the basses and sopranos, for example. They sing in unison but manage to draw attention to the human skill of the singer and thus necessarily away from God. The soloists take this a step further: they bask in the limelight afforded by the silence of the choir. Then there are those who are moody or nursing a grudge and do not sing at all, disturbing the unity of song with the protest of silence. In all this, Bonhoeffer observes, we need not worry too much about those who are "unmusical," for when the community is spiritually attuned, there are far fewer of those than we would imagine.

The reason we need not worry about the unmusical is that

> unison singing is much less a musical than a spiritual matter. . . . It is the voice of the church that is heard in singing together. It is not I who sing, but the church. However, as a member of the church, I may share in its song. Thus all true singing together must serve to widen our spiritual horizon. It must enable us to recognize our small community as a member of the great Christian church [*Christenheit*] on earth and must help us willingly and joyfully to take our place in the song of the church with our singing, be it feeble or good.[212]

In emphasizing the beauty of the ethos of unity, manifested in the congregation's single address to God, Bonhoeffer revives an insight that has been taken for granted in much of the church's history. It was only on the eve of the Reformation that the assumption began to be questioned that the church's prayer is always communal, and thus that the absent must still join communal prayers in form and time even if they are spatially separated.[213] In time, this questioning gave rise to the belief that "private" prayers were not just allowed but preferred,[214] leaving modern Christians unprotected from the atomizing forces of modernity.

---

212. Bonhoeffer, *Life Together*, pp. 67-68.

213. Benedict, *Rule of St. Benedict*, p. 50.

214. Robert Taft, *The Liturgy of the Hours in the East and West: The Origins of the Divine Office and Its Meaning for Today* (Collegeville, MN: Liturgical Press, 1986), pp. 301-4.

This close examination of how the singing of psalms focuses the church on Christ gives us an ethically rich theological interpretation of a practice that we tend to think of primarily in aesthetic terms.[215] In so doing, we expose the familiar and acrimonious debates about styles of worship music as a sign of a church that is estranged from the theological heart of the practice. This allows contemporary arguments about church music to be redirected away from fruitless squabbles about the aesthetics of music to a firm focus on the aesthetics of political harmony and the importance of collective meditation on God's word. The aesthetic pleasure of the church's praise is properly its ability to facilitate *political* harmony. In singing we exist as one "many" held together in Christ, to whom and in whom we sing. We unite as a body in the confession that we must go on discovering its rationality, into which we must process as a community.

Finding a denunciation of sin amidst such praise comes as a jolt to modern Christians. Is this not out of place in a song of praise? Eric Zenger points out that such reactions suggest that moderns find imprecatory psalms distasteful because we are either ignorant of radical evil or not offended by it.[216] Francis Watson says that such reactions refuse Scripture's "proper vocation, which is to represent, in frail human language, a divine communicative action which does not arise from among ourselves, but addresses us from without."[217] In focusing, in conclusion, on human wickedness, the psalmist uncouples the parallel of humans and animals by resolving it into a direct focus on human sin. It is human wickedness that mars creation's order. The animal and created spheres are freed of their metaphorical linkage with chaos.[218] The chaos that matters is human rebellion, rather than all the natural forces at work in the world that humans wish to blame for their suffering. God is not threatened by the most fearsome of beasts, who are elsewhere depicted as praising him (Ps. 148; Job 12:7), which leaves only human beings to repent and be obliterated as sinners by the one with whom there is forgiveness (Ps. 130:4). Traditional Jewish[219] and Christian exegesis read this as a prayer that "sinners" be extinguished by having their "sins" extinguished from the earth (the

---

215. Jenson also relocates music from the realm of aesthetics to social relations, a move implied but not made explicit in Bonhoeffer's treatment. Jenson, *Systematic Theology,* pp. 234-36.

216. Erich Zenger, *God of Vengeance: Understanding the Psalms of Divine Wrath,* trans. Linda Maloney (Louisville: Westminster John Knox, 1996), ch. 3.

217. Watson, *Text and Truth,* p. 124. This makes it all the more puzzling that Watson can conclude of Ps. 137:8-9: "Christian victims of oppression could never legitimately appropriate this psalm in its entirety, however extreme their sufferings; and its use in Christian liturgical contexts can in no circumstances be justified" (p. 121).

218. Brown, *Seeing the Psalms,* p. 162.

219. Braude, *The Midrash on the Psalms,* p. 178.

Hebrew carries the sense of "spent," "exhausted," "completed").[220] Those who feed on God's Spirit cannot wish the extinction of any of his creatures, but they can passionately pray for the eradication of injustice they have suffered (Ps. 58-59; 68:1-2), and that all injustices be swallowed up into the new creation brought about by Christ's sacrifice. Full Christological, pneumatological, and ecclesiological weight should be given to the fact that this is a prayer for God to complete the work he has begun in drawing the rebellious in from the desert of self-obsession to create a new creation perfectly united in praise (Rev. 5:13). If it is, we need not fear the totalizing erasure of all difference in this extinguishing of sin, because, as we have seen, difference shorn of its rebellion now finds its true form in Christ.

To sing this is to confess that evil is not a privation of the good, but of praise. That this privation is the sin against the Holy Spirit is emphasized by the psalm's opening and closing blessings. Because this is a prayer to God, it discourages us from looking around to judge our neighbors as it convicts us in the singing that we are a mixture of obedience and disobedience. Its imprecation against sin is thus a prayer of sadness at negation, our oblivion and self-referential refusal to praise. Saved by this song of praise, we are sustained in it by our imprecations against sinners — against ourselves as sinners.

Therefore, before its final blessings, the psalm engages us in a prayer for an end to all unrighteousness and rebellion, offering us an open-ended hope for the end of evil and temptation. Even though evil is now God's sport, terrifying and yet at times used to feed his faithful, it is doomed to perish: "Then I saw a new heaven and a new earth; for the first heaven and the first earth had passed away, and the sea was no more" (Rev. 21:1). This final drying eradicates the earth's seas, springs, and rivers of rebellion (Rev. 16:3-4). It is the triumph of Yahweh's "eternal Gospel," which calls all creation to recognize the Creator by worshiping him (Rev. 14:7), so ending the persecution of the saints (Rev. 16:6).

The judgment of the old creation is not an annihilating second flood (Gen. 6:11-13, 17) but the final destruction of the destroyers of creation. It is through this judgment that the rainbow by which God promised Noah that he would never again destroy the earth (Gen. 9:13-17) finally becomes the permanent rainbow around God's throne (Rev. 4:3).[221] Yahweh has made good on his promise to Noah to ensure that a flood will never again destroy human life by subduing and so renewing through Christ the sea of rebellious nations

220. "I have no pleasure in the death of the wicked, but that the wicked turn from his way and live" (Ezek. 33:11).

221. Cf. Bauckham, *The Theology of the Book of Revelation*, pp. 51-53.

(Ps. 2; Rev. 17). It is because of this judgment that the book of Revelation can reveal to us the praise of Abraham in its final form, displaying the completion of the work of the cross and the consummation of Pentecost. In this final song the request to remove sinners has died away, and the church glories in having been purified as Christ's bride (Rev. 19:6-8).

> Then I heard what seemed to be the voice of a great multitude,
> like the sound of many waters
> and like the sound of mighty thunder peals,
> crying out, 'Hallelujah!
> For the Lord our God the Almighty reigns.
> Let us rejoice and exult and give him the glory,
> for the marriage of the Lamb has come,
> and his bride has made herself ready;
> to her it has been granted to be clothed with fine linen, bright and pure'
> — for the fine linen is the righteous deeds of the saints.

Here the components of creation praised in Psalm 104 are portrayed in their fullness: the saints' song is sustained by drinking directly from God's Spirit (Rev. 21:6; 22:1-2) and enlightened directly from the Son without the created garments of sun, moon, or temple (Rev. 21:22-26). The song thus provides us with final clarity about the two stories of God's work, whose praise makes the Christian ethos possible. One story is of material creation, beginning in Genesis 1, sustained by God through time and judged in the last days to prepare the way for the new creation. The other is its inner story, in which God creates ever anew by claiming individuals for praise. In this story God rescues humans for praise, ending not in judgment but in the weak cry from the depths rising and strengthening to push out all idolatries, swelling finally into a chorus around the divine throne that is cleansed of all hesitation, pride, and self-consciousness.

By offering these accounts and the words that train us to sing of them, the Psalms cut across the boundaries established by the metaphors that shape our common perceptions and relocate our sense of how all things hold together. This continual remaking is completed only in our seeing God face to face. In the meantime, their comprehensive and interwoven range of metaphors keeps a steady focus on God's works of power and deliverance, thus providing a place for faith to wrestle with God and to discover how all human truth partakes in this cosmic harmony. Such a moral theology begins with a full-bodied volitional, practical, and intellectual exploration of the practical steps necessary to follow the divine advent.

Praise takes us inside God's works. It reveals God's daily care in providing the food that sustains living creatures, and the time, space, and embodiment in which all creation exists. He makes human sociality possible by providing, renewing, and reclaiming language. He sustains this social space by setting up political authorities and maintaining peace. At the heart of human political life is the church, a community that learns from Scripture how to praise, with all creation, the divine inexhaustibility. In the church, the twisted sociality that expresses the ethos of self-interest, fear, and tribalism is remade into a political order whose *telos* is the discovery of the divine ethos of diversity in mutuality. It is a renewal sustained by the divine gift of Scripture, through which God invites and facilitates human praise. In praise the communion of saints continually rediscovers that God uses our faltering collaboration to bring humanity in tune with himself.

Epilogue

This equation encapsulates the biblical and ethical topography developed herein:

> One of the scribes asked him, "Which commandment is the first of all?" Jesus answered, "The first is, 'Hear, O Israel: the Lord our God, the Lord is one; you shall love the Lord your God with all your heart, and with all your soul, and with all your mind, and with all your strength.' The second is this, 'You shall love your neighbor as yourself.' There is no other commandment greater than these." (Mark 12:28b-30)

This means:

> Let the peace of Christ rule in your hearts,
>   to which indeed you were called in the one body.
>   And be thankful.
> Let the word of Christ dwell in you richly,
>   teach and admonish one another in all wisdom,
>   and sing psalms and hymns and spiritual songs
>   with thankfulness in your hearts to God.
> And whatever you do, in word or deed,
>   do everything in the name of the Lord Jesus,
>   giving thanks to God the Father through him.
>   Colossians 3:15-17

References

Adorno, Theodor. *Minima Moralia: Reflections from Damaged Life.* Translated by E. F. N. Jephcott. London: Verso Editions, 1978.

Allen, Leslie. *Word Biblical Commentary: Vol. 21, Psalms 101–50.* Revised edition. Nashville: Thomas Nelson, 2002.

Althaus, Paul. *The Theology of Martin Luther.* Translated by Robert Schultz. Philadelphia: Fortress Press, 1966.

Arendt, Hannah. *The Human Condition.* Chicago: University of Chicago Press, 1958.

Augustine. *The City of God against the Pagans.* Edited and translated by R. W. Dyson. Cambridge, UK: Cambridge University Press, 1998.

———. *Confessions.* Translated and introduced by Henry Chadwick. Oxford: Oxford University Press, 1991.

———. *Expositions of the Psalms.* 6 vols. Translation and notes by Maria Boulding. Edited by John E. Rotelle. New York: New City Press, 2000-2004.

———. *The Retractions, The Fathers of the Church: A New Translation.* Volume 60. Translated by Mary Bogan. Washington: Catholic University of America Press, 1968.

———. *St. Augustin: Prolegomena: St. Augustine's Life and Work, Confessions, Letters: Nicene and Post-Nicene Fathers.* Volume I. Edited by Philip Schaff. Edinburgh: T&T Clark, 1996.

———. *The Trinity.* Edited by John Rotelle. Translated by Edmund Hill. New York: New City Press, 1991.

Bader, Günter. *Psalterium affectum palestra: Prolegomena zu einer Theologie des Psalters.* Tübingen: J. C. B. Mohr (Paul Siebeck), 1996.

Banner, Michael. *Christian Ethics and Contemporary Moral Problems.* Cambridge, UK: Cambridge University Press, 1999.

Barnett, Victoria. "The Quest for the Historical Bonhoeffer." Paper presented at the American Academy of Religion, 2005.

Barth, Karl. *The Christian Life: Church Dogmatics IV.4. Lecture Fragments.* Translated by Geoffrey Bromiley. Edinburgh: T&T Clark, 1981.

————. *Church Dogmatics.* 14 vols. Edited by G. W. Bromiley and T. F. Torrance. Edinburgh: T&T Clark, 1936-1977.

————. *Community, State and Church: Three Essays by Karl Barth.* Translated by Will Herberg. New York: Anchor Books, 1960.

————. *The Epistle to the Philippians.* Translated by James Leitch. London: SCM Press, 1962.

————. *The Epistle to the Romans.* Translated by Edwyn Hoskyns. London: Oxford University Press, 1953.

————. *The Epistle to the Philippians: 40th Anniversary Edition.* Introductory essays by Bruce McCormack and Francis Watson. Louisville: Westminster John Knox Press, 2002.

————. *Erklärung des Johannes Evangelium (Kapital 1–8).* Edited by Walther Fürst. Zurich: TVZ, 1976.

————. *The Holy Spirit and the Christian Life: The Theological Basis of Ethics.* Translated by R. Birch Hoyle. Foreword by Robin Lovin. Louisville: Westminster John Knox Press, 1993.

————. *Protestant Theology in the Nineteenth Century: Its Background and History.* New edition. Introduction by Colin Gunton. Grand Rapids: Eerdmans, 2002.

————. *The Resurrection of the Dead.* Translated by H. J. Stenning. London: Hodder and Stoughton, 1933.

————. *A Shorter Commentary on Romans.* Translated by D. H. van Daalen. London: SCM Press, 1959.

Bartholomew, Craig, Jonathan Chaplin, Robert Song, and Al Wolters, eds. *A Royal Priesthood? The Use of the Bible Ethically and Politically: A Dialogue with Oliver O'Donovan.* Carlisle: Paternoster Press, 2002.

Bartholomew, Craig, Mary Healy, and Karl Moller, eds. *Out of Egypt: Biblical Theology and Biblical Interpretation.* Carlisle: Paternoster Press, 2004.

Bauckham, Richard. *The Theology of the Book of Revelation.* Cambridge, UK: Cambridge University Press, 2005.

Bayer, Oswald. *Promissio: Geschichte der reformatorischen Wende in Luthers Theologie.* Göttingen: Vandenhoeck, 1971.

Bethge, Eberhard. *Dietrich Bonhoeffer: Theologian, Christian, Contemporary.* Translated by E. Mosbacker, P. and B. Ross, F. Clarke, W. Glen-Doepel. London: Collins, 1970.

Biggar, Nigel. *The Hastening That Waits: Karl Barth's Ethics.* Oxford: Clarendon Press, 1993.

Birch, Bruce. *Let Justice Roll Down: The Old Testament, Ethics, and Christian Life.* Louisville: Westminster John Knox Press, 1991.

Birch, Bruce, and Larry Rasmussen. *Bible and Ethics in the Christian Life.* Revised version. Minneapolis: Augsburg Publishing House, 1989.

Bluhm, Heinz. *Martin Luther: Creative Translator.* St. Louis: Concordia Publishing House, 1965.

Bock, Darrell. *Luke: Vol. 1: 1:1–9:50.* Grand Rapids: Baker Books, 1994.

Bonhoeffer, Dietrich. *Creation and Fall: A Theological Exposition of Genesis 1–3.* Dietrich

Bonhoeffer Works 3. Edited by Martin Rüter, Ilse Tödt, and John W. de Gruchy. Translated by Douglas Stephen Bax. Minneapolis: Fortress Press, 1997.

———. *Dietrich Bonhoeffer's Meditations on the Psalms*. Edited and translated by Edwin Robertson. Grand Rapids: Zondervan, 2002.

———. *Discipleship*. Dietrich Bonhoeffer Works 4. Edited by Martin Kuske, Ilse Tödt, Barbara Green, and Reinhard Kraus. Translated by Barbara Green and Reinhard Krauss. Minneapolis: Fortress Press, 2001.

———. *Ethics*. Dietrich Bonhoeffer Works 6. Edited by Ilse Tödt, Heinz Eduard Tödt, Ernst Feil, and Clifford Green. Translated by Reinhard Krauss, Charles West, and Douglas Scott. Minneapolis: Fortress Press, 2005.

———. *Fiction from Tegel Prison*. Dietrich Bonhoeffer Works 7. Edited by Renate Bethge, Ilse Tödt, and Clifford Green. Translated by Nancy Lukens. Minneapolis: Fortress Press, 2000.

———. *Letters and Papers from Prison*. Enlarged edition. Edited by Eberhard Bethge. London: SCM Press, 1971.

———. *Life Together and Prayerbook of the Bible*. Dietrich Bonhoeffer Works 5. Edited by Gerhard Müller, Albrecht Schönherr, and Geffrey Kelley. Translated by Daniel Bloesch and James Burtness. Minneapolis: Fortress Press, 1996.

———. *Meditating on the Word*. Edited and translated by David McI. Gracie. Cambridge, MA: Cowley Publications, 1986.

———. *Reflections on the Bible: Human Word and the Word of God*. Translated by Eugene Boring. Peabody, MA: Hendrickson, 2004.

———. *Voices in the Night: The Prison Poems of Dietrich Bonhoeffer*. Edited and translated by Edwin Robertson. Grand Rapids: Zondervan, 1999.

Braude, William, trans. *The Midrash on the Psalms*. 2 vols. New Haven: Yale University Press, 1959.

Brown, Francis. *The Brown-Driver-Briggs Hebrew and English Lexicon*. Peabody, MA: Hendrickson, 1999 (reprint of 1906 ed.).

Brown, Peter. *Augustine: A Biography*. London: Faber and Faber, 1975.

Brown, William. *Seeing the Psalms: A Theology of Metaphor*. Louisville: Westminster John Knox Press, 2002.

———. *The Ethos of the Cosmos: The Genesis of Moral Imagination in the Bible*. Grand Rapids: William B. Eerdmans, 1999.

Brueggemann, Walter. *The Message of the Psalms: A Theological Commentary*. Minneapolis: Augsburg Publishing House, 1984.

———. *Old Testament Theology: Testimony, Dispute, Advocacy*. Minneapolis: Fortress Press, 1997.

Buber, Martin. *Right and Wrong: An Interpretation of Some Psalms*. Translated by Ronald Smith. London: SCM, 1952.

Burnett, Richard. *Karl Barth's Theological Exegesis: The Hermeneutical Principles of the Römerbrief Period*. Grand Rapids: Eerdmans, 2004.

Busch, Eberhard. *Karl Barth: His Life from Letters and Autobiographical Texts*. Translated by John Bowden. Grand Rapids: Eerdmans, 1994.

Calvin, John. *Commentary on the Book of Psalms*. 4 vols. Translated by James Anderson. Grand Rapids: Baker Book House, 1989.

Cavanaugh, William. *The Theopolitical Imagination: Discovering the Liturgy as a Political Act in an Age of Global Consumerism.* London: T&T Clark, 2002.

―――. *Torture and Eucharist: Theology, Politics and the Body of Christ.* Oxford: Blackwell Publishers, 1998.

Charry, Ellen. *By the Renewing of Your Minds: The Pastoral Function of Doctrine.* Oxford: Oxford University Press, 1997.

Childs, Brevard. *Biblical Theology of the Old and New Testaments: Theological Reflections on the Christian Bible.* Minneapolis: Fortress Press, 1993.

―――. *Introduction to the Old Testament as Scripture.* Philadelphia: Fortress Press, 1979.

Conrad, Joseph. *The Nigger of the Narcissus and Other Tales.* London: Oxford University Press, 1975.

Cosgrove, Charles. *Appealing to Scripture in Moral Debate: Five Hermeneutical Rules.* Grand Rapids: Eerdmans, 2002.

Coyzis, David. *Political Visions and Illusions: A Survey and Critique of Contemporary Ideologies.* Downers Grove, IL: InterVarsity Press, 2003.

Cragie, Peter. *Word Biblical Commentary: Vol. 19, Psalms 1–50.* Waco, Tex.: Word Books, 1983.

Crüzemann, Frank. *The Torah: Theology and Social History of the Old Testament Law.* Translated by Allan Mahnke. Edinburgh: T&T Clark, 1996.

Cunningham, Mary Kathleen. *What Is Theological Exegesis? Interpretation and Use of Scripture in Barth's Doctrine of Election.* London: Continuum International Publishing Group, 1995.

Daley, Brian. "Is Patristic Exegesis Still Usable? Some Reflections on Early Christian Interpretation of the Psalms." In *The Art of Reading Scripture.* Edited by Ellen Davis and Richard Hays. Grand Rapids: Eerdmans, 2003.

Davis, Ellen, and Richard Hays, eds. *The Art of Reading Scripture.* Grand Rapids: Eerdmans, 2003.

de Gruchy, John. "Eberhard Bethge: Interpreter Extraordinaire of Dietrich Bonhoeffer." Paper presented at the American Academy of Religion, 2005.

De Moor, Johannes C., and Wilfred Watson, eds. *Verse in Ancient Near Eastern Prose.* Neukirchen-Vluyn: Neukirchener Verlag, 1993.

Demson, David. *Hans Frei and Karl Barth: Different Ways of Reading Scripture.* Grand Rapids: Eerdmans, 1997.

Eaton, John. *The Psalms: A Historical and Spiritual Commentary with an Introduction and New Translation.* London: T&T Clark International, 2003.

Ebeling, D. Gerhard. *Wort und Glaube.* 3rd ed. Tübingen: J. C. B. Mohr, 1967.

Eco, Umberto, Richard Rorty, Jonathan Culler, and Christine Brooke-Rose. *Interpretation and Overinterpretation.* Edited by Stefan Collini. Cambridge, UK: Cambridge University Press, 1992.

Evans, C. F. *Saint Luke.* London: SCM, 1990.

Fitzgerald, John. "Haustafeln." In *Anchor Bible Dictionary* III, H-S. New York: Doubleday, 1992.

Fitzmyer, Joseph. *Luke the Theologian: Aspects of His Teaching.* London: Geoffrey Chapman, 1989.

Fodor, James, and Stanley Hauerwas. "Performing Faith: The Peaceable Rhetoric of God's Church." In Stanley Hauerwas, *Performing the Faith: Bonhoeffer and the Practice of Nonviolence,* pp. 79-109. Grand Rapids: Baker Books, 2004.

Fokkelman, Jan. *Narrative Art and Poetry in the Books of Samuel: A Full Interpretation Based on Stylistic and Structural Analyses.* 4 vols. Assen, the Netherlands: van Gorcum, 1981-1993.

———. *Reading Biblical Narrative: A Practical Guide.* Translated by Ineke Smit. Leiden: Deo Publishing, 1999.

———. *The Psalms in Form: The Hebrew Psalter in Its Poetic Shape.* Leiden: Deo Publishing, 2002.

Fowl, Stephen. *Engaging Scripture: A Model for Theological Interpretation.* Oxford: Blackwell, 1998.

Fowl, Stephen, and L. Gregory Jones. *Reading in Communion: Scripture and Ethics in the Christian Life.* Grand Rapids: Eerdmans, 1991.

Fox, Kate. *Watching the English: The Hidden Rules of English Behaviour.* London: Hodder and Stoughton, 2004.

Goldingay, John. *Models for Interpretation of Scripture.* Grand Rapids: Eerdmans, 1995.

Grant, George. *English Speaking Justice.* Notre Dame: University of Notre Dame Press, 1974.

Green, Joel B., and Max Turner, eds. *Between Two Horizons: Spanning New Testament Studies and Systematic Theology.* Grand Rapids: Eerdmans, 1999.

Gunkel, Hermann. *Die Psalmen.* Göttingen: Vandenhoeck & Ruprecht, 1926.

———. *The Psalms.* Translated by T. H. Horner. Introduction by J. Muilenberg. Philadelphia: Fortress Press, 1967.

Gunkel, Hermann, and J. Begrich. *Einleitung in die Psalmen: Die Gattungen der religiösen Lyrik Israels.* Göttinger Handkommentar zum AT. Göttingen: Vandenhoeck & Ruprecht, 1933.

Gunton, Colin. *Yesterday and Today: A Study of Continuities in Christology.* 2nd ed. London: SPCK, 1997.

Hall, Amy Laura. "Better Homes and Children: The Brave New World of Meticulously Planned Parenthood." *Books and Culture* (Nov./Dec. 2005): 18-20.

———. *Conceiving Parenthood.* Grand Rapids: Eerdmans, forthcoming.

Oxford: Blackwell, 2004.

Hauerwas, Stanley. *The Peaceable Kingdom: A Primer in Christian Ethics.* Notre Dame: University of Notre Dame Press, 1983.

———. *Performing the Faith: Bonhoeffer and the Practice of Nonviolence.* Grand Rapids: Baker Books, 2004.

Hauerwas, Stanley, and Samuel Wells, eds. *The Blackwell Companion to Christian Ethics.* Haynes, Stephen R. "Bonhoeffer and the Jews: Bethge and Beyond." Paper presented at the American Academy of Religion, 2005.

———. *The Bonhoeffer Phenomenon: Portraits of a Protestant Saint.* Minneapolis: Fortress Press, 2004.

Hays, Richard. *The Moral Vision of the New Testament: Community, Cross, New Creation: A Contemporary Introduction to New Testament Ethics.* San Francisco: HarperSanFrancisco, 1996.

Hegel, G. W. F. *Encyclopaedia of the Philosophical Sciences in Outline and Critical Writings.* Translated by E. Behler. New York: Continuum, 1990.

———. *Lectures on the Philosophy of Religion. Volume III: The Consummate Religion.* Translated by Peter C. Hodgson. Berkeley: University of California Press, 1985.

———. *Science of Logic.* Translated by H. D. Lewis. Atlantic Highlands, NJ: Humanities Press International, 1969.

Heidegger, Martin. *Being and Time: A Translation of* Sein and Zeit. Translated by Joan Stambaugh. Albany: State University of New York Press, 1996.

Higton, Mike. *Christ, Providence and History: Hans W. Frei's Public Theology.* London: T&T Clark International, 2004.

Holladay, William. *The Psalms through Three Thousand Years: Prayerbook of a Cloud of Witnesses.* Minneapolis: Fortress Press, 1996.

Horn, F. W. "Holy Spirit." Translated by Dietlinde Elliot. In *The Anchor Bible Dictionary* III, H-J. Edited by David Freedman. New York: Doubleday, 1992.

Jackson, Rebecca, Kimberly Gibson, Yvonne Wu, and Mary Croughan. "Perinatal Outcomes in Singletons Following In Vitro Fertilization: A Meta-Analysis." *Obstetrics & Gynecology* 103 (2004): 551-63.

Jenson, Robert. *Systematic Theology.* 2 vols. Oxford: Oxford University Press, 1999.

Jonas, Hans. *The Imperative of Responsibility: In Search of an Ethics for the Technological Age.* Translated by Hans Jonas and David Herr. Chicago: University of Chicago Press, 1984.

Kant, Immanuel. *Practical Philosophy.* Translated and edited by Mary Gregor. Cambridge, UK: Cambridge University Press, 1999.

Kelly, Geffrey. Review of *The Bonhoeffer Phenomenon: Portraits of a Protestant Saint. International Bonhoeffer Society Newsletter* 87 (Fall 2005): 4-6.

Kelsey, David. *Proving Doctrine: The Uses of Scripture in Modern Theology.* Harrisburg: Trinity Press International, 1999.

Kerr, Fergus. *Theology after Wittgenstein.* Oxford: Basil Blackwell, 1986.

Kierkegaard, Soren (Johannes Climacus). *Concluding Unscientific Postscript to Philosophical Fragments, Kierkegaard's Writings, XII.1.* Translated and edited by Howard Hong and Edna Hong. Princeton, NJ: Princeton University Press, 1992.

———. *Philosophical Fragments: Kierkegaard's Writings, VII.* Translated and edited by Howard Hong and Edna Hong. Princeton, NJ: Princeton University Press, 1985.

Kirschstein, Helmut. *Der souveräne Gott und die heilige Schrift: Einführung in die Biblische Hermeneutik Karl Barths.* Aachen, Germany: Shaker Verlag, 1998.

Klein, Ralph. *Word Biblical Commentary: 1 Samuel.* Waco: Word Books, 1983.

Knight, Douglas. "Liturgy as Exorcism." Online publication. http://www.douglasknight.org/mambo/content/view/51/38/.

———. "Speaking Humanity." In Murray Rae and Steve Holmes, eds., *The Person of Christ.* London: Continuum International Publishing Group, 2005.

Kraus, Hans-Joachim. *Psalms: A Continental Commentary.* 2 vols. Translated by Hilton Oswald. Minneapolis: Fortress Press, 1993.

———. *Theology of the Psalms.* Translated by Keith Crim. Minneapolis: Augsburg, 1986.

Levinas, Emmanuel. *Beyond the Verse: Talmudic Readings and Lectures.* Translated by Gary Mole. London: Athalone, 1994.

———. *Nine Talmudic Readings.* Translated with introduction by Annette Aronowicz. Bloomington: Indiana University Press, 1990.

Lewis, C. S. *Reflections on the Psalms.* London: Geoffrey Bles, 1958.

Lindbeck, George. *The Nature of Doctrine: Religion and Theology in a Postliberal Age.* Philadelphia: Westminster Press, 1984.

Lohfink, Norbert, and Erich Zenger. *The God of Israel and the Nations: Studies in Isaiah and the Psalms.* Translated by Everett Kalin. Collegeville, MN: Liturgical Press, 2000.

Lohse, Bernhard. *Martin Luther's Theology: Its Historical and Systematic Development.* Translated Roy A. Harrisville. Edinburgh: T&T Clark, 1999.

Longenecker, Richard. *New Testament Social Ethics for Today.* Grand Rapids: Eerdmans, 1984.

Luther, Martin. "Auslegung vieler schooner Sprüche göttlicher Schrift, daraus Lehre und Trost zu nehmen, welche der ehrwürdige Herr Doktor Martius Luther vielen in ihre Bibeln geschrieben." In *Luther deutsch: die Werke Martin Luthers in neuer Auswahl für die Gegenwart, vol 5: Die Schriftauslegung.* Edited by Kurt Aland. Göttingen: Vandenhoeck & Ruprecht, 1990.

———. *Luther's Works.* American Edition. 55 vols. Edited by Jaroslav Pelikan and Helmut T. Lehman. St. Louis: Concordia Publishing House; Philadelphia: Fortress Press, 1955-1986.

MacDonald, Nathan. "The *Imago Dei* and Election: Reading Gen 1:26-28 and Old Testament Scholarship with Karl Barth." (Unpublished paper).

MacIntyre, Alasdair. *Three Rival Versions of Moral Inquiry.* London: Gerald Duckworth and Co., 1990.

Markus, R. A. *Saeculum: History and Society in the Theology of St. Augustine.* Revised edition. Cambridge, UK: Cambridge University Press, 1988.

Marquard, Odo. *Apologie des Zufälligen: Philosophische studien.* Stuttgart: Philipp Reclam, 1986.

Marshall, I. Howard. *The Gospel according to Luke: A Commentary on the Greek Text.* Exeter: Paternoster Press, 1978.

Martin, Francis. "The Psalms as a Particular Mode of Revelation." *Nova et Vetera* 3, no. 2 (Spring 2005): 279-94.

Matera, Frank. *New Testament Ethics: The Legacies of Jesus and Paul.* Louisville: Westminster John Knox Press, 1996.

Mays, James Luther. *The Lord Reigns: A Theological Handbook to the Psalms.* Louisville: Westminster John Knox Press, 1994.

McAuliffe, Jane Dammen. "Reading the Qur'an with Fidelity and Freedom." American Academy of Religion Presidential Address, 2004. *Journal of the American Academy of Religion* 73:3 (September 2005): 615-35.

McCann, J. Clinton. *A Theological Introduction to the Book of Psalms: The Psalms as Torah.* Nashville: Abingdon Press, 1993.

McClellan, James, III, and Harold Dorn. *Science and Technology in World History: An Introduction.* Baltimore: Johns Hopkins University Press, 1999.

McClendon, James, and James Smith. *Convictions: Diffusing Religious Relativism.* Revised edition. Valley Forge: Trinity Press International, 1994.

McDonald, J. Ian. *The Crucible of Christian Morality.* London: Routledge, 1998.

McGlasson, Paul. *Jesus and Judas: Biblical Exegesis in Barth.* Atlanta: Scholars Press, 1991.

McKim, Donald, ed. *The Cambridge Companion to Luther.* Cambridge, UK: Cambridge University Press, 2003.

Meeks, Wayne. *The Moral World of the First Christians.* London: SPCK, 1987.

Milbank, John. *Theology and Social Theory: Beyond Secular Reason.* Oxford: Blackwell, 1990.

Mildenberger, Friedrich. *Biblische Dogmatik: Eine Biblische Theologie in dogmatischer Perspecktive.* 3 volumes. Stuttgart: W. Kohlhammer, 1997.

Milgrom, Jacob. *Leviticus: A New Translation with Introduction and Commentary.* 3 vols. New York: Doubleday, 1999-2001.

Miller, Patrick. *Interpreting the Psalms.* Philadelphia: Fortress Press, 1986.

Minkoff, Howard, Kathleen Powderly, Frank Chervenak, and Lawrence McCullough. "Ethical Dimensions of Elective Primary Cesarean Delivery." *Obstetrics & Gynecology* 103 (2004): 387-92.

Minkoff, Howard, and Richard Berkowitz. "The Myth of the Precious Baby." *Obstetrics & Gynecology* 106 (2005): 607-9.

Mitchell, David C. *The Message of the Psalter: An Eschatological Programme in the Book of Psalms.* Sheffield, UK: Sheffield Academic Press, 1997.

Mowinckel, Sigmund. *The Psalms in Israel's Worship.* 2 vols. Oxford: Oxford University Press, 1962.

Mudge, Lewis S., ed. *Essays on Biblical Interpretation.* Philadelphia: Fortress Press, 1980.

Murray, John. *Principles of Conduct: Aspects of Biblical Ethics.* London: Tyndale Press, 1957.

Nietzsche, Friedrich. *The Birth of Tragedy and Other Writings.* Edited by Raymond Geuss and Ronald Speirs. Translated by Ronald Speirs. Cambridge, UK: Cambridge University Press, 1999.

Nolland, John. *Word Biblical Commentary: Vol. 35a, Luke 1–9:20.* Dallas: Word Books, 1989.

Oberman, Heiko. *Luther: Man between God and the Devil.* Translated by Eileen Walliser-Schwarzbart. New York: Image Books, 1992.

O'Donovan, Oliver. *The Problem of Self-Love in St. Augustine.* New Haven: Yale University Press, 1980.

———. *The Ways of Judgment.* Grand Rapids: Eerdmans, 2005.

Ogletree, Thomas. *The Use of the Bible in Christian Ethics.* Philadelphia: Fortress Press, 1983.

Owen, John. *The Works of John Owen.* 23 vols. Edited by William Goold. Edinburgh: Banner of Truth Trust, 2000.

Ozment, Steven. *A Mighty Fortress: A New History of the German People.* New York: HarperCollins, 2004.

Patte, Daniel. *Ethics of Biblical Interpretation: A Reevaluation.* Louisville: Westminster John Knox Press, 1995.

Pence, Gregory. *Classic Cases in Medical Ethics: Accounts of the Cases That Have Shaped Medical Ethics, with Philosophical, Legal, and Historical Backgrounds.* New York: McGraw-Hill, 1990.

Pleins, J. David. *The Psalms: Songs of Tragedy, Hope and Justice*. Maryknoll, NY: Orbis, 1993.

Preuss, Samuel James. *From Shadow to Promise: Old Testament Interpretation from Augustine to the Young Luther*. Eugene, OR: Wipf and Stock, 1999.

Prinsloo, Willem. "The Psalms." In *Eerdmans Commentary on the Bible*. Edited by James Dunn and John Rogerson. Grand Rapids: Eerdmans, 2003.

Prothero, Rowland. *The Psalms in Human Life*. London: John Murray, 1909.

Richter, Sandra. *The Deuteronomistic History and the Name Theology: lᵉakkēn šᵉm\ô šām in the Bible and the Ancient Near East*. Beihefte zur Zeitschrift für die alttestamentliche Wissenschaft 318. Berlin/New York: Walter de Gruyter, 2002.

Ricoeur, Paul. *From Text to Action: Essays in Hermeneutics 2*. London: Athlon Press, 1991.

Ringleben, Joachim. "Metapher und Eschatologie bei Luther." *Zeitschrift für Theologie und Kirche* 100.2 (2003): 223-40.

Rist, John. *Augustine: Ancient Thought Baptized*. Cambridge, UK: Cambridge University Press, 1996.

Rogers, Eugene. *Sexuality and the Christian Body: Their Way into the Triune God*. Oxford: Blackwell, 1999.

Sacks, Jonathan. *The Politics of Hope*. London: Jonathan Cape, 1997.

Sauter, Gerhard. "Das Gebet als Wurzel des Redens von Gott." *Glaube und Lernen* 1 [Göttingen: Vandenhoeck & Ruprecht] (May 1986): 21-37.

―――. *Gateways to Dogmatics: Reasoning Theologically for the Life of the Church*. Grand Rapids: Eerdmans, 2003.

―――. "Reden von Gott im Gebet." In Gerhard Caspar, ed., *Gott nennen: Phänomenologische Zugänge*, pp. 219-42. Freiburg im Breisgau: Alber Verlag, 1981.

Schaefer, Konrad. *Psalms: Berit Olam Studies in Hebrew Narrative and Poetry*. Edited by David Cotter. Collegeville, MN: Liturgical Press, 2001.

Schüssler Fiorenza, Elisabeth. *In Memory of Her: A Feminist Theological Reconstruction of Christian Origins*. 2nd edition. London: SCM Press, 1995.

―――. *Rhetoric and Ethic: The Politics of Biblical Studies*. Minneapolis: Fortress Press, 1999.

Schweizer, Eduard. *The Good News according to Luke*. Translated by David Green. London: SPCK, 1984.

Seybold, Klaus. *Introducing the Psalms*. Translated by R. Graeme Dunphy. Edinburgh: T&T Clark, 1990.

Siker, Jeffrey. *Scripture and Ethics: Twentieth Century Portraits*. Oxford: Oxford University Press, 1997.

Smalley, Beryl. *The Study of the Bible in the Middle Ages*. Notre Dame, IN: University of Notre Dame Press, 1978.

Stringfellow, William. *An Ethic for Christians in a Strange Land*. Eugene, OR: Wipf and Stock, 2004.

Taft, Robert. *The Liturgy of the Hours in the East and West: The Origins of the Divine Office and Its Meaning for Today*. Collegeville, MN: Liturgical Press, 1986.

Tanner, Beth LaNeel. *The Book of Psalms through the Lens of Intertextuality*. New York: Peter Lang, 2001.

Tate, Marvin. *Word Biblical Commentary: Vol. 20, Psalms 51–100.* Waco: Word Books, 1990.

Taylor, Charles. *Sources of the Self: The Making of the Modern Identity.* Cambridge, MA: Harvard University Press, 1989.

Terrien, Samuel. *The Psalms: Strophic Structure and Theological Commentary.* Grand Rapids: Eerdmans, 2003.

Trudinger, Peter. *The Psalms of the Tamid Service: A Liturgical Text from the Second Temple.* Leiden: Brill, 2004.

Ulrich, Hans G. *Eschatologie und Ethik: Die theologishe Theorie der Ethik in ihrer Beziehung auf die Rede von Gott seit Friedrich Schleiermacher.* München: Christian Kaiser Verlag, 1988.

———. "Fides Quarens Intellectum: Reflections toward an Explorative Theology." Translated by Brian Brock. *The International Journal of Systematic Theology* 8:1 (2006): 42-54.

———. *Wie Geschöpfe leben: Konturen evangelisher Ethik.* Münster, Germany: Lit Verlag, 2005.

Verhey, Allen. *The Great Reversal: Ethics and the New Testament.* Grand Rapids: Eerdmans, 1984.

Von Harnack, Adolph. *History of Dogma.* 7 vols. Translated by Neil Buchanan. New York: Dover Publications, 1961.

Von Rad, Gerhard. *Old Testament Theology.* 2 vols. Translated by D. M. G. Stalker. New York: Harper and Row, 1965.

Wannenwetsch, Bernd. "Caritas fide formata. 'Herz und Affekte' als Schlüssel zu 'Glaube und Liebe'." *Kerygma und Dogma* 45 (2000): 205-24.

———. "Ecclesiology and Ethics." In Gilbert Meilaender and William Werpehowski, eds., *The Oxford Handbook of Theological Ethics,* pp. 57-73. Oxford: Oxford University Press, 2005.

———. "'Members of One Another': *Charis,* Ministry and Representation: A Politico-Ecclesial Reading of Romans 12." In Craig Bartholomew, Jonathan Chaplin, Robert Song, and Al Wolters, eds., *A Royal Priesthood? The Use of the Bible Ethically and Politically: A Dialogue with Oliver O'Donovan.* Carlisle, UK: Paternoster Press, 2002.

———. *Political Worship: Ethics for Christian Citizens.* Oxford: Oxford University Press, 2004.

———. "Representing the Absent in the City: Prolegomena to a Negative Political Theology according to Revelation 21." In L. Gregory Jones, Reinhard Hütter, and C. Rosalee Velloso Ewell, eds., *God, Truth, and Witness: Engaging Stanley Hauerwas.* Grand Rapids: Brazos Press, 2005.

———. "Singen und Sagen: Zur musisch-musicalishen Dimension der Theologie." *Neue Zeitschrift für Systematische Theolgie und Religionsphilosophie* [Berlin: Walter De Gruyter] 46 (2004): 330-47.

———. "Walking the Ten Words: Exploring the Moral Universe through the Decalogue." Unpublished paper.

———. "What Is Man? That You Are Mindful of Him! Biotechnological Aspirations in the Light of Psalm Eight." In *Farmington Papers*. Edited by Ralph Waller. Oxford: Farmington Institute for Christian Studies, 2004.

Watson, Francis. *Agape, Eros, Gender: Towards a Pauline Ethic*. Cambridge, UK: Cambridge University Press, 2000.

———. "Mistranslation and the Death of Christ: Isaiah 53 LXX and Its Pauline Reception" (forthcoming).

———. *Paul and the Hermeneutics of Faith*. London: T&T Clark International, 2004.

———. *Text and Truth: Redefining Biblical Theology*. Edinburgh: T&T Clark, 1997.

———. *Text, Church and World: Biblical Interpretation in Theological Perspective*. Grand Rapids: Eerdmans, 1994.

Webb, Stephen H. *Re-Figuring Theology: The Rhetoric of Karl Barth*. Albany: State University of New York Press, 1991.

Webster, John. *Barth's Ethics of Reconciliation*. Cambridge, UK: Cambridge University Press, 1995.

———. *Barth's Moral Theology: Human Action in Barth's Thought*. Grand Rapids: Eerdmans, 1998.

———. Editorial. *International Journal of Systematic Theology* 5, no. 2 (July 2003): 131-32.

———. *Word and Church: Essays in Christian Dogmatics*. Edinburgh: T&T Clark, 2001.

Westermann, Claus. *Praise and Lament in the Psalms*. Translated by K. R. Crim and R. N. Soulen. Atlanta: John Knox, 1981.

Wiley, H. Orton. *The Epistle to the Hebrews*. Revised edition. Kansas City: Beacon Hill Press, 1984.

Wittgenstein, Ludwig. *Philosophical Investigations*. Translated by G. E. M. Anscombe. Oxford: Basil Blackwell, 1968.

———. *Wittgenstein's Lectures, Cambridge, 1930-1932*. Edited by Desmond Lee. Oxford: Basil Blackwell, 1980.

Wolff, Hans Walter. *Anthropologie des Alten Testaments*. München: Christian Kaiser Verlag, 1973.

Work, Telford. *Living and Active: Scripture in the Economy of Salvation*. Grand Rapids: Eerdmans, 2002.

Yoder, John Howard. *Preface to Theology, Christology and Theological Method*. Introduction by Stanley Hauerwas and Alex Sider. Grand Rapids: Brazos Press, 2002.

Yoder, John Howard. *The Politics of Jesus*. 2nd edition. Grand Rapids: Eerdmans, 1994.

Zenger, Erich. *God of Vengeance: Understanding the Psalms of Divine Wrath*. Translated by Linda Maloney. Louisville: Westminster John Knox Press, 1996.

Zimmerli, Walther. *Man and His Hope in the Old Testament*. Naperville, IL: Alec R. Allenson, Inc., 1968.

———. "Zwillingspsalmen." In *Wort, Leid, und Gottesspruch: Beiträge zu Psalmen und Propheten*. Edited by J. Schreiner. Würzburg: Echter Verlag, 1972.

Index of Names

Adorno, Theodor, 283-84
Allen, Leslie, 323
Aristotle, 20, 26
Augustine, xi-xiii, 99-164; embodying spiritual food, 338-39; eschatological perception, 319, 322; ethics, and divine grammar, 249, 253, 266; ethos of salvific confession, 163-64; hermeneutics, 106-26; Holy Spirit and interpretation, 169; and Luther, 165-67, 170, 185, 187, 195, 202, 263-64; meditation, 336; singing, intratextual exegesis, 273; singing, reorienting affections, 275, 328-29, 353, 355; on social order, 308-9; Taylor and, 130-32, 163; waiting for God, 299

Barth, Karl, 56, 60; on creation, 215, 313-14, 319, 348; creation and reconciliation, 89, 94; negative eschatology, 206-7; personhood, 231; Scripture and theology, 52-53, 63-65, 68, 71-73; and social order, 46n.11, 48
Bayer, Oswald, 168, 185, 313
Bethge, Eberhard, 27, 79, 177
Birch, Bruce, 20-26, 31-34, 36, 41
Bonhoeffer, Dietrich, 71-95, 255, 351; exegetical theology, 71-88; law and revelation, 319; mandates, ethics as a path, 89-95; poetry, 177; praise, uniting church, 358-59; reading Scripture, 63-64; theological development, 26-27
Brown, William, 308

Buber, Martin, 72

Calvin, John, 250, 320, 334, 341, 349
Cavanaugh, William, 261
Charry, Ellen, 162
Childs, Brevard, 53-58, 62, 70, 99, 101
Cosgrove, Charles, 3-4, 11-15, 17

Dibelius, Martin, 44

Eco, Umberto, 268

Feuerbach, Ludwig, 230-32
Fowl, Stephen, 23-31: on Bonhoeffer, 26-27, 93; Holy Spirit and discernment, 28-31; moral self-criticism, 23-24, 34; practical wisdom, 26; saints, 25-27, 32

Gunkel, Hermann, 101

Habermas, Jürgen, 6
Hall, Amy Laura, 215-16
Hauerwas, Stanley, 33
Hays, Richard, 39-42, 55, 92, 275; and focal images, 46-47, 49-50, 251-53
Hegel, G. W. F., 311n.78
Heidegger, Martin, 267

Jenson, Robert, 246, 257, 273
Jones, L. Gregory, 23-28: on Bonhoeffer, 26-27, 93; moral self-criticism, 23-24, 34; practical wisdom, 26; saints, 25-27, 32

Index of Subjects

Index of Scripture References